Microsoft® Project 2002
Bible

Microsoft® Project 2002 Bible

Elaine Marmel

Hungry Minds™

Best-Selling Books • Digital Downloads • e-Books • Answer Networks • e-Newsletters • Branded Web Sites • e-Learning

New York, NY ✦ Cleveland, OH ✦ Indianapolis, IN

Microsoft® Project 2002 Bible

Published by
Hungry Minds, Inc.
909 Third Avenue
New York, NY 10022
www.hungryminds.com

Library of Congress Control Number: 2002100341

ISBN: 0-7645-3653-2

Printed in the United States of America

10 9 8 7 6 5 4 3 2 1

1B/SU/QU/QS/IN

Distributed in the United States by Hungry Minds, Inc.

Distributed by CDG Books Canada Inc. for Canada; by Transworld Publishers Limited in the United Kingdom; by IDG Norge Books for Norway; by IDG Sweden Books for Sweden; by IDG Books Australia Publishing Corporation Pty. Ltd. for Australia and New Zealand; by TransQuest Publishers Pte Ltd. for Singapore, Malaysia, Thailand, Indonesia, and Hong Kong; by Gotop Information Inc. for Taiwan; by ICG Muse, Inc. for Japan; by Intersoft for South Africa; by Eyrolles for France; by International Thomson Publishing for Germany, Austria, and Switzerland; by Distribuidora Cuspide for Argentina; by LR International for Brazil; by Galileo Libros for Chile; by Ediciones ZETA S.C.R. Ltda. for Peru; by WS Computer Publishing Corporation, Inc., for the Philippines; by Contemporanea de Ediciones for Venezuela; by Express Computer Distributors for the Caribbean and West Indies; by Micronesia Media Distributor, Inc. for Micronesia; by Chips Computadoras S.A. de C.V. for Mexico; by Editorial Norma de Panama S.A. for Panama; by American Bookshops for Finland.

For general information on Hungry Minds' products and services please contact our Customer Care department within the U.S. at 800-762-2974, outside the U.S. at 317-572-3993 or fax 317-572-4002.

For sales inquiries and reseller information, including discounts, premium and bulk quantity sales, and foreign-language translations, please contact our Customer Care department at 800-434-3422, fax 317-572-4002 or write to Hungry Minds, Inc., Attn: Customer Care Department, 10475 Crosspoint Boulevard, Indianapolis, IN 46256.

For information on licensing foreign or domestic rights, please contact our Sub-Rights Customer Care department at 212-884-5000.

For information on using Hungry Minds' products and services in the classroom or for ordering examination copies, please contact our Educational Sales department at 800-434-2086 or fax 317-572-4005.

For press review copies, author interviews, or other publicity information, please contact our Public Relations department at 317-572-3168 or fax 317-572-4168.

For authorization to photocopy items for corporate, personal, or educational use, please contact Copyright Clearance Center, 222 Rosewood Drive, Danvers, MA 01923, or fax 978-750-4470.

Hungry Minds™ is a trademark of Hungry Minds, Inc.

About the Author

Elaine Marmel is president of Marmel Enterprises, Inc., an organization that specializes in technical writing and software training. She routinely employs project management software and skills to manage critical business projects, and otherwise spends most of her time writing. Elaine has authored or coauthored more than 20 books about software, including Project, Word for Windows, Word for the Mac, Quicken for Windows, Quicken for DOS, 1-2-3 for Windows, Lotus Notes, and Excel. Elaine is a contributing editor to the monthly magazines *Inside Peachtree for Windows* and *Inside QuickBooks for Windows*.

Elaine left her native Chicago for the warmer climes of Florida (by way of Cincinnati, Ohio; Jerusalem, Israel; Ithaca, New York; and Washington, D.C.) where she basks in the sun with her PC, her dog, Josh, and her cats, Cato and Watson. Elaine also sings in the Toast of Tampa, an International Champion Sweet Adeline barbershop chorus.

Credits

Acquisitions Editor
Laura Carpenter VanWinkle

Project Editor
Amanda Munz Peterson

Technical Editor
Jim Kelly

Copy Editor
Rebekah Mancilla

Editorial Manager
Ami Frank Sullivan

Vice President, Technical Publishing
Richard Swadley

Vice President and Publisher
Mary Bednarek

Project Coordinator
Regina Snyder

Graphics and Production Specialists
Beth Brooks, Sean Decker,
Heather Pope, Jeremey Unger,
Mary Virgin

Quality Control Technicians
Laura Albert, David Faust,
John Greenough, Andy Hollandbeck,
Susan Moritz, Carl Pierce

Permissions Editor
Laura Moss

Media Development Specialist
Marisa Pearman

Illustrator
Anthony Bunyan

Proofreading and Indexing
TECHBOOKS Production Services

To my mom with love for all her understanding and support.

Preface

Managing projects can be as exciting as scheduling the next space shuttle or as mundane as planning routine production-line maintenance. A project can be as rewarding as striking oil or as disastrous as the maiden voyage of the Titanic. Projects can have budgets of $5 or $5,000,000. One thing that all projects have in common, however, is their potential for success or failure — the promise that if you do it right, you'll accomplish your goal.

Why You Need This Book

Microsoft Project is a tool for implementing project management principles and practices that can help you succeed. That's why this book provides not only the information about which buttons to press and where to type project dates, but also the conceptual framework to make computerized project management work for you.

How it's designed

This book strives to offer real-world examples of projects from many industries and disciplines. You'll see yourself and your own projects somewhere in this book. A wealth of tips and advice show you how to address, control, and overcome real-world constraints.

+ **As a tutorial.** You can use *Microsoft Project 2002 Bible* as a linear tool to learn Project — from the ground up.

+ **As a reference.** You can put it on the shelf and use it as your Project reference book, to be pulled down as needed — for advice, information, and step-by-step procedures.

Either way, this book is designed to enrich your Microsoft Project experience and to make you a better project manager.

Who it's for

Unlike word processing or spreadsheet software, many of you may have come to project management software never having used anything quite like it before. You may also have used earlier versions of Project or other project management software.

✦ **If you're new to project management.** This book is for you. The early chapters explain the basic concepts of computerized project management and what it can do for you, so that you have a context for learning Project.

✦ **If you're experienced with project management.** This book is also for you. It explains what's new in the latest version of Project and shows you techniques for using the software that you may not have considered before.

You will benefit most from this book if you have at least a basic understanding of the Windows environment, have mastered standard Windows software conventions, and are comfortable using a mouse. But beyond that, you need only the desire to succeed as a project manager, which this book will help you do.

The Special Features of This Book

To help you maximize your use of this book, I've included many special features in its design and conception. The following sections show you how they work.

Formatting conventions

To streamline your learning experience, I've used the following formatting conventions:

✦ Text you're asked to type. When you're asked to enter text into a Project schedule, for example, it appears in **boldface**.

✦ When using the mouse. A click indicates a left mouse-button click and right-click indicates a right mouse-button click. Double-click designates two quick, successive clicks of the left mouse button.

✦ Keystroke combinations. These look like this: Alt+Tab. Hold down the first key and, without letting it go, press the second key.

✦ Menu commands. These are shown with the command arrow — for example, Choose File ➪ Open.

✦ New terms. When a new term or concept is introduced, it appears in *italic*.

Margin icons

Throughout the book, I've included special icons in the margins to call your attention to added information, shortcuts and advice, warnings about potentially disastrous courses of action, the new features of Project 2002, references to additional wisdom, and how to access the wonderful software on the CD-ROM that accompanies this book. Here's how they look:

Sagacious Sidebars

Sidebars, such as this one, are departures into background details or interesting information. They're designed so you may read around them if you're in a hurry to accomplish a specific task.

When you have the time for a more comprehensive approach to the subject, however, the concepts that you find in sidebars may prove invaluable — providing the context and depth necessary to a fuller understanding of Project's functions.

 Note The Note icon signals additional information about a point under discussion or background information that may be of interest to you.

 Tip A tip is a bit of advice or a hint to save you time and indicate the best way to get things done.

 New Feature This icon highlights a new feature in Project 2002.

 Cross-Reference These helpful icons clue you in to sources of additional information on a topic under discussion. They point to another chapter or a specific heading elsewhere in the book.

 On the CD-ROM The CD-ROM icon flags helpful software and templates that you'll find on the accompanying CD-ROM.

How This Book Is Organized

This book is organized in the way that you will use Microsoft Project. It begins with some basic concepts, progresses through the features that you need to build a typical schedule, and then track its progress. The later chapters provide more advanced information for customizing Project, using it in workgroup settings, and taking Project online.

Part I: Project Management Basics

Part I of the book explains the basic project management concepts and terminology that you'll need in order to learn Project. In Chapter 1, you take a look at the nature of projects themselves, how Microsoft Project can help you control them, and the life cycle of a typical project. In Chapter 2, you get your first glimpse of the Project software environment.

Part II: Getting Your Project Going

Here's where you learn about the type of information that Project needs in order to do its job. In Chapter 3, you begin to build your first schedule and add tasks in an outline structure. In Chapter 4, you assign timing and construct timing relationships among those tasks. In Chapter 5, you begin assigning people and other resources to your project; this chapter is also where you learn to determine how these resources add costs to a project and how to handle issues such as overtime and shift work.

Part III: Refining Your Project

Before your project is ready for prime time, you need to tweak some things, just as you check spelling in a word-processed document. Chapter 6 explains how to view that information to gain perspective on your project, and Chapter 7 helps you to manipulate and customize views to make them work for you. Chapter 8 shows you how to make your project schedule look more professional by formatting the text and modifying the appearance of chart elements. The next two chapters delve into the tools that Project provides to resolve conflicts in your schedule. Chapter 9 explores resolving conflicts in the timing of your schedule, so you can meet your deadlines. Chapter 10 considers the issue of resolving resource conflicts, such as overworked people and underutilized equipment.

Part IV: Tracking Your Progress

Here's where you get the payoff for all your data entry and patient resolution of problems in your schedule. After you set your basic schedule and the project begins, you can track its progress and check data on your status from various perspectives. Chapter 11 gives you an overview of the tracking process. Chapter 12 shows you how to track progress on your individual tasks and view that progress in various ways. Chapter 13 is where you explore the power of generating reports on your projects for everyone from management to individual project team members. Chapter 14 gives advice and methods for analyzing your progress and making adjustments as needed to stay on schedule and within your budget.

Part V: Working in Groups

Most projects worth the effort of tracking in Project aren't done by a single person; workgroups, teams, and committees often form a day-to-day working project team. Chapter 15 shows you how to set up multiple projects to run concurrently or to consolidate smaller projects into larger schedules, and Chapter 16 describes how to keep members of your workgroup in touch using an e-mail workgroup. In Chapters 17 through 19, learn how to use Project's web-based tools and manage projects using Project Server, Microsoft's web-based project-managed solution.

Part VI: Advanced Microsoft Project

Part VI provides advice and information to make your use of Microsoft Project easier. Learn about customizing the Project environment in Chapter 20. Chapter 21 provides information on macros, which are simple programs that enable you to record and automatically play back series of steps that you use frequently, thus saving you time and effort. Chapter 22 deals with importing and exporting information into and out of Project. Importing information from other software can save you the time and expense of reentering existing data. And, in Chapter 23, you'll find some case studies that show you ways in which Project has been used by a variety of companies.

Appendixes

Appendixes B–D provide resources and other additional materials to make your work easier. Appendix A covers the contents of and installation for the companion CD-ROM, which contains trial software, time-saving templates, and a Web page with links to sites of interest in the project management world — including sites to partners of Microsoft Project.

Project Management Glossary

The glossary at the end of the book contains many specifically project management terms and concepts that have evolved over time. These terms are defined when they are first used in the book, but you may want to look them up at a later date. Use this handy alphabetical listing to do so.

Acknowledgments

No man (or woman) is an island, and this book is the product of the efforts of several people. Thank you, Laura Carpenter VanWinkle, for your support and for making things easier in general. Thank you, Amanda Munz Peterson, for keeping me sane. Thank you, Jim Kelly, for keeping me technically accurate and for adding insight. Thank you, Rebekah Mancilla, for keeping the manuscript readable. And thank you, Travis Silvers, for all the support from your department in setting up a Windows 2000 Server and you, Marisa Pearman, for producing the Web page for the CD. Last, thank you to the contributors who provided sample software for the readers on the book's CD. You all helped me make this a better book than I could have produced by myself.

Contents at a Glance

Contents

Part V: Working in Groups   417

Project Management Basics

I n this section, you are introduced to projects and the basic structure and functioning of Microsoft Project. First, you'll get a very basic overview of program management concepts. Your interaction with Microsoft Project Professional begins with understanding the differences between Project Standard and Project Professional; then, you'll take a tour of the product, and look over the new features of Project 2002.

The Nature of Projects

Everybody does projects. Building a tree house is a project; so is putting a man on the moon. From the simplest home improvement to the most complex business or scientific venture, projects are a part of most of our lives. But exactly what is a project, and what can you do to manage all of its facets?

Some projects are defined by their randomness. Missed deadlines, unpleasant surprises, and unexpected problems seem to be as unavoidable as the weekly staff meeting. Other projects have few problems. Nevertheless, the project that goes smoothly from beginning to end is rare. Good planning and communication can go a long way toward avoiding disaster. And although no amount of planning can prevent all possible problems, good project management enables you to deal with those inevitable twists and turns in the most efficient manner possible.

In this chapter, you begin exploring tools and acquiring skills that can help you become a more efficient and productive project manager. The goal of this chapter is to provide a survey of what a project is, what project management is, and how Microsoft Project 2002 fits into the picture.

Understanding Projects

When you look up the word *project* in the dictionary, you see definitions such as "plan" and "concerted effort." A project in the truest sense, then, isn't a simple one-person effort to perform a task. By this definition, getting yourself dressed — difficult though that task may seem on a Monday morning — isn't a project.

A project is a series of steps, often performed by more than one person. In addition:

✦ **A project has a specific and measurable goal.** You know you have finished the project when you have successfully met your project goal.

✦ **Projects have a specific time frame.** The success of a project is often measured by how successfully the project has been completed within the amount of time allotted to it.

✦ **Projects use resources.** Resources aren't just people; resources can include money, machinery, materials, and more. How well these resources are allocated and orchestrated is another key measure of a project's success or failure.

✦ **All projects consist of interdependent, yet individual, steps called *tasks*.** No piece of a project exists in a vacuum. If one task runs late or over budget, it typically affects other tasks, the overall schedule, and the total cost.

By their nature, projects are dynamic. They can last for months or even years. In addition, projects tend to grow, change, and behave in ways that you can't always predict. Consequently, you, as a project manager, have to remain alert to the progress and vagaries of your projects or you will never reach your goals. Documentation and communication are your two key tools for staying on top of a project throughout its life.

Exploring project management

Project management is a discipline that examines the nature of projects and offers ways to control their progress. Project management attempts to organize and systematize the procedures in a project to minimize the number of surprises you may encounter.

Project management and project managers concern themselves with certain key areas:

✦ Scheduling

✦ Budgeting

✦ Managing resources

✦ Tracking and reporting progress

To manage these aspects of projects, certain tools have evolved over the years. Some of these are conceptual, such as the *critical path*; others involve specific formats for charting progress, such as a *Gantt Chart*. The following sections introduce some key project management concepts and tools.

Critical path and slack

The critical path marks the series of tasks in a project that must be completed on time in order for the overall project to stay on schedule. For example, suppose that you are planning a going-away party at your office. You have three days to plan the party. Here are some of the tasks involved and their time frames:

Task	Duration
Signing the goodbye card	Three days
Ordering food	One day
Reserving a room	One hour
Buying a goodbye gift	One day

The shortest task, reserving a room, takes only one hour. Assuming that plenty of rooms are available for holding the party, you can delay reserving the room until the last hour of the third day. Delaying this task won't actually cause any delay in holding the party — as long as you accomplish this task by the end of the longest task, which is getting everyone to sign the goodbye card. Therefore, the task of reserving a room isn't on the critical path. However, you can't delay the task of signing the goodbye card, which is projected to take three days to accomplish, without delaying the party. Therefore, the card-signing task is on the critical path. (Of course, this example is very simple; typically, a whole series of tasks that can't afford delay form an entire critical path.)

The following points further define and clarify these concepts:

✦ *Slack,* also called *float,* is the amount of time you can delay a task before that task moves onto the critical path. In the preceding example, the one-hour-long task — reserving a room — has slack. This task can slip a few hours, even a couple of days, and the party will still happen on time. However, if you wait until the last half-hour of the third day to reserve a room, that task will have used up its slack and will then move onto the critical path.

✦ *Critical path* changes as the project progresses. Remember that a critical path is a means of prioritizing tasks that have no leeway in their timing to ensure that they don't run late and affect your overall schedule. Knowing where your critical path tasks are at any point during the project is crucial to staying on track. Figures 1-1 and 1-2 show the same schedule — first with all tasks displayed and then filtered to show only the tasks on the critical path.

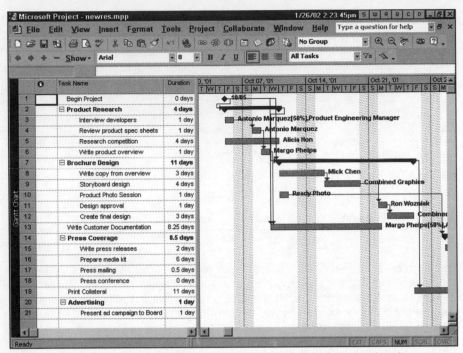

Figure 1-1: Tasks with slack displayed alongside those on the critical path

Cross-Reference   See Chapter 7 to learn how to filter for only critical tasks and for more information about changing the view of your project.

Durations and milestones

Most tasks in a project take a specific amount of time to accomplish. Tasks can take anywhere from five minutes to five months. The length of time needed to complete a task is called the task's *duration*. You should always try to break the long tasks in a project down to smaller tasks of shorter duration so that you can track their progress more accurately. For example, break a five-month-long task into five, month-long tasks. Checking off the completion of the smaller tasks each month reduces the odds of a serious surprise five months down the road — and makes you feel like you're actually getting something done.

Some tasks, called *milestones*, have no (zero) duration. Milestones are merely points in time that mark the start or completion of some phase of a project. For example, if your project involves designing a new brochure, the approval of the initial design may be considered a milestone. You can assign a duration to the process of routing the design to various people for review, but assigning a length of time to the actual moment when you have everyone's final approval is probably impossible. Therefore, this task has a duration of zero — that is, approval of the design is a milestone that simply marks a key moment in the project.

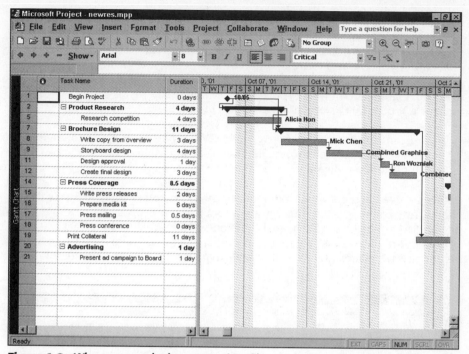

Figure 1-2: When you apply the appropriate filter, only the tasks that can't afford any delay will appear in your schedule.

Resource-driven schedules and fixed-duration tasks

Some tasks take the same amount of time — no matter how many people or other resources you throw at them. Flying from San Francisco to New York is likely to take five hours, regardless of how many pilots or flight attendants you add. You can't speed up a test on a mixture of two solvents that must sit for six hours to react by adding more solvent or by hiring more scientists to work in the laboratory. These tasks have a *fixed duration*, meaning that their timing is set by the nature of the task (these tasks are also called *fixed tasks*).

On the other hand, the number of available resources can affect the duration of some tasks. For example, if one person needs two hours to dig a ditch, adding a second person will likely cut the time in half. The project still requires two hours of effort, but two resources can perform the task simultaneously. Tasks whose durations are affected by the addition or subtraction of resources are called *resource-driven tasks*.

Note In real-world projects, this calculation is seldom so exact. Because people have different skill levels and perform work at different speeds, two people don't always cut the time of a task exactly in half. In addition, the more people you add to a task, the more communication, cooperation, and training may be involved. Although Microsoft Project handles additional assignments of resources as a strictly mathematical calculation, you can still use your judgment of the resources involved to modify this calculation somewhat (see Chapter 10).

Diagrams that aid project management

Gantt charts, network diagrams, and work breakdown structures (WBS) are tools of project management that have evolved over many years. These tools are simply charts that you can use to track different aspects of your project. Figure 1-3 shows a Microsoft Project Gantt Chart, and Figure 1-4 shows a Microsoft Project network diagram. Figure 1-5 shows a typical WBS, although Microsoft Project does not include a WBS chart as one of its standard views.

On the CD-ROM You can purchase an add-on product (WBS Chart for Project) to create a WBS chart from a Microsoft Project file. The CD-ROM included with this book features a sample of the program.

Before people used computers to manage their projects, managers drew these charts. Any self-respecting project war room had a ten-foot network diagram, WBS, or Gantt Chart tacked to the wall. By the end of the project, this chart was as marked up and out-of-date as last year's appointment calendar. Thankfully, project management software makes these charts easier to generate, update, and customize.

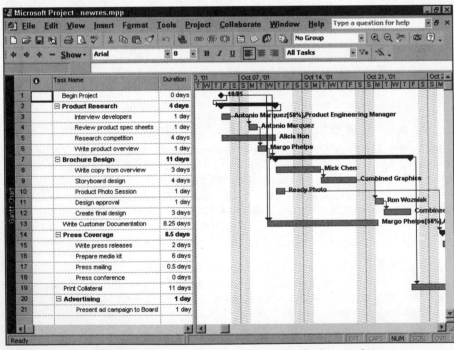

Figure 1-3: The Gantt chart bars represent timing of tasks in a project.

Figure 1-4: The network diagram resembles a flowchart for work in a project.

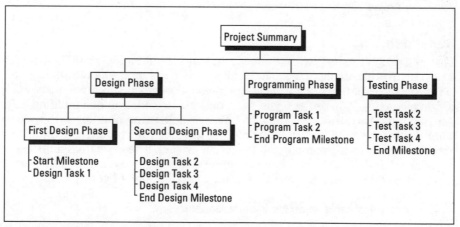

Figure 1-5: The work breakdown structure chart reminds you of a typical company organization chart.

A Gantt Chart represents the tasks in a project with bars that reflect the duration of individual tasks. Milestones are shown as diamond-shaped objects.

You can learn more about the various elements of the Gantt Chart in Chapter 2. For this chapter's purposes, you simply need to know that a Gantt Chart enables you to visualize and track the timing of a project.

Network diagrams, on the other hand, don't accurately detail the timing of a project. Instead, a network diagram shows the flow of tasks in a project and the relationships of tasks to each other. Each task is contained in a box called a *node*, and lines that flow among the nodes indicate the flow of tasks.

In Project 98 and prior versions of Project, network diagrams were called PERT charts. PERT stands for *Program Evaluation and Review Technique*. The Special Projects Office of the U.S. Navy devised this method for tracking the flow of tasks in a project when it was designing the Polaris submarine in the late 1950s.

The U.S. Defense establishment uses the "work breakdown structure" (WBS) as its primary tool for managing projects and describes the WBS in Military Standard (MIL-STD) 881B (25 Mar 93): "A work breakdown structure is a product-oriented family tree composed of hardware, software, services, data and facilities . . . [it] displays and defines the product(s) to be developed and/or produced and relates the elements of work to be accomplished to each other and to the end product(s)."

Project doesn't contain a PERT chart view; however, on the CD-ROM you'll find a sample version of PERT Chart EXPERT, a program that converts the information in any Project file to a PERT view.

Dependencies

The final project management concept that you should understand is dependencies. The overall timing of a project isn't simply the sum of the durations of all tasks, because all tasks in a project don't usually happen simultaneously. For example, in a construction project, you must pour the foundation of a building before you can build the structure. You also have to enclose the building with walls and windows before you lay carpeting. In other words, project managers anticipate and establish relationships among the tasks in a project. These relationships are called *dependencies*. Only after you have created tasks, assigned durations to them, and established dependencies can you see the overall timing of your project.

Chapter 4 covers several kinds of dependencies.

Managing projects with project management software

Many people manage projects with stacks of outdated to-do lists and colorful hand-drawn wall charts. They scribble notes on calendars in pencil, knowing that — more often than not — dates and tasks will change over time. They hold meetings, meetings, and more meetings to keep everyone in the project informed. People have developed these simple organizational tools because projects typically have so many bits and pieces that no one can possibly remember them all.

To manage any project, you need some set of procedures. Project management software automates many of these procedures. With project management software, you can:

✦ **Plan upfront.** By pre-planning the various elements of your project, you can more accurately estimate the time and resources required to complete the project.

✦ **View your progress.** By examining your progress on an ongoing basis from various perspectives, you can see whether you are likely to meet your goal.

✦ **Recognize conflicts.** By identifying time and resource conflicts early, you can try out various what-if scenarios to resolve them before they get out of hand.

✦ **Make adjustments.** You can make adjustments to task timing and costs, and automatically update all other tasks in the project to reflect the impact of your changes.

✦ **Generate professional-looking reports.** You can create reports on the status of your project to help team members prioritize and help management make informed decisions.

With improved workgroup, intranet, and e-mail capabilities, Microsoft Project also makes communication and cooperation among workgroup members much easier and more productive.

 Cross-Reference Project 2002 expands the capabilities of Project Server, which is Project's tool to manage projects on the Web. For more details, see Chapters 18 and 19.

What's required of you

Many people contemplate using project management software with about as much relish as they contemplate their next visit to the dentist. They anticipate hours of data-entry time before they can get anything out of the software. To some extent, that vision is true. You have to provide a certain amount of information about your project for any software to estimate schedules and generate reports, just as you have to enter numbers for a spreadsheet to calculate a budget or a loan payback schedule.

On the other hand, after you enter your basic project information into Microsoft Project, the ongoing maintenance of that data is far easier than generating handwritten to-do lists that become obsolete almost immediately. In addition, the accuracy and professionalism of reports that you generate with Project can make the difference between a poorly managed project and a successful one. In addition, as with a quarterly budget that you create with spreadsheet software, after you enter the data, Project performs its calculations automatically.

So, exactly what do you have to do to manage your project with Microsoft Project? To create a schedule in Microsoft Project, you must enter the following information about your tasks:

✦ Individual task names

✦ Task durations

✦ Task dependencies

To track the costs of these tasks, you add certain information about resources, including:

✦ The list of human and material resources and their costs for both standard and overtime hours

✦ The assignment of resources to specific tasks

To track a project over its lifetime, you need to enter the following information:

✦ Progress on tasks

✦ Changes in task timing or dependencies

✦ Changes in resources — that is, resources that are added to or removed from the project

✦ Changes in resource time commitments and costs

What Microsoft Project can do to help

Even though you still must enter a great deal of information into your project schedule, Microsoft Project has various shortcuts that can help you automate this chore.

✦ **Project templates.** If you often do similar types of projects, you can create project templates with typical project tasks already in place; you can then modify the templates for individual projects.

You can take advantage of sample project templates on this book's companion CD-ROM. These templates represent a cross-section of typical industries and project types.

✦ **Automating repeated tasks.** If you have tasks that repeat throughout the life of a project, such as weekly meetings or regular reviews, you can create a single repeating task and Project will duplicate it for you.

Project 2002 supports importing task information from Outlook and Excel.

✦ **Import existing task lists.** You can create projects from tasks that you've set up in Outlook or you can use Excel to start your project and then easily import the spreadsheet into Project.

See Chapter 3 for more information about starting projects in Outlook and Excel and then moving them into Project 2002.

✦ **Workgroup tracking.** You can use workgroup features that enable individual team members to enter and track progress on smaller pieces of the project. By tracking with this method, no individual person has an overwhelming amount of data entry to do. Also, team members feel more accountable and involved in the project.

See the chapters in Part V of this book, "Working in Groups," for detailed information about working in groups.

✦ **Macros.** You can take advantage of Microsoft's Visual Basic language to build macros that automate repetitive tasks, such as generating weekly reports.

See Chapter 21 for more information about using macros to speed your work.

The Life Cycle of a Project

Projects typically consist of several phases. Understanding the nature of each phase can help you to relate the features of Microsoft Project to your own projects.

Identifying your goal and the project's scope

Before you can even begin to plan a project, you have to identify the goal, which isn't always as obvious as it sounds. Various participants may define a project's goal differently. In fact, many projects fail because the team members are unwittingly working toward different goals. For example, is the team's goal to perform a productivity study, or to actually improve productivity? Is the outcome for your project to agree on the final building design, or is it to complete the actual construction of the building? As you analyze your goal and factor in the perspectives of other team members, make sure that your project isn't actually just one step in a series of projects to reach a larger, longer-term goal.

To identify your goal, you can use various communication tools, such as meetings, e-mail, and conference calls. Most importantly, you should conduct a dialogue at various levels (management through front-line personnel) that gets ideas on the table and answers questions. Take the time to write a goal statement and circulate it among the team members to make sure that everyone understands the common focus of the project.

Note   Be careful not to set a long-range goal that is likely to change before the project ends. Smaller projects or projects that have been broken into various phases are more manageable and more flexible.

After you understand your goal, you should also gather the information you need to define the project's *scope*. This endeavor may take some research on your part. The scope of a project is a statement of more specific parameters or constraints for its completion. Project constraints usually fall within the areas of time, quality, and cost, and they often relate directly to project deliverables.

The following are some sample goal and scope statements:

Project A:

✦ **Goal:** To locate a facility for our warehouse.

✦ **Scope:** By October 15, to find a modern warehouse facility of approximately 5,200 square feet, with a lease cost of no more than $3,000 per month, and in a location convenient to our main office.

Project B:

✦ **Goal:** To launch a new cleaning product.

✦ **Scope:** Includes test marketing the product, designing packaging, and creating and launching an advertising campaign. The launch must be completed before the end of the third quarter of 2002 and must cost no more than $750,000.

Notice that the second scope statement designates major phases of the project (test marketing, designing packaging, and an ad campaign). This statement provides a starting point for planning the tasks in the project. In fact, you may eventually decide to break this project into smaller projects of test marketing, designing packaging, and launching an advertising campaign. Writing out the scope of the project may encourage you to redefine both the goal and the scope to make the project more manageable.

Tip   Keep your goal and scope statements brief and to the point. If you can't explain your goal or scope in a sentence or two, then your project may be overly ambitious and complex. Consider breaking it into smaller projects.

Writing a simple goal and scope statement ensures that you've gathered key data, such as deliverables, timing, and budget, and that you and your team agree on the focus of everyone's efforts. These activities are likely to occur before you ever open a Microsoft Project file.

Planning

When you understand the goal and scope of a project, you can begin to work backwards to determine the steps you need to take to reach the goal. Look for major phases first, and then break each phase into a logical sequence of steps.

Planning for resources is one aspect of planning the entire project. Resources can include equipment of limited availability, materials, individual workers, and groups of workers. Take into account various schedules and issues, such as overtime, vacations, and shared resources between projects. Time, money, and resources are closely related: You can save time with more resources, but resources typically cost money. You need to understand the order of priority among time, quality, and money.

Note   There's truth to the old joke: Time, budget, or quality — pick two. Throwing resources (which usually become costs) at a schedule can decrease the time but can also cause loss of quality control. Stretching out the time can improve quality but usually causes resource conflicts and added costs. Microsoft Project helps you see the trade-offs among these three important criteria throughout the life of your project.

Planning is the point at which you begin to enter data in Microsoft Project and see your project take shape. Figure 1-6 shows an initial Microsoft Project schedule.

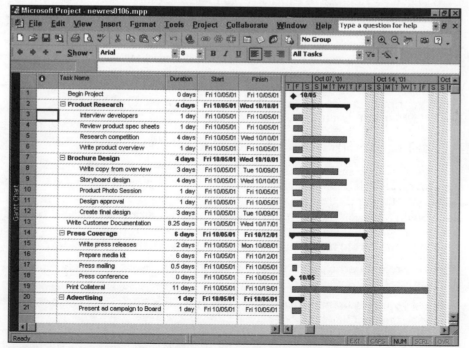

Figure 1-6: The outline format of a Project schedule clearly shows the various phases of your project. Notice that dependencies among tasks have not yet been established; every task starts at the same time, which isn't always possible.

Revising

Most of the time, you send an initial project schedule to various managers or coworkers for approval or input so that you can refine it, based on different factors. You can use the reporting features of Microsoft Project to generate several drafts of your plan.

Chapter 13 explains more about the reports available in Project.

Be prepared to revise your plan after everyone has a chance to review it. You may want to create and save multiple Project files to generate what-if scenarios based on the input you receive. Seeing your plans from various perspectives is a great way to take advantage of Project's power.

Finding resolutions to conflicts in timing and resource allocation is another aspect of planning and revising. Project helps you pinpoint these conflicts, which may include:

✦ A team member or resource booked on several projects at once

✦ A task beginning before another task that must precede it

✦ Unusually high use of expensive equipment in one phase that is throwing your budget out of whack

This book contains many tricks and techniques for resolving conflicts. Chapters 9 and 10, in particular, focus on using Microsoft Project features to resolve scheduling and resource problems.

When your project plan seems solid, you can take a picture of it, called a *baseline*, against which you can track actual progress.

Chapter 11 explains how to set (and, if necessary, clear) baselines.

Tracking

You should try to nail down your tracking methods before your project begins:

✦ Do you want to track your progress once a week or once a month?

✦ Do project participants actually track their own work or merely report their progress to you?

✦ Do you want to roll those smaller reports into a single, less-detailed report for management?

Knowing how you will track your project's progress, and who needs to know what and when, helps your team establish efficient tracking mechanisms from the outset, which reduces frustration.

The Microsoft Project schedule shown in Figure 1-7 uses the Tracking Gantt view to show the original baseline (the bottom bar of each task) tracked against actual progress (the top bar of each task).

Tip You can save interim baselines of a schedule at various points during your project. This approach helps you see where major shifts occurred and shows how you accommodated those shifts.

Figure 1-7: The darker portion of each upper task bar and the percentage figure to the right of each upper task bar indicate the percentage of each task that is complete.

Learning from your mistakes

Learning project management software isn't like learning to use a word processor. Project management entails conceptual layers that transcend the tools and features of the software. Having the experience and wisdom to use these features effectively comes from repeated use. You probably won't be a proficient Microsoft Project user right out of the gate. You have to work through one or more projects before you really know the most effective way to enter information about your project. You can expect to develop efficient tracking methods over time. Don't worry — it took you time to learn all you know about managing projects. If you pay attention to what goes on during your projects when you first implement Microsoft Project schedules, then you can learn from your mistakes.

Microsoft Project enables you to review your projects and see clearly where you estimated incorrectly, made adjustments too slowly, or didn't break phases into manageable chunks. Project keeps your original schedule's baseline in a single file, along with interim baselines and your final tracked schedule. When planning future projects, you can use these older baselines to help gauge the duration of tasks, the cost of certain items, how many resources are too many resources, and how many resources aren't nearly enough.

In the end, you'll be a more successful and efficient project manager. You can easily show your boss the specific actions that you've taken to avoid problems and provide solutions. In addition, you'll have the tools you need to help you and your manager understand the issues you face and get the support you need.

Summary

This chapter presented a survey of the discipline known as "project management" and explained the role that project management software can play to help you manage projects.

✦ Projects involve a stated goal, a specific time frame, and multiple resources (which can include people, equipment, and materials).

✦ Project management seeks to control issues of time, quality, and money.

✦ Critical path, slack, task durations, milestones, fixed tasks, resource-driven tasks, and dependencies are project management elements that help you build and monitor a project.

✦ Project management software can assist you in planning, tracking, and communicating with team members and reporting on projects with tools such as Gantt Charts and network diagrams.

✦ Although using Project takes some effort on your part, this effort pays off in increased productivity and efficiency.

✦ Projects typically have five phases: Setting the goal and defining scope, planning, revising, tracking, and reviewing to learn from your mistakes.

Chapter 2 takes a closer look at the Project environment and provides information about some of the tools that you can use to manage a project.

✦   ✦   ✦

Exploring the Microsoft Project Environment

CHAPTER 2

✦ ✦ ✦ ✦

In This Chapter

Taking a first look at Project

What's new in Project 2002

✦ ✦ ✦ ✦

Microsoft Project has come a long way in the past few years. It now sports an interface that makes managing a project almost as easy as maintaining your personal calendar. If you're a user of other Microsoft products, such as Word or Excel, the menus and tools in Project will, happily, look like old friends. And although Project's many views can be a bit overwhelming at first, they enable you to choose the perspective you need to monitor the progress of your project at any given time.

This chapter introduces Project's environment, as well as the powerful tools that Project places at your disposal. You practice moving among different views and work with some of the tools and onscreen elements that you can use to create schedules.

Taking a First Look at Project

Beginning with Project 2002, two versions of Microsoft Project will be available off the shelf. You can purchase Project 2002 Standard or Project 2002 Professional. These products differ only in the way that they support Project Server, which is Project's tool to manage projects on the Web.

Note   Project Server is the new name for Project Central and is now sold as a separate product; you won't find it on the Project 2002 CD like you did with Project 2000 and Project Central.

What Is Project Server?

Project Server enables you to manage projects on your company's intranet or on the Internet — and only the manager must actually install and use Microsoft Project. Everyone else on the project uses Project Web Access, the Web-based product that connects to the Project Server database that contains your project data. You open Project Web Access by typing the URL to the Project Server database into Internet Explorer 5.5 (or later version). Using Project Web Access *instead of* Microsoft Project, resources can:

✦ View a project's Gantt Chart

✦ Receive, refuse, and delegate work assignments

✦ Update assignments with progress and completion information

✦ Attach supporting documentation, such as budget estimates or feasibility studies to a project

✦ Receive notices about task status

✦ Send status reports to the project manager

Project managers can do even more than resources. For example, by using Project Server, project managers have access to a company-wide resource pool (called the Enterprise Resource Pool) that tracks resource allocations across projects. If a project manager finds that a specific resource is unavailable, the project manager can define the requirements for the job and let Project Server tools search the Enterprise Research Pool to find another resource with the same skills.

Project Server has been expanded beyond the capabilities of Project Central; however, the features and functions that you see in Project Server depend on the version of Project 2002 that you are using — Project Standard or Project Professional. If you are using Project Standard, you will find Project Server's features and capabilities about the same as those of Project Central and Project 2000. If you are using Project Professional 2002, you will have access to the entire suite of features available in Project Server. In this book, we'll assume you're using Project Professional.

Cross-Reference   See Chapters 18 and 19 for more information on the expansion of Project Server from Project Central.

Note   If you are not connected to Project Server, you'll see no difference in functionality between Project 2002 Standard and Project 2002 Professional. You will see commands in Project 2002 Professional that you won't see in Project 2002 Standard, but the commands won't be available for use.

Cross-Reference   See Chapters 18 and 19 for more information about Project Server and Project Web Access.

Although Microsoft Project doesn't come with Microsoft Office software, it is a member of the Microsoft Office family. Consequently, Project uses the standard Microsoft Office menu and toolbar structure and contains some of the familiar Microsoft Office tools.

Tip If you've used Outlook, Microsoft's organizer, e-mail, and calendar program, you'll recognize the bar on the left of the screen that enables you to switch among views and functions in the software. Project calls this feature the View Bar. You can choose to hide or display the View bar. Open the View menu; if a check appears next to View Bar, Project displays the View Bar. Click View Bar to remove the check and hide the View Bar.

Note The figures throughout this book don't show the View Bar.

Starting Project

When you open Microsoft Project from the Programs folder of the Windows Start menu, Project initially displays the main screen for Project 2002, as shown in Figure 2-1. This screen includes a new "goal-based user interface," called the *Project Guide*. The Project Guide is composed of both the Project Guide pane on the left side of the screen and the Project Guide toolbar.

Tip If Project does not appear on your Windows Start menu, you can use the Run command on the Start menu. Run the file `Winproj.exe`, which is found in the Microsoft Project folder on your hard drive. You can also open Project by double-clicking a project file in a directory contained in the My Computer area. Project files are saved with the extension .mpp.

Note If your organization uses Project Server, you may be prompted to connect to it or work offline before you see the Project Information dialog box. In this book, we'll work offline until Chapter 18.

New Feature The Project Guide pane and Project Guide toolbar use wizards to walk you through the necessary steps for creating projects.

At this point, you can use the Project Guide toolbar and the Project Guide pane to begin building your project. Click a link in the Project Guide to start a wizard in the Project Guide pane that walks you through the process suggested by the link. For example, if you click the Define the project link, Project starts the Define the Project wizard, as shown in Figure 2-2. The Project wizard consists of four steps; the first step helps you to establish the starting date for your project. After setting the date, click the right arrow at the top of the pane or click Save and go to Step 2 at the bottom of the Project Guide pane.

Tip The Project Guide has a toolbar that you can use; right-click any toolbar and choose Project Guide.

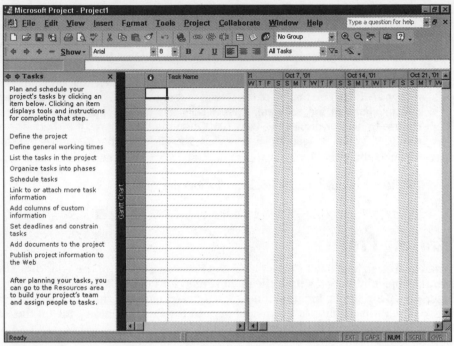

Figure 2-1: Project 2002's new goal-based user interface — Project Guide — helps you build your project. The buttons on the Project Guide toolbar control the information that appears in the Project Guide pane.

Figure 2-2: Clicking the Define the project link starts the Define the Project wizard in the Project Guide Task pane.

If you decide that you don't want to use the Project Guide (perhaps it eats up too much screen real estate for your taste, for example) you can hide the pane. To temporarily hide the pane, click either the X in the upper-right corner of the pane. To turn off the Project Guide feature, open the Options dialog box (choose Tools ➪ Options) and click the Interface tab. Then, remove the check from the Display Project Guide box.

Cross-Reference See Chapter 20 for more information on setting options in Project.

After you've hidden the pane, you see the blank Project screen in the Gantt Chart view, as shown in Figure 2-3.

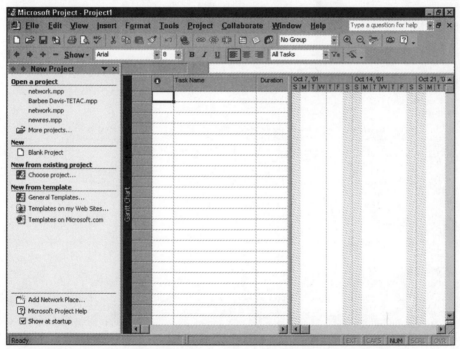

Figure 2-3: A blank project contains no project information; when you enter information in the Gantt view, the split pane displays the data both textually and graphically.

Project always opens a new project schedule in the Gantt view. You see other views throughout this book, but you're likely to spend a great deal of your time in the Gantt view. This view offers a wealth of information about your project in a single snapshot. In most table views, you find a fill handle, which you can use to populate columns, just as you use a fill handle in Excel.

For a detailed look at the other views available in Project, see Chapter 6.

Examining the Gantt Chart view

The Gantt Chart view has two main sections: the Gantt table and the Gantt Chart. After you enter task information, the Gantt table (in the left pane) holds columns of information about your project, such as task name, duration, start date, and more. The Gantt Chart (in the right pane) is a graphic representation that helps you see the timing and relationships among tasks, as shown in Figure 2-4.

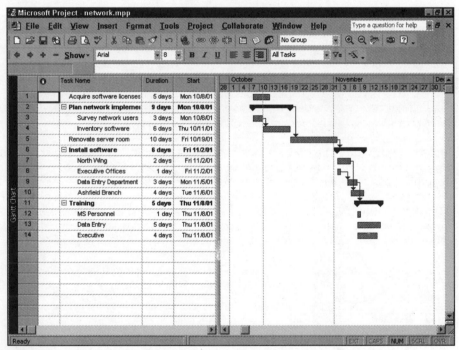

Figure 2-4: A sample project with task details in the Gantt table and bars representing tasks in the Gantt Chart.

The timescale along the top of the Gantt Chart acts like a horizontal calendar. Think of it as a ruler against which you draw the tasks in your project. Instead of marking off inches, however, this ruler marks off the hours, days, weeks, and months of your project. Notice that the chart displays two timescales: the major timescale along the top and a minor timescale beneath it. These two timescales help you to see the two levels of timing at once, such as the day and hour or the week and day.

Note   You can customize your timescale to show unusual time increments, such as thirds of months, or you can make the timescale display larger on your screen. In Figure 2-5, I customized the timescale to show week increments. Double-click the timescale itself to display the Timescale dialog box. You can adjust these and other settings for the major and minor timescale on the Timescale tab. Also note that Project uses default settings for the number of hours in a workday, days in a week, and so on. To adjust these settings to display or hide nonworking days, you can use the settings on the Nonworking Time tab in the Timescale dialog box.

Cross-Reference   In Chapter 3, I explain how to modify the calendars that control a project.

You can modify what you see onscreen in the Gantt view, and Project will carry those modifications to other views. After you practice moving among these views, you'll be able to see information about timing, budget, or resource assignments in detail, or you can look at just the big picture. You also can customize what each view shows you, depending on what you need to see. For example, you can use the divider that runs between the Gantt table and Gantt Chart to adjust how much of the window that each pane occupies. Dragging this divider to the right reveals more columns of data about your project in the Gantt table. Dragging the divider to the left displays more of the project's task bars in the Gantt Chart.

In addition to modifying how much of each pane you display onscreen, you can zoom in or out to view larger or smaller time increments for different perspectives of your project's schedule. You can show smaller time increments in the Gantt Chart by clicking the Zoom In button, or you can show larger increments of time by clicking the Zoom Out button. A daily perspective on a three-year project enables you to manage day-to-day tasks, whereas a quarterly representation of your project may be more useful when you're discussing larger issues with your management team.

Notice that the two panes of the Gantt Chart view have their own sets of scroll bars at the bottom of the window. To perform actions on information, you must use the appropriate scroll bar and select objects in the appropriate pane.

Using Project menus

The menus in Project 2002, which you access via the menu bar at the top of the screen, work like the menus in Office 2000 and Office XP; by default, commands are available "on demand." That is, when you open a menu, you see a small subset of commands that Microsoft believes you'll use most often. In addition, at the bottom of the menu, you see a pair of downward-pointing arrows, as shown in Figure 2-5. If you highlight the pair of arrows (or pause for a few moments), Project displays the other commands that usually appear on the menu, as shown in Figure 2-6. After you select a command, that command appears on the menu as soon as you open the menu.

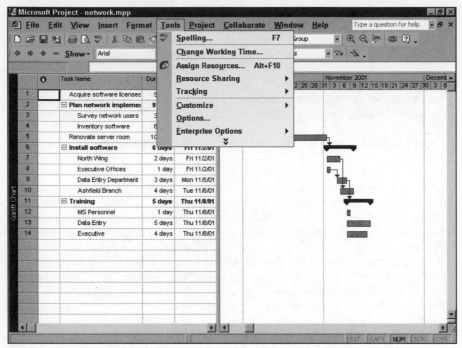

Figure 2-5: Initially, only a subset of commands appears on a menu.

You can change this menu behavior so that all commands appear on a menu when you open it. To do this, use the Customize dialog box.

Cross-Reference   The Customize dialog box is described in detail in Chapter 20.

Several of the menus in Project offer commands that are probably quite familiar to you, such as Save, Print, and Copy. Other menus on the menu bar are very specific to the tasks that you perform with Project.

Table 2-1 shows the various types of functions that you can perform from each menu.

Figure 2-6: When you pause or click the down arrow at the bottom of the menu, the rest of the menu commands appear.

Table 2-1	
Microsoft Project Menus	
Menu	**Types of Functions Available**
File	Open and close new and existing files; save and print files; adjust page setup and document properties; and route files to e-mail recipients.
Edit	Cut, copy, and paste text or objects; manipulate data with Fill, Clear, and Delete commands; link and unlink task relationships; and locate information with Find, Replace, and Go To commands.
View	Select various default views of your project; access standard report formats; choose to display or hide various toolbars; use the Zoom feature; or enter header and footer information.
Insert	Insert new tasks, another Project file, or columns in views; also insert various objects into your schedule, including drawings, Excel charts, Word documents, media clips, and even hyperlinks to Web sites.

Continued

Table 2-1 *(continued)*	
Menu	*Types of Functions Available*
Format	Adjust the appearance of text, task bars, the Timescale display, or the overall appearance of a view's layout.
Tools	Run or modify Spelling and AutoCorrect functions to proofread your schedule; access workgroup features; establish links between projects; and modify your working calendar or resources. You can also customize standard views and functions with the Organizer, Options, or Customize commands, or record macros and initiate tracking functions. If you're using Project 2002 Professional, you can set Enterprise options.
Project	Display task or project information or notes, or use commands to sort or filter tasks to see specific details. You can also control outlining features of your project tasks from here.

The remaining two menus, Window and Help, contain commands to arrange windows onscreen and access Help features, respectively.

 See Chapter 3 for more information on the Help system in Project.

Microsoft has placed corresponding tool symbols and keyboard shortcuts (such as Del or Ctrl+F) next to the menu commands, as shown in Figure 2-7. This display helps you to learn the various ways to get things done more quickly in Project. Notice also that the main menus sometimes open up submenus (also called *side menus* or *cascading menus*). A black arrow to the right of a command indicates the presence of a side menu. Also, if you choose a menu command followed by an ellipsis, such as "Find..." or "Replace...," Project displays a dialog box.

Figure 2-7: Tool symbols appear to the left and keyboard shortcuts appear to the right of commands on Project menus. Submenus offer more choices, and dialog boxes appear if you click a menu command followed by an ellipsis.

Examining the toolbars

You're probably already familiar with tools in Windows programs and the way in which they appear by category on toolbars. When you open Project, two default toolbars are visible: the Standard toolbar and the Formatting toolbar, as shown in Figure 2-8.

Figure 2-8: The Standard toolbar and the Formatting toolbar are the default toolbars in Project.

You may see both toolbars appearing on one row when you open Project; in this case, you'll also notice that you don't see all the tools displayed in Figure 2-8. You can change the appearance so that the toolbars appear on two rows, as I've done throughout this book. If you choose to keep both toolbars on one row, you can access the buttons that don't appear by clicking the More Buttons down arrow, which appears at the end of each toolbar, and then clicking the button that you want to use.

Tip   If you hover your mouse over the More Buttons down arrow, a screen tip appears to help you identify it.

Cross-Reference   To change the appearance of the toolbars in Project, use the Customize dialog box, which is discussed in Chapter 20.

In some software programs, the tools available to you are context-sensitive; that is, they change according to the function that you're performing. In Project, the default toolbars are fairly consistent. Some tools become unavailable when you perform different functions or change views; in such cases, the tools appear grayed out, and nothing happens when you click them.

Note   If you insert an object into your project from another Microsoft application, such as Excel or PowerPoint, the other program's environment replaces the toolbars and menus in Project when you select that object. Therefore, you can use the other program's tools to modify the object without leaving Project. The toolbars and menus in Project reappear when you click anywhere outside the inserted object.

In addition to the Standard and Formatting toolbars, Project contains several other toolbars, which sometimes appear automatically when you're performing certain types of activities. However, you also can display any of these toolbars at any time by choosing View ➪ Toolbars and choosing from the toolbar side menu.

Tip   These toolbars appear as floating toolbars when you choose to display them. You can move floating toolbars anywhere on your screen by dragging their title bars. Alternatively, you can anchor any floating toolbar at the top of your screen near the default toolbars; to do so, simply drag the toolbar (using its title bar) to the top of the screen. Conversely, you can convert the Standard and Formatting toolbars into floating toolbars; to do so, just click anywhere on a toolbar (not directly on a tool, however) and drag it to any position on your screen.

Entering information

Several views or portions of views in Project, such as the Gantt table, use a familiar spreadsheet-style interface. Information appears in columns and rows. The intersection of a column and a row is an individual cell. Each task in your project has an ID number, indicated by the numbers that run down the left of the spreadsheet. You can enter information either in dialog boxes or directly into cells. When you select a cell, the Entry bar displays the information in the cell.

Cross-Reference   For more information on entering information in dialog boxes, see Chapter 4.

New Feature When you press the Delete key, Project no longer deletes an entire row; instead it deletes just the selected cell.

If you've ever used Microsoft Excel or one of the other popular spreadsheet programs, you already know how to enter and edit information in Project. When you begin typing in a cell, the insertion point appears in the cell to the right of any text that you enter. To edit text in a cell, click once to select the cell, and then press F2 or click a second time at the location in the cell where you want to begin editing. If you press F2, the insertion point appears at the right edge of the text in the cell. If you click a second time, the insertion point appears in the cell at the location where you clicked the second time.

As you enter information into a cell, the information also appears in the Entry bar, which runs along the top of the screen directly under the Formatting toolbar. The Entry bar in Project serves the same purpose as the Entry bar in Excel. You can type new text or edit existing text by clicking anywhere within the text in the Entry bar. Two buttons on the left of the bar enable you to cancel or accept an entry, as shown in Figure 2-9.

Figure 2-9: You can enter or edit text in individual cells or in the Entry bar.

Cross-Reference Chapter 4 covers entering and editing text in greater detail.

Changing views

Project offers multiple views in which you can display project information. A single view can't possibly show all the information that you need to see regarding timing, relationships among tasks, resource allocations, and project progress. In fact, each type of information requires special kinds of graphical and textual displays for you to interpret them accurately. Think of a project as a small business. As in any business, different people attend to various aspects of the work. The accounting department thinks mainly of the costs of doing business. The plant supervisor focuses on deadlines and having enough machinery to get the job done. Your human resources department thinks of people — their salaries, hours, benefits, and so on. As the owner of your project, you are likely to wear all these hats (and more) during the project. With Project, instead of changing caps as you move from one responsibility to another, you can simply switch to another view to see your work from a different perspective. Each view helps you to focus on a different aspect of your project. The View bar or the View menu enables you to jump from view to view, as shown in Figure 2-10.

Figure 2-10: The View bar offers several predefined views of your project.

The View bar contains icons for eight views; click the down arrow near the bottom of the bar to see them all. When you move down the View bar, an up arrow appears near the top of the bar so that you can return to the top of the View bar. You can display any of the views listed here by clicking it in the View bar. Similarly, the View menu contains commands for the same eight views; you can display any of the views listed on the View menu by clicking the command.

At the bottom of the View bar and on the View menu, you can see an item called *More Views*. Click More Views to open the More Views dialog box, as shown in Figure 2-11.

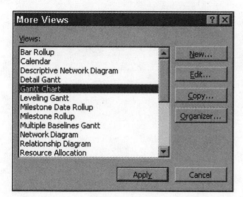

Figure 2-11: The More Views dialog box lists 24 built-in views — and you can add your own as well.

In Chapter 6, you learn more about which view you should use to gain a specific perspective on your project. In Chapter 7, you learn how to create custom views by clicking New in the More Views dialog box.

What's New in Project 2002

Rather than describing all the new features in Project 2002 at this point in the book, the following section describes just a few of them — and then provides a table that shows you where you can find more information in this book on other new features.

You can easily find the new features in the chapters in which I discuss them in detail. Simply look for the *New Feature* icon that appears next to this paragraph.

As I mentioned earlier, Project is not part of Office XP, but Project is part of the Office family. For this reason, you'll see some of the same interface features, such as Smart Tags and side panes, in Project 2002 that you find in Office XP. You'll also see feedback indicators whenever you make a change that is undoable. For example, in Figure 2-12, I changed the number of days originally set for the task. The Duration cell contains a small triangle, indicating the feedback. When you pass the mouse pointer over the cell, you'll see an icon; if you click the icon, Project will provide feedback — often explanations of calculations or alternative actions that you might take. Typically, you'll see feedback indicators if you make changes to resource assignments, edit the work, units, or duration, start, or finish of a task, or delete the task name.

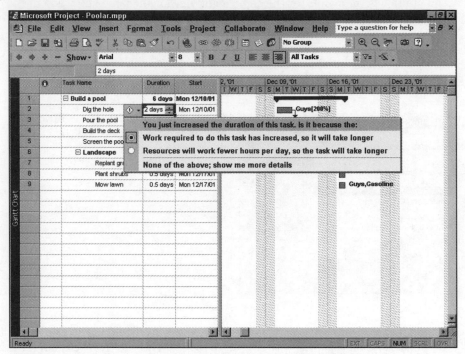

Figure 2-12: Feedback indicators provide you with additional information when you take various actions in Project.

Project 2002 contains some small "ease of use" changes, which are displayed in the following list:

✦ **The Delete key no longer deletes an entire row by default; instead, it deletes the contents of the current cell.** To delete a row, you can click the SmartTag that will appear, as shown in Figure 2-13, or you can select the row (by clicking the number of the row) and press Del.

✦ **You can change header row height in table views.** Move the mouse pointer underneath the row that you want to resize and, when the mouse pointer becomes a two-headed arrow pointing up and down, drag to the desired height.

✦ **By default, Project 2002 now wraps text in header row cells; you can turn this option off.** Open the View menu and click Tables. Then click More Tables and choose the table that you want to modify. Click Edit, and in the Table Definition dialog box that appears, as shown in Figure 2-14, remove the check from the Auto-Adjust Header Row Heights box.

Figure 2-13: Unlike prior versions, Project 2002 deletes the currently selected cell by default; you can use a SmartTag to choose to delete an entire row.

Figure 2-14: You can control whether text wraps in the header row of a table from the Table Definition dialog box.

✦ **You now have three timescale labels available in views with timescales.** For example, see the Gantt Chart view shown in Figure 2-15.

Cross-Reference   See Chapter 4 to learn how to set the timescale.

Figure 2-15: You can now set the timescale using three levels of detail.

✦ **You can open and modify Project 2002 files in Project 2000 and then reopen the file in Project 2002.** Fields and features new to Project 2002 won't be available or visible in Project 2000, but they will reappear when you reopen the project in Project 2002.

Project Server has many new features, as you'll see in Chapters 18 and 19. For example, you can use the Portfolio Modeling feature in the Project Server database to interactively tests changes to projects or staffing and view the impact of the changes. In the current version, you can save your results, but you cannot apply them directly to a project. (My crystal ball suggests that you watch for expansion of this feature in the next release of Project.)

Table 2-2 provides a list of other new features in Project — and includes the chapter in which you can find information about the new feature.

Table 2-2
New Features in Project 2002

Feature	Chapter	Special Note
SmartTags	2	
Project Guide	2, 3	
Calendar wizard	3	
Import Outlook and Excel tasks	3	
New Project wizard	3	
Assignment dialog box	5	
Generic resource	5	
Resource Availability Graph	5	Available also in Project Web Access if you are using Project Professional and Project Server
Printing View Totals	6	
Multiple Baselines and New Baseline Rollup Options	11	
Tracking Setup wizard	11	
Calculation Options	12	
Additional Earned Value fields and calculation options	14	
Attach supporting documents to projects	18	Available only if you are using Project Professional and Project Server
Check projects in and out to control access to enterprise projects	19	Available only if you are using Project Professional and Project Server
Notifications	19	Available only if you are using Project Professional and Project Server
To-Do List	18	Available only if you are using Project Professional and Project Server
Track Issues related to projects	18	Available only if you are using Project Professional and Project Server
Enterprise Custom Fields	19	Available only if you are using Project Professional and Project Server
Enterprise Global	19	Available only if you are using Project Professional and Project Server

Continued

Table 2-2 *(continued)*		
Feature	*Chapter*	*Special Note*
Enterprise Resources and Enterprise Resource Global	19	Available only if you are using Project Professional and Project Server
Project Server Accounts	19	
Resource Substitution Wizard	19	Available only if you are using Project Professional and Project Server
Resource View	19	Available only if you are using Project Professional and Project Server
Team Building	19	Available only if you are using Project Professional and Project Server
Versions	19	Available only if you are using Project Professional and Project Server
Import/Export Mapping Wizard	22	

Summary

This chapter introduced the Project 2002 environment and the many ways in which you can display project information. This chapter also described the following techniques:

✦ Understanding the Project screen

✦ Using Project menus and toolbars

✦ Entering information in your project

Chapter 3 covers how to get help in Project and how to save Project files.

✦   ✦   ✦

Getting Your Project Going

In this part of the book, you'll create your first new project. You'll define tasks in an outline structure and establish task timing, constraints, and dependencies. You'll then learn how to create resources, assign costs to them, and assign resources to tasks — all preliminary to identifying the costs associated with your project.

Creating a New Project

Now that you have some project management concepts under your belt and you've taken a stroll around Project's environment, you are ready to create your first schedule. Before you type a single date into a Project schedule, however, you must first assemble the relevant information about your project. Then you can open a new Project file and begin to build your project tasks by using a simple outline structure.

In this chapter, you begin to build your first Project schedule and learn how to take advantage of Project's various Help features. At the end of the chapter, you learn how to save your project.

Gathering Information

As you learned in Chapter 1, several elements must be in place before you can begin to build a project schedule. First, you must understand the overall goal and scope of the project so that you can clearly see the steps that lie between you and that goal. You'll find delineating the major steps involved a good place to start. Don't worry about the order of the tasks at this point — just brainstorm all the major areas of activity. For example, consider a project such as organizing an annual meeting for your company. Here are some possible steps that you may take:

   ♦ Book the meeting space

   ♦ Schedule speakers

   ♦ Arrange for audiovisual equipment

   ♦ Order food

   ♦ Send out invitations

   ♦ Mail out annual reports

The last item on that list raises the question of scope: Is it within the scope of your project to create the annual report or should you simply obtain copies of a report from the marketing department, for example, and mail them out to stockholders before the meeting? In some corporations, the person responsible for organizing the annual meeting also is responsible for overseeing the production of the annual report. Be sure to answer these questions of scope and responsibility at this stage of your planning.

For this example, you can assume that another department is creating the annual report. You simply need to make sure that someone mails copies of the report to all stockholders before the annual meeting.

Determining detail tasks

After you have prepared a list of major tasks, break them down into more detailed tasks. Take one of the items on the list — "Order food," for example — and consider how you can break down this task. How detailed should you get? Here's one possible breakdown of the "Order food" task:

✦ Create a budget

✦ Determine a menu

✦ Select a caterer

  • Send out requests for bids

  • Receive all estimates

  • Review estimates and award contract

✦ Give final headcount to caterer

✦ Confirm caterer one week ahead

Could you do without the detailed tasks under "Select a caterer"? Do you need more detail under "Create a budget"? Those decisions are up to you, based on your knowledge of your project and procedures. However, here are some points to keep in mind:

✦ Create tasks that remind you of major action items, but don't overburden yourself with items of such detail that keeping track of your schedule becomes a full-time job. That's the purpose of daily to-do lists.

✦ Include milestones to mark off points in your project. For example, the "Review estimates and reward contract" task under the summary task "Select a caterer" is a milestone — it marks a point in time by which you want to have made a major decision. If that time comes and goes and you haven't selected the caterer, will missing this deadline affect other subsequent tasks? If so, including that milestone could be vital to your success.

✦ Include tasks that management will want to know about because you'll use the Project schedule to report progress. If your boss wants to see that you've sent out a purchase order to the caterer per your new Accounting department procedures, you may want to include the task (even if you don't think that this level of detail is important).

Establishing time limits

After you have an idea of the tasks involved in your project, you need to have some idea of their timing. Should you allow two weeks for caterers to reply with bids? Not if you have only three weeks to organize the meeting. You may want to approach determining task timing by building an initial schedule in Project, assigning time to tasks, and seeing how close you can come to your deadline. If you're way off, you can go back and tweak the timing for individual tasks until your schedule works.

You may be tempted to trim time off your tasks to make them fit a deadline, but this approach tends to produce an unrealistic schedule. What is the solution? Use the initial schedule to convince your boss that you need more time, money, or resources to complete this project on time. If he or she wants to trim time from a specific task to meet the deadline, you may have grounds to ask for more help.

At this early planning stage, get any information that you need to assign timing to tasks; for example, contact vendors or subcontractors to get their timing estimates, which you need to reflect in your schedule. If your project has a drop-dead completion date, you should be aware of it. However, leave it to Project to show you whether your estimates work in an overall schedule.

Lining up your resources

Before you can build a Project schedule, you must understand what resources are available to you, as well as their costs. You don't necessarily have to know these resources by name, but you should know, for example, that your project needs three engineers at a cost of $75 per hour and one piece of earth-moving equipment at a daily rental cost of $450.

You need to identify these resources and assign them to individual tasks early in the project-planning process. Find out anything you can about the availability of these resources: Are some resources available only half-time for your project? Will all of the engineers be unavailable during the third week of August because of a professional conference? Research the cost and availability of resources as much as possible as you begin to build a project.

For more information about identifying resources and assigning them to individual tasks, see Chapters 5 and 19.

Looking at dependencies

Finally, before you enter project information into a schedule, be aware of relationships among tasks. Does the CEO have to approve the menu before you book the caterers? Are you required to wait three weeks after applying for a permit before starting construction on a building? If your project faces issues involving the order and relationships of tasks, you will save yourself some headaches down the line and build a more realistic schedule if you can identify these obstacles now.

Opening a Project File

You can start a project file in a couple of different ways; in this section, you'll first see the "usual" way to start a file. Then, I'll cover using templates with project files.

Opening a project file — the usual way

Okay, you've done your homework. You've made some notes about your upcoming project's tasks, timing, resources, and dependencies. You're ready to start building your first schedule in Project. On the Windows Start menu, highlight Programs and choose Microsoft Project. You'll see the main Project window, where you can begin building a task outline.

 Note   When you first open Microsoft Project — depending on how you have your Enterprise options set — you may be prompted to connect to Project Server or work offline. To work offline, simply click My Computer and then click the Work Offline button.

 Cross-Reference   To learn how to set Project Server options, see Chapter 19.

Other ways to open or start projects

You can base your project on one of the templates that became available in Project 2000. Templates contain "standard" information to help you get started quickly. Instead of entering tasks, you may need only to edit tasks. Open the File menu and click New. In the New Project task pane that appears, click the template that you want to use.

 Tip   If you don't see the template, click General Templates to display the Templates dialog box. From the Project Templates tab, select the template that you want to use.

 Note   You may need your Project 2002 CD to install the template.

If you want to open a project that you previously saved, use the New Project task pane again. (If you don't see the New Project task pane, open the File menu and click New.) If you see the project that you want to open listed in the Open a project section of the New Project task pane, click the project name, as shown in Figure 3-1.

Otherwise, click More projects to open the project.

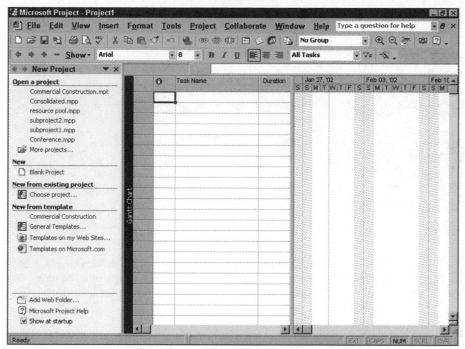

Figure 3-1: The New Project task pane appears on the left side of the Project window and enables you to create new projects from templates or to open existing projects.

Note   If you're using Project Server, you'll see the Open from Microsoft Project Server window to choose a project available through Project Server. If your project is not stored in the Project Server database, click the Open from File button and then navigate to the folder where you saved your project.

Establishing Basic Project Information

Use the Project Information dialog box, shown in Figure 3-2, to supply basic information about the new project that you want to set up.

Figure 3-2: The Project Information dialog box tracks basic information about each project.

Tip   You can make the Project Information dialog box appear automatically whenever you start a new project by checking the Prompt for project info for new projects box on the General tab of the Options dialog box. Choose Tools ➪ Option to open the dialog box.

You can enter the following eight pieces of information in the Project Information dialog box:

✦ **Start date.** If you set a start date for the project, all tasks begin on that date until you assign timing or dependencies to them.

✦ **Finish date.** If you know a final deadline, you can enter it here and then work backward to schedule your project. You must change the setting in the Schedule from field to make this option available.

✦ **Schedule from.** You can build schedules from completion to start by setting this field to Project Finish Date. Alternatively, you can build your schedule from the start date forward by accepting the default setting, Project Start Date.

✦ **Current date.** Project uses your computer clock for the default entry in this field. If you want to use a different date, change the date in this field. You can adjust this setting to generate reports that provide information on your project as of a certain date or to go back and track your project's progress from an earlier date.

✦ **Status date.** This field performs earned value calculations and identifies the complete-through date in the Update Project dialog box; Status Date also enables Project to place progress lines in your project. If you leave the status date set at NA, Project sets the status date equal to the current date set on your computer clock and calendar.

✦ **Calendar.** You can select the calendar on which to base your schedule. The Standard calendar is the default — it schedules eight hours of work, five days a week.

✦ **Priority.** Starting in Project 2000, you can establish a priority for each project in addition to setting priorities for tasks — a numerical value between 1 and 1,000. The project level priority plays a role when you use shared resources across multiple projects. Setting a project priority helps you to better control how resource leveling adjusts tasks when you share resources across projects.

✦ **Enterprise Custom Fields.** If your organization is using Project Server, you may need to assign values to project-level custom fields or outline codes defined in the Project Server database. You'll see an asterisk (*) next to any required custom field or outline code.

Enter either a start or finish date — only one will be available to you, depending on the choice you've made in the Schedule from field. If you schedule from the project Start date, Project will default the constraint type for all new tasks to As Soon As Possible (ASAP). And, as you'd expect, if you schedule from the project Finish date, Project will default the constraint type for all new tasks to As Late As Possible (ALAP).

To enter one of these dates, click the down arrow next to the text box. (The arrow is not available if the Schedule from field isn't set for that choice.) Select a date from the pop-up calendar, as shown in Figure 3-3.

Caution If you decide to schedule backwards from the Finish date, Project can't use tools such as resource leveling to resolve conflicts in your schedule.

You can change the project's start date during the planning phase, trying out alternative what-if scenarios by modifying this field. As you build your tasks going forward, Project indicates the finish date dictated by the length of your tasks and their timing relationships. When you're satisfied with the overall time frame, you can set the start date that works best when you're ready to begin.

Tip If you have already begun the project, you can set the start date to a date in the past to accurately reflect the real start date. Tasks on the Gantt Chart appear to have occurred before the current date line.

Figure 3-3: Use the arrow keys at the top of this calendar to choose other months.

If you know the date by which something must be completed (as with the annual meeting project, for example, or a Christmas party that must happen on December 25), you can schedule tasks by moving backward from the finish date. When you do this, Project builds the tasks going back in time. You may be surprised when Project generates a schedule telling you that you should have started three weeks earlier to finish in time. In that case, you can either add resources to get the work done faster or reduce the scope of the project.

Cross-Reference   In Chapters 9 and 10, you'll read about techniques that you can use to help you resolve scheduling and resource problems.

When beginning a new schedule, you will typically accept the default settings for Current date and Status date. After your project is under way, changing these default settings affects project tracking and the material generated in project reports.

For now, you can leave all the default settings (that is, scheduling from the start of the project, having the current date be today, and starting the project today, as well as basing your schedule on the standard calendar). Click OK to close the Project Information dialog box.

Looking at Project Calendars

The Project Information dialog box enables you to set the basic parameters of the project's timing. Those parameters and the information that you're about to enter for specific tasks are based on the base calendar.

You can create a base calendar for each group of resources in your project. For example, if the plant employees work a 9-hour day from 6:00 a.m. to 3:00 p.m., and the office employees work an 8-hour day from 8:00 a.m. to 5:00 p.m., you can create two base calendars. When you assign one day of an office employee's time, Project understands it to be an 8-hour day. In the Project Information dialog box, you designate whether you want your project to use a standard, 24-hour, or Night Shift calendar for most of your work assignments.

If you're using Project Standard, the preceding information is absolutely true. If you're using Project Professional, it's *almost* all true. When using Project Professional, you can create your own base calendars (for both projects and tasks) if you're working offline and storing the project locally (not in the Project Server database). If you store the project in the Project Server database, then you can create base calendars only if the administrator has given you the rights to do so.

Project also supports resource calendars and task calendars in which you can set exceptions to base calendars for specific resources or to tasks in your project whose work hours are different from the rest of the resources or tasks.

You learn more about task calendars in Chapter 4 and more about resource calendars in Chapter 5.

Setting calendar options

Project makes default assumptions about certain items that form the basis of the default base calendar (or the project calendar). For example, Project assumes that the default week contains 5 working days and 40 working hours. Project uses this calendar for resources unless you assign a different calendar to them. You can see the assumptions that Project uses on the Calendar tab of the Options dialog box.

The Calendar tab of the Options dialog box does not affect scheduling; the options that you see in this dialog box show you the defaults that Project will use to convert durations into corresponding time amounts. For example, if you enter 1mo for a task's duration, Project assumes that you are allotting one month (which is equal to 20 days) for that task.

To view the default calendar options, choose Tools ⇨ Options. Click the Calendar tab in the Options dialog box, as shown in Figure 3-4.

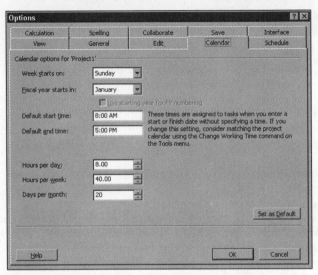

Figure 3-4: By reviewing the settings on the Calendar tab in the Options dialog box, you ensure that you and Project are speaking the same language when you enter task duration information.

Caution   Any changes that you make to these options apply to the current schedule only. To save your changes across all schedules, click the Set as Default button on the Calendar tab.

You can select any day of the week as your start day. For example, if you run a restaurant that closes on Sundays and Mondays, you may want to designate a work-week of Tuesday through Saturday. In that case, you will set the Week starts on field to Tuesday.

If your company uses a fiscal year other than the calendar year (January through December), you may want to set the Fiscal year starts in option. This setting is especially useful when you generate reports showing costs per quarter or year.

The final five settings on the Calendar tab of the Options dialog box enable you to designate specific start and end times for each day, the number of hours in a day and in a week, and the number of days in a month. For example, you can set the workday to start at 9:00 a.m. and end at 6:00 p.m., assign 9 hours to your workday (no lunch for you!), and end up with a 45-hour week.

Setting schedule options

You also can modify the way in which Project enters task information. In the Options dialog box (if it isn't open, choose Tools ➪ Options), click the Schedule tab to change the default settings for entering tasks, as shown in Figure 3-5. On this tab, you determine the default unit of time for entering task durations (the default is days), work time (hours), and whether new tasks start on the project start date or the current date. For example, if you are working on a five-year project in which most tasks run for months — not days — you may want to change the default setting for the Duration Is entered in field. If you prefer to have any new tasks begin no earlier than the current date, you can adjust the setting for New tasks. As you gain experience in entering information, you will find ways to customize Project to match your work style.

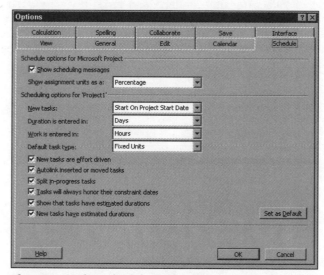

Figure 3-5: The Schedule tab is where you modify the default settings for entering tasks.

When you are satisfied with the settings on the Schedule tab, click OK to close the Options dialog box.

Creating a new calendar

The Standard calendar may not work for your project under all circumstances. You may find that all members of a specific group of resources work on the same calendar, but their calendar is different from the Standard calendar. For a group such as this, you can create a special resource calendar.

You use calendars to manage task schedules; you also can modify the calendars of resources to mark time when they aren't available. In Chapter 4, you'll read more about task calendars; in Chapter 5, you'll learn more about resource calendars.

For example, suppose that you run a print shop and each project that you complete requires you to use the printing press, but the press requires cleaning and maintenance each week for two hours on Thursday afternoon. To make sure that each printing project considers the maintenance requirement of the printing press, you can create a "Press" calendar that considers the need to shut the press down for cleaning and maintenance. Then you can assign the Press calendar to the Press Time task that you create for each project.

As previously mentioned, if you're using Project Standard, everything you're about to read works automatically. However, if you're using Project Professional, you can create your own base calendars (for both projects and tasks) if you're working offline and storing the project locally and not in the Project Server database. If you store the project in the Project Server database, then you can create base calendars only if the administrator has given you the rights to do so. Also, the privilege to create base calendars doesn't permit you to change the Standard calendar.

To create a new, project-wide calendar, open the Tools menu and click Change Working Time to display the Change Working Time dialog box, as shown in Figure 3-6.

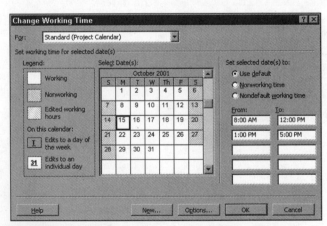

Figure 3-6: By default, Project displays the settings for Standard (Project Calendar) in the Change Working Time dialog box.

If other calendars exist, you'll see them listed in the For list box. You can create a custom calendar by clicking the New button. Project displays the Create New Base Calendar dialog box, as shown in Figure 3-7.

Figure 3-7: From the Create New Base Calendar dialog box, you can create a copy of an existing calendar or you can create a new Standard calendar.

If you want to model your calendar on an existing calendar, select the existing calendar from the Make a copy of drop-down box. Provide a name for the new calendar in the Name box.

Tip
By default, Project suggests that you copy the calendar that you were viewing when you chose the New button. In particular, I suggest that you make a copy of the Standard calendar rather than modifying it. That way, you'll always be able to use the original Standard calendar if you need it.

Click OK to create the new calendar and then make changes to it in the Change Working Time dialog box. To change the working hours for a particular day, make sure that you use the For list box to select the calendar that you want to change, and then make changes. The Legend on the left side of the dialog box identifies Working, Nonworking, and Edited working hours, and Nondefault days or hours for this calendar.

Using standard Windows selection techniques, select the dates that the resource will be on vacation.

Note
To select contiguous days, click the first day. Then press the Shift key as you click the last day that you want to select. To select noncontiguous days, press Ctrl as you click each day that you want to select. Scroll up to see an earlier month; scroll down to see a later month. To select all Sundays, click the letter that corresponds to the day. Project selects all Sundays in all months.

Make the necessary changes in the From and To text boxes or use the Set Selected Date(s) To option buttons. Because you set an exception to the regular schedule, the dates (or days) that you selected appear underscored in the calendar; in Figure 3-8, all Thursdays and Tuesday, January 15 are not using the default calendar. Even if you don't select a particular date, you can tell that the day contains nonstandard working hours by comparing the shading for the date to the Legend.

Tip
You don't need to select the Non-default working time option button if you're changing the hours for a particular day. Although the dialog box continues to show that the Use default option is selected, Project automatically selects the Nondefault working time option button.

Tip
Reselecting a date and clicking the Default Working Time button returns the date to its original scheduled time on that date; therefore, selecting Default Working Time for Sundays means "don't schedule work on Sundays."

Figure 3-8: Project marks exceptions to the typical schedule with an underscore.

Entering Tasks

To begin building a project, enter the major steps to reach your goal in roughly the same order that you expect them to occur. (Don't worry if you're not quite accurate about the sequence of events; Project makes it easy to reorganize tasks in your schedule at any time.)

New Feature   You can use the Project Guide to help you enter Tasks. Display the Project Guide toolbar (simply right-click any toolbar and click Project Guide) and click the Tasks button. In the Project Guide pane, click the List Tasks In The Project link. You'll see helpful information on entering tasks.

For the sample project (organizing a corporate annual meeting), follow these steps to create your first task — booking the meeting space:

1. Click the Task Name column in the first row of the Gantt table.

2. Type **Book Meeting Space**. The text appears in the cell and in the entry bar above the Gantt table.

3. Press Enter to accept the text.

Tip   You also can accept an entry in a cell by clicking the check mark button located to the left of the entry bar, by pressing a directional arrow key on your keyboard to move to another cell, by clicking another cell with your mouse pointer, or by pressing Tab.

Information begins to appear in your schedule. For example, Project lists the task name in the Task Name column and makes a corresponding entry in the Duration column; the question mark in the Duration column represents an estimated duration. (Remember the default setting in the Schedule tab of the Options dialog box? The default length of new tasks is estimated at one day.) According to the Start column, the task begins today; in addition, a task bar reflects the one-day duration of the task graphically.

Cross-Reference Chapter 4 contains more information about estimated durations.

If you use the scroll bar located at the bottom of the Gantt table to move to the right, you see the Finish Date entry. Because this is a one-day task, it will be completed by the end of the day.

Tip You also can drag the bar that divides the Gantt table from the Gantt Chart to expand the visible area of the Gantt table.

Using either your mouse pointer or the down-arrow key on your keyboard, move to the second row in the Task Name column and enter **Schedule Speakers** as the next task. Then enter the following tasks in the next four rows: **Arrange for Audio/Visual Equipment, Order Food, Send Invitations,** and **Mail Annual Reports.** Your schedule should now look like the schedule shown in Figure 3-9.

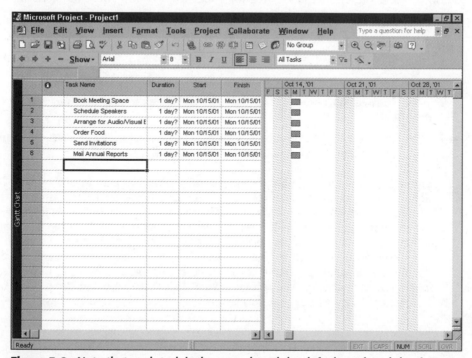

Figure 3-9: Note that each task is the same length by default, and each begins on the project start date.

Adding Subtasks

After you enter the major tasks in your project, you can begin to flesh out the details by adding subordinate tasks, also referred to as *subtasks*. When you add subtasks, the upper-level task becomes a summary task. Summary tasks and subtasks provide an easy-to-apply outline structure for your schedule.

Project's outline approach also enables you to display and print your project information with various levels of detail. For example, with only summary tasks showing, you see a higher-level overview of the project that you may want to present to management. On the other hand, you can reveal the details of only one or two phases of a project so that you can discuss those tasks with the people who will be performing them. The outline structure gives you a lot of flexibility in working with your schedule.

New Feature

You can use the Project Guide to help you organize your project outline. On the Project Guide toolbar (to display the toolbar, right-click any toolbar and then click Project Guide), click Tasks. Then click the Organize Tasks into Phases link.

When you insert a new task, it appears above the currently selected task. Begin by adding subtasks under the Book Meeting Space task. Follow these steps to insert a new task:

1. Click the Schedule Speakers task.

2. Choose Insert ⇨ New Task. Row 2 becomes a blank row, and all the other tasks move down one. Your cursor rests in the new task row.

3. Type **Request purchase order** and click the check mark button to accept the new task.

4. Click the Indent button on the Formatting toolbar (it looks like a right-facing arrow) to indent the subtask, as shown in Figure 3-10.

Note

Summary tasks appear in boldface type and subtasks appear in normal type by default; however, some people like to differentiate these task types even more. In traditional outlining, the capitalization of items may vary, depending on their level. For example, you can capitalize the first letters of all the words in the summary tasks (headline style) and capitalize only the first letter of the first word in the subtasks (sentence style), as in this example. The choice is yours; however, if you decide to use some special effect as you enter text, be consistent so that others looking at your schedule will recognize your system. And if others are to work on your schedule, make sure that they follow the formats you have established.

Indent button

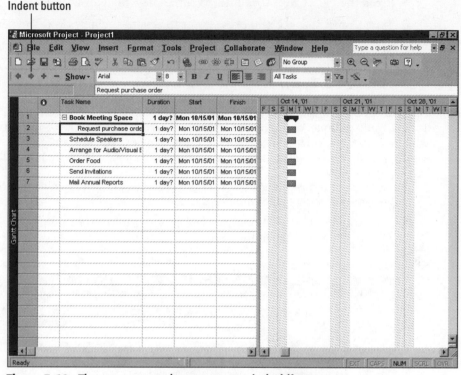

Figure 3-10: The summary task now appears in boldface type.

Notice that the summary task (Book Meeting Space) now displays a solid black line on the Gantt Chart with a down-arrow shape marking its beginning and end. When a task becomes a summary task (that is, when it contains subtasks), the timing of the summary task reflects the total amount of time required to complete the subtasks. If a task has a duration assigned to it and you make it into a summary task, the timing of the subtasks overrides the assigned duration. If you change the timing of a subtask, the summary task duration changes to reflect the change.

You can add other subtasks by following these steps:

1. Click the Schedule Speakers task.

2. Press the Insert key on your keyboard (which is a shortcut alternative to using Insert ➪ New Task). A new blank row appears.

3. Type **Select room** and press Enter to accept the new task. The new task uses the same level of indentation as the task above it.

4. Press the Insert key on your keyboard. A new blank row appears.

5. Type **Confirm space** and press Enter to accept the new task. The new task uses the same level of indentation as the task above it.

6. Press Insert.

7. Type **Order flowers** and press Enter to accept the new task.

Each of these new tasks indents to the subordinate level. However, the third new task is not a subtask of the Book Meeting Space summary task. To move the task higher in the outline hierarchy, you can simply select the new task and use the Outdent button on the toolbar, but try using your mouse to move it as follows:

1. Move your mouse over the Order flowers task until the mouse pointer becomes a two-way pointing arrow.

2. Drag the task to the left until a thick gray line indicates that it is lined up with the upper-level tasks in the outline, as shown in Figure 3-11.

Figure 3-11: You can use your mouse to drag tasks in or out in the outline hierarchy.

3. Release the mouse button to complete the move.

Your schedule now looks like the schedule shown in Figure 3-12. Adding details is as simple as inserting new tasks wherever you want them and then moving them in or out in the outline structure.

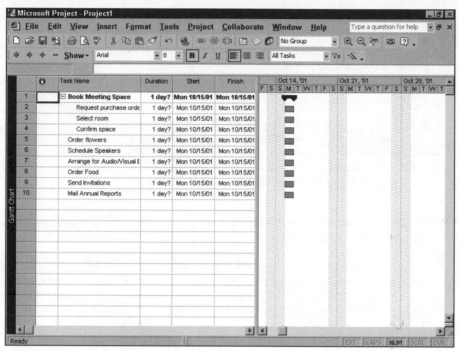

Figure 3-12: The outline structure enables you to see summary and subtasks as manageable chunks of work.

Saving Project Files

Of course, you should always save your work frequently. With the often mission-critical information centralized in a Project file, frequent saving is even more important. When saving Project files, you have the option of setting up protection for them. You also can save your files as templates; that is, files on which you can base other schedules.

Saving files

To save any Project file for the first time, open the File menu and click Save or click the Save tool on the Standard toolbar. In the Save As dialog box, specify the name of the file, where to save the file, and what format you want to use, as shown in Figure 3-13.

Figure 3-13: Use the buttons and tools of the File Save dialog box to tell Project where to save a file and what format to use.

Tip   Project 2002 and Project 2000 share the same file format — you can open Project 2002 files in Project 2000.

Cross-Reference   The format of Project 2002 files is the same as Project 2000 files, but the format of Project 2000 files is different from the format of Project 98 files. You can, however, save Project 2002 files as Project 98 files. You even can set Project 2002's default save format to Project 98 files. See Chapter 20 for more information.

In the File Name box, type a name for the file. Click the arrow at the right edge of the Save in list box to display a hierarchy of your computer's drive and directory organization. Click the Up One Level tool to move up one level in that hierarchy. Or use one of the Save in buttons (History, My Documents, Desktop, Favorites, or Web Folders) to select a folder in which to save the file. To place this project file in a new folder, navigate to the drive or folder in which you want Project to store the new folder and then use the Create New Folder tool.

Note   After you save a project for the first time, you can simply click the Save button to save the file; Project won't display this dialog box. If you want to change a setting or save the file with a new name, choose File ➪ Save As to display this dialog box again.

By default, Project saves files in Project 2002 format with the extension .mpp. If you want to save a file in a different format, such as a Microsoft Access database (.mdb) or a Project 98 file (also .mpp), you can select that format in the Save as type drop-down list. After you enter a filename and designate its location and file type, click Save to save the file.

Tip   Clicking the ODBC button enables you to export Project data to an ODBC database.

Project displays the Planning Wizard if you haven't set a baseline for the project. If you're ready to set a baseline, change the option in the dialog box to save your file with a baseline; otherwise, accept the defaults and click OK to save your project without setting a baseline.

Cross-Reference To read more about baselines, see Chapter 11.

Saving files as templates

One format in the Save as type selection is template. Template files have an extension of .mpt. The template feature is especially useful in project management because your projects are often similar to ones that precede or follow them. A template file saves all the settings that you may have made for a particular project, such as formatting, commonly performed tasks, and calendar choices. Keeping template files on hand can save your coworkers (and yourself) from having to reinvent the wheel each time you want to build a similar project.

You may ask, "Can't I just save my previous project's file with a new name and use that for my next project?" Yes, you can, but after you track progress on tasks, opening that final project file and stripping it back to its baseline settings is a cumbersome routine.

Saving the initial schedule as a template on which you can build new schedules is a much better approach. To create a new schedule, simply open the template and save the file as a standard Project file with a new name.

Protecting files

Some projects are as top secret as an FBI file. In a case such as this, some people within the organization — and certainly people from outside the organization — should not have access to the details. If your projects fit this mold, you need a way to keep your Project files secure from prying eyes. You can set a measure of security for Project 2002 files by clicking the Tools button in the File Save dialog box and choosing General Options to display the Save Options dialog box, as shown in Figure 3-14.

Figure 3-14: Don't use your phone extension, birthday, or spouse's name as a password — such passwords are much too easy to break!

Tip

What kind of passwords should you use? Consider two factors: You must be able to remember the password, and you must make it something that the average person won't be able to guess. (No password is perfect; if someone really wants to break into your files, he or she will.) Try using passwords such as an address or phone number that you had as a kid; information that you remember but others are not likely to know.

Assigning the Protection password safeguards the file from being opened. Only someone with the assigned password can open a file protected in this way. The Write reservation password, on the other hand, permits anyone to open the file without a password, but as a *read-only* file (that is, no one else can make any changes to the file). Finally, if you check the Read-only recommended option, Project displays a message recommending that anyone opening the file not make changes to it. However, this choice doesn't actually prevent someone from making changes.

Caution

Both the Protection and Write reservation passwords are case-sensitive. If you assign a password of JoeS, you can't open the file if you type in joes.

Closing Project

When you're finished working in Project, you can save your files as described previously and then use one of the following methods to close the program:

✦ Click the Close button in the upper-right corner of the Project window.

✦ Choose File ➪ Exit.

If you haven't saved any open files, Project prompts you to do so.

Working with a Project Outline

After you build the outline, reorganizing the sequence of individual tasks is easy. You also can manipulate the outline to show more or less detail about your project. Outlining features work the same way in many software products; for example, Word for Windows, PowerPoint, and Project — all Microsoft products — have the same outlining tools and features. In Project, you can (as you may expect) move, copy, hide, and display tasks.

Adjusting tasks in an outline

To move tasks in an outline, you can cut and paste (as you will see in Steps 1 through 4), or you can drag and drop (as you will see in Steps 9 and 10). You also can change the relative position of tasks in the hierarchy of the outline by promoting or demoting them (outdenting or indenting). In Steps 5 through 8 and 11 and 12, you see examples of promoting and demoting tasks.

To move tasks, you must first select them. Use any of the following techniques to select tasks:

Tip You can select a task by clicking its Gantt bar.

✦ To select a single task, click its ID number.

✦ To select several contiguous tasks, select the first task. Then hold down the Shift key and click the last task that you want to select.

✦ To select several noncontiguous tasks, hold down the Ctrl key as you click the ID numbers of the tasks that you want to select.

It's important to remember that — although you can move tasks wherever you like — when you move a summary task, its subtasks move with it. So, to move a subtask on its own to another location in the outline, you first must promote (outdent) it to the highest task level.

Moving subtasks up one level can be a little tricky. For example, to move the task "Request purchase order" under the task "Order Food," you must first promote "Request purchase order" to the highest level. When you do so, however, the other subtask under "Book Meeting Space" (that is, "Confirm space") becomes subordinate to "Request purchase order." Moving the upper task also moves its subordinate. To avoid this problem, promote the "Confirm space" task so that it is no longer subordinate, move the "Request purchase order" task where you want it to be located, and then go back and demote "Confirm space" to be subordinate, once again, to the "Book Meeting Space" task. In the beginning, this process is a little confusing, so get some practice by trying the steps that follow.

Tip To move a summary task on its own, you must first promote all its subtasks to a higher level.

Try reorganizing tasks using both the toolbar tools and your mouse by following these steps:

1. Click the ID number (in the leftmost column) for the task "Order flowers." Project highlights (selects) the entire row.

2. Click the Cut tool on the Standard toolbar.

3. Click the Gantt bar for Send Invitations. Project selects the row.

4. Click the Paste tool on the Standard toolbar. The "Order flowers" task appears selected in its new location above the task "Send invitations."

5. Move the mouse pointer over the subtask name, "Request purchase order," until the pointer becomes a double arrow.

Tip When you first place the mouse pointer over the task name, you won't have much time to view the double arrow; Project displays a gray screen tip containing the task name. If you're patient, the screen tip will disappear and the double arrow will reappear.

6. Press and hold down the left mouse button while you drag the task to the left. A gray vertical line appears onscreen, indicating that you are promoting a task in the outline hierarchy. When you release the mouse button, your schedule should look like the schedule shown in Figure 3-15.

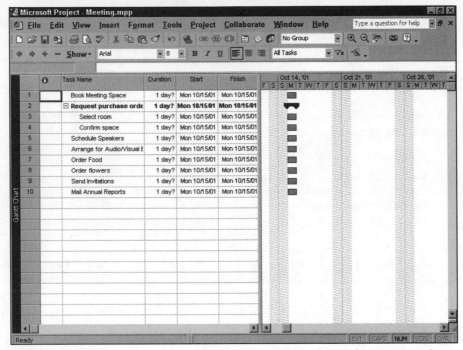

Figure 3-15: When you outdent a task, you may shift the hierarchy structure of subtasks beneath it.

Tip   Dragging a task to the right demotes the task in the project outline. You'll see the same gray vertical line when you promote or demote tasks.

7. Select both "Select room" and "Confirm space." Move the mouse pointer over either of the subtask names until the pointer becomes a double arrow.

8. Drag the tasks to the left to outdent them.

9. Click the ID number of the task "Request purchase order."

10. While using the mouse to point at the ID number, drag the "Request purchase order" task below the "Order food" task. A horizontal gray line indicates the new position as you drag.

11. Click the Indent button on the Formatting toolbar to make the task subordinate.

12. Select the "Select room" and "Confirm space" tasks and click the Indent button.

Your schedule now has two tasks with subtasks beneath them, as shown in Figure 3-16. Moving subtasks around your outline can be a little cumbersome. Don't despair — in a well-planned outline, you are much more likely to move summary tasks and their subtasks as a unit.

Tip   You also can move a subtask without taking other subtasks with it by moving the designated task to the bottom of the list of subtasks before outdenting it. This approach saves you the step of outdenting subsidiary subtasks.

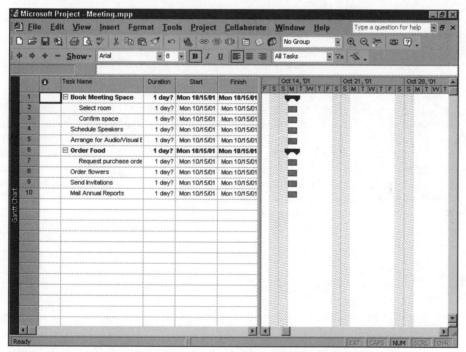

Figure 3-16: Both "Book meeting space" and "Order food" have subtasks beneath them.

Copying tasks

Copying tasks also is simple to do and can come in very handy while building a project outline. For example, suppose that you were entering tasks in a project to test various versions of a compound to see which works best as a fixative. You may repeat the same series of tasks ("Obtain compound sample," "Test in various environments," "Write up test results," "Analyze results," and so on) several times. Instead of typing those tasks 10 or 20 times, you can save time by copying them.

To copy tasks, you must first select them. Use any of the following techniques described in the previous section. You can copy tasks in two ways:

✦ Use the Edit, Copy and Edit, and Paste commands (or their corresponding tools on the Standard toolbar) to copy the selected task(s) to another location.

Tip   Remember, to copy a summary task and its subtasks, you need only select the summary task and copy it. Project automatically copies the summary's subtasks for you.

✦ Hold down the Ctrl key while you drag the task(s) to another location. Release the mouse button to complete the copy.

If you have several repetitive phases of a project, such as the development and production of several models of a single product, you can use the fill handle to copy the tasks. In Figure 3-17, you see three tasks: Design, Development, and Production. To copy the group of tasks, select their task names. Place the mouse pointer over the fill handle in the lower-right corner of the selection; the mouse pointer changes to a plus sign (+). Drag the fill handle down until you have selected the group of rows that you want to contain the repetitive tasks.

Mouse pointer dragging the fill handle

Fill handle

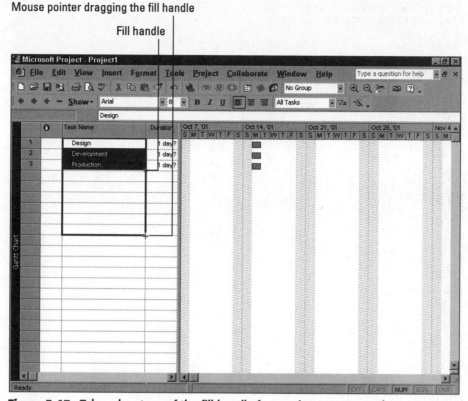

Figure 3-17: Take advantage of the fill handle for contiguous copy tasks.

Caution The fill handle copies tasks into a contiguous range; if the range already contains information, however, using the fill handle to copy overwrites the existing information. To avoid the problem, insert blank rows in the project before using the fill handle. Select the task that you want to appear beneath the new row and choose Insert ⇨ New Task. To insert more than one blank row, select the number of rows that you want to insert before choosing Insert ⇨ New Task.

When you release the mouse pointer, Project copies the tasks into the selected range, as shown in Figure 3-18.

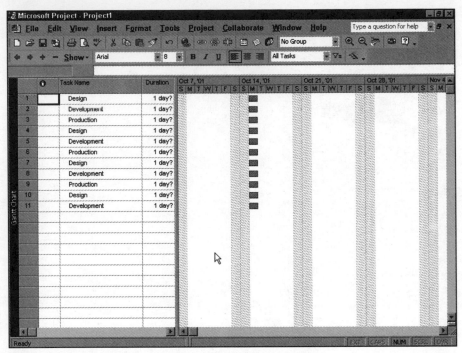

Figure 3-18: Project fills the range with the selected tasks.

Tip   Suppose that you're using WBS codes and you set up the WBS codes to automatically assign codes when you create new tasks. When you copy tasks by using any of the methods described, Project automatically assigns incremental WBS codes to the new tasks.

Displaying and hiding tasks

The outline structure enables you to view your project at different levels of detail by expanding or collapsing the summary tasks. You can use the Show button on the Formatting toolbar to quickly hide or display subtasks based on their outline level, as shown in Figure 3-19. By using the Show button, you also can quickly display all the detail tasks in your schedule.

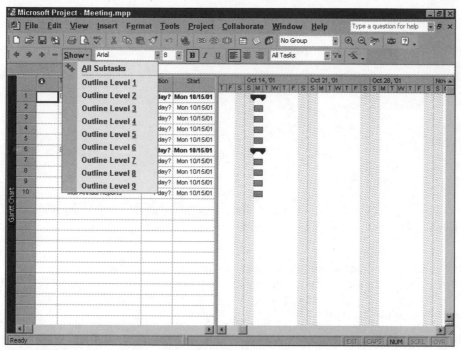

Figure 3-19: Use the Show button on the Formatting toolbar to easily determine the level of detail that you want to view in a project.

Figure 3-20 shows a small box with a minus sign (-) that appears to the left of each summary task. This symbol indicates that all subtasks are in view. If you click the minus sign, any subtasks disappear from view and a plus sign appears next to the summary task name. The plus sign indicates that the task is associated with some hidden detail tasks. Click the plus sign to reveal the "hidden" subtasks.

Figure 3-20: You can expand or collapse any task that has a subtask.

How many levels of detail can an outline have? Just about as many as you need. For example, the schedule shown in Figure 3-20 has several levels of detail regarding the annual meeting example. Any task that has subtasks also has the plus and minus sign mechanism for displaying or hiding them.

Caution   Using too many levels of outline indentation (usually more than three or four) makes it difficult to see your entire schedule onscreen. In fact, a very detailed project outline may indicate that you need to rethink the scope of the project and break it into smaller, more manageable projects.

You can use the hide and show features of the outline to focus on just the amount of detail you want. You can take the same schedule from Figure 3-20, for example, and show just the highest level of detail for a report to management to summarize project activity, as shown in Figure 3-21.

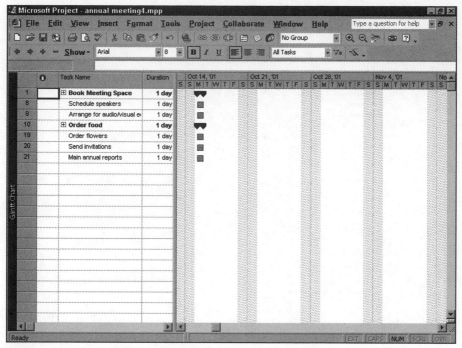

Figure 3-21: The detailed tasks are now hidden. The plus symbols and the summary-style task bar, however, indicate that there's more here than meets the eye.

Getting Help

As you begin to build tasks in a schedule, you're likely to have questions about using Project 2002 that the Help system can answer. Project's Help is similar to the Help feature in Office 2002 products. If you've used any Microsoft Office product, the Help environment in Project will be very familiar.

If you click the Office Assistant button located on the end of the Standard toolbar, you'll see an animated Paperclip and a bubble in which you can type an English language-like question, as shown in Figure 3-22.

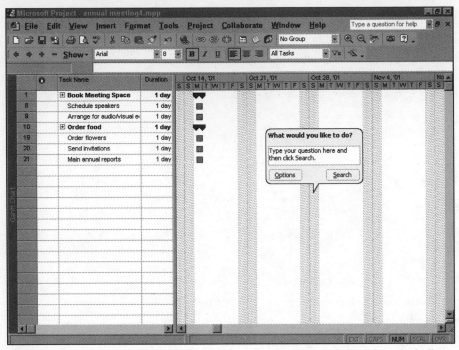

Figure 3-22: The Paperclip, which answers questions typed into its thought balloon.

The Help character annoys many people, however, so Project offers two different ways in which you can avoid it:

✦ **Bypass it.** You can choose Contents and Index from the Help menu.

✦ **Turn it off.** You can turn off the Office Assistant; clicking the Office Assistant button becomes the equivalent of choosing Help, Contents and Index. To turn off the Office Assistant, click the Office Assistant button on the Standard toolbar to display the Office Assistant. In the bubble, click the Options button to display the Office Assistant Options dialog box, as shown in Figure 3-23. Remove the check from the Use the Office Assistant checkbox on the Options tab.

Make sure this box is empty to hide the Office Assistant

Figure 3-23: To turn off the Office Assistant, remove the check from the first box in this dialog box.

Note If you decide later that you again want to use the Office Assistant, choose Help ➪ Show Office Assistant.

Using the Help system

The Contents and Index option on the Help menu takes you to the Help Welcome window. You find three tabs in the Help window:

✦ **The Contents tab.** Lists topic areas that you can open, level by level, until you reach the specific information that you require. This feature is similar to working your way through a table of contents in a book to find a particular topic.

✦ **The Answer Wizard tab.** Enables you to type questions and search for Help topics.

✦ **The Index tab.** Provides a searchable index of topics and subtopics. Like a book index, you can look up a specific term or phrase by finding it in an alphabetical listing.

The Contents tab

Figure 3-24 shows the Contents tab of the Help Topics dialog box. You can use this tab to locate information by general topic areas. When you open any of these topics, Help takes you to a list of subtopics. By narrowing down these subtopics, you eventually get to the information that you want.

Figure 3-24: The Contents tab provides general topic areas to help you locate what you need.

The Contents tab is simply a way to get help if you know the general topic that you want to learn about but perhaps don't know enough about the terminology to type a specific phrase or term in the Index. The Contents tab and the Index tab often bring you to the same information screen. For example, if you select the topic "Creating a Project Hierarchy Using Outlining," double-click to display subtopics, and then select the subtopic "Indent and outdent tasks into summary tasks and subtasks," the Contents tab displays the same information as the Index tab displayed in the previous example.

Tip   Use the buttons across the top of the Help information screen. You can display or hide the Contents, Answer Wizard, and Index tabs; go Back to the previously displayed screen; print a topic; or display Options for Help.

The Answer Wizard tab

When you select the Answer Wizard tab on the Help window, you see a pane where you can type a question, as shown in Figure 3-25. When you click Search, Help displays topics relevant to your question. You can then select a Help topic to display.

Figure 3-25: Use the Answer Wizard to get help by posing a question.

The Index tab

The Index tab shown in Figure 3-26 enables you to type or choose a keyword and then display information about it.

Follow these steps to locate information on Project's outlining feature. (If you haven't already opened the Contents and Index area of Help, do so now by choosing Help ➪ Contents and Index and then selecting the Index tab.)

1. Type the letters **ou**. Help displays keywords in the middle of the tab that begin with the letters you typed; the first is "outdent."

2. Type the letters **tl**. Project narrows down to the topic "outline." This "quick pick" functionality enables you to type only as many letters as Project needs to identify the topic. You also can use the scroll bar and mouse to scroll through keywords and select topics.

3. Click the Search button at the top of the Index tab. Help displays the topics associated with the keyword, and the actual Help information for the first topic in the list.

4. Click a topic to read the Help information for it.

Figure 3-26: Use the Index tab to search for help using keywords, much the way you'd use the index of a book. Several topics may exist for any keyword in the Help Index.

Note Help information often contains steps required to complete a procedure. In addition, a "Find related help" hyperlink takes you to related topics when you click it. Finally, the Help text may contain hyperlink text, a button to show you how to accomplish some task, and even demos.

Tip You can split set up your screen so that Help appears on one side and Project on the other, enabling you to use the information in Help to walk through a complicated or lengthy procedure. Click the Auto Tile button on the Help toolbar to set up your screen this way. The Auto Tile button is the leftmost button on the Help toolbar.

Finding online help

If you're connected to the Internet, you can find a world of support, information, and even freeware, shareware, or products-for-a-price that work along with Project.

 This book's companion CD-ROM includes several products from third-party vendors that work with Project to enhance it.

Choose the Office on the Web command to follow a link to the Microsoft Office Assistance Center Web site. At this site, you can find things such as update information, files to download, and a link to a list of software companies that provide add-on products or specialize in the use of Microsoft Project. If you have a technical question about Project, you can click Assistance to use Online Support or to look up articles on Microsoft Project stored in Microsoft's Knowledge Base. You also can find links on this page to the Microsoft Project Newsgroups, the Microsoft Project Resource Kit, and the Solution Provider Database.

Summary

In this chapter, you started to build your first project by creating summary tasks and subtasks. You learned about the following aspects of Project:

✦ Gathering the data that you need to begin creating your schedule

✦ Entering Project information and setting up some calendar defaults

✦ Creating summary and subtasks

✦ Saving files and closing Project

✦ Working with the outlining hierarchy to assign WBS codes and move, copy, and display subtasks

✦ Using the Help system to search for information and obtain online help

In Chapter 4, you begin to add details about task types, add timing, and establish relationships among your tasks.

✦   ✦   ✦

Building Tasks

Hessiod, that classic Greek project manager, once said, "Observe due measure, for right timing is in all things the most important factor." You could do worse than to use this truism from around 700 B.C. as your personal project management mantra today. When it comes to projects, timing is, indeed, everything.

In Chapter 3, you created several tasks and used the outlining feature of Project to organize them. But every task in your schedule has the default length (one estimated day), and they all occur on the very same day. In essence, you have listed the steps to get to your goal, but with no related timing, your schedule may as well be a shopping list.

You have to add durations to your tasks; in other words, you must establish how long (or how many hours of effort) each task will take. However, timing consists of more than determining how many hours, days, or weeks it takes to complete each task. Timing for your project becomes clear only when you've set a duration for each task and when you've established the relationships, called *dependencies*, among the tasks. Only then can you accurately predict the amount of time that you will need to complete the project.

Establishing Timing for Tasks

Your boss asks how long it will take to write that report, and you tell her it'll be about a week. Your coworker calls and asks when you'll be finished repairing the computer network, and you tell him it'll take another day. You make estimates about task durations every day. You know your own business, and you're probably pretty good at setting the timing for everyday tasks based on many factors.

Exactly how do you figure out the timing for a task in a project? The method is virtually identical to the seemingly automatic process that you go through when someone asks you how long it will take to complete a task, such as placing an order for materials. For example:

1. You estimate that you will spend about 40 minutes doing the research and performing the calculations to determine how many square feet of lumber you'll need for the job.

2. You consider how long the actual task (placing a phone order for materials) will take. This duration could be a matter of only minutes, but if you factor in playing a few rounds of phone tag, you may want to allow half a day.

3. You also think about what's involved in getting a purchase order. With your system, cutting a purchase order can take up to four days. Some of that time requires your presence, but most of it consists of waiting.

So how long is your task? You could say you need exactly 4 days, 4 hours, and 40 minutes; but just to be safe, you should probably allow about 5 days. In addition, Project has some issues specific to task timing that you need to understand to estimate task durations accurately.

By default, Project creates *resource-driven* tasks. Here's a simple example. You have to plant a tree. One person needs two hours to plant a tree. If you add another person (another resource), together they need only one hour to complete the task. That is, two resources, each putting in an hour of effort, complete the two hours of effort in only one hour. With resource-driven scheduling, when you add resources, the task timing becomes shorter; if you take resources away, the task takes longer to complete. The resource-driven method is Project's default scheduling method, and Project refers to these resource-driven tasks as *fixed-unit* tasks.

Caution   The reduction of time required on a resource-driven task is strictly a mathematical calculation in Project: Ten people get work done in one-tenth the time of one person. However, whenever two or more people work on a task, the time savings are seldom so straightforward. You must also factor in the time for those people to communicate, miscommunicate, hold meetings, and so on.

Fixed-work and fixed-duration tasks

You also can use the *fixed-duration task* in Project. The number of resources does not affect the timing of this type of task. If you want to allow a week for a committee to review the company's new ad campaign — no matter how many people are on the committee — the task has a fixed duration. You can't shorten the task's duration by adding resources to it. In fact, adding people to the review process may lengthen it because their effort has no impact on getting the work done more quickly, but coordinating their efforts can add time.

To Pad or Not to Pad?

Although most people agree that delays are inevitable and that you should allow for them, people who schedule projects accommodate these delays in various ways.

Some schedulers build in extra time at the task level, adding a day or two to each task's duration — just in case. Unfortunately, padding each task may leave you with an impossibly long schedule, and may suggest to your boss that you're not very efficient. Why should it take two days to run a three-hour test? It doesn't — but because you know that setting up the test parameters properly the first time is an error-prone process, you allow a couple of workdays to complete the testing. Just make sure your boss understands that you're building a worst-case scenario; when you bring the project in early, he or she will be glad to share the praise.

Some project managers add one long task, maybe two weeks or so in duration, at the end of the schedule, and they name it something like Critical Issues Resolution Period. This task acts as a placeholder that covers you if individual tasks run late. This approach can help you see how the overall time left for delays is being used up as the project proceeds. For example, if the final two-week task is running a week late because of earlier delays, you know that you've eaten up half of the slack that the task represents.

Or, you can build a schedule with best-case timing. Then you can document any problems and delays that occur, and request additional time as needed. In the case of a project that you must complete quickly, you may need to work this way. However, best-case timing sets you up for potential missed deadlines.

Which approach should you use? Possibly a combination; for example, try building a best-case schedule. If the completion date is one week earlier than your deadline, by all means add a little time to the tasks that are most likely to encounter problems, such as those performed by outside vendors.

The *fixed-work task* was a task type that became available in Project 98. When you create a fixed-work task, you set the duration of the task, and Project assigns a percentage of effort sufficient to complete the task in the time allotted for each resource that you assign to the task. For example, if you assign three people to work on a one-day task, Project would say that each person should spend 33 percent of his or her time on the task to complete it in one day.

Effort-driven tasks

For fixed-duration and fixed-unit tasks, you can tell Project to modify the percentage of total work allocated to each resource, based on the number of assigned resources if the number of resources changes. In effect, you create an effort-driven task. The work required to complete the task remains the same, but Project redistributes the work equally among all assigned resources.

Note By default, fixed-work tasks are effort-driven. You can choose to make fixed-duration and fixed-unit tasks effort-driven if you want, or you can make Project retain the original allocation of work.

In this chapter, I use Project's default settings: the durations that you assign to tasks are resource-driven. Therefore, a five-day task requires five days of resource effort to complete.

Cross-Reference In Chapter 5, you learn more about how resource assignments modify task timing.

Assigning Task Timing

You now understand the basics of estimating task timing, and you understand how task timing relates to effort expended on the task by resources. The actual process of assigning durations is quite simple. To assign a duration to a task, you can use one of the following three methods:

✦ Use the Task Information dialog box to enter and view information about all aspects of a task, including its timing, constraints, dependencies, resources, and priority in the overall project.

✦ Enter a duration in the Duration column of the Gantt table.

✦ Use your mouse to drag a task bar to the required length.

Using the Task Information dialog box

Follow these steps to assign durations from the Task Information dialog box:

1. Display the Gantt Chart view (open the View menu and click Gantt Chart).

2. Double-click a Task Name to open the Task Information dialog box, as shown in Figure 4-1.

Tip You can also click the Task Information button on the Standard toolbar, or right-click either the Task Name or the task's Gantt bar and select Task Information to display this dialog box.

Figure 4-1: If you double-click an already-entered task name, that name appears in the Name field in this dialog box; if you double-click a blank task name cell, you can fill in the name here.

3. Use the arrows in the Duration field to reduce or increase the duration from the default setting of one day. Each click changes the duration by one day.

You may have noticed that Project uses estimated durations by default for tasks when you type the duration into the Gantt table — you saw a question mark (?) next to each duration. When you establish a task's duration in the Task Information dialog box, place a check in the Estimated box to make the duration of the task estimated. Use estimated durations when the time frame for the task isn't firm; you can easily display tasks with estimated durations by using a new filter in Project (see Chapter 6 for more information about filters).

4. Click the Duration field and highlight the current entry to enter a duration in increments other than a day.

Project 2000 first gave you the ability to specify a duration in months. Project uses the Calendar tab of the Options dialog box to determine the number of days in a month.

5. Type a new duration by using the following abbreviations: *m* for minutes, *h* for hours, *w* for weeks, and *mo* for months.

6. Click OK to establish the task duration. For example, the Gantt Chart task bars shown in Figure 4-2 reflect the new task lengths.

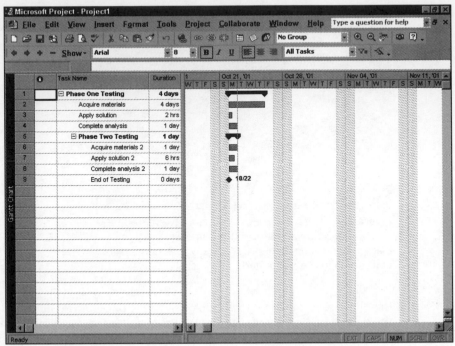

Figure 4-2: Task bars become more meaningful after you assign durations.

Using the Gantt table

To enter a task's duration on the Gantt table, simply click the Duration column and type in the duration. Even though you've set the default to use estimated durations, when you type a duration on the Gantt table, Project assumes that you want an actual instead of an estimated duration — unless you type a question mark (?).

Tip   You can change Project's default behavior (and use actual instead of estimated durations) on the Schedule tab of the Options dialog box — see the next section for more information.

You can type in a duration in a few different ways. For example, Project recognizes all of the following entries as three weeks: 3 w, 3 wks, 3 weeks.

Tip   If you want to assign the same duration to several contiguous tasks, type the duration once and then use the fill handle in the Duration column to copy the duration to the other tasks.

Start and Finish Versus Duration

You could use the Start and Finish fields in the Task Information dialog box to set a start date and finish date for the task, rather than entering a duration. However, if you use the Start and Finish dates, Project uses only working days in that date range. If you enter a duration, Project calculates the beginning and end of the task, taking into consideration weekends and holidays for you. These two methods could have different results.

For example, suppose you have a four-day task that starts on December 23, 2002. Here's how that week looks on a calendar:

Sun	Mon	Tues	Weds	Thurs	Fri	Sat
22	23	24	25	26	27	28

December 25, 2002 falls on a Wednesday. If you entered 12/23/02 as the Start date and 12/26/02 as the Finish date, Project would calculate that as a three-day task (assuming that your company closes for Christmas) with work on December 23, 24, and 26. However, if you enter four days in the Duration field, the calculated Start and Finish dates would be 12/23/02 and 12/27/02, respectively, taking into account both the Christmas holiday and a weekend. In this example, the workdays are December 23, 24, 26, and 27.

If a task has immutable timing, such as a Christmas celebration on Christmas day, use the Start and Finish fields. If you're definite about how many workdays a task will require, but not the days on which the work will occur, use the Duration field to set timing and let Project calculate the actual work dates based on the calendar.

Using your mouse and the task bar

Finally, follow these steps to adjust a task's duration using your mouse and the task bar:

1. Place your mouse pointer on the right edge of a task bar until the pointer becomes a vertical line with an arrow extending to the right of it.

2. Click and drag the bar to the right. As you do, Project displays the proposed new task duration and finish date, as shown in Figure 4-3.

3. Release the mouse button when the duration that you want appears in the information box.

Mouse pointer

Figure 4-3: If you're a visually oriented person, dragging task bars to change durations may be the best method for you.

Setting scheduling options

You aren't limited to entering resource-driven tasks or estimated durations on the Gantt table. You can change the default task type and other default scheduling settings for your project. Choose Tools ➪ Options and click the Schedule tab of the Options dialog box to change the default settings for entering tasks, as shown in Figure 4-4.

In this dialog box, you determine the default unit of time for entering task durations (the default is days), work time (hours), and whether new tasks start on the project start date or the current date. For example, if you are working on a five-year project in which most tasks run months — not days — you may want to change the default setting for the "Duration is entered in" field. If you prefer to have any new tasks begin no earlier than the current date, you can adjust the setting for New tasks. To enter actual durations instead of estimated durations, remove the check from the last checkbox on the Schedule tab.

Figure 4-4: Use the Schedule tab of the Options dialog box to change Project's default behavior for scheduling.

As you gain experience in entering information, you will find ways to customize Project to match your work style. When you are satisfied with the settings in the Schedule tab, click OK to close the Options dialog box.

Assigning a calendar to a task

Task calendars became available in Project 2000. You can assign a calendar to a task by using the same steps to create the Press calendar described in Chapter 3; choose Tools ➪ Change Working Time to display the Change Working Time dialog box. Click the New button to create the calendar and provide a name for the new calendar. Select the dates that won't be "standard" and make the appropriate changes. Click OK to save the calendar.

Cross-Reference For more detailed steps on creating a new calendar, see Chapter 3.

To assign a calendar to a task, double-click the task name to open the Task Information dialog box for that task. Click the Advanced tab and open the Calendar list box to a special calendar for the task, as shown in Figure 4-5.

Figure 4-5: Assign a calendar to a task from the Advanced tab of the Task Information dialog box.

Creating milestones

Managers often use milestones to mark key moments in a project, such as the completion of a phase or the approval of a product or activity. In Project, milestones are tasks that usually have zero duration. The symbol for a milestone on the Gantt Chart is a diamond shape. For example, the diamond in the Gantt Chart shown in Figure 4-6 indicates that the End of Testing task is a milestone.

A task doesn't have to have a zero duration to be a milestone; you can mark any task as a milestone. On the Advanced tab of the Task Information dialog box, place a check in the Mark Task as Milestone checkbox. In this case, the task duration won't change to zero; however, the element representing it in the Gantt Chart changes from a bar, reflecting the task's duration, to a milestone diamond symbol, representing the task as a moment in time.

Note   For milestones with durations longer than zero, the diamond appears at the end of the duration.

Timing for summary tasks

How do you assign durations for summary tasks? You don't. Remember, summary tasks simply roll up the timing of their subtasks. Therefore, they don't have any timing of their own. If three subtasks occur one right after the other and each is three days long, the summary task above them takes nine days from beginning to end. If you open the Task Information dialog box for a summary task, most timing settings appear gray, indicating that they're not available.

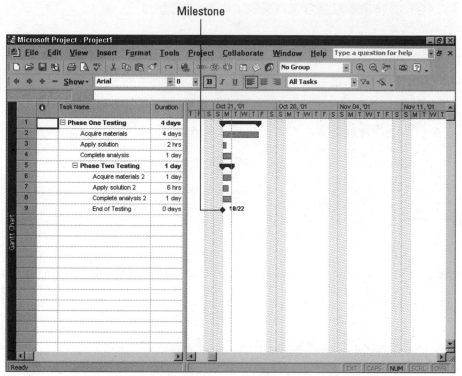

Figure 4-6: A milestone typically marks a noteworthy point in your project; a milestone is often a task of no duration.

Using Recurring Tasks

Projects quite often have tasks that occur on a regular basis: weekly staff meetings, quarterly reports, or monthly budget reviews are examples of these recurring tasks. Rather than have you create, for example, 20 or so weekly staff-meeting tasks over the life of a five-month project, you can use Project's recurring-task feature. This feature enables you to create the Meeting task once and assign a frequency and timing to it. Follow these steps to create a recurring task:

1. Because Project inserts tasks above the selected task, select the task that you want to appear below the recurring task and choose Insert ⇨ Recurring Task to open the Recurring Task Information dialog box, as shown in Figure 4-7.

2. Type a name for the recurring task.

3. Set the task duration in the Duration field; for example, does the meeting run for two hours, or does a report take a day to write?

Figure 4-7: If a task occurs at regular intervals during the life of a project, you can save yourself time by creating it as a recurring task.

4. Set the occurrence of the task by selecting one of the Recurrence pattern option buttons: Daily, Weekly, Monthly, or Yearly. Depending on the recurrence that you select, the timing settings to the right of the control buttons change. Figure 4-8 shows the Monthly settings.

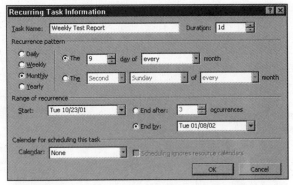

Figure 4-8: Daily, Weekly, Monthly, and Yearly occurrences require you to make slightly different choices.

5. Select the appropriate settings for the recurrence frequency. For a Weekly setting, place a check next to the day(s) of the week on which you want the task to occur; for example, the task shown in Figure 4-7 occurs every Tuesday. For Monthly or Yearly, set the day of the month on which you want the task to occur; the task in Figure 4-8 occurs on Day 9 of every month.

Note

For a Daily task, you have only one choice: whether you want it to occur every day or only on scheduled workdays. For example, if you want to schedule a computer backup for every day of the week — regardless of whether anyone is at work — you can have the task occur every day. (Ask your MIS department how to automate the process so that it occurs even when nobody is at work.)

6. Set the *Range of recurrence* — the period during which the task should recur — by entering Start and End after or End by dates. If you need to repeat a test weekly for only one month of your ten-month project, you could set Start and End after or End by dates that designate a month of time.

Tip

If you set the End after number of occurrences, Project calculates the date range required to complete that many occurrences of the recurring task and automatically displays the ending date in the End by box. This method can be useful if one of these events falls on a holiday: Project schedules one extra occurrence of the task to compensate. For a weekly staff meeting, you probably don't want to schedule an extra meeting because of a holiday; you can just skip that meeting or schedule it on a different day. On the other hand, if you must repeat a test 16 times during the project cycle, you will want to add one more occurrence of the Test task to compensate for the holiday. Therefore, set the number of occurrences rather than the time range.

7. Click OK to create the task. Project creates the appropriate number of tasks and displays them as subtasks under a summary task with the name you supplied in Step 2; note the recurring task symbol in the Indicators column of the Gantt Chart shown in Figure 4-9.

Figure 4-9: Task bars appear for each occurrence of the recurring task in the Gantt Chart.

Mysterious Icons in the Indicator Column

The symbol next to each Weekly Test Report task in the schedule shown in Figure 4-9 represents a task with a timing constraint applied. Project applies this constraint automatically as you enter settings for the recurring task.

If you move your mouse pointer over one of these symbols as you can see in the figure included here, you can see an explanation of that constraint; for example, the each Weekly Test Report task has a Start No Earlier Than constraint, based on the timing that you set in the Recurring Task Information dialog box. The first recurring task can start no earlier than the From date entered there, and each task occurs weekly thereafter. You learn more about setting timing constraints in the next section.

Establishing Constraints and Deadline Dates

Constraints affect the timing of a task relative to the start or end of your project or to a specific date. Setting a deadline date in Project provides you with a visual reminder if you don't complete a task by the deadline date that you establish.

Understanding constraints

Project sets all tasks you create to start, by default, with an As Soon As Possible constraint. Barring any dependency relationships with other tasks (see the "Establishing Dependencies Among Tasks" section later in this chapter), the task would start on the first day of the project. You can set other constraints:

✦ **As Late As Possible.** This constraint forces a task to start on a date such that its end occurs no later than the end of the project.

✦ **Finish No Earlier Than/Finish No Later Than.** This constraint sets the completion of a task to fall no sooner or later than a specific date.

✦ **Must Finish On/Must Start On.** This constraint forces a task to finish or start on a specific date.

✦ **Start No Earlier Than/Start No Later Than.** This constraint sets the start of a task to fall no sooner or later than a specific date.

Only the Must Finish On/Must Start On settings constrain a task to start or end on a particular date; all the other settings constrain the task to occur within a certain time frame.

Using deadline dates

Starting in Project 2000, you can also establish a deadline date for a task. The deadline date differs from a constraint in that Project doesn't use the deadline date when calculating a project's schedule. Instead, the deadline date behaves as a visual cue to notify you that a task finished after the deadline date, as shown in Figure 4-10. Be aware that you won't see any indicator if you complete the task prior to the deadline date.

Although deadline dates won't affect the calculation of a project schedule, they will affect a Late Finish date and the calculation of total slack for the project. Also be aware that you can assign both a deadline date and a constraint to a task. In a project that you schedule from a beginning date, a deadline date has the same effect as a Finish No Later Than constraint. If you assign deadline dates to tasks in projects that you schedule from an ending date, those tasks will finish on their deadline dates unless a constraint or a dependency pushes them to an earlier date.

Missed deadline date indicator

Figure 4-10: When you set a deadline date for a task and you don't finish the task before the deadline, Project displays an indicator to alert you that the task finished later than you specified.

Setting constraints and deadline dates

You set constraints on tasks in your project by using the Advanced tab of the Task Information dialog box, shown in Figure 4-11. Select a constraint type from the Constraint Type drop-down list. For all settings in the Type list other than As Late As Possible and As Soon As Possible, designate a date by typing in a date or by clicking the arrow next to the Constraint Date field and choosing a date from the drop-down calendar that appears. Set a deadline date by clicking the arrow next to the Deadline field and choosing a date from the drop-down calendar that appears.

Figure 4-11: Click the arrow next to the Constraint
type field to see the various constraints.

Under what circumstances would constraints be useful? Consider these situations:

✦ A project involves preparing a new facility for occupancy, and you want the
final inspection of that facility to happen as late as possible.

✦ The approval of a yearly budget must finish no later than the last day of the
fiscal year, ready to begin the new year with the budget in place.

✦ Billing of a major account must start no sooner than the first day of the next
quarter so that the income doesn't accrue on your books this quarter.

✦ Presentation of all severance packages for laid-off employees must finish on
the day a major takeover of the company is announced.

Deadline dates would be useful when:

✦ You need to prepare the annual budget by a deadline date to ensure approval
in time to begin the new year with the budget in place.

✦ You need to prepare severance packages for laid-off employees so that you
can present them on the day a major takeover of the company is announced.

You see how constraints and dependencies interact in establishing the timing of
tasks later in this chapter in the "Establishing Dependencies Among Tasks" section.

Manipulating the Gantt Chart to View Timing

After you enter several tasks and task durations, you'll probably want to manipulate the timescale in the Gantt Chart to view information about these tasks using different increments of time. Use any of the following methods to modify the appearance of items in your Gantt Chart:

✦ Adjust the amount of the window that the Gantt table and the Gantt Chart use by moving your mouse pointer over the divider line until it becomes the two-directional arrow pointer. Drag the divider to the right or left to adjust the amount of the window taken up by the two panes.

✦ Modify the width of columns in the Gantt table so that you can see more columns onscreen by moving your mouse pointer over a column's right edge until you see the two-directional arrow pointer. Drag the column edge to the right or left to make it larger or smaller.

✦ Double-click the column heading and change the column width in the Column Definition dialog box that appears. Also use this dialog box to change the title and alignment of the column title.

 New Feature   You can now set the timescale to view three levels instead of just two levels.

✦ Modify the increments of time displayed in the timescale itself either by double-clicking the timescale or by choosing Format ➪ Timescale. The Timescale dialog box appears, as shown in Figure 4-12. You can change the units for the top tier, the middle tier, and the bottom tier. These adjustments enable you to concentrate on a particular period in your project or to view larger increments with less detail. The Count field controls how many instances of the unit Project marks off on your Gantt Chart.

Figure 4-12: In the Timescale dialog box, adjust the units to display and how many to include.

Figure 4-13, for example, shows a top tier timescale in months and a middle tier timescale in weeks, and a bottom tier timescale in days. The Count for each is 1: one month with each of its four or five weeks shown, and each week's seven days shown.

Figure 4-13: When you specify one week in the Count field of the Timescale dialog box, Project marks off every week on the portion of the timescale that displays weeks.

If you change the Count for the middle tier — weeks — to 2, the weekly timescale displays two-week increments, as shown in Figure 4-14. To show more of the project onscreen, consider eliminating the bottom tier of the timescale, as shown in Figure 4-15.

Tip To shrink the timescale even more (that is, to see more of your project onscreen) use the Size setting in the Timescale dialog box. This setting enables you to view the timescale at a percentage of its full size.

Figure 4-14: Changing the Count field for weeks to 2 causes Project to mark off weeks in two-week chunks.

Starting in Project 2000, you can independently set the use of the fiscal year for any tier of the timescale. To make this feature work, you should set up a fiscal year calendar. Use the detailed steps discussed in Chapter 3 or the overview steps reviewed previously in this chapter in the "Assigning a Calendar to a Task" section. As you create the new calendar, make sure you click the Options button in the Change Working Calendar dialog box to display the Calendar tab of the Options dialog box. Then, change the starting month from January to your fiscal year's starting month.

Figure 4-15: You can compress the Gantt bars of your project so that you see more of the project on-screen by adjusting the timescale.

Entering Task Notes

You can attach notes to individual tasks to remind you of certain parameters or details for the task. For example, if a task involves several subcontractors, you may want to list their contact information here so it's close at hand when you're working on the project schedule. Or use the Notes field to document company regulations relative to that type of procedure. When you add a note to a task, you can display the note onscreen and include the note in a printed report.

Cross-Reference

You can also attach notes to individual resources and to their assignments, as you will learn in Chapter 5.

To enter a note for a task, follow these steps:

1. Double-click a task to open the Task Information dialog box.

2. Click the Notes tab to display it, as shown in Figure 4-16.

3. Type your note in the area provided. You can use the tools identified in Figure 4-16 to format your note text.

4. Click OK to attach the note to your task.

Figure 4-16: The Notes tab provides simple word processing, such as tools for formatting your notes.

A Note icon now appears in the Indicators column of the Gantt table, as shown in Figure 4-17. Move the mouse pointer over this icon to display the note.

Figure 4-17: Project automatically adds an icon for the note to the Indicators column.

You can print notes along with your schedule. To do so, follow these steps:

1. Choose File ➪ Page Setup.

2. Click the View tab to display the settings shown in Figure 4-18.

Figure 4-18: Notes appears on a separate page after printing your Gantt Chart when you place a check next to Print notes.

3. Click the Print notes checkbox to have Project print notes for tasks.

4. Click OK.

Cross-Reference
You learn more about printing schedules in Chapter 7.

Establishing Dependencies Among Tasks

Whereas constraints tie tasks to the project start or end or to particular dates, dependencies tie tasks to the timing of other tasks in the project. Dependencies are central to visualizing the true length of a project.

Dependencies exist because all tasks in a project rarely can happen simultaneously; usually, some tasks must start or finish before others can begin. Tasks overlap for many reasons: the inability of resources to do more than one task at a time, the lack of availability of equipment, or the nature of the tasks themselves (you can't start construction until you receive a construction permit). You can't really know the total time that you will need to complete a project until you establish durations and dependencies. For example, a project that comprises five 10-day-long tasks with no dependencies among the tasks takes 10 days to complete. But, if the tasks must happen one after the other, the project requires 50 days.

Understanding dependencies

A task that must occur before another task is a *predecessor task*. The task that occurs later in the relationship is a *successor task*. A task can have multiple predecessors and successors. Tasks with dependency relationships are *linked*. Gantt Charts show these links as lines running between task bars; an arrow at one end points to the successor task. Some dependency relationships are as simple as one task ending before another can begin. However, some relationships are much more complex. For example, if you're moving into a new office and the first task is assembling cubicles, you don't have to wait until all the cubicles are assembled to begin moving in furniture. You may work in tandem, using the first morning to set up cubicles on the first floor. Then you can begin to move chairs and bookcases into the first-floor cubicles while the setup task continues on the second floor.

Understanding the interactions between constraints and dependencies

Both constraints and dependencies drive the timing of a task. Consider for a moment how constraints and dependencies may interact when you apply one of each to a task. Say that you have a task — to open a new facility — that has a constraint set so that it must start on June 6. You then set up a dependency that indicates the task should begin after a task — fire inspection — that is scheduled for completion on June 10. When you try to set up such a dependency, Project displays a Planning Wizard dialog box, like the one shown in Figure 4-19. This dialog box indicates a scheduling conflict. Project displays this dialog box when a conflict exists among dependencies or between constraints and dependencies.

Figure 4-19: Multiple dependencies or a combination of dependencies and constraints can cause conflicts in timing.

If a conflict exists between a constraint and a dependency, the constraint drives the timing of the task; the task does not move from the constraint-imposed date. You can modify this functionality by choosing Tools ➪ Options. On the Schedule tab of the Options dialog box, remove the check from the Tasks Will Always Honor Their Constraint Dates checkbox. When you change this option, dependencies — rather than constraints — determine timing.

See Chapter 9 for more information about resolving timing conflicts.

You can create dependencies in one of three ways:

✦ You can select two tasks and use the Link Tasks command on the Edit menu or the Link Tasks button on the Standard toolbar. The first task that you select becomes the predecessor in the relationship.

✦ You can open the successor task's Task Information dialog box and enter predecessor information on the Predecessors tab.

✦ You can use your mouse button to click the Gantt bar of a predecessor and drag to the Gantt bar of a successor to create a link to a successor task.

If you want to link a whole range of tasks to be consecutive (one finishes, the next begins, and so on down through the list of tasks), select the range of tasks (drag from the ID number of the first task to the ID of the last task). Then use the Link Tasks button or the Link Tasks command in the Edit menu to create a string of such relationships at one time.

Allowing for overlap and delays

Although many dependency relationships are relatively clear-cut — Task A can begin only when Task B is complete, or Task C can start only after Task B has started — some are even more finely delineated. These relationships involve overlap and delay (delay is also called *lag time*).

To understand these two concepts, consider these examples. Suppose that your project tests a series of metals. In the first task, you apply a solution to the metal, and in the second task, you analyze the results. However, time can be a factor, so you want the analysis to begin only when several days have passed after the application of the solution. You build in a delay between the finish of the first task (the predecessor) and the start of the second (the successor). Figure 4-20 shows a relationship with some lag between the two tasks; the line between the two tasks indicates the dependency, and the space between the bars indicates the gap in time between the finish of one and the start of the next.

You create lag time using the Predecessors tab of the Task Information dialog box.

Lag

Figure 4-20: After you apply the solution, you must wait four days to analyze the results.

Note   Some people prefer to build a task to represent lag, rather than to establish a dependency relationship. For example, instead of placing a dependency between application of the solution and analysis, you can create a three-day-long task called Solution Reaction Period. Then create a simple dependency relationship between Solution Reaction Period and the analysis so that the analysis task won't begin until Solution Reaction Period is complete. Adding the lag tasks can generate a very long schedule with multiple tasks and relationships to track. But in a simpler schedule, this approach enables you to see relationships as task bars. You can try both methods, and see which works best for you.

Another test in your project involves applying both a solution and heat. You first want to apply the solution for three hours and then begin to apply heat as well. Notice the overlap between the tasks: the predecessor task — applying the solution — begins at 8:00 a.m. and runs to 2:00 p.m.; the successor task — applying heat — begins three hours after the start of the predecessor task, at 11:00 a.m. The project shown in Figure 4-21 has some overlap between tasks.

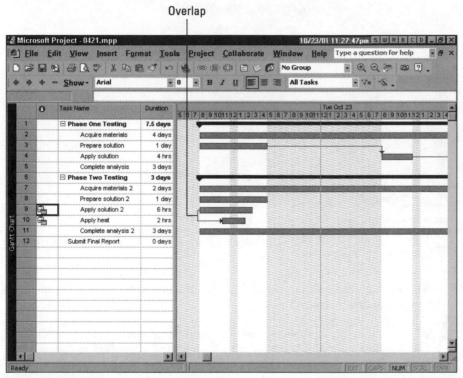

Figure 4-21: Some overlap occurs between the application of the solution and the application of the heat in this testing project.

Note   I set up a task calendar that ignores lunchtime so that both tasks could continue uninterrupted (the icons in the Indicator column represent the task calendar), and I changed the timescale so that you can see the hours of a day.

Dependency types

Four basic dependency relationships define the relationship between the start and finish of tasks: start-to-finish, finish-to-start, start-to-start, and finish-to-finish. You can set these dependency relationships on the Predecessors tab of the Task Information dialog box, as shown in Figure 4-22.

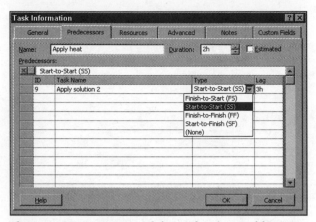

Figure 4-22: Four types of dependencies enable you to deal with every variable of how tasks can relate to each other's timing.

Tip   Use the Lag column on the Predecessors tab of the Task Information dialog box to create lag time between tasks.

The first timing mentioned in each relationship name relates to the predecessor task and the second to the successor. Therefore, a start-to-finish dependency relates the start of the predecessor to the finish of the successor, and a finish-to-start relationship relates the finish of the predecessor to the start of the successor. Project refers to these relationships by their initials, such as *SS* for a start-to-start relationship.

Tip   As you view the figures in the following sections, take note of the direction that the arrow points between tasks; the direction of the arrow provides important visual clues about the type of dependency.

Finish-to-start (FS)

A finish-to-start relationship is the most common type of dependencies and is, in fact, the only relationship that you can create by using your mouse or Link Tasks tool or command. In the finish-to-start relationship, the successor task can't start until the predecessor task finishes. Examples of this relationship are:

✦ You must write a report before you can edit it.

✦ You must have a computer before you can install your software.

In Figure 4-23, you see examples of the FS relationship in which the successor task can start as soon as its predecessor is finished. The following tasks have a finish-to-start relationship:

Task 2 and Task 3

Task 3 and Task 4

Task 4 and Task 5

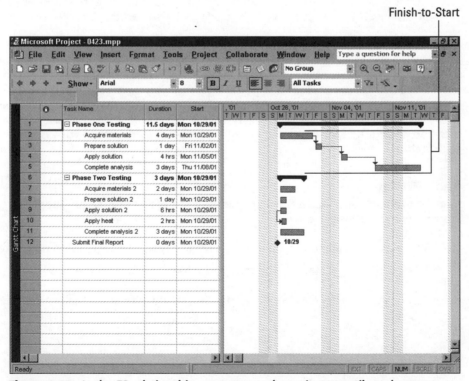

Figure 4-23: In the FS relationship, successor tasks can't start until predecessor tasks finish.

Note The relationship between Tasks 4 and 5 also contains some lag time added in a previous section, "Allowing for Overlap and Delays."

Start-to-finish (SF)

With the start-to-finish relationship, the successor task cannot finish until the predecessor task starts. Here are some examples:

✦ You can finish scheduling production crews only when you start receiving materials.

✦ Employees can start using a new procedure only when they have finished training on it. If the use of the new procedure is delayed, you also want to delay the training so that it occurs as late as possible before the implementation.

Note Can you set up this start-to-finish example as a finish-to-start relationship? Not really. The idea is to allow no delay between training and implementation. If you set the new procedure to start only when the training finishes, the new procedure can start any time after the training ends, depending on how other relationships may delay it. If the training task has to finish just before the other task starts, delays of the later task (implementation) also delay the earlier task. This fine distinction will become clearer when you see projects in action.

Figure 4-24 shows a start-to-finish relationship between acquiring materials for Phase 2 Testing and completing the analysis of Phase 1 Testing. Assuming the test results of Phase 1 determine the materials you'll need for Phase 2, you really can't begin acquiring materials for Phase 2 Testing until you have completed the analysis of Phase 1 Testing. Notice the direction of the arrow connecting the two tasks; it provides a visual clue of the type of dependency that exists between the tasks. In fact, the direction of the arrow in *all* dependencies provides you with valuable information.

Start-to-start (SS)

In a start-to-start relationship, the successor can't start until the predecessor starts. Consider these examples:

✦ When you start getting results in an election, you can begin to compile them.

✦ When the drivers start their engines, the flagger can start the race.

Refer to Figure 4-24 to see a start-to-start relationship with some built-in lag time.

Start-to-Finish

Figure 4-24: The successor task can't finish until the predecessor task starts.

Finish-to-finish (FF)

In the finish-to-finish dependency, the successor task can't finish until the predecessor task finishes. For example:

✦ You finish installing computers at the same time that you finish moving employees into the building so that they can begin using the computers right away.

✦ Two divisions must finish retooling their production lines on the same day so that the CEO can inspect them at the same time.

Suppose that, in Phase 2 of the testing in Figure 4-25, you can begin preparing the solution (Prepare solution 2) while you're still acquiring materials (Acquire materials 2); however, you can't finish preparing the solution until you finish acquiring the materials. Therefore, set up a finish-to-finish dependency between the two tasks to make sure that you don't finish preparing the solution if you experience a delay acquiring materials.

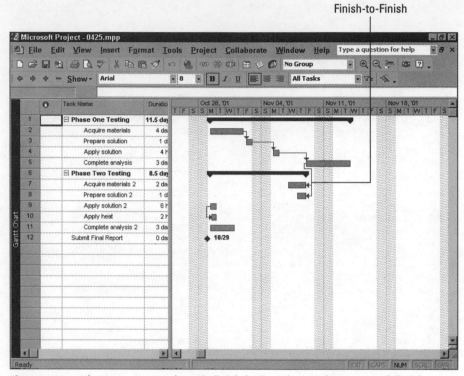

Figure 4-25: The successor task can't finish before the predecessor task finishes.

Establishing dependencies

As mentioned previously, you can set dependencies in a few different ways. If you use the tasks on the Gantt Chart to set dependencies, you must establish finish-to-start relationships. To establish more complex relationships, including delay and overlap, use the Task Information dialog box.

Note   You can set dependencies between two summary tasks or between a summary task and subtask in another task group using a finish-to-start or a start-to-start dependency. You cannot use any other type of dependency, and you cannot set dependencies between a summary task and any of its own subtasks.

Setting finish-to-start dependencies

With the Gantt Chart displayed, you can use your mouse, the Link Tasks tool, or the Link Tasks command from the Edit menu. You can use any of these methods to set a simple finish-to-start relationship:

1. Place your mouse pointer over the predecessor task until the pointer turns into four arrows pointing outward.

2. Drag the mouse pointer to the second task. An information box describes the finish-to-start link you are about to create, as shown in Figure 4-26.

3. Release your mouse button when you're satisfied with the relationship, and Project establishes the link.

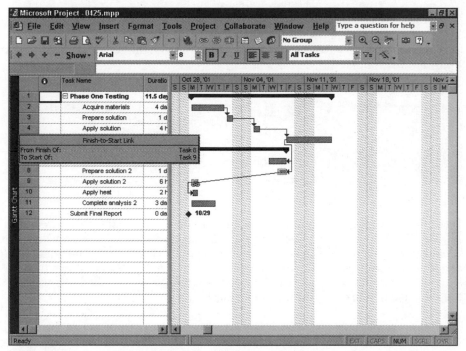

Figure 4-26: The relationship isn't established until you release the mouse button. If you have second thoughts, just drag back to the predecessor task before releasing your mouse.

To use the Link Tasks tool or command, simply follow these steps:

1. Select the tasks that you want to link. To select adjacent tasks, drag through their ID numbers in the Gantt Chart table. To select non-adjacent tasks, hold Ctrl as you click the ID numbers of the tasks that you want to link.

Note   Starting in Project 2000, you also can select non-adjacent tasks by holding Ctrl as you click their Gantt bars.

2. Click the Link Tasks tool, or Choose Edit ➪ Link Tasks. Project establishes the link.

Setting other types of dependencies

You can use either the Task Information dialog box or the Task Dependency dialog box to set any type of dependency. Use the Task Dependency dialog box, as shown in Figure 4-27, to establish dependency types or lag times between tasks. To open the Task Dependency dialog box, double-click the line that connects the tasks that you want to change.

Figure 4-27: Use this dialog box to establish task *f*dependencies or lag time.

From the Task Information dialog box, in addition to establishing dependencies and lag times, you also can set overlap times. If you choose to use the Task Information dialog box, open the dialog box for the successor task and build the relationship on the Predecessors tab.

Follow these steps to create a task dependency:

1. Double-click the task that you want to make a successor. When the Task Information dialog box appears, select the Predecessors tab if it's not already displayed.

2. Click the Task Name column; an arrow appears at its far end.

3. Click the arrow to display the drop-down list of task names, as shown in Figure 4-28.

4. Click the task that you want to identify as the predecessor to this task.

Figure 4-28: Every task that you create for your project appears on this list.

5. Click the Type field; a list box arrow appears.

6. Click the arrow to display a list of dependency types.

7. Click the type of dependency that you want to establish, such as start-to-start or start-to-finish.

To establish a dependency with no delay or overlap, click OK at this point to create the relationship. If you want to establish any delay, click the Lag column and supply an amount of time for the delay. If you want to establish overlap, simply enter a negative number in the Lag column. For example, if you want the successor to finish one week before the predecessor finishes, use a finish-to-finish relationship and type **1 week** in the Lag column.

Viewing Dependencies

After you've established several dependencies in a project, you can study them in several ways. You can, of course, open each task's Task Information dialog box and look at the relationships listed on the Predecessor tab. You can also view the lines drawn between tasks to see dependencies. Finally, you can scroll to the right in the Gantt table, or you can reduce the size of the Gantt Chart to see more of the Gantt table and display the Predecessors column, as shown in Figure 4-29. This column lists any relationships, using the two-letter abbreviations for the dependency type and positive and negative numbers to show lag and overlap.

Figure 4-29: Display the Predecessors column to show all the relationships for a task.

Deleting Dependencies

Here are several techniques for deleting dependencies:

✦ Open the Task Information dialog box for the successor task, select the Predecessors tab, click the task name for the link you want to break, and press Delete on your keyboard.

✦ Display the Predecessors column in the Gantt table, click the Predecessors cell for the successor task, and either press Delete to delete all relationships or edit the predecessor information in the cell or in the entry bar.

✦ Select the tasks involved in the dependency you want to delete and click the Unlink Tasks tool, or choose Edit ➪ Unlink Tasks.

✦ Double-click the dependency line and click the Delete button in the Task Dependency dialog box.

Note   If you delete a dependency, the task bars may shift accordingly to reflect any new timing.

Summary

In this chapter, you read more about the timing of tasks, including how to set task durations and dependencies. You know how to:

✦ Differentiate between resource-driven and fixed scheduling

✦ Establish task durations

✦ Assign calendars to tasks

✦ Create recurring tasks

✦ Establish constraints and deadline dates

✦ Adjust the timescale to view task durations

✦ Add and view task notes

✦ Set, view, and delete dependencies

In Chapter 5, you begin to assign resources to tasks and to learn more about the relationship between resource assignment and task timing.

✦   ✦   ✦

Creating Resources and Assigning Costs

The management portion of the term "project management" suggests that you are overseeing and, supposedly, controlling what goes on during the project's lifetime. In the last chapter, you learned how to build the tasks that comprise the project. Now you need to identify the resources for each task. Some tasks require people only; other tasks may also require equipment.

As you create resources, you'll see that various rates are associated with a resource. As you assign the resource to a task in your project, Microsoft Project automatically begins to calculate the cost of your project.

Understanding Resources

Resources are the people, supplies, and equipment that enable you to complete the tasks in your project. In versions prior to Project 2000, you could define only *work resources* — people or equipment that consume time when working on a task. When you set up work resources, you define the amount of time that they have to spend on a project (100 percent is full-time). Similarly, when you assign a work resource to a task, you indicate the amount of time that you want the work resource to spend on the task (100 percent is full time).

Project 2000 added *material resources* — items that are consumed while working on a project. Material resources use . . . well, materials like gasoline or wood — as opposed to time. When you assign a material resource to a task, you specify the amount of the material resource that you intend to use in units appropriate for the material resource. You also can indicate whether the amount of material used is based on time; for example, the number of gallons of water used when watering a lawn depends on the amount of time that you run the water and the number of gallons per hour that flow from the faucet. Or, you can indicate that the amount of material is fixed; for example, you need five 2 × 4's to construct a bench — regardless of how long you take to build the bench.

New Feature Starting in Project 2002, you can define generic resources and assign them to tasks when you don't know the actual resources that may exist.

Starting in Project 2002, you can define *generic resources* — resources (as defined by you) that describe the skills you need for a task when you don't know what specific resources are available. Although this generic resource feature was designed to work in conjunction with the Resource Substitution Wizard and Enterprise Resources (available in Project Server), you may find generic resources handy even if you don't use Project Server. For example, you can use generic resources when you don't care *who* does the work — you simply want to track the work completed on a project.

Cross-Reference If you're using Project Server, you also can take advantage of three other related features. You can define Enterprise Resources — resources available company-wide for projects. You can use Team Builder to help you select resources for your project from the Enterprise Resource pool, and you can use the Resource Substitution Wizard to replace generic resources with actual resources. Read more about Enterprise Resources, Team Builder, and the Resource Substitution Wizard in Chapter 19.

Resources cost money and therefore affect the cost of the project. To manage a project effectively, you should define resources and assign those resources to tasks in the project. Thus, you need to know how Project uses those resource assignments to change the duration and length of your project.

Tip If you expect to use the same resources for several projects, consider setting up the resources in a special project that contains no tasks. Then you can use Project's resource pooling feature and the "resource project" to share resources across multiple projects. This approach enables you to set up resources once and then use them repeatedly on many different projects. For more information about resource pooling and managing multiple projects, see Chapter 15. If you use Project Server, consider setting up Enterprise Resources. See Chapter 19 for more information about Enterprise Resources.

How resources work

By defining and then assigning resources, you accomplish several goals:

✦ You can keep track of the tasks being performed by resources — because Project identifies the resources assigned to each task.

✦ You can identify potential resource shortages that may force you to miss scheduled deadlines and possibly extend the duration of your project.

✦ You can identify underutilized resources. If you reassign these resources, you may be able to shorten the project's schedule.

When the tasks that you create are effort-driven — Project defines all new tasks as effort-driven by default — the resources that you assign to a task affect the duration of the task. For example, if you assign two people to do a job, the job typically gets done in less time than if you assigned only one person to the job. But, you ask, what about the cost? Does the use of additional resources increase the project's cost? Perhaps yes — perhaps no. You may find that completing the project in less time (by using more resources) saves you money because you can accept more projects. Or you may be eligible for a bonus if you complete the project earlier than expected, and the bonus may cover or exceed the cost of the additional resources you used.

How Project uses resource information to affect the schedule

For effort-driven tasks, Project uses the resource information you provide to calculate the duration of the task and, consequently, the duration of the project. However, if you set up a task with a fixed duration, Project ignores the resources assigned to the task when calculating the duration of the project. Similarly, if you don't assign resources, Project calculates the schedule using only the task duration and task dependency information that you provide.

See Chapter 4 for information on task durations and task dependencies.

Assigning a resource to a task can affect the duration of the project because work on the task can't begin until the resource is available. Project uses a resource calendar to define the working days and times for a resource, but the resource's availability also depends on other tasks to which you have assigned the resource.

If the work assigned to a resource exceeds the time available, Microsoft Project assigns the resource to the task and indicates that the resource is overallocated. This technique enables you to see the problem and decide how to fix it.

You also have the option of assigning costs to resources when you define them, as you'll see in "Creating a Resource List" later in this chapter.

How Project gathers cost information

When you assign costs to resources and then assign resources to tasks, Project can calculate the cost of a project. In addition to resource-associated costs, Project also handles fixed costs, which you learn more about near the end of this chapter.

Assigning costs enables you to monitor and control the money that you're spending on a project. Project shows you where and how you are spending your money; this information enables you to control when a project's costs accrue, which, in turn, helps you to schedule your bill payment. The cost-related information that Project provides helps you to verify the following items:

✦ The cost of resources and materials for any task

✦ The cost of any phase of your project, as well as the cost of the entire project

 Tip   Cost information that you gather on one project may help you to calculate bids for future projects.

Creating a Resource List

 Note   If you intend to upload this project into Project Server, you may want to assign resources from the Enterprise Resource pool, a company-wide group of resources. See Chapter 19 for details on assigning resources from the Enterprise Resource pool.

Project gives you the option of creating resources one at a time, as you think of them, or entering all (or most) resources by using the Entry table of the Resource Sheet. To display the Resource Sheet, shown in Figure 5-1, click the Resource Sheet button on the View bar or choose View ➪ Resource Sheet. By default, Project displays the Entry table of the Resource Sheet.

 Note   You can switch tables by clicking View ➪ Table and then selecting from the submenu that appears. Each table contains columns pertinent to its name; for example, the Cost table shows columns pertaining to a resource's cost.

 Tip   If you want to add resources to your project that exist elsewhere (such as your company Address book or in Microsoft Project Server), click the first link on the Resource page of the Project Guide.

If you use the Resource Sheet to define most of the resources for your project, the actual process of assigning resources goes much faster because you don't have to stop to create the resource first. Also, using the Resource Sheet is a safe way to define resources; the visual presentation helps you avoid accidentally creating the same resource twice. For example, if you define Vickey and Vicki, Project sees two resources, even though you may have simply misspelled the name the second time.

You can enter the basics for the resource by filling in the Resource Sheet; simply press the Tab key to move from field to field (cell to cell). The Resource Sheet shown in Figure 5-1 does not show all the fields described in this section; scroll to the right to see the rest of the Entry table of the Resource Sheet.

 Tip   You can customize the Resource Sheet to show many additional fields that you may want to set up for each resource. For example, if you need to manually enter e-mail addresses for each resource, you can add the E-mail Address column to the Resource Sheet.

Cross-Reference

See Chapter 7 to learn how to insert a column in a table.

Figure 5-1: The Resource Sheet displays a list of the resources available to your project.

New Feature

As part of the Project Guide, you can have Project walk you through the process of creating resources. The Resources page of the Project Guide, visible in Figure 5-1, appears when you switch to the Resource Sheet view or when you click the Resources button on the Project Guide toolbar. Click a link to walk through the associated steps.

A *field* is a cell in a table into which you type appropriate information. All table and form views contain fields. Each field on the Resource Sheet serves a specific purpose:

✦ **Indicators.** Although you can't type in the Indicators field, icons appear here from time to time. Some of the icons appear as Project's response to an action that you've taken. For example, you may see an indicator for an overallocated resource. In other cases, the indicator appears because you entered a note about the resource. See the "Adding Notes to a Resource" section later in this chapter for more information.

Tip

If you point at an indicator, Project displays the information associated with the icon.

✦ **Resource Name.** Type the name of the resource. For manpower, you can type a person's name or you can type a job description, such as Product Analyst 1 or Product Analyst 2.

✦ **Type.** Use this column to specify whether you're defining a human or material resource. Project refers to human resources as "Work."

✦ **Material Label.** For material resources, specify the unit of measure. You can set up any label that you want; you can use minutes for long distance, feet for lumber, or miles for gasoline.

✦ **Initials.** Type initials for the resource, or accept the default that Project provides, which is the first letter of the resource name. This designation appears on any view to which you add the Initials field. Typically, a resource's name appears, but you can customize the view to display initials if you prefer.

✦ **Group.** Assign resources to groups if they share some common characteristic, such as job function. Then you can use this field as a filtering or sorting mechanism and display information about the group (a particular job function) as opposed to a specific resource. Just type a name to create a group.

Tip   Be sure to spell the name the same way each time if you want to filter or sort by group.

✦ **Max. Units.** Project expresses the amount of the work resource you have available for assignment as a percentage. For example, 100 percent equals one unit, or the equivalent of one full-time resource; 50 percent equals one-half of a unit, or one-half of a full-time resource's time; and 200 percent equals two full-time resources.

✦ **Std. Rate.** The standard rate is the rate you charge for regular work for a resource. Project calculates the default rate in hours; you can, however, charge a resource's work in other time increments (for work resources, you can use minutes, days, weeks, or years; for material resources, think of the charge as per unit based on the Material label). To specify a time increment other than hours, type a slash and then the first letter of the word representing the time increment. For example, to charge a resource's use in days, type **/d** after the rate that you specify.

✦ **Ovt. Rate.** The overtime rate is the rate you charge for overtime work for a work resource. Again, Project calculates the default rate in hours, but you can change the default unit the same way you changed it for the Standard Rate.

✦ **Cost/Use.** In the Cost/Use column (read that as "cost per use"), supply a rate you use to charge a one-time rate for a resource. Use this rate for costs that are charged on a per/unit basis (such as material costs), rather than on some time-related basis.

✦ **Accrue At.** This field specifies how and when Microsoft Project charges resource costs to a task at the standard or overtime rates. The default option is Prorated, but you also can select Start or End.

  • If you select Start and assign that resource to a task, Project calculates the cost for a task as soon as the task begins.

  • If you select End and assign that resource to a task, Project calculates the cost for the task when the task is completed.

  • If you select Prorated and assign that resource to a task, Project accrues the cost of the task as you complete scheduled work.

Tip   If you set a cost per use rate for a resource and assign that resource to a task, Project always charges the cost of the resource at the beginning of a task.

✦ **Base Calendar.** Base calendar identifies the calendar that Project should use when scheduling the resource. The calendar identifies working and nonworking time. Project assumes that each resource uses the Standard calendar, but, as you'll read later in this chapter, you can create calendars for resource groups (perhaps to handle shift work) or you can modify an individual resource's calendar to reflect vacation or other unavailable time (such as jury duty).

✦ **Code.** You can use this field as a catchall field to assign any information that you want to a resource, using an abbreviation of some sort. For example, suppose your company uses cost-center codes; you may want to supply the cost-center code for the resource in the Code field. You can sort and filter information by the abbreviations that you supply in the Code field.

Note   After you create a resource, Project displays the resource's ID number on the very left edge of the Resource Sheet, to the left of the Indicators column.

Modifying Resource Information

You just learned a quick way to set up a resource — by typing on the Resource Sheet. In addition, you can use the Resource Information dialog box to fine-tune your resource's definition.

Use the Resource Information dialog box to modify resource information. To display the Resource Information dialog box, double-click any resource on the Resource Sheet or choose Project ➪ Resource Information. Then click the General tab.

You already provided most of the information on this tab on the Resource Sheet, so this section discusses the fields in the dialog box that didn't appear by default on the Entry table of the Resource Sheet.

Assigning a communication method

Use the E-mail field, shown in Figure 5-2, to supply the e-mail address of a resource. You must fill in this field if you want to use Project's workgroup feature, which enables users to assign, accept, or decline work electronically. You can make a selection from the Workgroup drop-down list to specify an electronic communication method.

Cross-Reference   See Chapter 16 for more about the e-mail workgroup feature. See Chapters 18 and 19 for more information about using Project and Project Server.

Figure 5-2: Use the General tab of the Resource Information dialog box to add information about a resource, such as an e-mail address or availability.

Specifying resource availability

Suppose that you set up a resource to represent a specific job, such as Intern, as shown in Figure 5-3. And suppose that you have more than one of this resource, but not at all times. Using the Resource Availability section, shown previously in Figure 5-2, you can specify the time periods for which the resource will be available. Figure 5-2 shows that five interns are available from October 22 through October 31, two interns are available for the first two weeks of November, and five interns are available from November 16 through November 30.

Note   Starting in Project 2000, you can contour the availability of resources. See Chapter 10 for more information.

E-mail and Project

If you're using a MAPI-compliant e-mail program, such as Outlook or Outlook Express, and you've stored the resource's e-mail address in your Address Book, you can click the Details button in the Resource Information dialog box to have Project look up the e-mail address for you. You can then copy the address from the Address Book, close the address book, and, in the E-mail field, press Ctrl+V to paste the address into the Resource Information dialog box.

However, I suspect you'll find it faster to use the "Specify people and equipment for the project" link on the Resources page of the Project Guide to enter e-mail addresses for resources. When you click the link, the page will change and present you with four options. Select the first one ("Add resources from the company Address Book"), click the Address Book link that appears, as shown in the figure, and follow the onscreen instructions.

Creating a generic resource

The Intern discussed in the previous section is, essentially, a generic resource. It's a job description, not a person. To mark a resource as generic, place a check in the Generic box on the General tab of the Resource Information dialog box (refer back to Figure 5-2). Your company may have set up custom fields in Project that apply to your generic resource; to assign the appropriate custom fields, click the Custom Fields tab and assign any appropriate values to your generic resource, as shown in Figure 5-3.

Cross-Reference   See Chapter 20 for more information about creating custom fields.

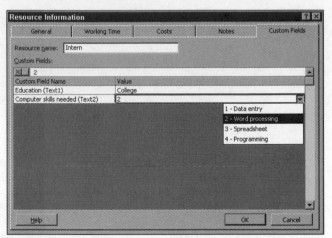

Figure 5-3: You can assign custom fields to generic resources that describe the skills required.

When you click OK to close the dialog box, you'll see an icon in the Indicator column like the one shown in Figure 5-4, signifying that the resource is generic.

Figure 5-4: Identify generic resources by the icon in the Indicator column.

Adding notes to a resource

Click the Notes tab of the Resource Information dialog box. The Notes text box shown in Figure 5-5 is a free-form text box in which you can type any information that you want to store about the resource. For example, you may want to store a reminder about a resource's upcoming vacation or an explanation about resource availability.

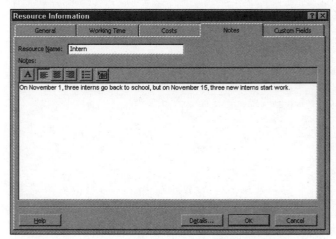

Figure 5-5: Use this text box to store any information about a resource.

After you type text in this box and click OK, a Note indicator icon appears in the Indicators column on the Resource Sheet, as shown in Figure 5-6.

Calendars and resources

As you learned in Chapter 3, Project uses a base calendar called the Standard calendar to calculate the timing of the project. When you first create a resource for your project, Project uses the Standard base calendar as the default (an 8-hour day, 40-hour week if you haven't changed this setting in the Project Information dialog box). As discussed in the preceding section, you can modify the dates that a resource is available; you also can modify working times. For example, you may want to change a resource's working hours, or you may want to block off a period of time — such as vacation time or a business trip — for a resource, making it unavailable during that period.

Note   The entire project has a Standard calendar, and each resource also has his or her individual Standard calendar.

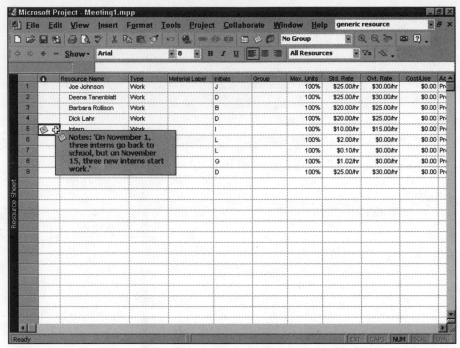

Figure 5-6: You don't need to reopen the Resource Information dialog box to read a note; instead, use the mouse to point at the indicator icon, and Project displays the contents of the note.

Modifying a resource's working hours

Suppose that a specific resource won't be available all day on a given day, or even on several specified days. For example, suppose that all the interns work from 1:00 p.m. to 6:00 p.m. To change the working hours of a resource, use the Working Time tab of the Resource Information dialog box. Double-click the resource on the Resource Sheet to open the dialog box. The resource's calendar appears with today's date selected. The Legend on the left of the dialog box identifies Working days, Nonworking days, Non-default working hours, and Exceptions. Select the dates your resource will not be available.

Note   To select contiguous days, click the first day. Then press the Shift key and click the last day that you want to select. To select noncontiguous days, press Ctrl as you click or drag over each day that you want to select. To select all of any day (for example, Sunday) click the letter of the day. Project selects all of those days, in all months.

Make the necessary changes in the From and To text boxes, as shown in Figure 5-7. The dates that you selected appear underscored in the individual's calendar because you set an exception to the regular schedule; the Legend shows you that the exception involves edited working hours.

Tip

You don't need to select the Non-default working time option button. While the dialog box continues to show that the Use default option is selected, in fact, Project automatically selects the Non-default working time option button.

Cross-Reference

To avoid overallocating a resource that works part of a day, level the resource on a day-by-day basis. Read more about handling overallocations in Chapter 10.

Figure 5-7: Select the dates you want to change. Project marks exceptions to the typical schedule with an underscore.

Blocking off vacation time

Human resources do take time off from work, and, to avoid overallocating a person by assigning work during a vacation period, you should mark vacation days on the resource's calendar.

Double-click the resource to display the Resource Information dialog box and click the Working Time tab. Find the date or dates that you want to block for vacation time by using the scroll bar next to the calendar. With the vacation dates selected, select the Nonworking time option. Click any other date on the calendar to cancel the selection; each date that you marked as vacation time appears with an underscore. Again, by comparing the date to the Legend, you can tell the reason for the exception.

Using Resources and Tasks

You've spent a lot of time in this chapter learning to define resources and fine-tune your resource definitions. Now you can finally assign resources to tasks. As noted earlier in this chapter, defining resources helps you to manage your project more effectively, both in scheduling and in cost.

Assigning resources to tasks

You can easily assign resources to tasks from the Gantt Chart view. Choose ➪ View ➪ Gantt Chart, or use the View bar to switch to the Gantt Chart view and then follow these steps:

1. Select the task to which you want to assign a resource. You can click the task bar on the Gantt Chart or you can click any column in the Gantt table.

2. Click the Assign Resources button or choose Tools ➪ Resources ➪ Assign Resources to open the Assign Resources dialog box, as shown in Figure 5-8.

Figure 5-8: Use the Assign Resources dialog box to assign a resource to the task identified at the top of the box.

3. Select the resource that you want to assign from the Resource Name list of the Assign Resources dialog box.

Tip   Did you forget to define a resource? You don't need to return to the Resource Sheet. Just type the name of the resource in the Resource Name column of the Assign Resources dialog box.

4. (Optional) If you're using Project Server and you intend to use Resource Substitution, in the R/D field, type an **R** for Request to indicate that any resource with the required skills can work on the task. You can also type a **D** for Demand to indicate that the selected resource is specifically required to work on the task.

Cross-Reference For more information about Resource Substitution, see Chapter 19.

5. Do one of the following to assign the amount of a resource:

- To assign any amount other than 100 percent of a resource, type the quantity of the resource as a percentage in the Units column. (Project defines units as percentages, so 100 percent equals one unit of the resource.)

- To assign 100 percent of a resource, leave the Units column blank. Project assigns 100 percent by default.

Note You don't need to type the percent (%) sign; Project assumes percentages. For example, if you type 50, Project converts your entry to 50%. However, you can't assign less than 1% of a resource's time.

6. Click Assign. Project places a check in the left-most column of the Assign Resources dialog box to indicate that the resource is assigned to the selected task.

7. Repeat Steps 3, 4, and 5 to assign additional resources or click Close.

Getting help while selecting resources to assign

New Feature Project 2002 contains some new options to help you select the best resource while making assignments.

You may have noticed a plus sign (+) next to "Resource list options" at the top of Figure 5-8. If you click the plus sign, the box expands, as shown in Figure 5-9, to provide you with ways to make selecting resources easier.

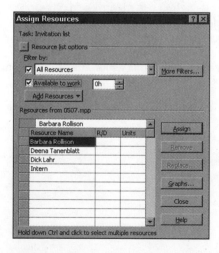

Figure 5-9: You can narrow your search for resources by filtering, and you can make additional resources available.

If you place a check in the Filter by box, Project makes available a long list of possible ways that you can limit the resource list. For example, you can search for only material resources or you can search for resources in a particular group (remember that you can assign resources to groups if they share a common characteristic). If you don't find the filter that you want to use, you can create your own filter by clicking the More Filters button and, in the More Filters dialog box that appears, click New.

Cross-Reference See Chapter 7 for information about creating custom filters.

If you place a check in the Available to work box, you can specify the number of hours that you need the resource. Project calculates the remaining available hours of each resource for the duration of the task and compares the results of the calculation with the number of hours that you specified. Resources with available hours equal to or greater than the value that you supplied appear in the list, along with the resources already assigned to the selected task.

Tip If you need a resource for 12 days, type **12d**, and Project will convert the value to 96 hours.

You can click the Add Resources button to display a list of sources from which you can select a resource: the active directory, your address book (if you use a MAPI-compliant e-mail program such as Microsoft Outlook or Outlook Express), or Microsoft Project Server — the items available and functioning in the list depend on your working environment.

Note The Active Directory is a Windows network feature; in a Windows network, the administrator can set up an active directory that contains a list of people and contact information for them.

The Assign Resources dialog box also contains a Graphs button that shows one of three graphs that you can use to help you select the best resource for the job. Be aware that none of these graphs relate particularly to a task for which you're considering assignment; instead, they focus on the resource.

Note Although you can select multiple resources to graph, this action may not be terribly useful when you're trying to select resources to assign to a task.

How Project Calculates "Available to Work" Hours

Project calculates the value for "available to work" hours using the resource's calendar, availability contour, and the duration of the task. Based on the resource's calendar, Project calculates the number of working hours for the selected task. Because the resource's availability may be reduced by the availability contour and by other assignments, Project multiplies available working hours by the availability contour value and then subtracts existing assignment work hours to determine "available to work" hours.

To see how this works, assume that you have a task to accomplish within a 10-day window and the calendar provides for an 8-hour workday. If Day 3 is a holiday and Days 6 and 7 are the weekend, you have only 7 days to complete the task. If you assign one resource full-time to this task, that resource would be allocated for 56 hours. But, if the resource's availability contour is set to 50 percent, the resource's availability is reduced to 28 hours. And, if the resource is already assigned to another task for 25 percent of the time on Days 1 and 2 (4 hours), the resource's "available to work" hours would be 24 hours.

The Work graph, shown in Figure 5-10, shows the amount of work (regardless of the task) assigned to the selected resource on a day-by-day basis.

Figure 5-10: On this graph, you see the amount of work assigned to the selected resource.

The Assignment Work graph, shown in Figure 5-11, breaks down the total workload of the resource that you're considering, showing you the resource's workload on the selected task, other tasks, and the resource's total availability based on the calendar. Using this graph helps you to see if you'll overallocate the resource by assigning it to this task.

Figure 5-11: Use this graph to avoid overallocating a resource.

The Remaining Availability graph, shown in Figure 5-12, shows you the resource's unassigned time.

 Note If you've overallocated a resource, you won't see a negative availability; the resource's availability will appear to be 0.

 Note You also can view this graph from the Resource Center in Project Web Access.

Figure 5-12: Use this graph to check a resource's availability.

Some tips about resource assignments

Use the following tips when assigning resources:

✦ **You can assign several different resources to the same task by simply selecting each resource.** You can select a single resource and immediately click Assign, or you can use standard Windows selection techniques to select several resources and then click Assign only once.

✦ **You can assign a resource to a task on a part-time basis by assigning less than 100 in the Units column.** The number that you type represents the percentage of working time that you want the resource to spend on the task.

✦ **You can assign more than one resource by assigning more than 100 in the Units column.**

✦ **You can consume material resources in two ways: fixed and variable.** When you use fixed consumption, you indicate that — no matter how long the task lasts — you'll use the same quantity of the material. For example, to build a swimming pool, you'll need two tons of concrete — no matter how long it takes you to pour the concrete. When you use variable consumption, you indicate that the length of the task does affect the amount of the material that you will use. For example, when you mow the lawn with a gas mower, the amount of gas you'll consume depends on how long you run the mower.

You designate fixed or variable consumption in the Units column of the Assign Resources dialog box. To differentiate between fixed and variable consumption, supply the rate at which you consume a variable resource. In Figure 5-13, gasoline is a material resource being consumed at a variable rate because I included the time frame used to measure consumption — the "per hour" designation.

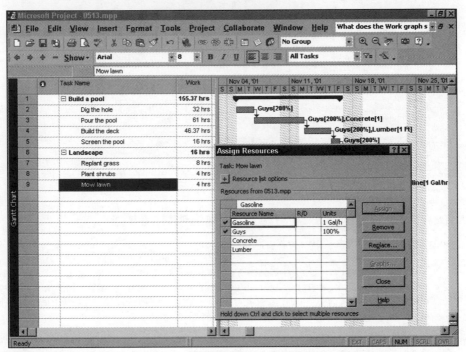

Figure 5-13: Indicate variable consumption by supplying the rate when you specify the amount you'll use.

After you assign a resource to a task, the resource name appears next to the task bar on the Gantt Chart by default. Depending on the task type that you set, you may be able to use resource assignments to modify individual task lengths and the entire project schedule. For example, if you assign additional resources to an effort-driven, fixed-unit task, Project shortens the duration of the task. As you learned in Chapter 4, the amount of work to be done doesn't change, but the extra concurrent effort shortens the time necessary to get the work done. Or if you assign a resource to work part-time on an effort-driven task, you may find that you can complete several tasks at the same time.

Tip   If you overallocate a resource by assigning more than you have available, Project displays the resource in red on the Resource Sheet view. Chapter 9 explains how to handle these problems.

Removing or replacing a resource assignment

To remove a resource assignment, select the task from which you want to remove
the resource assignment using the Gantt Chart view. Then click the Assign
Resources button or choose Tools ➪ Resources ➪ Assign Resources to display the
Assign Resources dialog box. Highlight the resource that you want to remove from
the task; you should see a check next to the resource in the left-most column of the
dialog box. Click Remove, as shown in Figure 5-14.

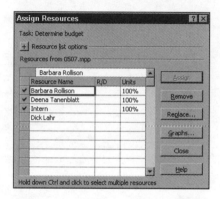

Figure 5-14: Remove resources from tasks by
selecting them in the Assign Resources dialog
box and clicking Remove.

You can be sure that at some point in your project you will want to move resource
assignments around. Here's the easy way to switch from one resource to another on
a particular task:

1. Select the task for which you want to switch resources.

2. Open the Assign Resources dialog box.

3. Highlight the resource you want to remove from the task; a check mark
   appears next to the assigned resource.

4. Select Replace. Project displays the Replace Resource dialog box, which
   enables you to easily select replacement resources, as shown in Figure 5-15.

5. Highlight each resource you want to assign and supply units.

6. Click OK.

Figure 5-15: The Replace Resource dialog box looks very similar to the Assign Resources dialog box.

Handling Unusual Cost Situations

Resources go hand in hand with tasks if you're trying to figure out how long it will take to complete a project. If you assign costs to your resources, those costs also affect the cost of your project. Assigning a cost to a resource, however, is not the only way to assign a cost to a project. For example, projects can have fixed costs associated with them. This section starts with a quick look at overall project costs and then focuses on handling unusual cost situations.

Looking at the project's cost

You've seen how to assign costs to resources. You've also seen how to assign resources to tasks — and, by the transitive property of equality (remember that one from high school algebra?), assigning a resource to which you have assigned a cost will cause your project to have a cost. Are you wondering what that cost is? From either the Gantt Chart view or the Resource Sheet view, choose Project ➪ Project Information to open the Project Information dialog box. Select Statistics to open the Project Statistics dialog box, as shown in Figure 5-16.

Figure 5-16: Check the cost of your project in the Project Statistics dialog box.

Cross-Reference Part IV covers tracking, recording actual work done, and analyzing and reporting on progress. Chapter 14 explains additional ways to view project costs. The following sections consider ways to assign unusual costs to a project.

Assigning fixed costs

This chapter has, to this point, focused on resources, and you have learned how to assign costs to a resource. But the costs of some tasks need to be calculated differently. In Project, you can assign a fixed cost to a task or you can assign a fixed resource cost to a task.

Assigning a fixed cost to a task

Some tasks are fixed-cost tasks; that is, you know that the cost of a particular task stays the same regardless of the duration of the task or the work performed by any resources on the task. For example, your catering service, as part of each job, washes linens. You own the washing machine, and you've done the calculation on the amount of water plus electricity (plus wear and tear) used each time you run the machine for a wash cycle. Or, you're renting a site for a meeting for a flat fee. In cases like these, you assign the cost directly to the task. If you assign a cost to a task, Project adds the fixed cost of the task to the cost of any resource work that you assign to the task when calculating costs for the project.

Note Remember that assigning a fixed cost to a task does not necessarily make the total cost of the task equal to the fixed cost that you assigned. You can, for example, assign more than one fixed cost as well as variable costs to a task.

To assign a fixed cost to a task, use the Gantt Chart view and apply the Cost table. Follow these steps:

1. Use the View bar to switch to the Gantt Chart view.

2. Choose View ⇨ Table:Entry ⇨ Cost to switch to the Cost table view of the Gantt Chart, as shown in Figure 5-17.

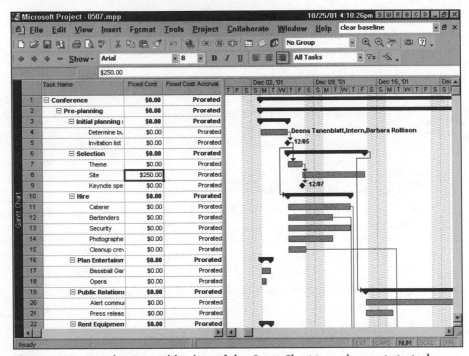

Figure 5-17: Use the Cost table view of the Gantt Chart to assign costs to tasks.

3. Select the task to which you want to assign a fixed cost.

4. Type the cost for that task in the Fixed Cost column and press Enter.

You can control the way Project accrues the fixed cost for a task from the Fixed Cost Accrual column. Your choices are Start, Prorated, and End. These choices have the same meaning as the accrual choices for resources discussed earlier in this chapter.

Tip   To control the way Project accrues all fixed costs, use the Calculation tab of the Options dialog box (choose Tools ⇨ Options).

Assigning a fixed resource cost to a task

Suppose that you hire a consultant to perform a task for a fixed amount of money; you can assign the consultant to the task as a fixed-cost resource.

1. Use the View bar to switch to the Gantt Chart view.

2. Choose View ➪ Table:Cost ➪ Entry to switch to the Entry table view of the Gantt Chart.

3. Select a task from the Task Name column.

4. Assign the resource to the task by using the steps explained earlier in this chapter. Don't worry about the number of units that you assign.

5. Choose Window ➪ Split.

6. Select the resource from the Resource Name column in the bottom pane.

7. Choose Format ➪ Details ➪ Resource Cost. A different pane appears at the bottom of the Gantt Chart.

8. Type **0** (zero) in the Units column for the resource and press Enter.

9. Type the fixed-resource cost in the Cost field. Figure 5-18 shows a fixed-resource cost for Dick Lahr.

10. Click OK.

Figure 5-18: Adding a fixed resource cost

Project adds a fixed-resource cost to other resource costs when calculating the total cost of a task, but the cost does not depend on the time that a resource spends working on the task.

> **Tip** Choose Window ⇨ Remove Split to close the bottom pane in the Gantt Chart view or drag the Split Bar.

Accounting for resource rate changes

In some situations, you must charge different rates on different tasks for the same resource. Or possibly, you expect a resource's rate to change during the life of your project. Project uses cost rate tables to accurately reflect resource costs as they change. On cost rate tables, you can identify up to 125 rates for a single resource, and you can identify the effective date of each rate. Cost rate tables help you to account for pay increases or decreases to resources during the life of your project and enable you to charge the same resource at different rates, depending on the task.

To assign multiple rates to a resource, use the Costs tab of the Resource Information dialog box. On the Resource Sheet view, double-click the resource for which you want to assign multiple rates. Click the Costs tab in the Resource Information dialog box, as shown in Figure 5-19.

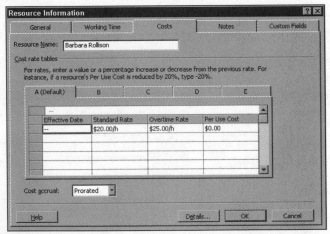

Figure 5-19: Use cost rate tables to assign different rates to a resource.

The Costs tab displays five cost rate tables (tabs A through E) that you can use to assign different rates to a resource for use on different dates throughout a project's life. On each cost rate table, you can enter up to 25 rates for the selected resource and indicate an effective date for each rate. Project uses the effective dates that you supply to apply the correct rate to a resource at different times during the project.

Tip　If you are specifying a new rate as an increase or decrease of an existing rate, you can specify the new rate in a percentage (such as +10% or -10%); Project calculates the value of the rate for you. You must enter the percent sign.

If you charge different amounts for resources depending on the type of work that they perform, you may want to use each cost rate table tab to represent sets of rates for different kinds of work.

To assign the correct resource cost rate table to a task, follow these steps:

1. Assign the resource to the task by using the Assign Resources dialog box, as you learned earlier in this chapter.

2. Choose View ➪ Task Usage or use the View bar to switch to the Task Usage view, as shown in Figure 5-20.

Figure 5-20: Task Usage view shows you the amount of time a resource is assigned to a particular task.

3. In the Task Name column, select the resource for which you want to select a cost table.

4. Click the Assignment Information button on the Standard toolbar to display the Assignment Information dialog box. Click the General tab, shown in Figure 5-21, to select a cost rate table.

5. Select the correct cost rate table from the Cost rate table drop-down list.

6. Click OK.

Figure 5-21: Use the General tab of the Assignment Information dialog box to select a cost rate table.

 Chapter 12 covers project costs in greater detail.

Summary

This chapter detailed more about using resources in Project, including how to create and assign resources. You've learned how to:

✦ Create a resource list

✦ Modify resource information, including using calendars for resources

✦ Assign resources to tasks and remove resource assignments

✦ Handle fixed costs, both for individual tasks and for resources

✦ Assign either a fixed or variable cost to a material resource

✦ Set up different rates for resources to account for pay increases or decreases or for charging resources at different rates on different tasks

In Chapter 6, you will learn the basics of using the standard views in Project.

✦   ✦   ✦

Refining Your Project

P A R T

III

In this part, you'll do a lot of work with views, which are the foundation for approaching your project from varying perspectives in order to analyze situations and isolate and solve problems. You'll learn about views in detail, and how to customize the appearance of your project. You'll also read about methods that you can use to resolve scheduling and resource problems.

Understanding the Basics of Views

A project is like a small business. As in any business, different people attend to various aspects of the work. The accounting department thinks mainly of the costs of doing business. The plant supervisor focuses on deadlines and having enough machinery to get the job done. Your human resources department thinks of people: their salaries, hours, benefits, and so on.

As the owner of your project, you are likely to wear all of these hats (and more) during the project. Changing views in Project is the practical way of changing hats. You switch to another view to see your work from a different perspective. Each view helps you to focus on a different aspect of your project.

Views in Project enable you to enter, organize, and examine information in various ways. Project provides a variety of views, and this chapter provides you with a basic understanding of the default views; the next chapter covers techniques that you can use to customize views and make them work for you.

What Is a View?

A *view* is a way to examine your project. Different views enable you to focus on different aspects of the project. Project uses three types of views, and typically uses them in combination:

   ✦ **Chart or graph views.** Present information by using pictures. You've already seen the Gantt Chart view, which is a chart view.

✦ **Sheet views.** Present information in rows and columns, similar to the way a spreadsheet program presents information. The Task Sheet view and the Resource Sheet view are both sheet views, and each row on the sheet contains all the information about an individual task or resource in your project. Each column represents a field that identifies the information that you're storing about the task or resource.

✦ **Forms.** Present information in a way that resembles a paper form. You saw the Task Form view in Chapter 4; a form displays information about a single item (or task) in your project.

Tip

Shortcut menus are available in many views. Right-click the view to see a shortcut menu.

You can modify the default views by switching what appears onscreen. You can also create custom views. The following two sections describe some common ways of manipulating views:

✦ Switching the table of any view that includes a table

✦ Adding or changing the details that appear in any view that contains a Details section

Cross-Reference

You also can create a combination view in which you actually see one format in one pane of the window and another format in another pane. Read more about creating custom views and combination views in Chapter 7.

Changing a table

If a view contains a table, you can use the Select All button to quickly switch to another table. The Select All button appears in the upper left of the table portion of the view. Right-click the Select All button to open the menu that appears in Figure 6-1.

Note

Project displays different choices on this menu, and the choices that you see depend on the view displayed when you opened the menu.

Choose More Tables to open the More Tables dialog box, which displays all the tables available in Project, as shown in Figure 6-2.

Note

The PERT tables won't appear in the More Tables dialog box until you've displayed PERT views. Read more about PERT views later in this chapter.

Changing a details section

You also can change the information that appears in the Details section of any view that displays a Details section (such as the Task Usage view). Choose any item from the list that appears when you choose Format ➪ Details, as shown in Figure 6-3.

Select All button

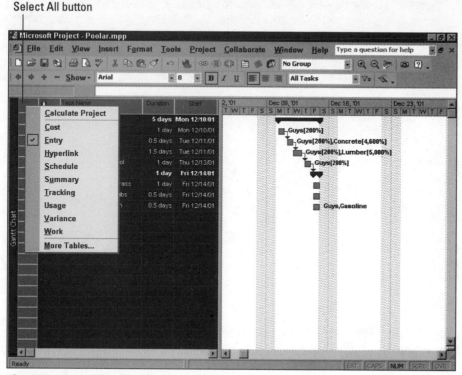

Figure 6-1: Switch tables by choosing from the menu that appears when you right-click the Select All button.

Figure 6-2: The More Tables dialog box shows the tables to which you can switch in the Task Usage view.

Note

Project adds rows to the Details section when you make selections from this menu. To remove a row, choose Format ➪ Details and select the item that you want to remove.

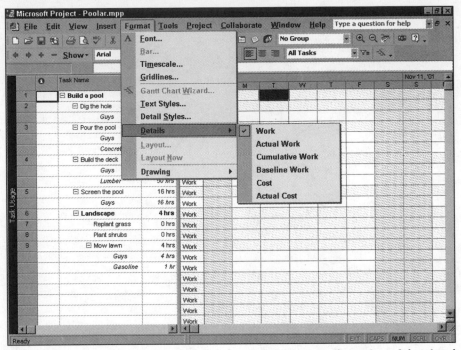

Figure 6-3: Change the information that appears in the Details section of the view by selecting from this list.

You can also use the Detail Styles dialog box (choose Format ➪ Detail Styles) in Figure 6-4 to add other information to the Details section.

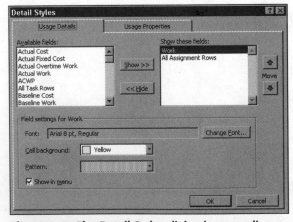

Figure 6-4: The Detail Styles dialog box supplies additional choices that you can display in the Details section of a view.

Examining Indicators

Indicators are icons that appear in the Indicator column on table views; the Indicator column appears to the right of the ID column. Indicators represent additional information about the row in which they appear. For example, your own notes appear in this field if you assign a note to a resource.

For more information about assigning notes to resources, refer to Chapter 5.

Different icons represent different types of indicators, as follows:

✦ **Constraint indicators.** These indicators identify the type of constraint assigned to a task. For example, a task can have a flexible constraint, such as Finish No Later Than, for tasks scheduled from the finish date. Or a task can have an inflexible constraint, such as Must Start On, for tasks scheduled from the start date. Constraint indicators also show that the task hasn't been completed within the time frame of the constraint.

✦ **Task type indicators.** Task type indicators may identify special conditions about a task, such as whether the task is a recurring task or whether the task has been completed. Task type indicators also identify the status of projects inserted in a task.

You can learn more about inserted projects in Chapter 20.

✦ **Workgroup indicators.** Workgroup indicators provide some information about the task and its resources. For example, a workgroup indicator can tell you that a task has been assigned but that the resource hasn't yet confirmed the assignment.

✦ **Contour indicators.** Contour indicators identify the type of contouring used to distribute the work assigned to the task.

You learn more about contouring in Chapter 10.

✦ **Miscellaneous indicators.** Miscellaneous indicators identify items, such as a note or a hyperlink, that you created, a calendar that's been assigned to a task, or a resource that needs leveling.

To identify the purpose of an indicator, point at it. Project tells you what the indicator means or displays additional information to remind you of important details.

Admiring the Views

The following is a list of the default views available in Project:

- ✦ Bar Rollup
- ✦ Calendar
- ✦ Descriptive Network Diagram
- ✦ Detail Gantt
- ✦ Expected Gantt (PERT)
- ✦ Gantt Chart
- ✦ Leveling Gantt
- ✦ Milestone Date Rollup
- ✦ Milestone Rollup
- ✦ Network Diagram
- ✦ Optimistic Gantt (PERT)
- ✦ PERT Entry Sheet
- ✦ Pessimistic Gantt (PERT)
- ✦ Relationship Diagram
- ✦ Resource Allocation
- ✦ Resource Form
- ✦ Resource Graph
- ✦ Resource Name Form
- ✦ Resource Sheet
- ✦ Resource Usage
- ✦ Task Details Form
- ✦ Task Entry
- ✦ Task Form
- ✦ Task Name Form
- ✦ Task Sheet
- ✦ Task Usage
- ✦ Tracking Gantt

Note   When you initially open the Views window, you'll see only 23 views listed. The four PERT views won't appear in the window until you use them. After you use them, they will also appear in the window.

Deciding which of Project's 27 built-in views (or any of your custom views) suits a particular purpose can be a little tricky. As you become more familiar with the features of Project and the way that you apply project management concepts and terms to Project, you'll get more comfortable selecting views by name. The View menu and bar list the eight most frequently used views. You'll find the other views in the More Views window; simply choose View ➪ More Views to see them.

Cross-Reference Project managers can view related information from Project Server in Project without switching between two windows. See Chapter 19 for more information.

The following sections describe how these views enable you to look at different aspects of your project. Notice the wealth of detail about your project that is available to you.

Tip To display any of these views, choose them from the View bar or right-click the View bar and choose More Views to select them from the More Views dialog box.

Calendar

The top selection on the View bar is the Calendar view, shown in Figure 6-5. The familiar format of the Calendar view makes it easy to use; a black box surrounds "today." Using a monthly calendar format, the Calendar view indicates the length of a task with a bar running across portions of days, or even weeks. On the Calendar view, nonworking days appear shaded. Although a task bar may extend over nonworking days, such as Saturday and Sunday in this example, the work of the task doesn't actually progress over those days. Don't forget that every project has a calendar (not to be confused with the Calendar view) that tells Project how to handle events, such as 24-hour shifts, weekends, and holidays off, over the life of your project.

The Calendar view is useful for entering a simple project and for reviewing what needs to be done on a given day. You can move from month to month by using the large arrow buttons in the right corner of the view, next to the current month name. Depending on your screen resolution, you can see slightly more than a month at a time onscreen by using the Zoom Out tool on the Standard toolbar while in Calendar view. Zoom Out shrinks the calendar to accommodate about a month and a half of your schedule.

Tip To modify the appearance of the Calendar view (for example, to shade working days and leave nonworking days clear), double-click anywhere on the calendar to open the Timescale dialog box and change the corresponding settings.

Detail Gantt

The Detail Gantt view shows a list of tasks and related information, as well as a chart that displays slack time and *slippage* as thin bars between tasks, as shown in Figure 6-6. Choose this view from the More Views dialog box (choose View ➪ More Views).

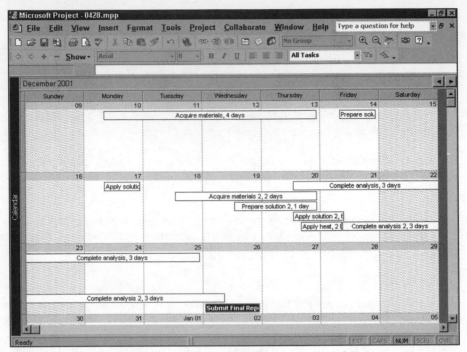

Figure 6-5: The Calendar view features a familiar, easy-to-read format.

The thin bar extending from the right edge of the second task shows slack time between the second and third tasks, and the thin bar that appears at the left edge of the second task represents slippage between the first task and the second task. The number of days appears in both cases. You can think of slack time as flexibility in the schedule. Slippage results when you save a baseline on a project initially, or when you record actual dates or durations for tasks, and the resulting actual finish dates or durations for the task are later than the baseline finish dates or durations.

This view is most useful for evaluating slack and slippage. The default table in the Detail Gantt view is the Delay table; use the techniques described earlier in this chapter to change the table.

You may want to incorporate the Task Details Form view in the bottom pane of the Detail Gantt view so that you can look more closely at the tasks associated with slippage or slack. Choose Window ➪ Split, or use the Split Bar to display the Task Details Form view in the bottom pane.

Note   You can create a combination view with the Detail Gantt view in the top pane and the Task Details Form view in the bottom pane that you can save and use later. See Chapter 7 for more details.

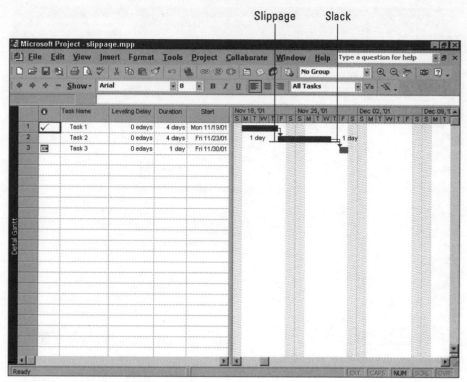

Figure 6-6: The Detail Gantt view

Gantt Chart

Chapter 2 covers the Gantt Chart view, shown in Figure 6-7, in detail. This view makes it easy for you to create a project, link tasks to create sequential dependencies, see how your project is progressing over time, and view tasks graphically while still having access to details.

Leveling Gantt

The Leveling Gantt view, shown in Figure 6-8, focuses on task delays. This view provides a graphic representation of delayed tasks while still providing task detail information. The chart portion of the view shows the effects before and after leveling. The default table that appears in the Leveling Gantt view is the Delay table, but you can change the table by using the techniques described earlier in this chapter. You can use the Delay table to add or remove delay time and see the effects of your changes.

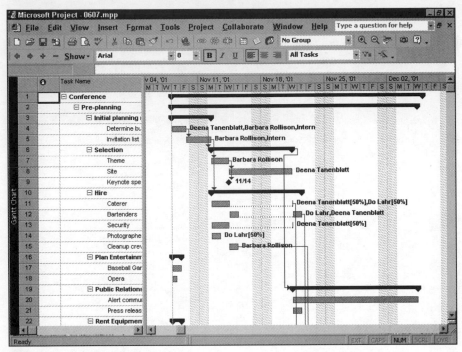

Figure 6-7: The Gantt Chart view

> **Note** *Leveling* is the process of resolving resource conflicts or overallocations by delaying or splitting certain tasks. You learn more about resource leveling in Chapter 10.

On this chart, you see the Theme task showing a leveling delay. The bar to the left of this task represents delay time, and the table indicates the number of days that the leveled task is delayed.

Tracking Gantt

The Tracking Gantt view is also based on the Gantt Chart view. The Tracking Gantt view provides a great visual way to evaluate the progress of individual tasks and the project as a whole. By using the Tracking Gantt view, you can see how your project has shifted from your original estimates and then decide how to adjust your plans to accommodate any delays. Theoretically, if a project ever goes faster than you've anticipated, you also can see the amount of extra time that you've bought yourself as a result of your efficiency. (However, projects so seldom go faster than projected that I won't show that option here!)

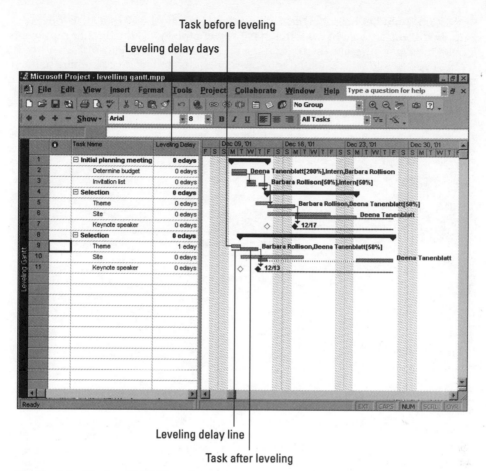

Figure 6-8: The Leveling Gantt view

Figure 6-9 shows a standard Gantt view of a project that has had some activity. The standard Gantt view shows the progress on tasks as a black bar within the baseline task bar. Tasks that depend on the completed tasks have been moved out to reflect any delays in actual work completed.

Figure 6-10, on the other hand, shows the same schedule displayed in the Tracking Gantt view using the Tracking table (the default table is the Entry table). The Tracking table enables you to update your project by supplying actual information. On the chart portion of the view, you see two bars for every task. The bottom bar shows baseline settings. The top bar reflects current scheduled start and finish dates if a task has not yet been started. If a task has been started — that is, if you have supplied some amount of work that has been completed — the top bar represents actual information, while the bottom bar represents baseline information. Project fills in the top bar and makes it solid to represent completed work; a hatching pattern appears in the top bar to represent unstarted work or work in progress. The bottom bars represent baseline task bars, which stay put; only actual work bars push out to reflect delays in timing.

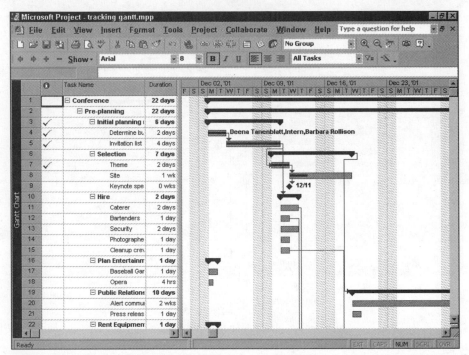

Figure 6-9: The standard Gantt view shows you the reality of your project timing at the moment, based on actual work done.

On the Tracking Gantt, you can see that the Determine Budget Invitation list and Theme tasks have been completed, and the Site task is 40 percent complete. No other tasks have been started, so the top bars on all other tasks represent scheduled start and finish dates, based on progress made so far in the project.

Figure 6-10: The Tracking Gantt view shows the discrepancy between your estimates and the real-world activity in your project.

Network Diagram

The Network Diagram became the name for the PERT Chart view you found in Project 98.

On the CD-ROM   Project doesn't really produce a PERT chart, but you can use an add-on product — PERT chart Expert. Try out a sample using the demo on the CD-ROM of this book.

The Network Diagram view shown in Figure 6-11 has less to do with timing than it has to do with the general flow of work and the relationships between tasks in your project. This view makes it easy for you to evaluate the flow of your project and check task dependencies.

Figure 6-11: The Network Diagram view

Each node on the Network Diagram view represents a task in your project. I used Project's Zoom command (View ➪ Zoom) to enlarge the node shown previously in Figure 6-12, so that you can see the details. A node contains the task name, duration, task ID number in the sequence of the project outline, start date, finish date, and, if assigned, the resource(s). The shape and color of each node represents different types of tasks — that is, critical tasks are red and have pointed sides, while noncritical tasks are blue and have more square sides. You can determine (and change) the meaning of node shapes in the Box Styles dialog box (choose Format ➪ Box Styles). The lines that flow between the nodes represent dependencies. A task that must come after another task is completed, called a *successor task*, appears to the right or sometimes below its predecessor.

You couldn't filter Project 98's PERT chart view; however, that feature was added in Project 2000. While viewing the Network Diagram, choose Project ➪ Filtered for: and select the filter that you want to use.

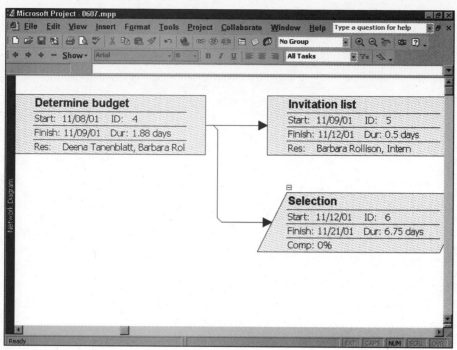

Figure 6-12: You can see task details when you examine the nodes of the Network Diagram.

You'll read more about filtering in Chapter 7.

Project 2002 enables you to group tasks in the Network Diagram view.

Starting in Project 2002, you can group tasks in the Network Diagram view, very similar to the way you can group in the Gantt view. Colored bands separate the nodes. For example, in Figure 6-13, you see tasks grouped by duration. Open the Project menu and point to Group to see the groups available by default — you also can create your own groups.

Figure 6-13: You can group tasks in a variety of ways on the Network Diagram.

You can now display indicators and custom fields in Network Diagram nodes. You add the node information to an existing node template or you create a new template. Follow these steps:

1. In the Network Diagram view, choose Format ⇨ Box Styles.

2. Click the More Templates button, as shown in Figure 6-14.

3. In the Data Templates box, edit one of the existing templates or create a new template from scratch.

4. In the Data Template Definition dialog box, click in the cell where you want either indicators or a custom field to appear; Project adds a list box indicator to the cell, thus enabling you to open the list and select the information that you want to appear in that cell of the node. In Figure 6-15, I'm adding the Indicators field to the nodes.

Figure 6-14: In the Box Styles dialog box, select the template that you want for the nodes in the diagram.

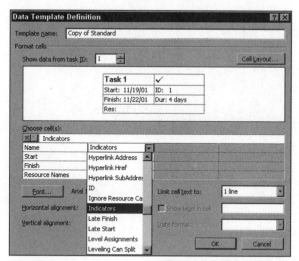

Figure 6-15: Add information to a cell of the Network Diagram node.

Note You can't edit the Standard template, but you can copy it, as I did in Figure 6-15.

5. Click OK to redisplay the Data Template dialog box.

6. Click Close to redisplay the Box Styles dialog box.

7. From the Data template list, select the template that you edited or created.

8. Click OK. You'll see the new field on appropriate nodes, as shown in Figure 6-16.

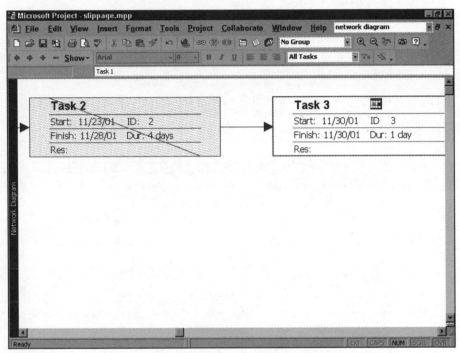

Figure 6-16: A Network Diagram that displays indicators in the nodes

Descriptive Network Diagram

The Descriptive Network Diagram, shown in Figure 16-17, is a cousin of the Network Diagram — and so focuses on the general flow of work and the relationships between tasks in your project.

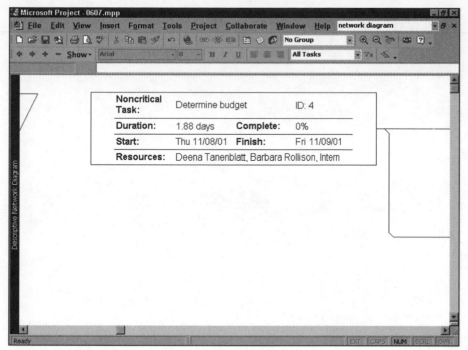

Figure 6-17: The Descriptive Network Diagram view

Like Network Diagram, each node on the Descriptive Network Diagram view represents a task in your project. If you compare Figures 6-12 and 6-17, you'll see more detail in the nodes of the Descriptive Network Diagram than you see in the Network Diagram; the Descriptive Network Diagram also indicates whether the task is critical and how complete the task is.

You can filter the Descriptive Network Diagram; simply choose Project ➪ Filtered for: and select the filter that you want to use.

Relationship Diagram

This special version of the Network Diagram view, shown in Figure 6-18, displays the current task in the center of the pane, with the task's predecessors to the left and successors to the right. When you are working on a large project, this graphic view helps you to focus on one task and the tasks linked to it.

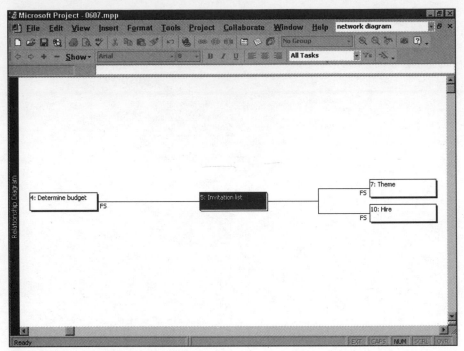

Figure 6-18: The Relationship Diagram

PERT analysis views

PERT analysis is sometimes called *what-if analysis*, and many project managers use this approach to estimate a probable outcome. The probable outcome that you estimate may be the duration of a task, its start date, or its end date. As a function of the estimating process, you specify the optimistic, pessimistic, and expected durations of tasks in your project. Then Microsoft Project calculates a weighted average of the three durations.

Note PERT stands for *Program Evaluation and Review Technique*. The Special Projects Office of the U.S. Navy devised this method of tracking the flow of tasks in the late 1950s.

As you may have guessed, PERT analysis has little to do with the PERT chart view that was available in Project 98 and earlier versions. But you can use four PERT analysis views in Project to help you make your estimates:

✦ PERT Entry Sheet

✦ Optimistic Gantt

✦ Expected Gantt

✦ Pessimistic Gantt

You can use the PERT Analysis toolbar, shown in Figure 6-19, to perform PERT analysis. Choose View ➪ Toolbars ➪ PERT Analysis to display the toolbar.

Optimistic Gantt

Pessimistic Gantt

PERT Entry Form

PERT Entry Sheet

Set PERT Weights

Calculate PERT

Expected Gantt

Figure 6-19: Use this toolbar to help you with PERT analysis tasks.

Tip

You'll need to use the PERT Analysis toolbar to display the four PERT views the first time; after you've displayed the views, you'll see them available in the More Views window.

PERT Entry Sheet

The PERT Entry Sheet view shown in Figure 6-20 focuses PERT analysis entirely on durations. Click the PERT Entry Sheet button on the PERT Analysis toolbar to display this sheet.

Using this sheet, you enter optimistic, expected, and pessimistic durations for each task. When you click the Calculate PERT button on the PERT Analysis toolbar, Project uses a weighted average of the numbers that you supply and calculates the probable duration of the task. Project displays the result in the Duration column for that task. Notice the duration of 3.75 days for the Invitation task; Project calculated this duration by using the weighted average of the numbers in the Optimistic Dur., Expected Dur., and Pessimistic Dur. columns for the task.

Figure 6-20: Use this view to focus on entering estimated durations for PERT analysis.

Optimistic Gantt

After you have entered optimistic, expected, and pessimistic durations in the PERT Entry Sheet view and calculated, you can view the optimistic results for your entire project in the Optimistic Gantt view. Click the Optimistic Gantt button on the PERT Analysis toolbar to display the Optimistic Gantt view. As its name implies, the Optimistic Gantt view, shown in Figure 6-21, is a variation of the Gantt Chart view; the Optimistic Case table is on the left side and Gantt bars are on the right. You can use this view to enter and evaluate the optimistic scenarios for task durations, start dates, and end dates.

Note   Initially, you may not see bars in any of the PERT Gantt views. While displaying any of these views, click the Calculate PERT button on the PERT Analysis toolbar again, and Project displays the bars.

If you prefer to work with start dates and end dates or to focus entirely on optimistic durations while estimating, you can use this view to enter and evaluate the optimistic scenarios for task durations, start dates, and end dates. If you use this approach, you also will need to supply the same type of information in the Expected Gantt view and the Pessimistic Gantt view before you click the Calculate button.

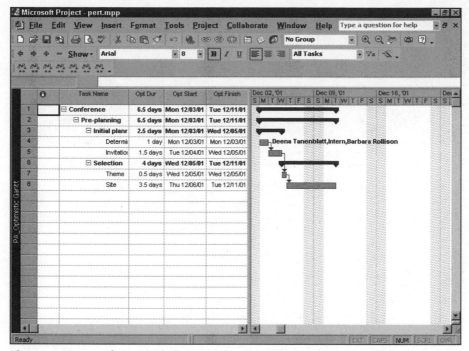

Figure 6-21: Use the Optimistic Gantt view to analyze optimistic task durations.

Expected Gantt

After you have entered optimistic, expected, and pessimistic durations on the PERT Entry Sheet and calculated, you can view the expected results for your entire project on the Expected Gantt view. Click the Expected Gantt button on the PERT Analysis toolbar to display the Expected Gantt view, as shown in Figure 6-22. Like its cousins — the Optimistic and Pessimistic Gantt views — the Expected Gantt view is a variation of the Gantt Chart view. Project displays the Expected Gantt table on the left side and Gantt bars on the right side.

If you prefer to estimate with start dates and end dates or to focus entirely on expected durations, you can use this view to enter and evaluate the expected scenarios for task durations, start dates, and end dates. If you use this approach, you also need to supply the same types of information on the Optimistic Gantt view and the Pessimistic Gantt view before you click the Calculate button.

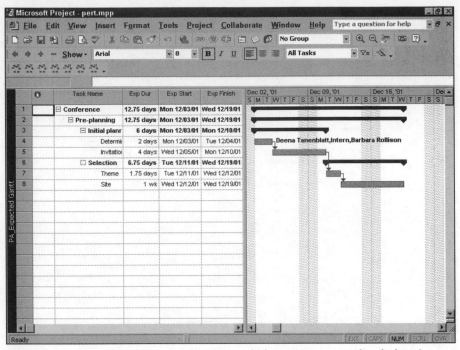

Figure 6-22: Use the Expected Gantt view to help create expected task durations.

Pessimistic Gantt

After you enter optimistic, expected, and pessimistic durations on the PERT Entry Sheet view and perform the calculations, you can view the pessimistic results for your entire project in the Pessimistic Gantt view. Click the Pessimistic Gantt button on the PERT Analysis toolbar to display the Pessimistic Gantt view, as shown in Figure 6-23. Like its cousins — the Expected Gantt and the Optimistic views — the Pessimistic Gantt view is also a variation of the Gantt Chart view. Project displays the Pessimistic Gantt table on the left and Gantt bars on the right. You can use this view to enter and evaluate the pessimistic scenarios for task durations, start dates, and end dates.

If you prefer to work with start dates and end dates or to focus entirely on pessimistic durations while estimating, you can use this view to enter and evaluate the pessimistic scenarios for task durations, start dates, and end dates. If you use this approach, you also need to supply start and end dates on the Expected Gantt view and the Optimistic Gantt view before you click the Calculate button.

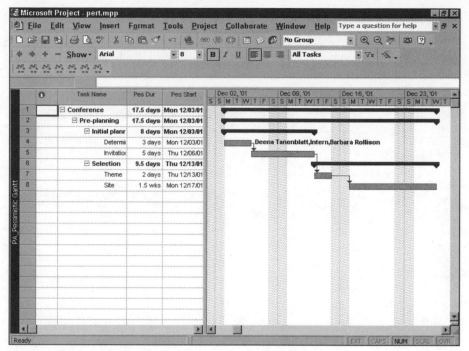

Figure 6-23: Use the Pessimistic Gantt view to help create pessimistic task durations.

PERT Weights

Project calculates a weighted average when you use PERT analysis. You can control the weights that Project applies to each scenario from the Set PERT Weights dialog box, as shown in Figure 6-24. Click the PERT Weights button on the PERT Analysis toolbar (second button from the right edge of the toolbar). Note that the values you enter must sum to 6 using the following formula:

```
(optimistic duration) + 4(expected duration) + (pessimistic duration) ≡ 6
```

You can use different weights to change the emphasis that Project applies to its calculation of each scenario.

Figure 6-24: Use the Set PERT Weights dialog box to adjust the weights that Project applies when making PERT calculations.

Resource Allocation

The Resource Allocation view is a combination view. For example, in Figure 6-25, the Resource Usage view appears in the top pane, and the Leveling Gantt Chart view appears in the bottom pane.

Figure 6-25: The Resource Allocation view displays resource allocation relative to the project timing.

Cross-
Reference
The Resource Usage view is covered later in this chapter, and the Leveling Gantt Chart view was covered earlier in this chapter.

The default table that appears on the Resource Usage view (the upper pane of the combination view) is the Usage table; the default table that appears on the Gantt Chart view (the lower pane of the combination view) is the Entry table. As you scroll the right side of the window, the top and bottom panes move together. You can use the techniques described earlier in this chapter to change either table.

Resource Form

The Resource Form view displays detailed information about one resource at a time, as shown in Figure 6-26.

Figure 6-26: The Resource Form view

Use the Next and Previous buttons in the upper-right corner of the window to display different resources; if you haven't sorted or filtered resources, Project shows them to you in ID number order.

Resource Graph

The Resource Graph view shows how a particular resource is being used on a project. You can use the Resource Graph view to spot and correct resources that are inappropriately allocated. Note that the Resource Graph view shows information for one resource at a time. To view a different resource, click the scroll arrows that appear below the left pane in this window. This view works well as part of a combination view.

The Resource Graph view highlights resource conflicts: people, equipment, or other resources that are being overworked or underutilized. Looking at the Resource Graph view as both a single and combination view can show you how assignments on individual tasks are affecting a resource's utilization on a project. Figure 6-27 shows the main Resource Graph view; Figure 6-28 shows the combination view with details at the bottom of the Project window of the tasks being performed. You can create this view by choosing Window ➪ Split.

Figure 6-27: The percentage of a person's available work time is tracked and displayed as overallocated and underallocated.

Project displays a resource's total work hours on any particular day as a bar. A bar that falls short of the 100 percent mark indicates that a resource isn't working full-time and may be underutilized. A bar that extends beyond 100 percent indicates that somebody is working too many hours in a day. The percentage of the workday that the resource is working appears at the bottom of the usage bars.

Note

Underutilization may indicate that a resource is busy with other projects the rest of that day, and overutilization may signal occasional and acceptable overtime. See Chapter 8 for more information about interpreting these bars. See Chapter 10 for more about resolving conflicts in resource time.

Figure 6-28: Displaying task information beneath a Resource Graph can help you to see which work assignments are keeping the resource busy.

Resource Name Form

The Resource Name Form view is a simplified version of the Resource Form view (compare Figure 6-29 with Figure 6-26). None of the cost information appears in this view, nor do you see the resources' maximum units, base calendar, group, or code.

You can use this view to set up basic information about resources for a project — this can give you a good idea about a resource's workload. Use the Previous and Next buttons to view different resources.

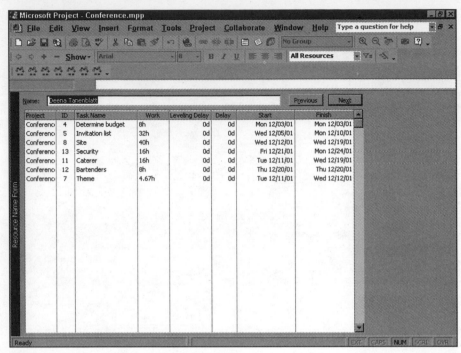

Figure 6-29: The Resource Name Form view

Resource Sheet

The Resource Sheet view shown in Figure 6-30 gives you a wealth of information about the resources assigned to your project, including standard and overtime rates, availability for overtime work, and fixed costs.

By assigning group designations to resources, such as Marketing, Facilities, or Temporary Help, you can use filters to study resource information for just one or two groups at a time.

This columnar interface is a great way to prepare to assign resources if, for example, you want to assign lower-cost people to most tasks and higher-cost people to certain mission-critical tasks. This view clearly shows to which group a resource belongs. If overallocations exist, you'll see a warning flag in the Indicator column on the far left of this view. Switch back to the Resource Graph to get details on these problems resource by resource.

The default table that appears on the Resource Sheet view is the Entry table, but you can change this table by using the techniques described earlier in this chapter.

Figure 6-30: You can view both standard and overtime rates in the Resource Sheet.

Resource Usage

The Resource Usage view shown in Figure 6-31 displays each resource and the tasks assigned to it. You can use the Resource Usage view to enter and edit resource information, and you can assign or reassign tasks to resources on this view by dragging the tasks between resources.

The Resource Usage view is also useful when you want to

✦ Check resource overallocations

✦ Examine the number of hours or the percentage of capacity at which each resource is scheduled to work

✦ View a resource's progress or costs

✦ Determine how much time a particular resource has for additional work assignments

The default table on the left side of this view is the Usage table. You can use the Table Selection button described earlier to switch to a different table. Similarly, you can use either the Format ⇨ Details or the Format ⇨ Detail Styles commands to add to or change the information that appears in the Details section. (Work is the default selection.)

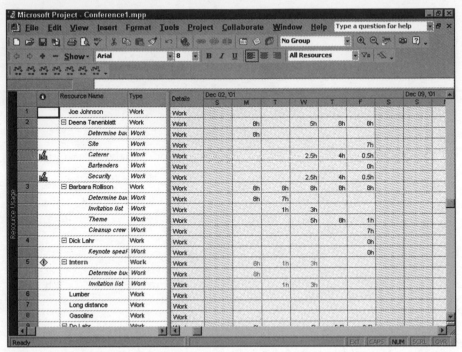

Figure 6-31: The Resource view organizes task assignments by resource so that you can easily figure out who's doing what and when in the Resource Usage view.

Rollup views

In Project 98, you could display symbols on a summary task bar that represented subtask dates: Effectively, you "rolled up" the subtasks onto a summary task bar when you collapsed the outline of the Gantt view. However, rollup wasn't an easy process in Project 98 because you needed to mark each individual task that you wanted to roll up.

Starting in Project 2000, you can allow for rollup behavior at a project level and avoid editing all the tasks. While viewing the Gantt Chart view of your project, choose Format ⇨ Layout. Project displays the Layout dialog box shown in Figure 6-32.

Place a check in the "Always roll up Gantt bars" checkbox; if you don't want see the rollup bars when you expand the project outline to view all tasks, also place a check in the "Hide rollup bars when summary expanded" checkbox.

Figure 6-32: Use this dialog box to enable rollup behavior for all tasks in your project.

Using the summary task bar

When you enable rollup behavior and collapse the outline, Project displays a summary task bar that contains symbols that represent subtask dates. Compare Figures 6-33, 6-34, and 6-35, which show various effects of collapsing the outline and rollup behavior. In particular, compare Figures 6-34 and 6-35.

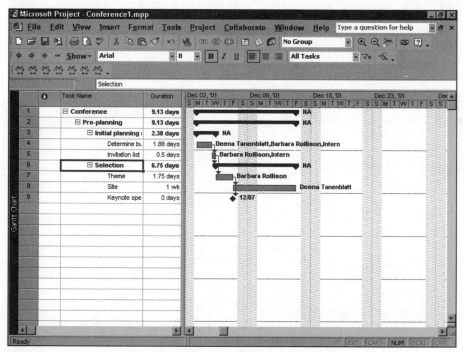

Figure 6-33: In this figure, the outline is completely expanded.

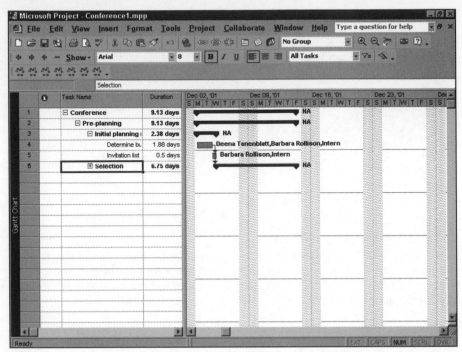

Figure 6-34: In this figure, I collapsed the outline for the Selection task, but I didn't enable rollup behavior.

Note   You can still specify rollup behavior at the task level so that Project doesn't roll up all tasks to summary bars when you collapse the outline. Remember that the changes you make in the Layout dialog box don't affect tasks whose rollup behavior you specified at the task level.

Using the Rollup_Formatting macro

Project contains a special macro called the Rollup_Formatting macro. When you run this macro, Project displays, on the Gantt Chart view, a summary bar that contains symbols that represent tasks; you can think of these tasks as rolled up onto the summary bar. This type of view helps you to create a summarized version of your project and makes important dates visible. Three new views help you to see your focus on your project's summary tasks:

✦ Bar Rollup

✦ Milestone Date Rollup

✦ Milestone Rollup

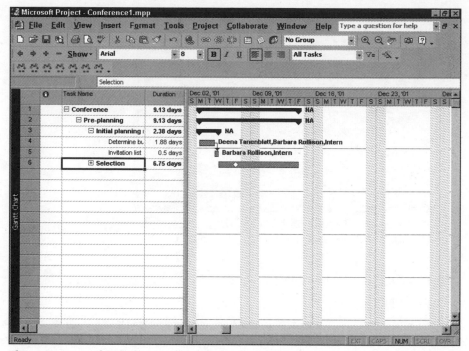

Figure 6-35: In this figure, I collapsed the outline for the Selection task and enabled rollup behavior.

Note A rollup view displays only the tasks that you format as rollup tasks in the Task Information dialog box. Remember, if you format rollup behavior for tasks in the Task Information dialog box, changing rollup behavior in the Layout dialog box (as discussed in the previous section) won't affect the appearance of your Gantt Chart.

This macro won't work unless you first mark tasks on the project as tasks that you want to roll up. Follow these steps to mark tasks and run the Rollup Formatting macro:

1. Select tasks in the Gantt Chart view.

Tip You can use Windows selection techniques to select several tasks simultaneously. Click the first task that you want to select. Then, to select contiguous tasks, press Shift and click the last task. Or to select noncontiguous tasks, press Ctrl and click each task.

2. Click the Task Information button on the Standard toolbar to open the General tab of the Multiple Task Information dialog box, as shown in Figure 6-36.

Figure 6-36: Use the General tab of the Multiple Task Information dialog box to mark tasks for rollup.

3. Place a check in the "Roll up Gantt bar to summary" checkbox.

4. Click OK.

5. Choose Tools ➪ Macros. Then choose Macros from the side menu to open the Macros dialog box, as shown in Figure 6-37.

Figure 6-37: Run macros from the Macro dialog box.

6. Select the Rollup Formatting macro and click Run. Project displays the Rollup Formatting dialog box, as shown in Figure 6-38.

Figure 6-38: Choose the style of formatting that you want for your rollup.

7. Select Bars to display rolled up tasks as bars, or select Milestones to display rolled up tasks as milestones, and click OK. Project displays the rolled up version of your project, as shown in Figure 6-39.

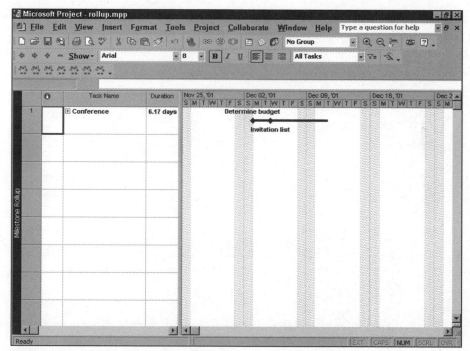

Figure 6-39: When you format rollup tasks as milestones, Project displays your project using the Milestone Rollup view.

Note

Using the Rollup Formatting macro can produce unpredictable results if your task start dates are close together. Task names may appear on top of one another — and be unreadable.

Switching rollup views

When you use the Rollup Formatting macro, Project displays only those tasks that you formatted for rollup. The table that you see in the sheet portion of all of these views is the Rollup table, but you can switch to another table by using the techniques explained earlier in the chapter. Figure 6-39 showed the Milestone Rollup view that Project displays if you selected Milestones in Step 7. If you select Bars in Step 7, Project displays the Bar Rollup view, as shown in Figure 6-40.

Figure 6-40: When you format rollup tasks as bars, Project displays your project using the Bar Rollup view.

 Tip

To redisplay all subtasks in a typical Gantt Chart view, click the Show button on the Formatting toolbar and choose All Subtasks.

Using the More Views dialog box (click the More Views button on the View bar), you can display the Milestone Date Rollup view, as shown in Figure 6-41.

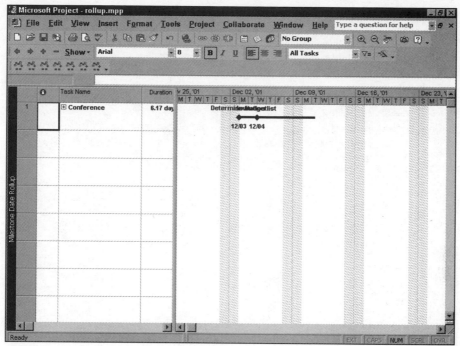

Figure 6-41: Use this view to see rollup tasks along with their start dates.

If your start dates are close together, Project overwrites the task names, thus making them difficult or impossible to read.

Task Details Form

The Task Details Form view closely resembles the Task Form view and the Task Name Form view. The Task Details Form view, shown in Figure 6-42, enables you to view and edit tracking information about one task at a time.

Use the Previous and Next buttons to switch from task to task. If you haven't sorted or filtered tasks, Project displays them in ID number order. The Task Details Form view is a good choice for part of a combination view.

Task Entry

The Task Entry view is a combination view. In Figure 6-43, the Gantt Chart view appears in the top pane, and the Task Form view appears in the bottom pane. To see information about a task in the Task Form view, select the task in the Gantt Chart view. You can see this view easily if you select the Gantt view and then choose Window ⇨ Split.

Figure 6-42: The Task Details Form view

Only the Gantt Chart view in the top pane uses a table. The default table is the Entry table, but you can use the techniques described earlier in this chapter to change the table.

Task Form

The Task Form view appears on the bottom portion of the Task Entry view, as shown previously in Figure 6-43. The Task Form view, shown in Figure 6-44, closely resembles the Task Details Form view, shown previously in Figure 6-42.

The Task Form view provides more resource information (such as costs) than the Task Details Form view, and the Task Details Form view provides more task information (such as predecessors) than the Task Form view. Use the Previous and Next buttons to switch tasks. The Task Form view also closely resembles the Task Name Form view.

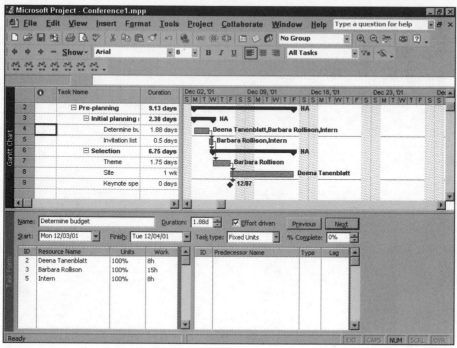

Figure 6-43: The Task Entry view

Task Name Form

The Task Name Form view is a cousin to the Task Details Form view and the Task Form view. This simplified version displays the basic characteristics of tasks, one task at a time, as shown in Figure 6-45.

Use the Previous and Next buttons to switch tasks. Again, if you compare Figures 6-42, 6-44, and 6-45, you can see how closely these views resemble each other. The Task Name Form view works well as part of a combination view.

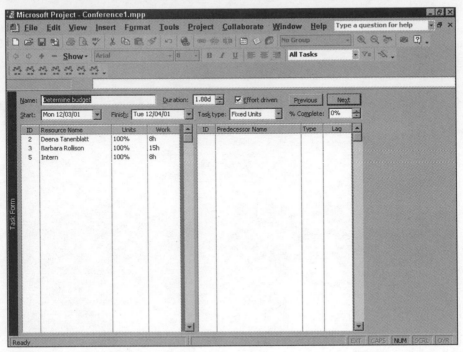

Figure 6-44: The Task Form view

Task Sheet

The Task Sheet view is the counterpart of the Resource Sheet view in that the Task Sheet view displays task information in a spreadsheet-like format. In this view, you can create tasks, link tasks (establishing dependencies), and even assign resources, as shown in Figure 6-46.

This view closely resembles the left portion of the Gantt Chart view and makes it easy to view tasks in chronological order. The default table that appears on the Task Sheet view is the Entry table, but you can use the techniques described earlier in this chapter to change the table.

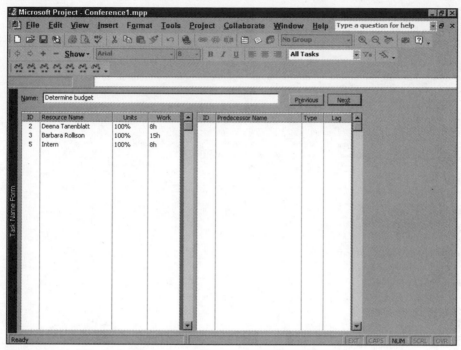

Figure 6-45: The Task Name Form view

Task Usage

This powerful view, shown in Figure 6-47, enables you to focus on how resources affect the task by showing resource assignments for each task. Use this view to organize resources by task, evaluate work effort and cost by task, and compare scheduled and actual work and costs.

Figure 6-46: The Task Sheet view helps you to see tasks in chronological order.

The default table for the left side of the view is the Usage table, but you can display other tables by using the Table Selection button, as described earlier in this chapter. Also, by default, Project shows Work in the Details section on the right; again, you can select any item from the Format Details menu or in the Details Styles dialog box. (Choose Format ➪ Detail Styles.)

Note How can you do 15.5 hours of work in one 8-hour day, as indicated in the sample project shown in Figure 6-47? Remember that this view shows total resource hours: As the figure shows, two people worked 7.5 and 8 hours, respectively.

Printing Your Project

When you print a project, you are printing a view. So, before you do anything, select the view that you want to print. If you're printing a sheet view, the number of columns that you see onscreen determines the number of columns that print. If the printed product requires more than one page, Project prints down and across; that is, the entire left side of your project prints before the right side prints.

Figure 6-47: The Task Usage view shows resources grouped under the tasks to which they are assigned.

Printing in Project is very similar to printing in any other Microsoft product. You can use the Print button on the Standard toolbar to print using default settings. And what are the default settings? They appear in two dialog boxes that you can view if you don't use the Print button.

Note You can also preview before printing, either by clicking the Preview button in the Print dialog box or by clicking the Print Preview button on the Standard toolbar.

Choose File ➪ Print to open the Print dialog box, as shown in Figure 6-48.

Note Starting in Project 2000, when you save the project file, Project retains the settings that you make in this dialog box for the timescale, including settings for "Print left column of pages only" and manual page breaks.

You can't open the Page Setup dialog box, shown in Figure 6-49, from the Print dialog box, but you can open the Page Setup dialog box either by choosing File ➪ Page Setup or by clicking the Page Setup button that is available in Print Preview. From the Page tab, you can set orientation and scaling. Using scaling, you may be able to fit the printed text onto one page.

Figure 6-48: From the Print dialog box, you can control, for example, the printer to which you print and the number of copies that you print.

Figure 6-49: The Page tab of the Page Setup dialog box

Note   Starting in Project 2000, you can set the first page number of the printed product. Suppose, for example, that your project is 10 pages long but you intend to print only pages 5 and 6. Typically, you'd want to number those pages as 1 and 2 — and you can do exactly that by setting the "First page number" box to 1.

From the Margins tab, shown in Figure 6-50, you can change the margins for your printed text and determine whether a border should appear.

Figure 6-50: The Margins tab of the Page Setup dialog box

From the Header tab, shown in Figure 6-51, you can define and align header information to appear on the top of every page that you print. Use either the buttons at the bottom of the box or the list box to add information that you want Project to update automatically, such as page numbers.

Figure 6-51: The Header tab of the Page Setup dialog box

You can include Project level fields in the header, footer, or legend of your printed product. From the appropriate tab of the Page Setup dialog box, use the Project Fields list box to select the field you want to include.

The Footer tab shown in Figure 6-52 works just like the Header tab. You can align and include the same kind of updating information in the footer on each page of your printed text.

Figure 6-52: The Footer tab of the Page Setup dialog box

The Page Setup dialog box changes just slightly, depending on the view that you were using when you opened the dialog box. For example, the Legend tab is available only when you're printing a Calendar, Gantt Chart view, or Network Diagram view, as shown in Figure 6-53. The Legend tab works just like the Header and Footer tabs, and you can align and include the same kind of updating information.

The View tab enables you to control what Project prints, such as all or only some columns, as shown in Figure 6-54.

 Project 2002 introduces the View tab.

Two new options in 2002 — Print column totals and Print row totals for values within print date range checkboxes — appear on the View tab and are checked by default in views where they are applicable: the Task Usage view and the Resource Usage view (the boxes will be unavailable in all other views). When you check the Print column totals checkbox, Project calculates totals in memory and adds a row to the printed page showing totals for timephased data, as well as for sheet data. You can take advantage of the Print row totals for values within print date range checkbox when you're printing a Usage view. Checking this box tells Project to add a column to the printed page that shows totals for the timephased data with the date range that you specify in the Print dialog box. The column totals print only on the last page, before any Notes pages, and row totals always print on a separate page after the timescale is complete.

Figure 6-53: The Legend tab of the Page Setup dialog box

Figure 6-54: The View tab of the Page Setup dialog box

Tip

In many cases, you can add a column to a table that gives you the same information you'll get in the row totals; the column will print where you place it, while the row totals print on a separate page.

Summary

This chapter covered the standard views available in Project. You:

✦ Saw a sample of each view

✦ Learned how to print in Project

Chapter 7 takes you beyond the basics in views; you learn how to customize and filter views and show other available information in views.

✦   ✦   ✦

Using Views to Gain Perspective

In Chapter 6, you saw samples of the built-in views that come with Project; and although you may never need any view other than the ones that come with Project, you're not limited to just those views. The potential for viewing information about your project is almost mind-boggling. In this chapter, you explore ways to make views work for you.

Customizing Views

You can customize the views in Project so that they show you the information that you need. Fiddle with the tables in views that contain tables or with the views themselves.

Changing tables

In views containing tables, you can make changes as simple as modifying the height of the rows or switching to a different table. Or, you can modify the appearance of the default table by moving columns around, hiding columns, or adding columns — and save your changes in a new table.

Changing row height

This advantageous feature helps you out whenever information is too wide to fit within a column; when you change the height of a row, the data wraps to fit within the taller row.

Note The capability to change the height of a row in a table is new to Project 2000.

Notice that the task names for Tasks 2 and 6, shown in Figure 7-1, don't fit within the Task Name column. If I increase the height of those rows, both names will wrap so that they will be visible, as shown in Figure 7-2.

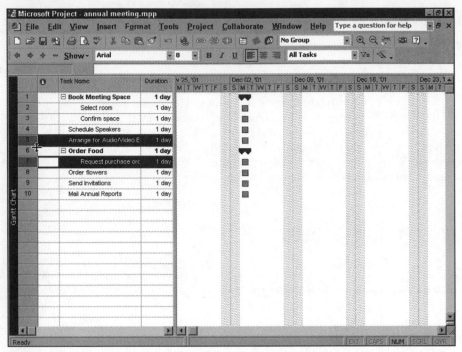

Figure 7-1: You can change the height of a row when the mouse pointer looks like a double-headed arrow.

To change the height of a row, select the row and move the mouse pointer into the Task ID number column at the bottom of the selected row. The mouse pointer changes to a pair of arrows pointing up and down (as shown previously in Figure 7-1). Drag down; when you release the mouse button, Project increases the height of the row and wraps any text in that row that didn't fit within its column.

Tip   To change the height of more than one row, select each row that you want to change. Use Windows selection techniques to select the rows. For example, to select two noncontiguous rows, click the ID of the first row; then press and hold Ctrl while you click the ID of the second row. When you change multiple rows simultaneously, Project assigns a uniform height to the selected rows.

Note   You can change row heights only in full row increments. In other words, you can make a row twice its original size but not one and a half times its original size.

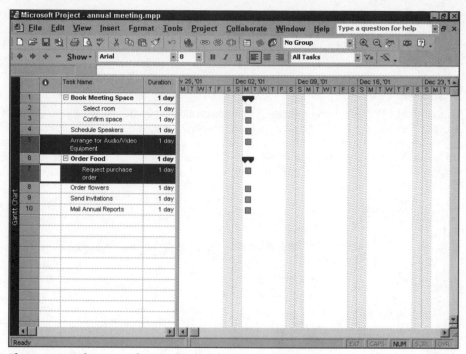

Figure 7-2: When you change the height of more than one row at a time, Project assigns a uniform height to all selected rows.

Hiding and inserting columns

You can temporarily remove a column from a table by hiding it. Right-click the column and choose Hide Column. Project doesn't remove the data in the column from the file; instead, the data is hidden from view. To see the column again (or to add a different column to your table), right-click the column heading that you want to appear to the right of the column that you're going to insert. Then, choose Insert Column from the shortcut menu that appears. You'll see the Column Definition dialog box, as shown in Figure 7-3.

Figure 7-3: Use this dialog box to add a column to your table.

Open the Field Name list box and select the name of the column that you want to add. You don't need to make any other changes; click Best Fit to make sure that Project provides enough space for the column title. Project inserts the column to the left of the selected column.

Switching tables

Tables don't appear in every view. For example, neither the Network Diagram view nor the Resource Graph view has a table displaying columns of information. However, views that have tables, such as any Gantt view or the Task Usage view, shown in Figure 7-4, also have a Select All button. Right-click the Select All button to list the standard tables you can display, as well as the More Tables options.

Select All button

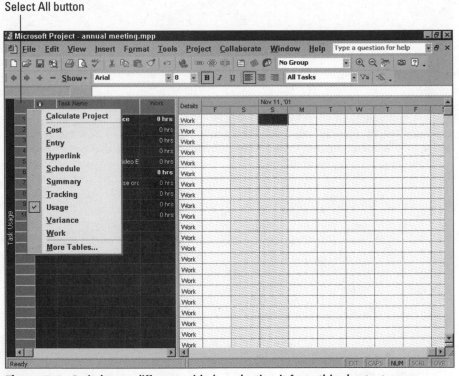

Figure 7-4: Switch to a different table by selecting it from this shortcut menu.

Tip   Clicking (instead of right-clicking) the Select All button selects all information in the table portion of the view.

Creating new tables or editing existing tables

As with views, Project has dozens of built-in tables, with a wide variety of information included to help you focus on issues of scheduling, resources, tracking, and so on. The More Tables window enables you to switch to tables that don't appear on the shortcut list of tables; you also can use the More Tables window to modify the fields of information displayed in the columns of tables, and even to create new tables. Creating new tables in Project is remarkably similar to editing existing tables; you use the same dialog box for both operations.

Note   How do you decide whether to create a new table or modify an existing one? If you can find a predefined table with a similar focus that has several of the fields that you want to include, start with a copy of that table. Then delete, rearrange, modify, or add fields as needed. If you can't find an appropriate model, you may need to create a new table. I suggest using a copy of the table because someone else using your schedule will expect to find the default fields in Project's original tables instead of the fields that you establish.

Suppose that the view will be more meaningful if the columns appeared in a different order than the order in which Project shows them. For example, many tables list baseline information first and then list actual information, resulting in this sequence of columns: Baseline Start, Baseline Finish, Actual Start, Actual Finish. Comparing this information may be easier if you create a table that presents the information in this order: Baseline Start, Actual Start, Baseline Finish, Actual Finish, and so on.

Or perhaps you'd like to add the table to the list of tables on the shortcut menu that appears when you right-click the Select All button. You may even want to add or delete some fields of information (columns) from the table. You can either edit an existing table or make a copy of it and edit the copy.

Caution   The More Tables window does not have a Table reset button; consequently, any changes that you make are permanent. I advise you to always make a copy of a table that you want to modify, rather than editing the original table. That way the original tables remain intact.

Follow these steps to create a new table or edit an existing table:

1. Choose View ➪ Table ➪ More Tables. Project displays the More Tables window, as shown in Figure 7-5.

2. Click the New button to create a new table. Or, select a table that you want to edit; you can use the Task or Resource choices at the top of the dialog box to display the type of table you need. Then click either the Edit button to edit the original table or the Copy button to edit a copy of the table. The Table Definition dialog box appears, as shown in Figure 7-6.

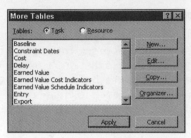

Figure 7-5: Select a table to use, edit, or copy from this dialog box.

Figure 7-6: Use the Table Definition dialog box to make changes to the appearance of a table. When you create a new table, no information appears in the bottom portion of the dialog box.

Note   If you create a copy, you may want to rename it in the Name box instead of using the default "Copy of" name Project supplies.

3. Enter a name for the table in the Name field. If you want to show this table in the shortcut menu that appears when you right-click the Select All button, select the "Show in menu" checkbox.

4. To add a field to the table, click a blank space in the area under the Field Name column; an arrow appears on the right side of the field. Click the arrow to display the drop-down list, as shown in Figure 7-7. Select a field name.

Figure 7-7: You can select fields of predefined information to build the columns in your table.

5. On the same row, click in the Align Data column. Project displays the default settings for alignment of data and title, as well as the width of the column. Click the arrow on the right side of the field; then select Left, Center, or Right alignment for the data in the column.

6. Click the Width column and, if necessary, modify the width of the column to accommodate the type of information that you think will typically go there.

Tip   If you aren't sure about the ideal column width, just accept the default. You can easily adjust column widths when the table is onscreen by dragging the edge of the column heading to the right or left.

7. Click the Title field and enter a title for the column if you don't want to use the default field name. Otherwise, skip this step.

8. Click the Align Title column and select a different alignment for the column title if you like.

9. Repeat Steps 4 through 8 to add more fields to your table. To edit your table, use the Cut Row, Copy Row, and Paste Row buttons to reorganize the order of fields in your table. Use the Insert Row and Delete Row buttons to add rows in between existing rows or remove existing rows.

10. If you have included any columns that include dates, such as Start or Finish information, you can modify the date format by using the drop-down list of choices in the Date format field. You can also modify the height of all the rows with the Row height setting.

Note The Header Wrapping field — a "yes or no" choice — controls whether long titles wrap within the column heading. If you set the Header Wrapping field to "No," Project will hide that portion of a column title that doesn't fit within the allotted space for the column.

11. If you want the first column of your table to remain onscreen while you scroll across your page, select the "Lock first column" checkbox. Typically, the Task ID column is the column locked in place in a table.

12. Click OK when you are finished. Then click Apply to display the new table on your screen.

Note By default, changes that you make to tables appear only in the current Project file. If you want new or edited tables to be available to other schedules, you must use the Organizer function in the More Tables dialog box to copy them to the `Global.mpt` file. See Chapter 20 for more information.

Working with views

As you learned in Chapter 6, views display a variety of information: tables with several fields of data, task bars, network diagram nodes, and so on. Microsoft has provided a plethora of views, meeting just about every information need. Nevertheless, you may want to create a variation on one of those views to look at information from a different perspective. For example, you can create a second Network Diagram view in which you set the nodes to display an entirely different set of information than the standard Network Diagram view. Then, rather than having to modify the nodes in the original Network Diagram view each time to see different information that you call on frequently, you can simply display the new view to use the alternative Network Diagram view. You can base an alternative view on any of the existing views and then change the information that Project displays by default to include only the information that you need.

Adding views

You can select a view from the View bar, or you can choose View ➪ More Views. Project gives you dozens of alternative views from which to select, as shown in Figure 7-8. When you create a new view, you can include it on the View bar or make it available in the More Views dialog box only.

Caution You can edit an existing view instead of creating a new view. But, like the More Tables dialog box, the More Views dialog box does not have a View reset button; consequently, any changes that you make are permanent. As I previously suggested, make a copy of a view that you want to modify, rather than editing the original view. That way the original views remain intact.

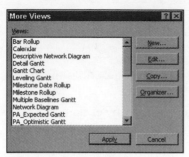

Figure 7-8: A wide selection of built-in views meets most informational needs.

To add a new view to your copy of Project, follow these steps:

1. Choose View ➪ More Views.

2. Click the New button in the More Views dialog box (shown previously in Figure 7-8). The Define New View dialog box appears, as shown in Figure 7-9.

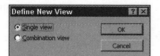

Figure 7-9: A simple choice awaits you in the Define New View dialog box: a single or combination view.

Tip   If you can, base your new view on a copy of an existing view — you'll have less to do to create the view.

3. Click the option button for a Single view and click OK. The View Definition dialog box opens, as shown in Figure 7-10.

Figure 7-10: Use this dialog box to name and describe your new view.

Note If you click the Combination view option button, the View Definition dialog box requests slightly different information.

4. Enter the Name of the new view. Choose a name that describes the information you'll show in the view.

5. Select a current view on which to base the new view by clicking the arrow to open the Screen drop-down list. Then choose a view name.

6. Do one of the following:

- If the screen that you chose in Step 5 gives you the option of selecting a table to include with it, select that table from the Table drop-down list shown in Figure 7-11.

- If the screen that you chose in Step 5 does not give you this option, go on to Step 7.

Figure 7-11: All the built-in tables and new tables that you have created appear on this list.

7. Open the Filter list box to choose a filter to apply to the view. By default, Project applies the All Tasks filter; therefore, all tasks appear in the view. To apply a selective filter so that Project highlights only filtered tasks, place a check in the Highlight filter checkbox at the bottom of the View Definition dialog box.

Note You can set filters to remove tasks from the display that don't meet the filtering criteria, or you can set filters to simply highlight the tasks that meet the criteria. If you want to reformat text that Project highlights as meeting filter criteria, choose Format ⇨ Text Styles. You learn more about these techniques later in this chapter.

8. Click the Show in Menu checkbox to make the new view available as a selection in the View bar and on the View menu. If you don't check this box, you must display the view by selecting it from the More Views dialog box.

9. Click OK and then click Apply to save the new view and display it onscreen.

Creating a combination view

You can manipulate views to see either a single or combination configuration. Combination views display the view that you've selected, as well as a second view that includes information about the selected task. Figure 7-12 shows the Network Diagram view with a combination of visual and textual information.

Figure 7-12: A combination view displays information for selected tasks.

You can display a combination in any view by moving your pointer to the split bar, shown in Figure 7-13, until the cursor becomes two horizontal lines with arrows; then double-click. You can also click and drag the split bar toward the top of your screen, or choose Window ⇨ Split. You can return to the simple Network Diagram view by double-clicking the split bar again.

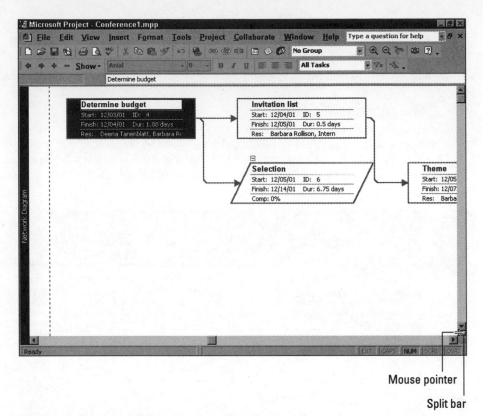

Mouse pointer

Split bar

Figure 7-13: When the mouse pointer appears in this shape, you can double-click to create a combination view.

Tip If you are displaying a combination view and you switch views, the new view also appears as a combination view. If you want to display a new view and have it occupy the full screen, choose Window ➪ Remove Split. You can always tell which portion of the split view you're in by the active view bar, a dark line that appears along the left edge of the view when you click the upper or lower view.

Suppose that you want to create a combination view that you can display at any time. Create a new combination view that includes the two views you want to see together.

1. Choose View ➪ More Views to display the More Views dialog box.

2. Click New to display the Define New View dialog box.

3. Choose the Combination view option to display the dialog box shown in Figure 7-14.

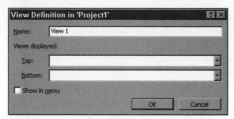

Figure 7-14: In the combination view version of the View Definition dialog box, select the two views to place onscreen.

4. Name the view and designate which view should appear on top of the screen and which view should appear at the bottom.

5. If you want to be able to display the view by choosing it from the View menu, place a check in the Show in Menu checkbox.

6. Click OK when you finish.

Ordering Tasks in a View

You can think of project management as the attempt to comprehend a large job by breaking the job into progressively smaller pieces — until the job is a collection of tasks. You want to organize the tasks so that you can estimate schedules, resource requirements, and costs. You can sort tasks and, starting in Project 2000, you can assign WBS codes or outline numbers to help you organize the project.

Sorting tasks

Sometimes, sorting information in a different way helps you to see things you might not have seen otherwise or even to get a better handle on a problem. In Project, you can sort a project from most views in almost any way that you want.

For example, in the Gantt Chart view, Project automatically sorts tasks by ID (see Figure 7-15). But you may find it easier to view your project information if you sort by Start Date. Choose Project ⇨ Sort ⇨ by Start Date and Project reorders the Gantt Chart view so that tasks are ordered by Start Date, as shown in Figure 7-16.

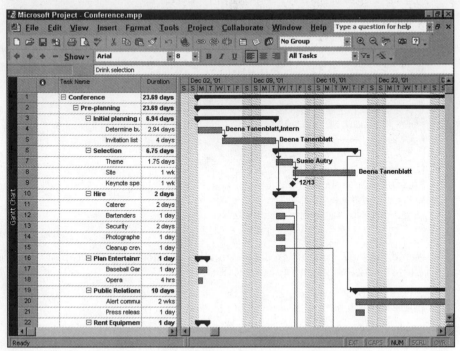

Figure 7-15: By default, Project sorts the Gantt view in Task ID order.

When you choose Project ➪ Sort, you see five common sort keys, as shown in Figure 7-17, but if you choose the Sort by command at the bottom of the menu, the Sort dialog box appears, as shown in Figure 7-18. From this dialog box, you can sort down to three levels. That is, if Project finds a "tie" at the first level, it will use the second sort that you specify to break the tie. And, if Project finds a "tie" at the second level, it will use the third sort you specify to break the tie. Using the checkboxes at the bottom of the dialog box, you can make your sort choices permanent by reassigning Task IDs, and you can choose to retain the outline structure of the project.

Figure 7-16: Using the Sort menu, you can sort a project by Task Start Date.

Creating WBS codes

The U.S. defense establishment initially developed the work breakdown structure (WBS), and you'll find it described in Section 1.6 of MIL-HDBK-881 (2 January 1998):

✦ A product-oriented family tree composed of hardware, software, services, data, and facilities. The family tree structure results from systems engineering efforts during the acquisition of a defense materiel item.

✦ A WBS chart displays and defines the product, or products, to be developed and/or produced. It relates the elements of work to be accomplished to each other and to the end product.

Figure 7-17: Choose one of these five common sort keys directly from the Sort menu.

Figure 7-18: You can set up a more complex sort structure for Project to use in the Sort dialog box.

More simply put, a WBS chart shows a numbered list of the tasks that you must complete to complete a project.

In Project 2002, you still can't produce a WBS graphic representation of your project similar to the one shown in Figure 7-19. You can, however, assign WBS codes to each task; WBS codes can be letters and numbers (or combinations of letters and numbers) that help you identify the relationship between tasks and organize the project.

Figure 7-19: The WBS chart is reminiscent of a company organization chart.

On the CD-ROM WBS Chart for Project, an add-on product for Project, creates a WBS chart from a Microsoft Project file. The CD-ROM that accompanies this book includes a sample of the program.

You can use any numbering system that you want for your WBS code structure. Suppose that you assigned codes to your project similar to the ones shown in Figure 7-20. The task numbered 1.1.2.3 identifies the first box in Level 2, the second box in Level 3, and the third box on Level 4 of the outline structure of the project. Although Project doesn't produce the graphic representation, it assigns the numbers based on the task's level within the project outline.

Figure 7-20: WBS numbering shows you the hierarchical relationship of tasks in the project.

To assign WBS numbers to a project, follow these steps:

1. Choose Project ➪ WBS ➪ Define Code. Project displays the WBS Code Definition dialog box. The Code preview box shows you the format of the WBS code you're designing as you design it — and therefore remains blank until you make selections in this dialog box.

2. Use the Project Code Prefix box to apply a prefix to all WBS codes that you assign. For example, you may want to use the initials of the project name.

3. In the Sequence column at the bottom of the box, select the type of character that you want to use for each level of the WBS code. In Figure 7-21, I've selected Numbers (ordered) for both Levels 1 and 2, but you can also include Uppercase or Lowercase letters; if you choose Characters (unordered), Project inserts an asterisk at that position of the WBS code.

Note   Using "Character" enables you to enter any characters that you want into that part of the WBS code. For example, suppose that you use a mask of Numbers (ordered) Length 1, Numbers (ordered) Length 1, Characters (unordered) Length 3. For any third level task, you can enter any three characters you want for the third part of the WBS. In the example, when you enter a third level task, you'll initially see a WBS of 1.1.***. However, you can change it to something like 1.1.a#3.

Figure 7-21: Use the WBS Code Definition dialog box to define the type of WBS code that you want to use.

4. Open the list box in the Length column and choose the length for the level of the WBS code. In Figure 7-21, I set Level 1 to two digits, but I allowed any number of digits for Level 2; you can choose Any, select from the predefined list of numbers 1-10, or type in any other number.

Note   For the technically curious, I tested 100, and Project accepted it, but using a 100-digit number in a WBS code isn't particularly practical.

5. In the Separator column, use the list box to select period (.), dash (–), plus (+), or slash (/) or type in any value that is not a number or a letter (such as =).

6. Repeat the previous steps for each level that you want to define.

7. Click OK when you finish.

Tip   You'll probably want to leave both the checkboxes checked at the bottom of the WBS Code Definition dialog box because they ensure that all tasks are assigned WBS codes and that the codes are unique.

The WBS codes don't appear by default on the Gantt Chart view; to view the WBS codes, you must add the WBS column. To add the WBS column to the left of the Task Name column, right-click the Task Name column. Project selects the column and displays a shortcut menu. Choose Insert Column from the shortcut menu, and Project displays the Column Definition dialog box. Open the Field Name list box and select WBS. If you want, change the alignment of data to Left. Then, click Best Fit to add the column to the worksheet portion of the Gantt Chart view, as shown in Figure 7-22.

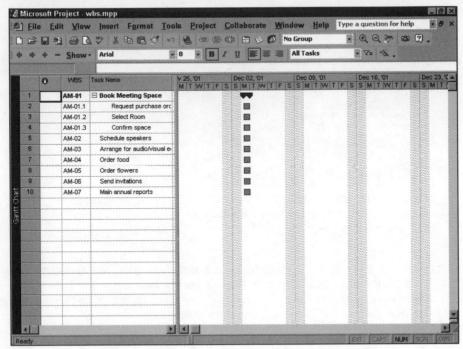

Figure 7-22: When you display the WBS column, Project displays the WBS codes for each task in your project.

Note   If you had added the WBS column *before* defining WBS codes, you would have seen outline numbering that corresponded to the task's position in the project outline.

Renumbering WBS codes

WBS codes *don't* automatically renumber themselves in all cases when you change the structure of the project outline, as shown in Figure 7-23. WBS Codes *will* automatically renumber themselves if you change the level of a task within the outline structure of the project. That is, if you drag a Level 1 task to a new Level 1 location or if you drag a subtask to a new location underneath its original parent task, both tasks will retain their original WBS code number. However, if you promote or demote the task, or if you move it so that it appears at a new level in the outline, Project will assign the task a new WBS code. You can test the premise by dragging "Select Room" so that it appears before "Request purchase order." Each subtask retains its original WBS code.

Figure 7-23: Because I moved tasks around, the WBS codes are no longer sequential.

There is one exception to the preceding rule. If you use the cut-and-paste method to move a task to a new location *at the same level in the outline*, Project assigns a new WBS code. Why? Because Project views cutting and pasting as the process of deleting one task and adding another task. If you set the options in the WBS Code Definition dialog box to generate new codes for new tasks and to verify uniqueness of WBS codes, Project generates a new WBS code for the task that you paste instead of reusing the WBS code of the task that you cut.

Note   If you're working on a government contract for which you and the government have agreed to a numbering scheme and you don't want WBS codes to change even if you move tasks around, use Outline codes, which are completely static. You can assign both an Outline code and a WBS code to a task. (You'll read about Outline codes later in this chapter.)

At times, however, you'll want to renumber the WBS codes, even though Project didn't renumber them automatically — and you can. In fact, you can renumber the entire project or only selected portions of the project. If you choose to renumber selected portions, you must select the tasks before starting the renumbering process.

Caution   You can't "undo" renumbering WBS codes, so save your project before you start this operation. That way, if you don't like the results, you can close the project without saving and reopen it in its original state before you renumbered.

To renumber all tasks in the project shown in Figure 7-23, follow these steps:

1. Choose Project ➪ WBS ➪ Renumber. Project displays the dialog box shown in Figure 7-24.

Figure 7-24: Use this dialog box to renumber the project.

2. Click OK. Project prompts you before renumbering.

3. Click Yes. Project reassigns all WBS numbers, as shown in Figure 7-25.

Figure 7-25: The WBS codes are again sequential after renumbering.

At this point, I'm going to hide the WBS column to keep the display as clean as possible.

Defining outline numbers

In the preceding section, I offered a scenario in which you're working on a government contract, and you and the government have agreed to a numbering scheme. In a case like this, you *don't* want WBS codes to change — even if you move tasks around. So, don't rely on WBS codes in Project; instead, use Outline codes, which are completely static.

Note
You can assign both an Outline code and a WBS code to a task.

Outline codes work similar to the way WBS codes work; however, outline codes are completely customizable, and they are not tied to the outline structure of your project. For example, you may want to assign a department code to a task so that you can view the project organized by department. Or, you may want to assign a company cost code to a task so that you can view tasks by cost code. And, you can create a list of valid outline codes for users to enter.

To define outline codes, follow these steps:

1. Choose Tools ➪ Customize ➪ Fields. Project displays the Customize Fields dialog box, as shown in Figure 7-26. Click the Custom Outline Codes tab.

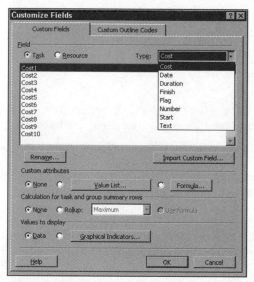

Figure 7-26: Select an outline code to customize.

Cross-Reference
Read more about customizing fields in Chapter 20.

2. Choose an Outline Code to customize.

3. To provide a meaningful name for the code, click the Rename button and type the new name. Then click OK to redisplay the Customize Fields dialog box.

4. Click the Define Code Mask button to display the Outline Code Definition dialog box shown in Figure 7-27.

Figure 7-27: The Outline Code Definition dialog box looks and operates like the WBS Code Definition dialog box.

5. In the Sequence column, select the type of character that you want to use for each level of the outline code.

6. In the Length column, use the list to choose the length for the level of the outline code.

7. In the Separator column, use the list box to select period (.), dash (–), plus (+), or slash (/), or type in any value that is not a number or a letter (such as =).

8. Repeat the previous steps for each level that you want to define.

If you simply want to create a mask for the outline code so that users use the correct format, you can click OK; you may want to place a check in the last checkbox to ensure that users enter outline codes that match the mask.

If you want to restrict the use of outline codes to a specific list of codes, you can click the Edit Lookup Table button in the Outline Code Definition dialog box to define permissible codes in the Edit Lookup Table dialog box, as shown in Figure 7-28.

On the first line, type a permissible outline code for Level 1. On the second line, type an outline code for Level 2 that is permissible under the outline code that you supplied for Level 1 and click the Indent button (the right arrow) at the top of the dialog box. On the third line, type another acceptable Level 2 outline code. If you need a Level 3 outline code under a Level 2 outline code, simply type the code on a blank line below the Level 2 outline code and click the Indent button again. To supply another Level 1 code, type the code and click the Outdent button (the left arrow) as many times as necessary, depending on the last code you entered.

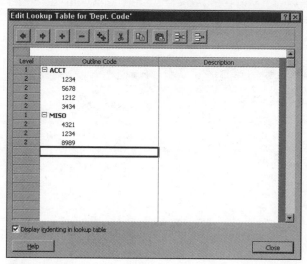

Figure 7-28: Use this dialog box to define the allowable lookup codes.

Repeat the process, filling in the acceptable outline codes. If you forget to include a code, highlight the code you want to appear *below* the code you'll add, and then click the Insert Row button at the top of the dialog box. And, if a code becomes invalid at some later date, reopen this dialog box, highlight the code, and click the Delete Row button.

Click the Close button to redisplay the Outline Code Definition dialog box. If you don't want to allow outline codes that don't appear in the lookup table, place a check in the "Only allow codes listed in the lookup table" checkbox. Then click the OK button to redisplay the Customize Fields dialog box, and click OK again to redisplay your project.

To display a column for an outline code, you follow the same process that you used to display the column for the WBS code. Right-click the column that you want to appear to the right of the Outline Code column and choose Insert Column. In the Column Definition dialog box, open the Field Name list box and select the outline code that you defined. Click Best Fit, and Project displays the column, but it's empty. Because outline codes don't follow an "ordered" pattern (in other words, alphabetical or numerical), Project has no way of knowing what outline codes to assign to any particular task. If you didn't create list entries, you can simply type the outline codes into the column.

Tip   Remember that outline codes may need to match the mask that you created.

If you did create list entries (and if you told Project to only allow outline codes listed in the lookup table) click in the column. You'll see a list box arrow; when you open it, the entries from the lookup table appear, as shown in Figure 7-29.

Figure 7-29: You can choose outline codes from the entries listed in the lookup table.

Filtering Views to Gain Perspective

Filters help you to focus on specific aspects of your project. For example, suppose that you want to view the tasks assigned to only certain resources or you want to display only the tasks on the critical path of your project. You can apply filters to views to limit the information you see and to help you focus on a particular issue.

Project filters come in two varieties: task filters, which enable you to view specific aspects of tasks, and resource filters, which enable you to view specific aspects of resources. In Table 7-1, you find a description of the default task filters, and in Table 7-2, you find a description of the default resource filters. Many of the filters perform similar functions.

Note

The Tasks with Deadlines filter and the Tasks with Estimated Durations filter (shown in Table 7-1) first appeared in Project 2000.

Table 7-1
Default Task Filters

Filter	Purpose
All Tasks	Displays all the tasks in your project.
Completed Tasks	Displays all finished tasks.
Confirmed	Displays the tasks on which specified resources have agreed to work.
Cost Greater Than	Displays the tasks that exceed the cost you specify.
Cost Overbudget	Calculated filter that displays all tasks with a cost that exceeds the baseline cost.
Created After	Displays all tasks that you created in your project on or after the specified date.
Critical	Displays all tasks on the critical path.
Date Range	Interactive filter that prompts you for two dates and then displays all tasks that start after the earlier date and finish before the later date.
In Progress Tasks	Displays all tasks that have started but haven't finished.
Incomplete Tasks	Displays all tasks that haven't finished.
Late/Overbudget Tasks Assigned To	Prompts you to specify a resource. Then, Project displays tasks that meet either of two conditions: the tasks assigned to that resource that exceed the budget you allocated for them, or the tasks that haven't finished yet and will finish after the baseline finish date. Note that completed tasks do not appear when you apply this filter, even if they completed after the baseline finish date.
Linked Fields	Displays tasks to which you have linked text from other programs.
Milestones	Displays only milestones.
Resource Group	Displays the tasks assigned to resources that belong to the group you specify.

Continued

Table 7-1 *(continued)*

Filter	Purpose
Should Start By	Prompts you for a date and then displays all tasks not yet begun that should have started by that date.
Should Start/Finish By	Prompts you for two dates: a start date and a finish date. Then Project uses the filter to display those tasks that haven't started by the start date and those tasks that haven't finished by the finish date.
Slipped/Late Progress	Displays two types of tasks: those that have slipped behind their baseline scheduled finish date and those that are not progressing on schedule.
Slipping Tasks	Displays all tasks that are behind schedule.
Summary Tasks	Displays all tasks that have subtasks grouped below them.
Task Range	Shows all tasks that have ID numbers within the range you provide.
Tasks with Attachments	Displays tasks that have objects attached or a note in the Notes box.
Tasks with Fixed Dates	Displays all tasks that have an actual start date and tasks to which you assign some constraint other than As Soon As Possible.
Tasks with Deadlines	Displays all tasks to which you have assigned deadline dates.
Tasks with Estimated Durations	Displays all tasks to which you have assigned an estimated duration.
Filter	Purpose.
Tasks/Assignments with	Displays the tasks or assignments that have overtimeOvertime.
Top Level Tasks	Displays the highest-level summary tasks.
Unconfirmed	Displays the tasks on which specified resources have not agreed to work.
Unstarted Tasks	Displays tasks that haven't started.
Update Needed	Displays tasks that have changes, such as revised start and finish dates or resource reassignments, and that need to be sent to resources for update or confirmation.

Filter	Purpose
Using Resource	Displays all tasks that use the resource you specify.
Using Resource in Date Range	Displays the tasks assigned to a specified resource that start after the first date you specify and finish before the second date you specify.
Work Overbudget	Displays all tasks with scheduled work greater than baseline work.

Table 7-2
Default Resource Filters

Filter	Purpose
All Resources	Displays all the resources in your project.
Confirmed Assignments	Available only in the Resource Usage view, displays only those tasks for which a resource has confirmed the assignment.
Cost Greater Than	Displays the resources that exceed the cost you specify.
Cost Overbudget	Calculated filter that displays all resources with a cost that exceeds the baseline cost.
Date Range	Interactive filter that prompts you for two dates and then displays all tasks and resources with assignments that start after the earlier date and finish before the later date.
Group	Prompts you for a group and then displays all resources belonging to that group.
In Progress Assignments	Displays all tasks that have started but haven't finished.
Linked Fields	Displays resources to which you have linked text from other programs.
Overallocated Resources	Displays all resources that are scheduled to do more work than they have the capacity to do.
Resource Range	Interactive filter that prompts you for a range of ID numbers and then displays all resources within that range.
Resources with Attachments	Displays resources that have objects attached or a note in the Notes box.
Resources/Assignments	Displays the resources or assignments that have overtime with Overtime.

Continued

Table 7-2 *(continued)*	

Filter	Purpose
Should Start By	Prompts you for a date and then displays all task and resources with assignments not yet begun that should have started by that date.
Should Start/Finish By	Prompts you for two dates: a start date and a finish date. Then Project uses the filter to display those tasks or assignments that haven't started by the start date and those tasks or assignments that haven't finished by the finish date.
Slipped/Late Progress	Displays two types of resources: those that have slipped behind their baseline scheduled finish date and those that are not progressing on schedule.
Slipping Assignments	Displays all resources with uncompleted tasks that are behind schedule because the tasks have been delayed from the original baseline plan.
Unconfirmed Assignments	Displays the assignments for which requested resources have not yet agreed to work.
Unstarted Assignments	Displays confirmed assignments that have not yet started.
Work Complete	Displays resources that have completed all of their assigned tasks.
Work Incomplete	Displays all resources with baseline work greater than scheduled work.
Work Overbudget	Displays all resources with scheduled work greater than baseline work.

Applying a filter to a view

By applying a filter to a view, you specify criteria that Project uses to determine what tasks or resources should appear in that view. Project then selects information to display and either highlights the selected information or hides the rest of the information. To apply a filter and hide all other information, follow these steps:

1. Display the view you want to filter.

2. Choose Project ➪ Filtered for.

3. Choose the filter that you want from the Filtered for side menu.

Note   Because Project enables you to apply task filters to task views only and resource filters to resource views only, the Filtered for hierarchical menu shows either All Task or All Resources, depending on the view that you displayed before starting these steps.

If you want to apply a filter that doesn't appear on the list, or you want to apply a highlighting filter, follow these steps:

1. Display the view you want to filter.

2. Choose Project ⇨ Filtered for ⇨ More Filters. Project displays the More Filters dialog box, as shown in Figure 7-30.

Figure 7-30: Use the More Filters dialog box to apply a filter that doesn't appear on the Filtered for list or to apply a highlighting filter.

3. Click the Task option button to select and apply a task filter; select the Resource option button to select and apply a resource filter.

Caution   Remember that Project won't let you apply a task filter to a resource view or a resource filter to a task view.

4. Select a filter name from the list.

5. Click Apply to apply the filter or click Highlight to apply a highlighting filter. If the filter that you want to apply is an interactive filter, type the requested values.

6. Click OK.

Tip   To turn off a filter, choose Project ⇨ Filtered for. Then choose All Tasks or All Resources, as appropriate.

Creating custom filters

If none of Project's default filters meet your needs, you can create a new filter or modify an existing filter by customizing a filter's criteria from the More Filters dialog box. To edit an existing filter, follow these steps:

1. Display the view that you want to filter.

2. Choose Project ⇨ Filtered for ⇨ More Filters to open the More Filters dialog box.

3. Select the option button of the type of filter you want to use: Task or Resource.

4. Highlight the filter that you want to modify and then click the Copy button. Project displays a Filter Definition dialog box similar to the one shown in Figure 7-31.

Figure 7-31: The Filter Definition dialog box enables you to edit an existing filter.

The More Filters dialog box does not have a Filter reset button; consequently, any changes that you make are permanent. For this reason, I advise you to click the Copy button to make a copy of a filter you want to modify, rather than clicking the Edit button to edit the original filter. That way, the original filters remain intact.

5. Click in the Field Name column; Project displays a list box arrow to the right of the field.

6. Select a field from the list.

7. Repeat Steps 5 and 6 for the Test column and supply a comparison operator.

8. Repeat Steps 5 and 6 in the Value(s) column and supply a filtering value.

9. Repeat Steps 5 through 8 for each criterion that you want to create; also supply an And/Or operator if you supply additional criteria. Remember, "And" means that the filter displays information only if the task or resource meets *all* criteria, whereas "Or" means that the filter displays information if a task or resource meets *any* of the criteria.

10. Click OK to redisplay the More Filters dialog box.

11. Click Apply to apply the filter.

> **Note**
>
> To create a new filter, click the New button in Step 4. In the Filter Definition dialog box, the name "Filter 1" appears in the Name box and no information appears at the bottom of the box. You need to supply a name for the new filter and some filtering criteria. If you want your new filter to appear in the Filtered for list, place a check in the Show in Menu checkbox.

Each line that you create in the Filter Definition dialog box is called a *statement*. If you want to evaluate certain statements together, but separate from other statements in your filter, group the statements into a set of criteria. To group statements, leave a blank line between sets of criteria, and select either operator in the And/Or field for the blank row.

If your filter contains three or more statements within one criteria group, Project evaluates all "And" statements before evaluating "Or" statements. Because versions of Project earlier than 98 did not work this way, using filters that you created in versions of Project prior to Project 98 may produce results that you don't expect in Project 2002. Also note, however, that across groups, Project evaluates "And" conditions in the order in which they appear.

Using AutoFilters

AutoFilters are similar to regular Project filters, but you can access them directly on the sheet of any sheet view instead of using a menu or a window. By default, the AutoFilters option is off when you create a project, but you can enable it by clicking the AutoFilter button on the Formatting toolbar.

When you enable AutoFilters, a list box arrow appears at the right edge of every column name in a sheet view. When you open the drop-down list, Project displays filters appropriate to the column, as shown in Figure 7-32.

> **Tip**
>
> You can turn on AutoFilters automatically for new projects that you create. Choose Tools ➪ Options and click the General tab. Place a check in the "Set AutoFilter on for new projects" checkbox.

AutoFilter button

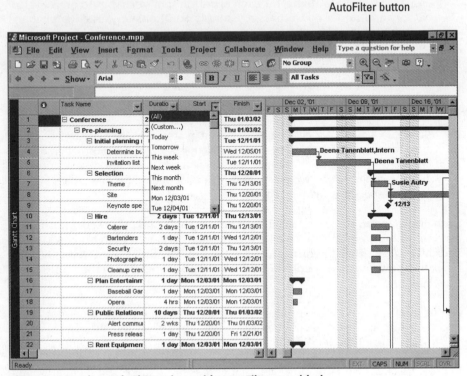

Figure 7-32: The Task Sheet view with AutoFilters enabled

Using grouping

Grouping is another technique that you can use to view information about your project. You may be able to solve a problem if you group tasks together by some common denominator. In Figure 7-33, I've grouped tasks by duration to help identify shorter versus longer tasks.

Project contains some predefined groups; to use one of these groups to arrange tasks in a view by the group common denominator, follow these steps:

1. Display the view that you want to use to group tasks.

2. Choose Project ➪ Group By.

3. Choose the group that you want from the Group By menu.

Note

Because Project enables you to group tasks only on task views and resources only on resource views, the Group By menu shows either task groupings or resource groupings, depending on the view you displayed before starting these steps.

Figure 7-33: Group tasks in a view to help you identify information about your project.

You're not limited to using the groups that appear on the Group By menu; you can group by almost any field. If you want to group in a way that doesn't appear on the menu, follow these steps:

1. Display the view that you want to use to group tasks.

2. Choose Project ⇨ Group by ⇨ More Groups. Project displays the More Groups dialog box, as shown in Figure 7-34.

Figure 7-34: Use the More Groups dialog box to apply a group that doesn't appear on the Group By list or to create a new group by copying and editing an existing group.

3. Click the Task option button to select and apply a task grouping; select the Resource option button to select and apply a resource grouping.

Tip

Remember that Project won't let you apply a task group to a resource view or a resource group to a task view.

4. Select a group name from the list.

5. Click Apply to apply the filter or click Edit or Copy to edit a group or make a copy of a group so that you can edit it.

Caution

Like its cousins, the More Groups dialog box does not have a Group reset button; consequently, any changes that you make are permanent. I advise you to click the Copy button to make a copy of a group that you want to modify, rather than editing the original group. That way the original groups remain intact.

6. If you simply want to apply a group, click OK. If you are creating a new group by copying an existing group, you'll see the Group Definition dialog box, as shown in Figure 7-35.

Figure 7-35: Use this dialog box to create a custom group based on an existing group.

7. Assign a name to the group that you're creating and place a check in the Show in Menu box if you want the group available from the Group By side menu.

8. Open the Field Name list box and select a field on which you want Project to group.

9. In the Order column, choose Ascending or Descending.

10. (Optional) Select a font for the grouping title information.

11. (Optional) Change the cell background and the pattern that Project displays for the field.

12. (Optional) Click the Define Group Intervals button to display the Define Group Interval dialog box, as shown in Figure 7-36. In this dialog box, you can control the grouping intervals Project uses.

Figure 7-36: Use this dialog box to specify the intervals at which you want Project to group the fields.

13. Place a check in the Show summary tasks box to include summary tasks in the grouping.

14. Click OK to save your choices and redisplay the More Groups dialog box.

15. Click Apply to apply the group you just defined.

New Feature Starting in Project 2002, you can group on assignment fields in Usage views.

Project 2002 enables you to group on assignment fields; follow these steps:

1. Choose Project ➪ Group by ➪ Customize Group By. You see the Customize Group By dialog box shown in Figure 7-37.

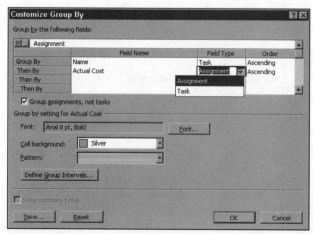

Figure 7-37: Use this dialog box to group by assignment fields.

2. Select the fields by which you wish to group.

3. Place a check in the "Group assignments, not tasks" checkbox.

4. In the Field Type column, select whether to group by assignment or by task.

Note   In the example, I started working from the Task Usage view. If you start working from the Resource Usage view, the name of the checkbox will change to refer to resources instead of tasks, and, in the Field Type list, you will choose whether to group by assignment or by resource.

5. Click OK. Project groups based the project on your selections.

Tip   To turn off grouping, choose Project ⇨ Group By. Then choose No Group.

Summary

This chapter covered techniques that you can use to get more information from Project's views. You learned:

✦ How to work with tables

✦ How to customize views

✦ How to order tasks in a view

✦ How to assign WBS codes and outline codes to tasks

✦ Methods for filtering information while working

✦ Methods for grouping information while working

You can use the skills you've learned here to make Project work in the way that's most comfortable for you.

Chapter 8 explains how to change the appearance of your project by formatting elements and inserting drawings and objects.

✦   ✦   ✦

Modifying the Appearance of Your Project

◆   ◆   ◆   ◆

In This Chapter

Changing Project's looks

Using the GanttChartWizard

Formatting elements one by one

Inserting drawings and objects

◆   ◆   ◆   ◆

After you enter the information for your project, you may want to take the time to format the individual elements of the schedule. After all, you may be working with this project for months or even years. Why not get it to look just right?

Project has dozens of ways to format the appearance of elements from text to task bars, link lines, and network diagram nodes. Some of these changes are practical; others simply provide shapes or styles that may be more pleasing to you. You can use color and insert drawings or pictures into your schedule to make a visual point. You can also copy pictures of your Project file into other Office documents — for example, to include in a report. So get ready: This chapter is where you can get creative!

Changing Project's Looks

Beyond the obvious motivation of making the lines and colors in your schedule more appealing, you may have a practical reason for modifying a schedule's appearance. You may, for example, want to do any of the following to make information about your project more accessible:

♦ Display information, such as the start and end dates or resources assigned to the task, in text form alongside task bars. This technique is especially useful for longer schedules in which a task bar may appear on the printed page far to the right of the task information in the Gantt table.

♦ Use a bolder color for any tasks on the critical path (tasks that, if delayed, will delay the final completion of the project). This method helps you keep an eye on tasks that are vital to meeting your deadline.

✦ Modify the display of baseline timing estimates versus actual progress on tasks so that you can more clearly see any divergence.

Starting in Project 2002, you can store multiple baselines; you may want to format your project schedule to more easily distinguish various baselines. See Chapter 11 for more information on multiple baselines.

✦ Display or hide dependency lines between tasks. In a project with many complex dependency relationships, multiple lines can obscure task bar elements or network diagram nodes.

In short, beyond mere cosmetics, paying attention to the format of your schedule elements can help you focus on your project. Keep in mind that these changes pertain only to the currently open schedule, and any changes that you make to the format of these elements appear both onscreen and on any corresponding printed versions of the project.

You can change formats whenever you like and then change them back again without changing the data in your project. For example, you may decide not to display dependency lines to print out a report of resource assignments for your boss because printing the lines can obscure the list of resources next to each task bar. You can always redisplay the dependency lines later.

Using the GanttChartWizard

You can make changes to specific elements in several Project views. However, the Gantt Chart view has its own wizard to help you format the various pieces. Running through the GanttChartWizard highlights some of the options.

Consistency Counts

Displaying an abundance of elements on a schedule can be a mixed blessing. For example, highlighting critical tasks, adding end shapes to task bars, and showing both baseline and actual lines as well as slack can result in a chart that is confusing. Remember that you're not formatting elements to satisfy your particular penchant for one color or another, but to make project information easier to read.

You'll help everyone in your organization read and understand Project schedules if you make the formatting consistent across your organization. The more your coworkers and management see the same formatting in various schedules, the more quickly they'll learn to read the symbols, and the less likely they are to misread a schedule. Set standards for formatting projects in your workgroup and your division (even across your whole company) and stick to them.

Note A *wizard* is an interactive series of dialog boxes that require you to answer questions or make selections. Project uses your input to create or modify some aspect of your project (in this case, the formatting applied to your Gantt Chart). The Microsoft Office family of products uses wizards to automate many functions.

You can use the GanttChartWizard from either the Gantt Chart view or the Tracking Gantt view. Because GanttChartWizard changes apply only to the project file that's open when you run the wizard, start by displaying the project that you want to format. Then follow these steps:

1. Click the GanttChartWizard button on the Formatting toolbar, or choose Format ➪ GanttChartWizard to start the wizard. A dialog box appears, as shown in Figure 8-1.

Figure 8-1: Step 1 of the wizard simply greets you and tells you what the wizard does.

Note The four buttons at the bottom of this dialog box appear at the bottom of each wizard dialog box. Click Cancel to leave the wizard without saving any settings, click Back to move back one step, and click Finish to complete the wizard based on the information that you've provided to that point.

2. Click Next to move to the next step. In the second wizard dialog box, as shown in Figure 8-2, indicate the category of information that you want to display. You can select only one item here. Try clicking each of the following choices to see a preview of its style on the left of the dialog box:

   • **Standard.** Shows blue task bars, black summary task bars, and a black line superimposed over the task bars to indicate progress on tasks

   • **Critical path.** The Standard layout with critical path tasks in red

   • **Baseline.** Displays baseline task bars and progress task bars separately, rather than superimposed as with the Standard setup, as shown in Figure 8-2.

- **Other.** Displays a drop-down list that contains several alternative, predefined chart styles for the categories of Standard, Critical Path, Baseline, and Status.

- **Custom Gantt Chart.** The wizard displays several additional screens to enable you to create a highly customized Gantt Chart.

Figure 8-2: The preview provides an idea of how each option formats your Gantt Chart.

3. Click the option button for Custom Gantt Chart and then click the Next button. The third wizard dialog box appears, as shown in Figure 8-3. In this dialog box, you choose whether to differentiate between critical and noncritical tasks.

Note   If you select any of the other options in the second dialog box of the GanttChartWizard, the remaining wizard dialog boxes deal with the elements that you want to display with the task bars, such as resource names, dates, or custom information. You also have an opportunity to designate whether Project should display lines between task bars to indicate dependencies.

Figure 8-3: Formatting critical and noncritical tasks differently can help you spot potential scheduling problems early.

4. Leave the default setting of Yes, and click Next to display the next wizard dialog box, shown in Figure 8-4. Here you can select a color, pattern, and end shape for the critical task bars.

Figure 8-4: End shapes delineate the two ends of task bars.

Tip

Highlighting critical tasks in a project helps you to pay special attention to them when reviewing or tracking progress. If you don't want to format the Gantt Chart to treat critical tasks differently, try using a filter to temporarily display only critical tasks, as you learned to do in Chapter 7.

5. Click each drop-down box and select the style options you want. When you're done, click Next. The dialog box that appears (not shown) resembles the dialog box shown in Figure 8-4; in this dialog box, you choose the color, pattern, and end shapes for noncritical task bars.

Caution

Be careful about selecting a solid pattern for task bars: Superimposed progress lines are typically a solid color (black) and may be hard to see against a solid task bar.

6. Pick a combination that you can differentiate easily from your critical task bar choices and then click Next. Figure 8-5 shows the next wizard dialog box, in which you select styles for summary task bars. The additional choice here of Bar style refers to the thickness of the bar.

Note

Be sure to make choices here that differentiate summary task bar styles from the choices you made for normal and critical tasks.

7. Click Next to see the next wizard dialog box, shown in Figure 8-6, in which you can select the color, pattern, and shape of milestone symbols. Select a shape for milestones that is different from the end shapes that you've chosen for task bars so that the milestones stand out clearly.

Figure 8-5: The thicker bar styles obscure the end shapes. If seeing end shapes is important, use the thinner style shown here.

Figure 8-6: Solid patterns make a milestone stand out; consider a bright color to make them easy to spot.

8. Click Next to display the next wizard dialog box, shown in Figure 8-7, and select the Baseline and slack options that you want to display. *Baseline* is a picture of the plan before you began tracking actual progress, and *slack* is any extra time a task can use up before it moves onto the critical path. In Figure 8-7, I chose the Baseline and slack option.

9. Click Next to view the next wizard dialog box in which you can choose the type of task information to display with your Gantt bars: Resources and dates (the end date only), Resources, Dates, None of the choices, or Custom task information. When you choose Dates, as I did in Figure 8-8, Project displays the start date and end date in the task bar area. If you choose this setting, you don't need to show the corresponding columns for start date and end date in the Gantt table, so this option can help you to modify the size of your schedule printout.

Figure 8-7: With this preview, you can begin to see how your choices will look.

Figure 8-8: Placing text alongside task bars can be very useful with larger schedules.

10. Click Next to display the next wizard dialog box (not shown) in which you specify whether to show link lines between tasks to represent dependency relationships. Leave the default setting to display the lines.

11. Click Next. This GanttChartWizard dialog box, shown in Figure 8-9, previews your formatting options. You can use the Back button to go back and make changes.

12. Click the Format It button to apply your choices. Project displays a final dialog box to tell you that your formatting is complete.

13. Click the Exit Wizard button to close the dialog box and see your changes.

When Enough Is Too Much

If you select Custom task information in the GanttChartWizard (refer to Figure 8-8), the wizard opens three consecutive dialog boxes. These three dialog boxes prompt you to display one set of information alongside normal task bars, another set on summary task bars, and a third set next to milestone tasks, respectively. The wizard also prompts you to display one set of data to the left of each task bar, one set to the right, and one inside the task bar itself. You could end up with nine pieces of information in and around your various task bars!

You make your selections from drop-down lists in these three dialog boxes. The information ranges from the task name, duration, and priority to percentage of work complete and types of constraints.

Obviously, if you display nine sets of data in and around task bars, your Gantt Chart will become unreadable. However, you may consider this scenario: Put the task name inside both summary and normal task bars, put the start date to the left and the finish date to the right of normal task bars, and put the cost of summary tasks to the right of their bars. (The final element is a total of the cost of all tasks beneath the summary tasks.)

You can also modify the information that is available to someone viewing your schedule by changing the columns displayed in the Gantt table pane of the Gantt Chart view.

Figure 8-9: If you don't like what you see, move back to the dialog box in which you made the original setting, change it, and then move forward to this dialog box again.

Formatting Elements One by One

The GanttChartWizard enables you to make changes to several common elements, such as summary task bars or dependency lines. But Project also enables you to format each of these elements separately, and to format them with even more options. You can change the style of many other elements in Project, including:

✦ Text used in your charts

✦ Boxes used in the Network Diagram Chart view

✦ Gridlines displayed in various views

Working with text

You may want to change text to be more readable; some people prefer a larger font, for example, to make views easy to read. Perhaps you want to use boldface for row and column titles or a distinctive font for summary tasks.

Note You format text the same way for any view. You can't format fonts in the Calendar view, but you can format categories of text.

You can make all of these changes and more in Project. You can even change all text in a certain category, or simply change the attributes of a single, selected piece of text in any Project table. For example, you may want to apply boldface to the task name of the milestone Grand Opening, but not to all milestone task names.

Caution The Undo function is not available when you make changes to fonts and other formatting features. You must manually return the text to its original settings if you're unhappy with the change.

Formatting selected text

To format selected text, follow these steps:

1. Move to any view that contains a table of columns (the Gantt Chart, Task Usage, or Resource Sheet views, for example).

2. Click the cell containing the text that you want to format. To format more than one adjacent cell, click the first cell. Then drag your mouse to highlight cells above, below, to the left, or to the right.

3. Choose Format ➪ Font to open the Font dialog box, shown in Figure 8-10. From the three lists across the top of this dialog box, you can select a new font; select a font style such as Italic or Bold (Regular is normal text that has neither italic nor bold applied); or change the font size. Click the Underline checkbox to apply underlining to text, or select a color from the Color drop-down palette. A preview of your selections appears in the Sample area.

4. If you prefer, you can use buttons on the Formatting toolbar to change font and font size or to apply bold, italic, or underline styles. And, you can preview fonts before you select them from the Formatting toolbar, as shown in Figure 8-11.

Figure 8-10: Project uses the standard Windows Font dialog box, so many settings are probably familiar.

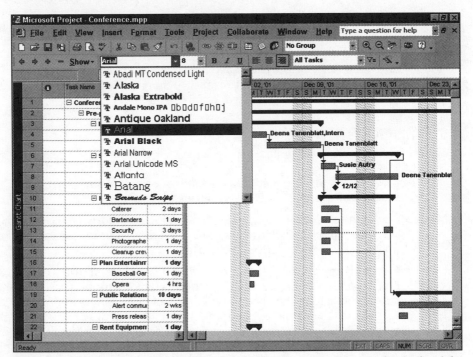

Figure 8-11: When you view the fonts in the Font list box, you see a facsimile of the font as it will appear if you choose it.

5. Click OK to save your changes.

Applying formatting to categories of text

You can use text styles to change the format of text for one cell in a table or to apply a unique format to an entire category of information such as all task names for milestones. Text styles are identical to the formatting options for text described in the preceding section, but you can apply text styles to specific categories of text.

Follow these steps to use text styles to modify text:

1. Choose Format ➪ Text Styles to open the Text Styles dialog box, shown in Figure 8-12.

Figure 8-12: The default in the Item to Change list box is All (that is, all the text in your project schedule).

2. Click the down arrow next to the Item to Change field to display the options. (This field is the only element that distinguishes the Text Styles dialog box from the Font dialog box you saw earlier.)

3. Use the scroll bar to move down the list. You can format text for categories such as row and column titles, summary tasks, tasks on the critical path, and milestones. Click a category to select it.

4. Select the settings that you want for the text, including the font, font size, style, color, and script. When you're done, click OK to apply the formatting.

Using the Items to Change list box, you can format categories of text to add emphasis to certain key items, such as critical tasks and milestones, or to make your schedule more readable by enlarging text or choosing easy-to-read fonts. Figure 8-13 shows a schedule with text styles applied to various elements, such as row and column headings, critical and noncritical tasks, and summary tasks.

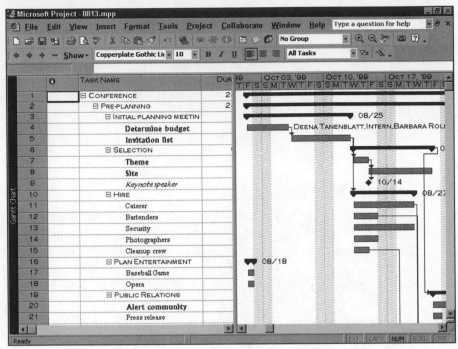

Figure 8-13: Italic font indicates critical tasks; summary tasks are in boldface.

Caution

Good advice bears repeating: Don't go overboard with multiple fonts on a single schedule. You can actually make a project harder to read by using too many fancy fonts. Avoid using more than one or two fonts in your schedule, and vary the text by using bold or italic or by modifying the font size between categories, rather than using many different fonts. Also, try to set up company standards for formatting so that all your project schedules have a consistent, professional look.

Changing taskbars

In addition to changing text styles in your schedule, you can modify the look of the task bars. You considered some of these changes when you used the GanttChartWizard. You can make changes to the shape, pattern, and color of bars, as well as to the style of shape that appears on either end of the taskbar.

Formatting taskbars

Formatting taskbars is similar to formatting text. You can format either an individual taskbar or a category of taskbars, such as milestones or critical tasks. You click a particular task and access the dialog box for formatting just that taskbar by choosing Format ➪ Bar. Alternatively, you can open the dialog box for formatting categories of taskbars by choosing Format ➪ Bar Styles. The actual settings that you can modify are the same either way.

Tip You can open the Format Bar dialog box by right-clicking the bar you want to modify and choosing Format Bar from the shortcut menu. You can open the Bar Styles dialog box by right-clicking a blank spot in the taskbar area of the Gantt Chart and choosing Bar Styles from the shortcut menu that appears.

Figure 8-14 shows the Format Bar dialog box; Figure 8-15 shows the Bar Styles dialog box. The bottom half of the Bar Styles dialog box has two tabbed sheets called Text and Bars. Counterparts to these tabbed sheets appear in the Format Bar dialog box and are called Bar Shape and Bar Text. The Bar Styles dialog box has a table from which you can designate the category of taskbar that you want to modify and the changes that you want to make.

Figure 8-14: You can modify the appearance of an individual taskbar to draw attention to it.

You can use the Bars tab at the bottom of the Bar Styles dialog box to set the shape, type or pattern, and color for the bar and its end shapes, as you did when you used the GanttChartWizard. Use the Text tab to add text to the chart portion of the Gantt Chart view. Follow these steps:

Note You can place text in more locations around a taskbar from the Bar Styles dialog box than you can by using the GanttChartWizard. This dialog box also enables you to place many more pieces of information near taskbars.

Entry bar   Tabs for bar formatting

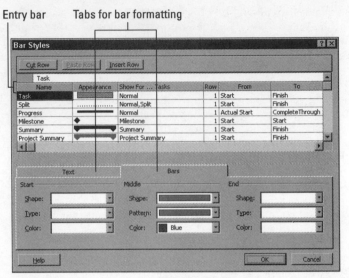

Figure 8-15: Use the Bars tab of the Bar Styles dialog box to change the appearance of an entire category of tasks.

1. Click the Text tab to select the information that you want to display to the left, right, above, below, or inside the selected category of taskbar, as shown in Figure 8-16.

2. Select the Name of the category of taskbar to which you want to add text. If necessary, make changes to the category in the Bar Styles table at the top of the dialog box. Immediately following these steps is an explanation of the type of information that appears in each column of the table.

3. At the bottom of the dialog box, select the location for the text that you want to add. Project displays a list box arrow at the edge of the box.

4. Select the text that you want to appear on the chart portion of the Gantt Chart view for the selected category.

5. Click OK to save your changes.

The columns in the Bar Styles table at the top of the dialog box are as follows:

✦ **Name.** This column specifies the taskbar category. To create a new taskbar category name, click the Insert Row button at the top of the dialog box and type in any name you like. This name appears in a legend for your chart when you print it.

✦ **Appearance.** This column provides a sample of the current formatting settings for the bar.

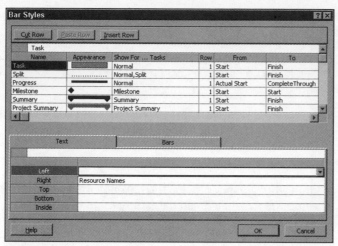

Figure 8-16: Be careful not to place too much information around taskbars or you'll create a cluttered, illegible Gantt Chart.

When you click in any of the next four columns, Project displays a list box arrow at the right edge of the column. Open the list box to identify valid choices for these columns.

✦ **Show For . . . Tasks.** This column defines the types of tasks that the specified formatting affects. You can specify the type of task to affect by selecting the category from a drop-down list or by typing a category name directly in the cell or in the entry bar. If you want to specify more than one category, add a comma (,) after the first type and then select or type a second category. For example, to specify Normal tasks that are critical and in progress as a new category of taskbar style, choose or type one of the following: Normal, Critical, In Progress.

You can type directly in a Bar Styles table cell; you don't need to type in the Entry bar.

✦ **Row.** The Row column specifies how many rows of bars (as many as four) that you want to display for each task. If you have only one row and you are showing a bar for both the baseline timing and progress, the bars overlap each other. If you want two separate bars, you need two rows. You also can add extra rows to accommodate text above or below taskbars.

Tip   If a task fits in several categories, what happens? Project tries to display multiple formatting settings. (For example, if one category is solid blue and the other is a pattern, you get a blue pattern.) If Project can't display the formats together, whichever item is higher in this listing takes over. To modify the formatting precedence, use the Cut Row and Paste Row features to rearrange the rows in the Bar Styles dialog box.

✦ **From and To.** These columns define the time period shown by the bar. The Progress bar, for example, shows the actual date that the task started and the amount of task completed through today. Select the time frames from drop-down lists in each of these fields.

Figure 8-17 shows a schedule with expanded rows; the baseline duration is displayed beneath normal taskbars, and the baseline finish date appears to the right of summary taskbars. To display the expanded rows and the baseline duration beneath normal tasks, I used the settings shown in Figure 8-18. In the top of the dialog box, I changed the Row setting for Task from 1 to 2; in the bottom of the dialog box, on the Text tab, I included Baseline Duration.

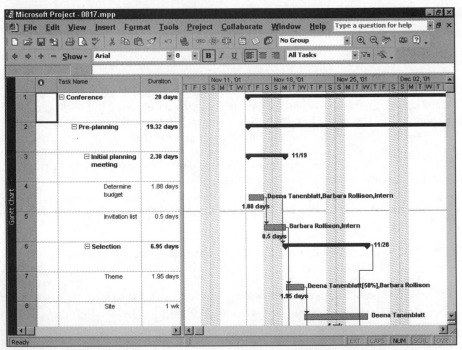

Figure 8-17: Adding rows to each task can make your schedule easier to read.

The settings in the Bar Styles dialog box enable you to modify, in great detail, the appearance of your schedule and how Project displays or prints it. If you print a legend along with your schedule, it reflects these changes. However, remember that modifying taskbar colors won't be of much use in black and white printouts of schedules, and creating too many kinds of formatting with too many variables can make your schedule difficult to read. The advice given previously about standardizing these settings across your organization holds for changes that you make to task bar formatting as well.

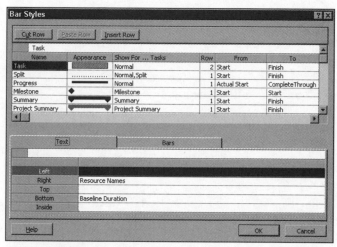

Figure 8-18: In the table, I changed the number of rows for normal tasks. At the bottom of the dialog box, I added Baseline Duration to the bottom row of normal tasks.

Changing the layout of the Gantt Chart

The layout of a Gantt Chart refers to the appearance of link lines, date formats used for information displayed near taskbars, the height of taskbars, and how Project displays certain characteristics of taskbars.

Note

In views other than the Gantt Chart view, layout affects slightly different elements. For example, in the Calendar view, layout affects the order in which Project lists multiple tasks on one calendar day and how it splits date bars. And, as you'll read in the next section, layout in the Network Diagram Chart view affects link lines and how Project handles page breaks.

To modify the layout, choose Format ➪ Layout. In the Gantt Chart view, the Layout dialog box appears, as shown in Figure 8-19.

Caution

If you have a short schedule with many tasks running only hours in length, don't round taskbars to whole days.

Figure 8-19: Because layout affects different elements in different views, the Layout dialog box for the Gantt Chart view is different than the Layout dialog box for the Network Diagram or Calendar views.

Here are the options to set for the Gantt Chart layout:

✦ **Links.** Click one of these option buttons to display either no link lines or to use one of the available styles. Remember, link lines graphically display dependency relationships among tasks. If you want to take a quick look at your schedule with no dependency information showing, use the no link lines choice in this dialog box.

✦ **Date format.** Use this drop-down list to select a date or time format. Two interesting date formats include a week number (W5/5 and W5/5/97 12:33 PM) of the year and the day of the week; therefore, W50/3/99 is December 15, 1999 (the third day of the fiftieth full week of the year 1999).

Be aware that your nation or industry may use conventions for numbering weeks that may result in different week numbers than Project 2000 produces.

✦ **Bar height.** Select a height in points for the bars in your Gantt Chart.

The checkboxes in the Layout dialog box have the following effects:

✦ Always Roll Up Gantt bars. This setting gives you the freedom to display your Gantt schedule by rolling up tasks onto summary bars.

✦ Hide Rollup bars when summary expanded. This checkbox works with the preceding checkbox to hide rollup behavior if your schedule is completely expanded.

See Chapter 6 for more on Project's rollup capabilities.

✦ Round bars to whole days. This option works well on longer schedules, but not as well on schedules with tasks that tend to run in hourly or half-day increments.

✦ Show bar splits. This option provides graphic representation on the Gantt Chart of split tasks.

Note

Split tasks are tasks that start, then stop for a time, and then start again. For example, if you expect to begin hiring employees for the project, but you know that your company imposes a two-week hiring freeze during the last two weeks of the year for accounting purposes, you can create a split task (see Chapter 9). The setting for splits in the Layout dialog box simply enables you to show the split task as separate task bars or one continuous task bar.

✦ Show drawings. If you place a check in this checkbox, Project displays drawings that you've inserted on your chart.

Make any choices in the Layout dialog box, and click OK to implement them.

Changing gridlines

Gridlines are those lines in your Gantt Chart and the Gantt table that mark off periods of time, rows and columns, pages in your schedule, and regular intervals in the chart. In Figure 8-20, gridlines mark off regular intervals across the chart; this format can help you read across the page on a long schedule. Also, the vertical line that marks the current date appears as a dashed line, rather than as the typical small-dotted line that you've seen in other figures in this chapter.

Figure 8-20: Displaying additional gridlines can make a schedule easier to read.

To modify gridlines, choose Format ➪ Gridlines. The dialog box shown in Figure 8-21 appears. In the "Line to change" list, the options Gantt Rows, Sheet Rows, and Sheet Columns enable you to set gridlines at regular intervals. For example, the project in Figure 8-20 has the Gantt Rows set to show at an interval of every four rows. You can change the line type and color only (not the interval) for the other choices in the "Line to change" list. To modify these settings, highlight the kind of line that you want to change and then select the desired settings from the Type and Color drop-down lists.

Figure 8-21: Only a few types of lines can be set at regular intervals.

Tip   If you do make substantial changes in the Gridlines dialog box, consider saving the file as a template for everyone else in your organization to use for their projects. This template not only saves you and your coworkers the effort of repeating the changes but also helps to enforce consistency throughout your organization.

Changing network diagrams

You can format the nodes in a network diagram, and you can control the layout of the network diagram. You can modify the style of text placed in network diagram boxes and control the number of fields per node. You can control the size and the shape of the node and adjust the thickness and color of the line that defines the box.

Formatting network diagram nodes

You can make modifications to the boxes that form the various nodes displayed in the Network Diagram Chart view similar to the way you can format taskbars in the Gantt Chart. You can format the color and line style of the box itself for each type of task. You also can control the number of fields that appear per node, the shape of the node, the horizontal and vertical alignment of text within the node, and the font used in each cell of the node. Use these settings to draw the reader's attention to categories of nodes that you want to emphasize.

Caution

As with task text and taskbars in the Gantt Chart view, you should be careful about keeping track of changes you make: The Undo feature doesn't work here. Project has its own color and line scheme for various types of tasks, and you run the risk of formatting one category to look just like another category by mistake. Because interpreting the information in a Project chart is so key to success, be very careful about changing formatting defaults.

Modifying node box styles

You can change the formatting of network diagram boxes individually, or you can change the formatting of a particular category of boxes. To change an individual box, select the box in the network diagram and choose Format ⇨ Box to display the dialog box shown in Figure 8-22.

Figure 8-22: To modify the appearance of a single box in the network diagram, use this dialog box.

Use the Shape box to select 1 of 10 shapes for the box; similarly, use the Color box to identify the color for the lines of the box and the Width box to specify the width of the box's border. You also can set the Background color and pattern for the node. Make changes and watch the Preview to determine the affects of your changes. When you finish, click OK to save the changes.

To format a category of box, such as all Critical Milestones, use the Box Styles dialog box shown in Figure 8-23. You can display this dialog box by choosing Format ⇨ Box Styles.

Figure 8-23: Use this dialog box to select a category of box to format.

Select the type of box that you want to format from the "Style settings for" list. The current settings for the box appear in the Preview. The rest of the options in this dialog box are the same as the options in the Format Box dialog box, except for the Set highlight filter style checkbox. You can filter information on the network diagram, as you learned in Chapter 7. Placing a check in the Set highlight filter style checkbox enables you to set the color Project uses when filtering tasks on the network diagram.

Tip   You should make the Name one of the pieces of information you display. Otherwise, the flow of tasks in the network diagram chart is nearly incomprehensible.

Formatting fields that appear on nodes

Network diagram nodes display the following information by default: Task Name, Duration, ID, Start and Finish dates, Percent Complete, and Resource Name, if assigned. However, you can display up to 16 pieces of information. For example, to focus on costs in today's staff meeting, change the network diagram node information to Task Name, Baseline Cost, Actual Cost, Actual Overtime Cost, and Cost Variance. If your manager wants a network diagram chart report so that he or she can see whether the project schedule is on track, change this information to Task Name, Critical, Free Slack, Early Finish, and Late Finish.

Caution   Although you can specify up to 16 pieces of information, beware of information overload. Providing too much information on a node will make the network diagram difficult to read and evaluate and your reader will miss your point.

Starting in Project 2002, you can include indicators and custom fields in network diagram nodes.

To modify the appearance of the information in a node, you can change the information included in a node, the font used to display the information, and the horizontal and vertical alignment of the information. Follow these steps:

1. Open either the Format Box or Box Styles dialog box.

2. Click the More Templates button. Project displays the Data Templates dialog box shown in Figure 8-24.

Figure 8-24: Select a template to modify or copy, or create a new template.

 A template contains previously established node format settings.

3. Highlight the template that you want to change and click the Edit button. Alternatively, you can create a new template by clicking the New button, or you can copy an existing template and make changes to the copy by clicking the Copy button. For this exercise, I'll copy the Standard template by clicking the Copy button. Regardless of the button that you click, Project displays the Data Template Definition dialog box shown in Figure 8-25.

 The picture at the top of the dialog box provides a preview of the current structure of the cell. In the figure, the node contains eight cells — two on each row and four in each column. Blank cells (one each in the top and bottom rows) are merged with nonblank cells.

Click here to change the contents of the cells in the node

Figure 8-25: Use this dialog box to change the information you show in network diagram nodes.

4. To change the contents of a cell of the node, click the corresponding cell in the middle of the dialog box. A list box arrow appears to the right of the cell; open the list box to select a new field for the selected cell.

5. To change the font for a particular cell, select that cell and click the Font button. A dialog box appears, from which you can select a new font, the font size, and font attributes, such as boldface or italics.

6. Use the Horizontal and Vertical alignment list boxes to change the alignment of text within its cell.

7. Use the "Limit cell text to" list box to specify the number of lines for each cell; a cell can be as many as three lines.

8. Click the "Show label in cell" checkbox to include an identifier in the cell for the type of information. For example, if you select the cell containing "Name" and then click the "Show label in cell" checkbox, the title of the task will contain "Name:" followed by the title of the task.

9. To increase or decrease the number of cells in the node, click the Cell Layout button to display the dialog box shown in Figure 8-26. From this dialog box, specify the number of cells for all nodes. After you click OK, Project redisplays the Data Template Definition dialog box with the appropriate number of cells available for formatting.

Figure 8-26: Use this dialog box to change the number of cells in a node.

10. Click OK to close the Data Template Definition dialog box; click Close to close the Data Templates window, and click OK to close the Box Styles dialog box.

Changing the layout of the network diagram

The layout controls available for the network diagram starting in Project 2000 have increased significantly over those previously available for the PERT chart available in Project 98 and earlier. As Figure 8-27 demonstrates, you can control the layout mode, the box arrangement, the link style and color, and several overall options for the network diagram.

Figure 8-27: You can control layout mode, box arrangement, and link style for the network diagram.

By default, Project automatically positions all boxes on the diagram, but you can choose to manually position the boxes.

Using the Arrangement list box, you can change the order in which Project displays the boxes. Choose from Top Down From Left, Top Down By Day, Top Down By Week, Top Down By Month, Top Down — Critical First, Centered From Left, and Centered From Top. The varying arrangements change the number of pages required to print your network diagram.

You also can change the row and column alignment and spacing, as well as row height and column width. Using checkboxes in the Box Layout section, you can hide or display summary tasks, keep tasks with their summaries, and adjust for page breaks.

You can control the style of the link lines, and you can choose to show arrows and link labels, which, by default, show the type of link dependency that exists between two tasks (Finish-to-Start, Finish-to-Finish, and so on). And, you can select different colors for both critical and noncritical links.

For more information on types of links, see Chapter 4.

For the network diagram as a whole (not the individual nodes) you can choose a background color and pattern. You also can mark in-progress tasks with half an X and completed tasks with an entire X. If you hide all information on the nodes except the ID, Project reduces the size of the nodes on your network diagram and therefore reduces the number of pages that will print. You can also choose to show page breaks, which appear as dotted lines onscreen in the network diagram view. In Figure 8-28, I've included link labels and hidden all task information except the ID. A page break appears at the right side of the diagram (not shown in the figure).

Remember, creating too many kinds of formatting with too many variables can make your schedule difficult to read. The advice given previously in this chapter about standardizing these settings across your organization holds for changes that you make to network diagram layouts as well.

Formatting the Calendar view

As I mentioned earlier in the chapter, you format text in the Calendar view the same way that you format text in any other view. Although you can't format the text of individual items in the Calendar view, you can use the Text Styles dialog box as described previously in this chapter to format categories of text.

In the Calendar view, you can format bar styles and you can change the layout of the calendar. This section explores those types of changes.

Figure 8-28: By adjusting the layout of the network diagram, you can dramatically change its appearance.

Formatting the Calendar entries

When you display the Calendar view, by default, entries appear in boxes that Project calls bars. You can, if you prefer, change the style of these bars. For example, you can make all critical tasks appear on the Calendar in red. Choose Format ➪ Bar Styles in the Calendar view to display the dialog box shown in Figure 8-29. Select a type of task from the list on the left. As you make changes in the Bar shape area and the Text area, watch the Sample at the bottom of the box for the effects of your changes.

In the Bar shape area, use the Bar type box to change display tasks using a Line, a Bar, or None — choosing None "hides" the selected task type from the Calendar view. If you choose Bar from the Bar type box, open the Pattern list box and select a pattern, which appears inside the box for the task type. If you want, choose a pattern for Project to display between split tasks from the Split pattern box. Place a check in the Shadow box to display a shadow behind a bar (this option is available only if you choose Bar from the Bar type box).

Figure 8-29: Use this dialog box to change the appearance of the Calendar view. Add different colors for different task types, or use a line instead of a box to represent the task's duration.

Place a check in the Bar rounding box to tell Project to draw the bar for tasks that take less than one day so that the task's duration is implied. For example, use bar rounding to tell Project to draw a bar that extends three-quarters of the width of the day to represent a task that takes .75 days. If you don't use bar rounding, Project doesn't try to imply the duration of the task by the length of the bar.

In the Text area, you can include Project fields for each task type; to include more than one field, separate fields with a comma (refer to Figure 8-29). Align the text with the bar or line using the Align list box. If you chose Bar as the Bar type, you can place a check in the Wrap text in bars checkbox; when you place a check in this box, Project wraps text so that it fits within the box. For example, if you show the task name and duration in the box, and the task name is fairly long but the task lasts only one day, Project will wrap the text so that the task takes more than one row when it appears on the calendar. You'll be able to read all displayed information about every task. If you don't place a check in the Wrap text in bars box, Project displays only as much information as it can fit in a box sized to match the task's duration. In the example just described, you may not see the entire task name, and you certainly won't see the task duration because the box will span only one day.

Changing the Calendar layout

Use the Layout dialog box, shown in Figure 8-30, to change the layout of tasks on the Calendar view. By default, Project displays tasks in the Calendar view using the current sorted order of tasks.

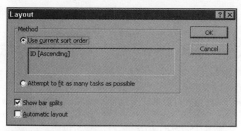

Figure 8-30: Use the Layout dialog box to change the way Project presents tasks in the Calendar view.

Cross-Reference You can read about sorting tasks in Chapter 7.

If you don't want tasks to appear in the Calendar view using the currently sorted order, choose the "Attempt to fit as many tasks as possible" option button. Project sorts tasks by Total Slack and then by Duration to try to fit the maximum number of tasks into the rows for a week without overlapping bars.

Remove the check from the Show bar splits checkbox to hide the designation for split tasks from the Calendar view. Place a check in the Automatic layout checkbox to have Project automatically adjust the Calendar view to accommodate new tasks that you add or tasks that you delete.

Inserting Drawings and Objects

We're living in the age of multimedia and MTV. Visual elements have a way of getting a message across that simple text often can't match. Statistics show that 75 percent of the world learns visually. In Project, you can insert graphic images (photos, illustrations, or diagrams, for example) in four places:

✦ In a Gantt Chart, in the taskbar area

✦ In notes (task, resource, or assignment)

✦ In headers, footers, and chart legends

✦ In resource or task forms

You also can copy your Project schedule into other Office products.

Copying pictures

Suppose that you've written a report in Microsoft Word and you would *really* like to include your Gantt Chart in the report. You can print it on a separate page, but you can also insert it as a picture in the appropriate place in your Word document. Or, suppose that you want to post a picture of your Project schedule on the Web. You can easily create a picture for either of these purposes.

Using the Copy Picture command, you can copy your Project schedule to the Windows Clipboard and then paste it into any application as a graphic image. Click the Copy Picture button on the Standard toolbar or choose Edit ➪ Copy Picture. The dialog box shown in Figure 8-31 appears. To copy the picture to the Clipboard, select the "For screen" option button in the Render image section and click OK. If the image you're copying will fit well into another document, Project simply copies the picture to the Windows Clipboard. But, if the picture you are copying is particularly large, Project warns you and displays a dialog box that gives you the opportunity to scale the picture before saving or pasting.

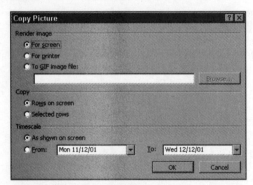

Figure 8-31: Choose "For screen" to copy a Project schedule to the Windows Clipboard.

After you've copied the picture, simply switch to the other document in which you want to place the picture and click the Paste button in that document. Figure 8-32 shows a Gantt Chart in Word.

When you use the Paste button, you place a graphic in your document; the graphic is not linked to Project in any way, so, from the program where you pasted the chart, you cannot:

✦ Edit the chart to make scheduling changes

✦ Double-click the image to open the chart in Project

Note   Even if you choose the Paste Special command, the image you copied from Project is exactly that — an image. It is not a Project file that you can link to from another application.

Figure 8-32: After you use the Copy Picture command to render an image for the screen, you can paste the image into any document.

To create a graphic image file that you can use on a Web page or in a document, select the To GIF image file option in the Copy Picture dialog box (shown previously in Figure 8-31). When you choose to render the image for a printer, Project copies the image to the Windows Clipboard but formats the image using your printer driver; if your printer is a black-and-white printer, the image will appear in shades of gray rather than the colors you see onscreen, like the one you see in Figure 8-33. If your printer is a color printer, the image will appear in color like it looks onscreen. You can view the image in the Clipboard Viewer applet that comes with Windows (refer to Figure 8-33) or you can copy it into another application.

Using visuals in schedules

Because project management is often a serious, information-oriented business, you don't want to overdo the visuals. Remember, both the Gantt Chart and the network diagram are visuals. And, pictures of bunnies and curly doodads aren't likely to sit well with the head of your engineering division. However, used judiciously, images can reinforce the information about your project and lend a professional look to your reports.

Figure 8-33: When you render the picture for a printer, Project places a "black and white" image of your project on the Windows Clipboard.

Consider using graphics in the following ways:

✦ Add a company logo to the header of your schedule so that it appears at the top of every page.

✦ Add a photograph of each of your key resources in their resource note. The photo helps you get to know all the team members on a large-scale project so that you can address them by name in meetings and in the hallway.

✦ If a particular task involves a schematic or diagram of a product, place a copy of the diagram in the task notes for reference.

 Placing graphics in a schedule can take up a big chunk of memory, making your file larger and possibly making calculation time longer; for this reason, use graphics on an as-needed basis.

✦ If your schedule has a key milestone, place a graphic suggesting success or accomplishment next to the milestone in the Gantt Chart. Every time you review your schedule with your team, you'll subconsciously focus on that goal and how close you're getting to it, which can boost morale.

 Graphic objects come in a variety of file formats, depending on the type of graphic and the program in which it was created. You can use scanned images, photo files, illustrations such as clip art, a chart you've created in a program such as Excel, a Word for Windows table, and even a video clip. Look on the Internet for sources for graphics files, or use the images available to the Microsoft Office family products.

Inserting visual objects

To insert an object into a header, footer, or legend, choose File ➪ Page Setup and click the appropriate tab. Use the Insert Picture button to open a dialog box that enables you to select a picture file to insert. For task notes, double-click the task to open the Task Information dialog box, select the Notes tab, and use the Insert Object button to insert a file.

Suppose, for example, that you've got an Excel worksheet that provides information you need for a budgeting task. You can insert the worksheet data on the Notes tab of the Task Information dialog box for the budgeting task. Follow these steps:

1. Double-click the task with which you want to associate the worksheet.

2. Click the Notes tab.

3. Click the Insert Object button. The Insert Object dialog box appears, as shown in Figure 8-34.

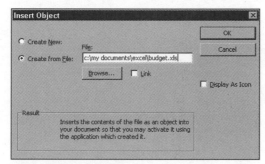

Figure 8-34: Select the file that you want to associate with a task.

4. Click the Create from File option.

5. Click the Browse button to select the worksheet.

6. Click the OK button. The worksheet information appears as a graphic on the Notes tab, as shown in Figure 8-35.

Suppose instead that you want to see a chart of the information on the Notes tab; logically, you create the chart on the worksheet and then try the preceding steps and get the entire worksheet — both numbers and chart. To place *just* the chart on the Notes tab, follow these steps:

1. Select the chart in Excel and click the Copy button to copy it to the Clipboard.

2. Switch to Project.

3. Open the Task Information dialog box for the appropriate task.

4. Click the Notes tab

5. Click the Paste button in Project. The chart alone appears on the Notes tab, as shown in Figure 8-36.

Tip   You can place any image directly on the Gantt Chart; don't open the Task Information dialog box. Instead, copy the image to the Clipboard and, after you switch to Project, click the Paste button.

Insert Object button

Figure 8-35: The information in the file appears as a graphic object on the Notes tab of the Task Information dialog box.

Note   If you are using a version of Office older than Office XP, you can use the Microsoft Clip Gallery to practice placing a graphic in a Project file. Clip art is a collection of line drawings in various styles. These images come in assorted categories, such as Business, Maps, Office, and Transportation. With Office XP, Microsoft made major changes to the way the Clip Gallery works; to use a clip from the Clip Gallery in Project, you will first need to insert the clip into an Office XP program and then copy it to the Windows Clipboard. Once the image resides on the Clipboard, you can copy it into Project as previously described.

Figure 8-36: You can copy any image you place on the Windows Clipboard into Project.

Using the Drawing toolbar

Project has a drawing feature that you can use to build simple diagrams or add shapes or text boxes to the Gantt Chart area of your Project file. For example, you may want to draw a circle around an important taskbar in your schedule to draw attention to it in a presentation. Or, suppose that you want to suggest cutting a task from the project; you may want to draw an X through the task to make your point, as shown in Figure 8-37. The formatting methods you learned earlier in this chapter enable you to create settings so that predefined information appears next to taskbars in your schedule. However, you must use the Drawing Text Box tool to enter your own text.

Figure 8-37: Consider using this type of drawing to display a project onscreen using an LCD panel, or at a trade show.

To display the Drawing toolbar shown in Figure 8-38, you can choose either View ➪ Toolbars and select the Drawing toolbar for display, or choose Insert ➪ Drawing.

Figure 8-38: The Drawing toolbar is a floating toolbar; drag it up near the Formatting toolbar if you want to dock it at the top of your screen, or click the dark blue bar at the top and drag to move it around your screen.

Here's how you can use the tools on the Drawing toolbar:

✦ To draw an object, click the Line, Arrow, Rectangle, Oval, Arc, or Polygon buttons and then click the taskbar area of the Gantt Chart. Holding down your mouse button, drag to draw the shape. When using the Polygon tool, you need to draw several segments to define the multisided shape, clicking at the end of each segment. To complete the polygon, double-click at the end of the last segment. With all the other tools, the shape appears automatically when you drag in one direction and release your mouse button.

✦ To create text anywhere around your taskbar, click the Text Box button and drag to draw a box. Your insertion point appears in the box whenever you select the box; you can type any text you like.

✦ To fill an object with color, click the Cycle Fill Color button on the Drawing toolbar repeatedly until you see the color that you want.

✦ To anchor a drawing object in the Gantt Chart to a particular task bar — so that if you move the task in the schedule the graphic moves with it — select the object and click the Attach to Task button on the Drawing toolbar. Click the Attach to task control button in the Format Drawing dialog box, shown in Figure 8-39, enter a task ID number, and enter the settings for the point on the taskbar at which you want to attach the object. Then click OK. (You can reach the Format Drawing dialog box at any time by choosing Format ➪ Drawing ➪ Properties.)

Tip   You can also use three tools on the Drawing toolbar with other types of graphic objects that you insert. The Draw, Cycle Fill Color, and Attach to Task buttons work with any selected object, such as clip art.

When you no longer need the Drawing toolbar, click the Close button in the upper-right corner to remove it.

Figure 8-39: You can also attach a graphic to a position on the timescale, rather than attaching it to a particular task. Place a graphic at a particular date on the timescale, for example.

Modifying graphics and drawings

You can also use the Format Drawing dialog box to format graphic object styles. To open this dialog box, right-click any object and choose Properties from the shortcut menu. You'll see the Size & Position tab initially, as shown in Figure 8-40. Click the Line & Fill tab to see the choices shown in the figure.

Use the Color and Line drop-down options on the left to assign a style of thickness and color to lines. Use the Fill Color and Pattern options to place a color and pattern, such as solid or thatched lines, inside an object.

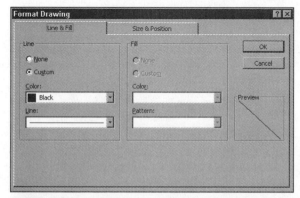

Figure 8-40: Rather than cycling through fill colors by using the button on the Drawing toolbar, you can select a fill color from a drop-down palette in the Line & Fill tab of the Format Drawing dialog box.

Tip   Fill color and pattern fill the inside of a drawn object and the background area of a clip art or other pre-drawn graphic object. The Preview box shown in Figure 8-40 demonstrates how a fill pattern surrounds the clip art object — filling the background of the object, rather than filling the object itself.

Resizing and moving drawings and other objects is similar to working with objects in other programs:

✦ **To resize an object.** Click the object to select it. Click any of the eight selection handles; drag inward to make the object smaller or drag outward to make the object larger.

✦ **To move an object.** Move your mouse pointer over the object until your cursor changes to four arrows. Click the object, hold down your mouse button, and drag the object anywhere in the Gantt Chart area. Release the mouse button to place the object.

Summary

In this chapter, you learned many ways to:

✦ Format text for individual selections or globally by category of task

✦ Format taskbars and the information displayed near them

✦ Format network diagram boxes and change the information that you display in the Network Diagram view

✦ Change the layout options for Gantt Chart taskbars and network diagram nodes

✦ Add gridlines to the Gantt Chart view

✦ Insert graphic objects and drawings in the Gantt Chart and in notes, or as a header and footer

Chapter 9 explains how to fine-tune timing to resolve scheduling conflicts.

✦   ✦   ✦

Resolving Scheduling Problems

Scheduling conflicts are the bane of the project manager's existence. Scheduling conflicts typically fall into two categories:

+ Your project is taking longer than you had planned.

+ Your resources are over-assigned.

This chapter considers the first problem and focuses on identifying and then resolving scheduling problems; Chapter 10 focuses on the second problem.

Scheduling conflicts announce themselves in a number of ways. Changing views and filtering information by using the techniques described in Chapters 6 and 7 may identify some glaring problem inherent in your original logic. For example, if you filter your project to view only incomplete tasks or slipping tasks, you may spot some problems. More likely, however, you'll unknowingly create a problem by using a *task constraint*, which is explained in the next section.

Resolving Scheduling Conflicts

Project provides several techniques that you can use to resolve scheduling conflicts. This section covers the following strategies:

+ Adding resources

+ Using overtime

+ Adding time

+ Adjusting slack

✦ Changing constraints

✦ Adjusting dependencies

✦ Splitting a task

Adding resources to tasks

Adding resources to a task can decrease the time necessary to complete the task. On the Advanced tab of the Task Information dialog box, which is shown in Figure 9-1, set the task type to Fixed Units. In this instance, adding resources to the task reduces the duration of the task. Also remember that a check appears by default in the Effort driven checkbox of the Task Information dialog box. When you use the Effort driven option, Project reallocates the work among the assigned resources.

Figure 9-1: The Advanced tab of the Task Information dialog box controls the task type and whether the task is effort driven.

Using overtime

In the best of all possible worlds, you have unlimited resources and you can add resources to resolve scheduling problems. After giving yourself a reality check, though, you'll discover that you don't have unlimited resources, and adding resources may not be an option. But you may be able to use overtime to shorten a task's duration, which is the next strategy that you can use to resolve scheduling problems.

Cross-Reference For information on resolving resource conflicts, see Chapter 10.

Overtime in Project is defined as the amount of work scheduled beyond an assigned resource's regular working hours. Overtime hours are charged at the resource's overtime rate. Overtime work does not represent additional work on a task; instead, it represents the amount of time spent on a task outside regular hours. For example, if you assign 30 hours of work and 12 hours of overtime, the total work is still 30 hours. Of the 30 hours, 18 hours are worked during the regular work schedule (and charged to the project at the regular rate), and 12 hours are worked during off hours (and charged to the project at an overtime rate). Therefore, you can use overtime to shorten the time that a resource takes to complete a task.

To enter overtime, follow these steps:

1. Select the Gantt Chart view from the View bar.

2. Choose Window ➪ Split to reveal the Task Form in the bottom pane.

3. Click the Task Form to make it the active pane.

4. Choose Format ➪ Details ➪ Resource Work. Project adds the Ovt. Work column to the Task form, as shown in Figure 9-2.

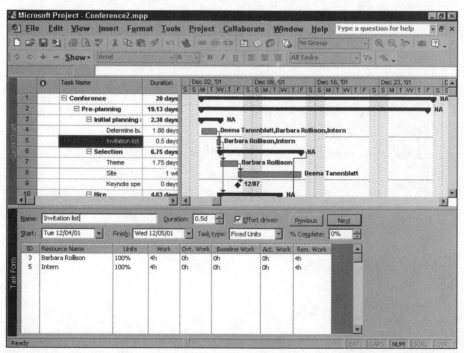

Figure 9-2: Use the Task form and display the Overtime (Ovt. Work) column to add overtime.

5. Move to the top pane and select the task to which you want to assign overtime.

6. Move to the bottom pane and fill in the overtime amount for the appropriate resource.

Tip   After you finish entering overtime, you can hide the Task form by choosing Window ➪ Remove Split.

Adding time to tasks

You can also solve scheduling conflicts by increasing the duration of a task. Again, in the best of all possible worlds, you have this luxury. In reality, you may not. But if you can increase the duration of a task, you may find that once-scarce resources are now available to complete the task — given its new timing.

As you know, you can change the duration from several different views, such as the Task Usage view or the Gantt Chart view. You can also use the Task Information dialog box to complete this task, as shown in Figure 9-3. To open the Task Information dialog box, double-click the task and use the Duration box to change the duration.

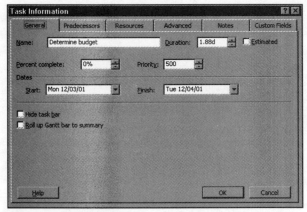

Figure 9-3: Change the duration from the Task Information dialog box.

Adjusting slack

Slack time is the amount of time that a task can slip before it affects another task's dates or the finish date of the project. *Free slack* is the amount of time that a task can be delayed without delaying any other task. Most projects contain *noncritical tasks with slack* — these tasks can start late without affecting the schedule. If you have slack in your schedule, you may be able to move tasks around to balance phases of the schedule that have no slack with phases that have too much slack. Therefore, you can use tasks with slack to compensate for tasks that take longer than planned or to help resolve over-assignment of resources.

Note   Slack values can also help you identify inconsistencies in the schedule. For example, you'll see a negative slack value when one task has a finish-to-start dependency with a second task, but the second task has a Must Start On constraint that is earlier than the end of the first task.

Almost by definition, you create slack time if you use the Must Start On constraint when you create your task. As you learned in Chapter 4, you set constraints on the Advanced tab of the Task Information dialog box, as shown in Figure 9-4. To display the Task Information dialog box, double-click the task in your schedule. When the dialog box appears, select the Advanced tab.

Figure 9-4: Constraints can often create slack time.

To avoid creating slack time, use the As Soon As Possible constraint whenever possible. To find tasks with slack time, follow these steps:

1. Choose View ➪ More Views to open the More Views dialog box.

2. Select Detail Gantt from the list, and then click Apply.

Tip   You can identify slack on the Gantt bars. Slack appears as thin lines extending from the regular Gantt bars.

3. Right-click the Select All button and select Schedule from the list of tables.

4. Drag the divider bar to the right to view more of the table. Now you can see the Free Slack and Total Slack fields, as shown in Figure 9-5.

Figure 9-5: You can find slack time on tasks by using the Detail Gantt view and the Schedule table.

Changing task constraints

Task constraints are the usual culprits when projects fall behind schedule. By default, Project uses the Planning Wizard to warn you when you are about to take an action that is likely to throw your project off schedule. For example, if you impose a Must Start On task constraint on a task with no slack time and with other tasks linked to it, Project displays the Planning Wizard dialog box, as shown in Figure 9-6.

Figure 9-6: The Planning Wizard appears by default when you apply a constraint that is likely to lengthen your project schedule.

Similarly, if you impose an illogical start date on a task when recording actual dates, Project displays a Planning Wizard dialog box that resembles the one shown in Figure 9-7. For example, you'll see a Planning Wizard dialog box if you accidentally enter a start date for Task 4 that is earlier than Task 3, and Task 4 is linked to and succeeds Task 3.

Figure 9-7: The Planning Wizard also warns you if you try to record a start date that will cause a scheduling conflict.

Notice that you can turn off the Planning Wizard warnings by placing a check in the Don't Tell Me About This Again checkbox at the bottom of the Planning Wizard dialog box. (Some people just don't like to have wizards popping up all the time.)

If you turn off the Planning Wizard, Project still warns you if you take actions that cause scheduling problems. Instead of the Planning Wizard, Project displays a more traditional message, as shown in Figure 9-8.

Figure 9-8: When you disable the Planning Wizard and take an action that may cause a scheduling problem, Project displays this warning message.

The message shown in Figure 9-8 refers to the Invitation List task, which is the predecessor task of the Theme task, as you can see in Figure 9-2. Project makes suggestions concerning actions that you can take to avoid the conflict — these suggestions all refer to the predecessor task. Notice also that, unlike the Planning Wizard, this message box does not give you the option of canceling your action.

So, although you may find the Planning Wizard annoying at some levels, it can actually save you effort at other levels. Sorry that you turned it off? To turn it on again, choose Tools ⇨ Options and click the General tab, as shown in Figure 9-9.

Figure 9-9: You can control whether the Planning Wizard appears from the General tab in the Options dialog box.

Place a check in the Advice from Planning Wizard checkbox, and then click the Advice About Errors checkbox to place a check in it. (You also can control the other types of advice that you receive in the same location.)

Adjusting dependencies

By changing task dependencies, you can tighten up the schedule and eliminate scheduling conflicts. If you inadvertently link tasks that don't need to be linked, you may possibly create a situation in which you don't have the resources to complete the tasks and as a result, the project schedule falls behind. If you discover unnecessary links, you can remove them. When you remove the dependencies, you may find holes in the project schedule where work can be performed but isn't. After you remove unnecessary dependencies, you may be able to move tasks around and fill those holes.

Reviewing dependencies is easiest if you use the Relationship Diagram view in the bottom pane of the Gantt view, as shown in Figure 9-10. The Relationship Diagram view shows you the selected task and its immediate predecessor and successor.

1. Choose Window ➪ Split.

2. Click the bottom pane.

3. Choose View ➪ More Views.

4. Select Relationship Diagram from the More Views window and click Apply.

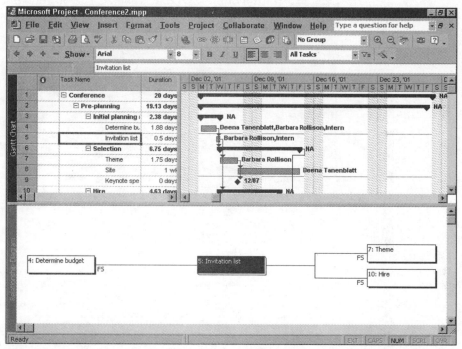

Figure 9-10: Use the Relationship Diagram view to review task dependencies.

Click each task in your project to review its dependencies. As you review the tasks, ask yourself the following questions:

✦ Do I really need to complete A before B begins?

✦ Could I perform them concurrently?

✦ Could I do one of them later without harming the project?

Splitting a task

Splitting a task can sometimes be the best way to resolve a scheduling conflict. You may not be able to complete the task on consecutive days, but you can start the task, stop work on it for a period of time, and then come back to the task. Project enables you to split a task any time you determine that you need to make this type of adjustment. Remember that splitting a task creates a gap, which you'll see in the task's Gantt bar. Follow these steps to split a task:

1. Switch to the Gantt Chart view.

2. Click the Split Task button on the Standard toolbar. The button appears to be pressed, the mouse pointer changes shape, and a screen tip tells you how to split a task, as shown in Figure 9-11.

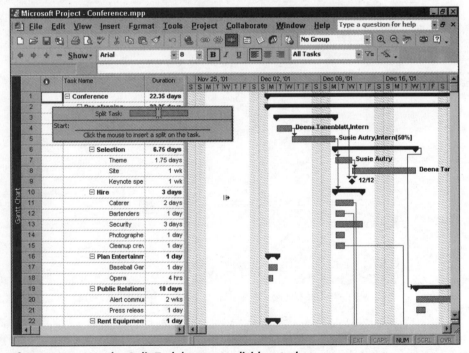

Figure 9-11: Use the Split Task button to divide a task.

3. Move the mouse pointer along the bar of the task that you want to split. As the mouse pointer moves, dates representing the split date appear in the screen tip.

4. Click when the screen tip shows the date on which you want to split the task; Project inserts a one-day split.

Tip   If you want the split to last longer than one day, drag to the right instead of clicking.

After you split a task, it will look similar to Task 8, as shown in Figure 9-12, with dotted lines appearing between the two portions of the split. If you decide that you want to remove a split, drag the inside portions of the split together so that they touch.

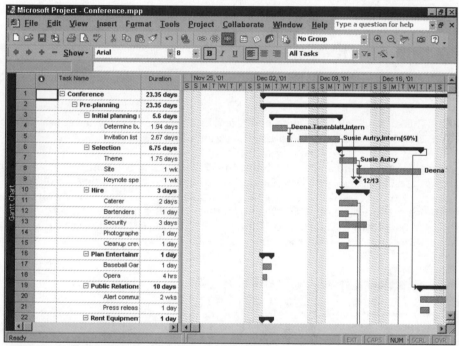

Figure 9-12: This Gantt Chart shows a split task.

Using the Critical Path to Shorten a Project

Earlier in this chapter, you examined ways to resolve the scheduling conflicts that develop for one reason or another. But what about simply shortening the time frame that you originally allotted for the entire project, and thus becoming a hero? How would you accomplish that goal? You'd evaluate — and try to shorten — the critical path.

The *critical path* shows the tasks in your project that must be completed on schedule in order for the entire project to finish on schedule — and these tasks are called *critical tasks*. Most tasks in a project have some slack, and you can delay them some without affecting the project finish date. However, if you delay critical tasks, you affect the project finish date. As you use the techniques described earlier in this chapter to modify tasks to resolve scheduling problems, be aware that changes to critical tasks will affect your project finish date.

Note   Noncritical tasks can become critical if they slip too much. You can control how much slack that Project allows for a task before defining the task as a critical task. Choose Tools ➪ Options and then click the Calculation tab. In the box labeled "Tasks are critical if slack is less than or equal to," at the bottom of the tab, enter the number of slack days.

Identifying the critical path

You'll see the critical path best if you use the GanttChartWizard to display the critical path in red.

Cross-Reference   This discussion of the GanttChartWizard focuses on displaying the critical path; see Chapter 8 for a more complete description of that wizard.

Open the View menu and select Gantt Chart. Then click the GanttChartWizard button on the Formatting toolbar (second button from the right edge) or choose Format ➪ GanttChartWizard. The first GanttChartWizard dialog box welcomes you to the GanttChartWizard. Click Next to move on to the next GanttChartWizard dialog box, as shown in Figure 9-13. Then select Critical path to describe the kind of information that you want to display on the Gantt Chart.

Figure 9-13: Select Critical path when you run the GanttChartWizard.

Subsequent dialog boxes in the GanttChartWizard enable you to select other types of information to display, such as resources and dates on Gantt bars and links between dependent tasks. All other choices that you make while running the GanttChartWizard are a matter of personal preference; when you finish, click the Format It button, and then click the Exit Wizard button.

When you view the Gantt Chart, all tasks in the project still appear, but tasks on the critical path appear in red.

Note

After you use the GanttChartWizard, you can switch to any view and critical tasks will appear in red. Try the Network Diagram view, for example; the critical tasks appear in red boxes.

If you prefer, you can use formatting to identify critical tasks. When you apply formatting to critical and noncritical tasks, this formatting appears on all views in which you can see taskbars. The formatting identifies critical tasks with a "Yes" in or near the bar of the tasks and noncritical tasks with a "No."

To apply formatting, follow these steps:

1. Display the Gantt Chart view.

2. Choose Format ➪ Bar Styles; Project displays the Bar Styles dialog box.

3. Select Task from the list at the top of the Bar Styles dialog box to apply formatting to noncritical tasks.

4. Click the Text tab at the bottom of the dialog box.

5. Select a position for the formatting: Left, Right, Top, Bottom, or Inside. When you click a position, a list box arrow appears.

6. Click the list box arrow and scroll to select Critical, as shown in Figure 9-14.

7. Click OK.

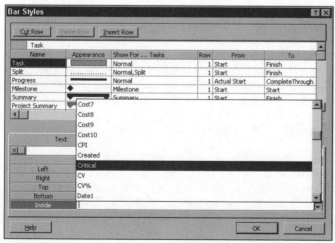

Figure 9-14: Use the Text tab of the Bar Styles dialog box to apply formatting that distinguishes critical from noncritical tasks.

After you apply the formatting, the Gantt Chart shows critical and noncritical tasks, as shown in Figure 9-15. Because I placed "critical" information inside task bars, "No" appears inside noncritical tasks, and "Yes" appears inside critical tasks.

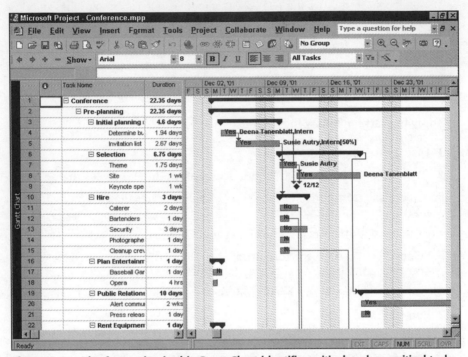

Figure 9-15: The formatting in this Gantt Chart identifies critical and noncritical tasks.

Even with formatting, this approach to identifying the critical path can be cumbersome if your project contains many tasks. Alternatively, you can identify the critical path by filtering for it. As Chapter 7 explains, you can apply the Critical filter to any task view to display only critical tasks, as shown in Figure 9-16. To apply the filter, display the view that you want to filter and choose Project ➪ Filtered for ➪ Critical or choose Critical from the Filter list box on the Formatting toolbar.

Tip   Filtering is a very effective tool to display only certain aspects of the project, but sometimes you need to view all the tasks in your project and still identify the critical ones. If you use formatting (your own or the formatting that is supplied by the GanttChartWizard), you can always identify critical and noncritical tasks — even if you are viewing all the tasks in your project.

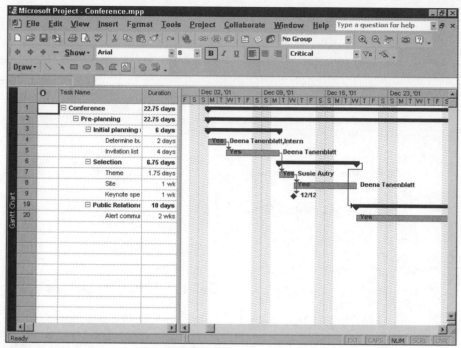

Figure 9-16: Filter to display only critical tasks.

Shortening the critical path

Shortening the time allotted on the critical path shortens your project's duration. The converse is also true; lengthening the time allotted on the critical path lengthens the project. In all probability, you, as the project manager, are also responsible (at least to some extent) for the cost of a project. Typically, the longer a project goes on, the more it costs. Therefore, shortening the critical path is often the project manager's goal.

Shortening a project's duration can result in an earlier finish. But it also can mean starting later. Obviously, the second alternative is riskier, particularly if you are not confident in your estimates. If you are new to project management, you probably should not plan to start later; instead, use project management tools to help you evaluate the accuracy of your estimating skills. Over time (and multiple projects), you'll know how accurate your estimates are and then you can take the risk of starting a project later than initially planned.

To reduce the time allotted on the critical path, you can:

✦ Reduce the duration of critical tasks

✦ Overlap critical tasks to reduce the overall project duration

To reduce the duration of critical tasks, you can:

✦ Reassess estimates and use a more optimistic task time. The PERT Analysis views can help you here.

✦ Add resources to a critical task. Remember, however, that the task must not be a fixed-duration task — adding resources to a fixed-duration task does not reduce the time of the task.

✦ Add overtime to a critical task.

To overlap critical tasks, you can:

✦ Adjust dependencies and task date constraints

✦ Redefine a finish-to-start relationship to either a start-to-start or a finish-to-finish relationship

After you know the techniques that you can apply to adjust the critical path, you need to ask the important question: What's the best way to identify tasks that you want to change and then make changes? The answer: Select a view and filter it for critical tasks only. I prefer the Task Entry view, which is a combination view of the Gantt Chart and the Task Form view, because the top pane displays a graphic representation of your project and the bottom pane displays most of the fields that you may want to change, as shown in Figure 9-17.

To set up this view, select the Gantt Chart view. The table that you apply to the Gantt Chart is a matter of personal preference; you may consider the Schedule table because it shows slack information. After you select the Gantt Chart view, choose Window ➪ Split. The Task Form appears in the bottom pane.

To filter for critical tasks, choose Project ➪ Filtered for ➪ Critical. Click each critical task to evaluate it and make changes in the Task Form at the bottom of the screen.

Tip   You also can sort your critical tasks by duration. That way, the critical tasks are in order from the longest to the shortest, and you can focus on trying to shorten longer tasks.

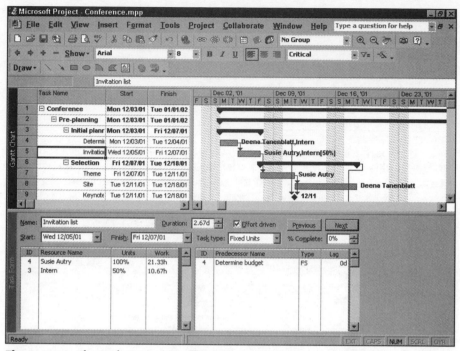

Figure 9-17: The Task Entry view, filtered for critical tasks, is probably the easiest view in which to work if you're trying to adjust the critical path.

Using Multiple Critical Paths

Project enables you to view more than one critical path in a project. This feature comes in handy when you have lots of tasks driving other tasks and you want to find out which ones are truly critical to finishing the network of tasks on time.

By default, when you view only one critical path, you're viewing the tasks that must be completed to finish the project on time. These tasks have no total slack (total slack is the amount of time you can delay a task without delaying the completion of the project).

Suppose, however, that your project contains lots of subtasks, and within the subtasks you have dependencies. You may start wondering, within a given network of tasks, which ones are really critical. In this case, view your project with multiple critical paths, where Project displays a separate critical path for each network of tasks.

Consider the project shown in Figure 9-18. In this figure, you see the following four networks of tasks:

✦ Network 1: Subtasks 1, 2, and 3

✦ Network 2: Subtask 4

✦ Network 3: Subtasks 5 and 6

✦ Network 4: Subtasks 7 and 8.

The critical path for the project appears with a cross-hatched pattern (onscreen, it's also red) and is driven by Network 4. Also notice that Network 1 is *not* part of the critical path. And although it may not be obvious, I've built slack into Network 1.

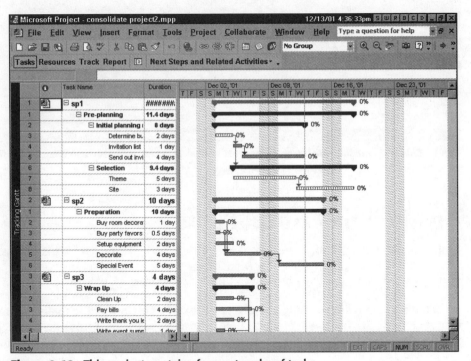

Figure 9-18: This project contains four networks of tasks.

When you display multiple critical paths, you see a critical path for each network of tasks, as shown in Figure 9-19. Notice that all the tasks in Networks 2, 3, and 4 appear critical, while only Subtask 3 of Network 1 appears critical. When you view multiple critical paths, Project calculates the critical path for each network of tasks. For each unique task, Project sets its late finish date equal to its early finish date. When a task has no links, like Network 2, it is critical because its late finish is equal to its early finish. If a network of tasks contains slack, like Network 4, some tasks won't be critical while others are critical. When you view multiple critical paths, you can determine which tasks within a network of tasks must be completed on time to avoid delaying the network.

Figure 9-19: When you view multiple critical paths, you see the critical tasks within each network of tasks in your project.

By default, Project displays only one critical path, but you can change this default. Choose Tools ➪ Options and click the Calculation tab to display the dialog box shown in Figure 9-20. Place a check in the "Calculate multiple critical paths" checkbox and click OK.

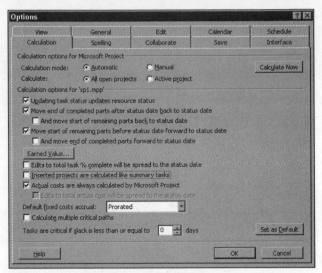

Figure 9-20: Display multiple critical paths within a project from the Calculation tab of the Options dialog box.

Summary

This chapter described the following techniques that you can use to resolve scheduling conflicts and shorten the length of your project:

✦ Adding resources to tasks

✦ Using overtime

✦ Adjusting slack

✦ Changing task constraints and dependencies

In Chapter 10 you learn how to resolve conflicts that occur with resources.

✦   ✦   ✦

Resolving Resource Problems

Resource allocation is the process of assigning resources to tasks in a project. Because the potential for resource overallocation always accompanies resource assignment, this chapter explores the causes of resource overallocation and suggests methods to resolve the conflicts.

Understanding How Resource Conflicts Occur

As you assign resources to tasks, Project checks the resource's calendar to make sure that the resource is working. However, Project doesn't assess whether the resource is already obligated when you assign the resource to a new task; Project enables you to make the assignment. Be aware, though, that the additional assignment may lead to overallocating the resource. Overallocation occurs when you assign more work to a resource than the resource can accomplish in the time that you've allotted for the work to be completed.

For example, if you assign Mary to work full-time on two tasks that start on the same day, you actually assign Mary to 16 hours of work in an 8-hour day — not possible unless Mary is a really dedicated employee who has no life outside work. On the other hand, if you have a group of three mechanics and you assign two mechanics to work on two tasks that start on the same day, you still have one spare mechanic and no overallocation.

Figure 10-1 shows a series of tasks under the Hire task that begin on the same day. By assigning the same resource to all of them, an overallocation is inevitable. And, overallocations can cause delays in the project schedule.

Figure 10-1: Assigning the same resource to tasks that run simultaneously causes an overallocation.

To calculate the scheduled start date for a task, Project checks factors such as the task's dependencies and constraints. Project then checks the resource's calendar to identify the next regular workday and assigns that date as the start date for the task. If you haven't assigned resources to the task, Project uses the project's calendar to calculate the next regular workday. But when Project calculates the task start date, it does not consider other commitments that the resource may have outside of the current project.

Spotting Resource Conflicts

Before you can resolve resource conflicts, you need to spot them. You can use views or filters to help you identify resource overallocation problems.

Using views to spot resource conflicts

Use a resource view, such as the Resource Sheet view or the Resource Usage view, to find resource conflicts. On these views, overallocated resources appear in red. In addition, a Caution icon appears in the Indicator column to signal an overassigned resource. You can see a message about the overallocation if you point at the icon with your mouse. To display the Resource Usage view that is shown in Figure 10-2, select Resource Usage from the View bar.

Figure 10-2: The Resource Usage view displays overallocated resources in red, and an icon appears in the Indicator column.

You also can see a graphic representation of a resource's allocation by switching to the Resource Graph view. To display the view shown in Figure 10-3, select Resource Graph from the View bar.

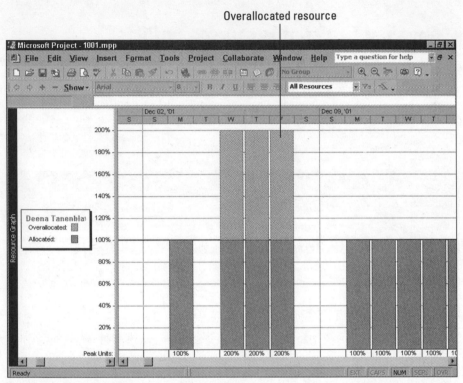

Figure 10-3: The Resource Graph view provides a picture of a resource's allocation.

The Resource Allocation view is useful for working with overallocations — a Gantt Chart in the lower pane shows the tasks assigned to the resource that you select in the top pane. Tasks that start at the same time overlap in the Gantt Chart pane; this view helps you pinpoint the tasks that are causing the resource's overallocation. The top portion of the view in Figure 10-4 shows that Barbara Rollison is overallocated on Wednesday, Thursday, and Friday, December 5, 6, and 7. If you examine Thursday, December 6, more closely, you'll notice that Barbara is scheduled to work 11 hours that day. In the bottom portion of the view, the two tasks to which she's assigned 100 percent of the time are Theme and Cleanup crew — and the Gantt view makes it easy to see the overlap of the two tasks on that Thursday.

Figure 10-4: The Resource Allocation view uses the Gantt Chart format to show the tasks assigned to the resource selected in the top pane.

To switch to the Resource Allocation view, choose View ➪ More Views and then select Resource Allocation.

Tip   To find the next resource conflict, click the Go To Next Overallocation button on the Resource Management toolbar. It's the third button from the left edge of the toolbar.

Using filters to spot resource conflicts

Filtering is another simple technique that you can use to resolve resource conflict problems. If you filter the Resource Usage view to display only overallocated resources, as shown in Figure 10-5, the problems become even more apparent. To filter the view, switch to it first by choosing View ➪ Resource Usage. Then open the Filter list box on the Formatting toolbar and choose Overallocated Resources or choose Project ➪ Filtered ➪ Overallocated Resources.

Figure 10-5: You can filter the Resource Usage view to show overallocated resources only.

Next, add the Overallocation field to the view to identify the extent of the resource's overallocation. Choose Format ➪ Details ➪ Overallocation. As Figure 10-6 shows, Project adds a row to the timescale portion of the view to show you the number of hours you need to eliminate to correct the overallocation.

Resolving Conflicts

After you find the overallocations, you need to resolve the conflicts. Project managers use several methods to resolve conflicts.

Changing resource allocations

If you play around with resource allocations, you can resolve a resource conflict. Adding a resource is one obvious way to resolve an overallocation. For example, suppose that Task 3 is an effort-driven task that has a resource conflict with Task 4; the two tasks don't run concurrently, but Task 3 is continuing when Task 4 is supposed to start. Suppose also that you need the same resource, Deena Tanenblatt, to work on both tasks. Adding a resource (Do Lahr) to Task 3 reduces the amount of time it takes to finish Task 3, which can eliminate Deena's conflict between Tasks 3 and 4.

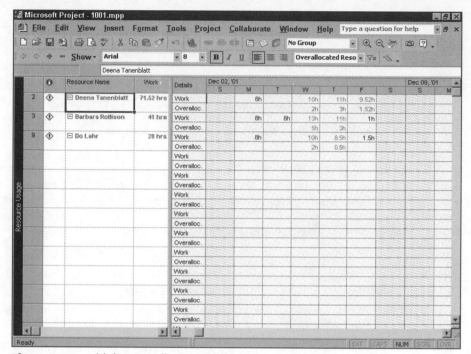

Figure 10-6: Add the Overallocation field to the Resource Usage view.

Cross-Reference

You can add a resource by using the techniques described in Chapter 5, or you can add a resource to a task by using the Resource Usage view (described later in this chapter).

Switching resources

You also can resolve resource conflicts by switching resources. You can use this technique when one resource is overallocated, but you have another resource available that's capable of doing the job. You switch resources by adding one and deleting the other from the task in question. When you want to switch resources, work in the Resource Usage view (refer to Figure 10-2; Figures 10-5 and 10-6 are also based on the Resource Usage view), where you can focus on resource conflicts.

First, examine the resource with the conflict, and in the upper pane, find the task from which you want to remove that resource. Then, click anywhere in the row of the task and press the Delete key on your keyboard. Project removes the task from the assigned resource — and, with luck, indicates that the resource no longer has a conflict.

Cross-Reference

If you're using Project Server, you can take advantage of the Resource Substitution Wizard to substitute generic resources automatically. See Chapter 19 for more details.

Adding a task to a resource

To add a task to a resource from the Resource Usage view, follow these steps:

1. Scroll down until you find the resource to which you want to add a task.

2. Click the row of any task to which you have already assigned the resource.

3. Press the Insert key on your keyboard. Project inserts a blank line.

4. Fill in the task name, and Project fills in the default duration for the task.

Adding or deleting a resource

You can add or delete a resource by using a number of techniques. For example, you can work in the Gantt Chart view and then split the view (choose Window ➪ Split) to display the Task Entry view (a combination of the Gantt Chart view in the top pane and the Task Form view in the bottom pane). Select a task in the Gantt Chart view and then:

✦ To add a resource, select the resource from the list box that appears when you click the Resource Name column of the Task Entry view.

✦ To delete a resource, select the resource's ID number in the Task Entry view and press the Delete key.

✦ To switch resources, use the Replace Resource dialog box (see Chapter 5 for more details).

Tip Working in the Gantt Chart view is effective, but the Resource Usage view helps you to focus on resource conflicts.

Scheduling overtime

You also can resolve a resource conflict by scheduling overtime for the resource. *Overtime* in Project is the amount of work scheduled beyond an assigned resource's regular working hours, and overtime hours are charged at the resource's overtime rate. Overtime work does not represent additional work on a task; instead, it represents the amount of time spent on a task during nonregular hours. By scheduling overtime, the resource may finish the task faster and therefore eliminate the conflict. As you learned in the last chapter, you assign overtime from the Gantt Chart view. Use the following steps:

1. Display the Gantt Chart view (choose View ➪ Gantt Chart).

2. Choose Window ➪ Split to switch to the Task Entry view and reveal the Task Form in the bottom pane.

3. Click the Task Form to make it the active pane.

4. Choose Format ➪ Details ➪ Resource Work. Project adds the Ovt. Work column, as shown in Figure 10-7, to the Task Form view. 0h means that you have not yet assigned overtime.

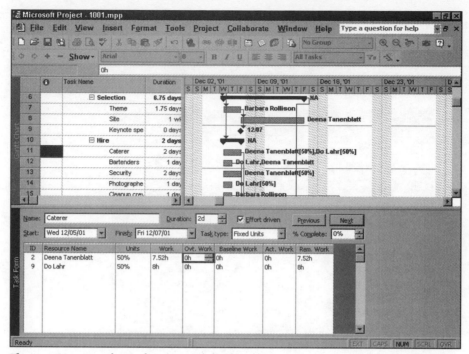

Figure 10-7: Use the Task Form and display the Overtime column to add overtime.

5. Select the task in the top pane to which you want to assign overtime.

6. Go to the bottom pane and fill in the overtime amount for the appropriate resource.

When you finish entering overtime, you can hide the Task Form by choosing Window ➪ Remove Split.

Redefining a resource's calendar

If your resource is a salaried resource, you may have the option of redefining a resource's calendar so that hours typically considered nonworking (and therefore charged at an overtime rate if worked) become working hours. If a resource has a conflict and the number of hours in conflict on a given day is low enough, you can eliminate the conflict by increasing the working hours for the resource for that day.

You can make this kind of change to any resource — Project won't stop you. But you need to consider the effects on the cost of your project. If you are paying a resource at an overtime rate for working during nonworking hours, then you don't want to change nonworking hours to working hours in Project. If you do, you will understate the cost of your project.

To change a resource's working calendar, go to the Resource Usage view. Identify the resource that has a conflict, and note the number of hours that the conflict involves. Double-click the resource that has a conflict to open the Resource Information dialog box for that resource. Click the Working Time tab to view that resource's calendar, as shown in Figure 10-8.

Figure 10-8: Use the Working Time tab of the Resource Information dialog box to change the standard working hours for the resource.

To change the standard working hours for a resource, follow these steps:

1. Click the first date on which the resource is overallocated.

2. Click the Use default option button.

3. Use the From and To boxes to set up nonstandard working hours for that day.

4. Repeat this process for each day that you want to change the work schedule for a particular resource.

5. Click OK when you finish.

Assigning part-time work

Suppose that a resource is assigned to several concurrent tasks and is also overallocated. Suppose also that you don't want to add other resources, switch to a different resource, or add overtime. You can assign the resource to work part-time on each of the tasks to solve the conflict, although the tasks may take longer to complete by using this method. Or, you may want to use this method in conjunction with additional resources to make sure that you can complete the task on time.

To assign a resource to work part-time, you can change the number of units of the resource that you apply to the task. By default, Project sets task types to Fixed Units; therefore, if you change the amount of time a resource works on a task, Project changes the duration of the task accordingly.

Note

If you want to retain the duration and assign a resource to work part-time on a task, you should change the task type to Fixed Duration. By making this change, however, you are indicating that the task can be completed by the resource in the allotted amount of time — effectively, you are shortening the amount of time that it takes to complete the task because you're applying less effort during the same time frame.

To change the task type to Fixed Duration, follow these steps:

1. Display the Resource Allocation view by using the More Views window (choose View ➪ More Views).

2. Click the task that you want to change in the upper pane. Project displays that task in Gantt format in the lower pane.

3. Double-click the task that you want to change in the lower pane. Project displays the Task Information dialog box. Click the Advanced tab, as shown in Figure 10-9.

4. Open the Task type list box and select Fixed Duration.

5. Click OK.

Figure 10-9: Use the Advanced tab of the Task Information dialog box to change the task type.

Now you can assign resources to work part-time on this task without changing the task's duration. Follow these steps:

1. In the Resource Allocation view, click a task in the top pane to which the over-allocated resource is assigned.

2. Click the Assignment Information button on the Standard toolbar or double-click the task to open the Assignment Information dialog box. You can see the General tab in Figure 10-10.

Figure 10-10: Use the Assignment Information dialog box to change a resource's workload to part-time.

3. Change the value in the Units box to reflect the percentage of time that you want the resource to spend on the task — in this case, the value should be lower than 100%.

4. Click OK.

Controlling when resources start working on a task

For cases in which you've assigned more than one resource to a task, consider staggering the times that the resources begin working on the task to resolve resource conflicts. When you delay a resource's start on a task, Project recalculates the start date and time for that resource's work on the task. To stagger start times for resources, work in the Task Usage view and follow these steps:

Note   This technique can extend the duration of the task, which may not be a viable option for you.

1. Choose View ➪ Task Usage.

2. Select the resource whose work time you want to delay in the Task Name column.

3. Click the Assignment Information button or double-click the resource. Project displays the General tab of the Assignment Information dialog box (as shown previously in Figure 10-10).

4. Change the dates in the Start or Finish boxes.

5. Click OK.

Delaying tasks by leveling resource workloads

If you have scheduled several tasks to run concurrently and you now find resource conflicts in your project, you can delay some of these tasks to level — or, spread out — the demands that you're making on your resources. Leveling is the process of resolving resource conflicts by delaying or splitting tasks to accommodate the schedules of assigned resources. You can ask Project to select the tasks to delay or split by using its leveling feature, or you can control the process manually by examining the project to identify tasks that you are willing to delay or split.

Automatic leveling

When Project does the leveling for you, it redistributes a resource's assignments and reschedules them according to the resource's working capacity, assignment units, and calendar. Project also considers the task's duration, constraints, and priority.

What is a task's *priority*? Well, in some circumstances, you want Project to level some tasks before it levels other tasks. You can do so by assigning different priority levels to tasks. By default, Project assigns all tasks a priority of 500. The higher the priority level you assign, the longer Project waits before leveling a task. So, before you start to use the automatic-leveling feature, consider how you want to prioritize tasks. To set a priority, follow these steps:

1. Choose View ➪ Gantt Chart.

2. Double-click the task for which you want to set a priority or select the task and click the Task Information button on the Standard toolbar. Project displays the Task Information dialog box.

3. Use the General tab to set a priority, as shown in Figure 10-11.

Tip

After you prioritize tasks — but before you level — you can sort tasks by priority to view the tasks that Project is most likely to level.

Figure 10-11: Set a priority for the task.

To level tasks automatically, follow these steps:

1. Choose Tools ➪ Level Resources to open the Resource Leveling dialog box, as shown in Figure 10-12.

Figure 10-12: From the Resource Leveling dialog box, you can set resource leveling options.

2. Select Automatic to have Project automatically level resources, if necessary, whenever you make a change to your schedule. Select Manual to perform leveling only when you select Level Now from this dialog box.

3. Use the "Look for overallocations on a . . . basis" list box to select a basis. The *basis* is a time frame, such as Day by Day or Week by Week. (The Indicator box in the Resource Usage view may contain a note suggesting the appropriate basis.)

4. Place a check in the "Clear leveling values before leveling" checkbox to make Project 2002 behave like Project 98 when leveling; that is, Project resets all leveling delay values to zero before leveling. If you remove the check from this box, Project 2002 does not reset leveling values but builds upon the values. During leveling, the scheduling for previously leveled tasks will probably not change.

5. In the "Leveling range for" area, select either to level the entire project or to level only for specified dates.

6. In the Leveling order drop-down list, select the order that you want Project to consider when leveling your project. If you choose "ID Only," Project delays or splits the task with the highest ID number. If you choose "Standard," Project looks at predecessor dependencies, slack, dates, and priorities when selecting the best task to split or delay. If you choose "Priority, Standard," Project looks first at task priority and then at all the items listed for the Standard leveling order.

7. Place a check next to any of the following options:

   • "Level only within available slack" to avoid changing the end date of your project

   • "Leveling can adjust individual assignments on a task" to have leveling adjust one resource's work schedule on a task independent of other resources working on the same task

   • "Leveling can create splits in remaining work" if you want leveling to split tasks to resolve resource conflicts

8. Click Level Now to apply leveling.

You can review the effects of leveling from the Leveling Gantt Chart view, as shown in Figure 10-13. Choose Views ➪ More Views ➪ Leveling Gantt and then click Apply. Project adds green bars to your Gantt Chart, which represent the duration of tasks before leveling. Depending on the nature of your project, Project may build more slack into your tasks.

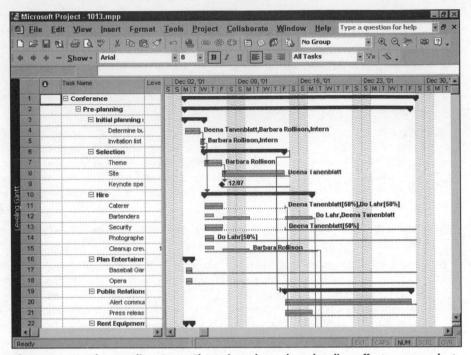

Figure 10-13: The Leveling Gantt Chart view shows how leveling affects your project.

To remove the effects of leveling, reopen the Resource Leveling dialog box (choose Tools ➪ Level Resources) and click Clear Leveling. A subsequent dialog box enables you to clear leveling for the entire project or for selected tasks only.

Note If you are scheduling from a finish date, you still can level to resolve resource conflicts. Project calculates the delay by subtracting it from a task's or assignment's finish date, causing the finish date to occur earlier.

Manual leveling

Manual leveling is especially handy when automatic leveling doesn't provide acceptable results. Manual leveling is also useful when you have just a few resource conflicts to resolve. To manually level resources in Project, use the Resource Allocation view and follow these steps:

1. Choose View ➪ More Views. From the More Views dialog box, highlight Resource Allocation, and click Apply.

2. Highlight the task that you want to delay in the top pane.

3. In the bottom pane, enter an amount in the Leveling Delay field. Project delays the task accordingly and reduces the resource's conflict.

Figures 10-14 and 10-15 show before and after pictures for manual leveling. I used a very simple situation to demonstrate the effects of manual leveling: I set up a project with only two tasks and one resource, and I assigned the same resource full-time to both tasks. Notice that manually leveling the second task delays the second task so that it starts when the first task finishes.

Figure 10-14: The Resource Allocation view before manually leveling.

Contouring resources

Contour is the term that Project uses to refer to the shape of a resource's work assignment over time. Contours come in several flavors; the most common are Flat, Back Loaded, Front Loaded, and Bell. The default contour is Flat, which means that a resource works on a task for the maximum number of hours that he or she is assigned to a task for the duration of the assignment. You can use different contours to control how much a resource works on a task at a given time — and possibly resolve a conflict.

Tip   Add the Peak Units field to the Resource Usage view to display the maximum effort — as distributed over time — that a resource is expected to work. This field is particularly useful when you have selected a contour other than the default (Flat).

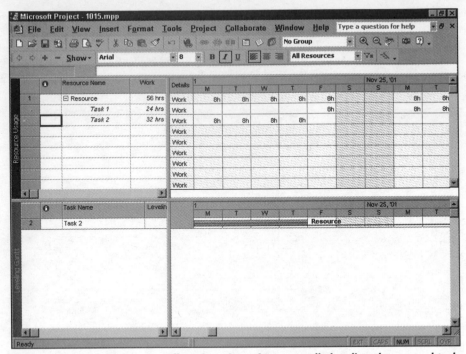

Figure 10-15: The Resource Allocation view after manually leveling the second task.

The Flat contour assigns a resource to work the maximum number of hours per time period throughout the duration of the task. By changing the contour, you can more accurately reflect the actual work pattern for the resource while working on a task.

When you think of contours, think of dividing each task into 10 equal timeslots. By using the various contours, Project assigns percentages of work to be done in each timeslot. Contours help you to assign work to a task, based on when the task requires the effort. For example, if a task requires less effort initially, consider using a Back Loaded contour. If a task requires most effort in the middle of the task, consider using a Bell, Turtle, or even an Early Peak contour.

Caution If you start changing contours from the default Flat contour, you may inadvertently create a resource conflict. Therefore, viewing the contours that you set can help you resolve resource conflicts.

Setting a contour pattern

To set a contour pattern, follow these steps:

1. Choose View ➪ Task Usage. In the sheet portion of the view, Project displays each task in your project with the resources assigned to it listed below the task, showing the number of hours per day that a resource is assigned to a task.

2. In the Task Name column, double-click the resource for which you want to apply a contour or select the resource and click the Assignment Information button on the Standard toolbar. Then click the General tab of the Assignment Information dialog box, as shown in Figure 10-16.

Figure 10-16: Use the General tab of the Assignment Information dialog box to select a contour.

3. Open the Work contour list box and select a contour.

4. Click OK.

Tip   To change the start and end dates for the resource's work on the task, use the Start and Finish list boxes.

When you select a contour other than Flat, an indicator appears next to the resource in the Indicator column. If you pass the mouse pointer over the indicator, Project identifies the contour applied to the resource, as shown in Figure 10-17.

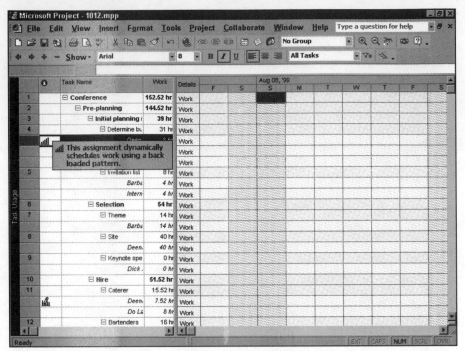

Figure 10-17: Project displays an icon in the Indicator column next to a resource for which you have chosen a contour other than Flat.

Tip   The same icon appears in the Indicator column in the Resource Usage view.

Here are a few points to keep in mind when working with contours:

✦ Suppose that you apply a contour other than the default Flat contour to a task and later you add new total work values to the task. Project automatically reapplies the contour pattern to the task and the resources by first distributing the new task work values across the affected time span, and then assigning new work values to the resources working on the task.

✦ If you set a contour and then change the start date of the task or the start date of a resource's work on the task, Project automatically shifts the contour and reapplies it to include the new date, thus preserving the pattern of the original contour.

✦ If you increase the duration of a task, Project stretches the contour to include the new duration.

✦ Suppose that you apply a contour other than the default contour to a task. If you manually edit a work value on the portion of a view displaying the contour, Project no longer applies the contour pattern automatically. However, you can reapply the contour to redistribute the new values.

✦ If you enter actual work and then change the task's total work or total remaining work, Project automatically redistributes the changes to the remaining work values and not to the actual work.

Contouring a resource's availability

Starting in Project 2000, you can contour a resource's availability. To contour a resource's availability, use the General tab of the Resource Information dialog box, as shown in Figure 10-18. In the Resource Availability box, set Available From and Available To dates for the selected resource. A particular resource may be available to work on your project only part-time for a specified time frame. Or, suppose that you have five computer programmers, but only three are available in August and one retires in September. Use the Resource Availability section to specify the availability of your resources, which will influence your project's schedule.

Figure 10-18: Set dates that represent the resource's availability so that you can assign the resource to a task by using only the dates that the resource is available.

Pooling resources

Finally, you can try to solve resource conflicts by using a *resource pool*. A resource pool is a set of resources that are available to any project. You can use resources exclusively on one project, or you can share the resources among several projects.

Typically, resource pooling is useful only if you work with the same resources on multiple projects and you don't use Project Server. Different project managers can share the same resources. Because resource pooling is so closely tied to the topic of managing multiple projects, I'll postpone further discussion until Chapter 19; in that context, you'll better understand the application of resource pooling to resolving resource conflicts.

If you're using Project Server, you won't need to use resource pooling; instead, you'll be more interested in using Enterprise resources and the Resource Substitution Wizard to resolve resource conflicts. See Chapter 18 for more information.

Summary

This chapter explained how to identify and resolve resource conflicts that can delay a project. The techniques involved include:

✦ Changing resource allocations

✦ Scheduling overtime

✦ Redefining a resource calendar

✦ Assigning part-time work

✦ Controlling resource start times

✦ Leveling resource workloads

✦ Contouring resources

In the next chapter, you learn the art of tracking your progress by comparing your project to its baseline.

✦   ✦   ✦

Tracking Your Progress

U p to this point in the book, you've been creating your project schedule — and, in general terms, estimating. You've estimated task durations, resource usage, and even the actual tasks needed to complete the project. In this part of the book, you'll begin to use tracking tools to help you evaluate your estimates so that you can improve your planning skills. You'll learn the basics of tracking, how to record "actual" information in Project, how to print reports, and how to analyze the cost of your project.

Understanding Tracking

This chapter marks something of a turning point in this book and in your use of Project. Up to this point, you've been in the planning phase: building a project schedule, entering tasks, adding resources, and shifting things around so that resource assignments don't conflict and so that tasks have the proper relationships to each other. You've even tweaked details such as text formatting and the appearance of taskbars. You now have a workable, good-looking project in hand — and now you are ready to start the project.

Tracking is the process of comparing what actually happens during your project to your estimates of what would happen. To track, you need to take a picture of your project schedule at the moment your planning is complete, called a *baseline*. But you also have to understand what steps are involved in tracking and how to set up efficient procedures to handle them.

New Feature Starting in Project 2002, you can store up to 11 baselines for any project.

Understanding the Principles of Tracking

A good plan is only half the battle. How you execute that plan is the key. Think of yourself as the quarterback in a football game. If you run straight down the field toward the goalpost, never swerving to avoid an oncoming opponent, you won't get very far. Project tracking is similar: If you don't swerve and make adjustments for the changes in costs and timing that are virtually inevitable in any human endeavor, you're not playing the game correctly.

Computerized project management greatly enhances your ability to quickly see problems and revise the plan to minimize any damage. Project enables you to compare what you thought would happen to what actually happens over the course of the project.

Estimates versus actuals

The plan that you've been building is an estimate of what can occur; it's your best guess (an educated one, hopefully) about how long tasks may take, how one task affects another, how many resources you need to complete the work, and what costs you expect your project to incur. Good project managers keep good records of their estimates and actuals to become better project managers. By comparing these two sets of data, you can see where your estimates were off and then use this information to make your next plan more realistic. You can also use data on actual costs and timing to make the changes in your strategy that are necessary to keep you on track and meet your current project's goals.

Tracking in Project consists of entering information about actuals, such as the actual start date, the actual finish date, and the actual duration of a task. You enter actual time worked by resources and actual costs incurred. When you enter information about actuals, Project shows you a revised schedule with projections of how the rest of the schedule is likely to play out, based on your actual activity.

Project managers usually track activity on a regular basis, such as once a week or every two weeks. This tracking includes information about tasks in progress, as well as about tasks that have been completed.

This tracking activity also enables you to generate reports that show management where your efforts stand at any given point in time. By showing managers the hard data on your project's status — rather than your best guess — you can make persuasive bids for more time, more resources, or a shift in strategy if things aren't going as you expected. Figure 11-1 shows a Tracking Gantt view using its default table, the Tracking table.

Cross-Reference   Chapter 12 explains the specific steps for updating a project to reflect actual progress.

Making adjustments as you go

Tracking isn't something you leave to the end of the project, or even to the end of individual tasks. Tracking tasks in progress on a regular basis helps you to detect any deviation from your estimates. The earlier you spot a delay, the more time you have to make up for it.

Tip   If Project determines that you're running late on a task, it automatically will move dependent tasks into the future.

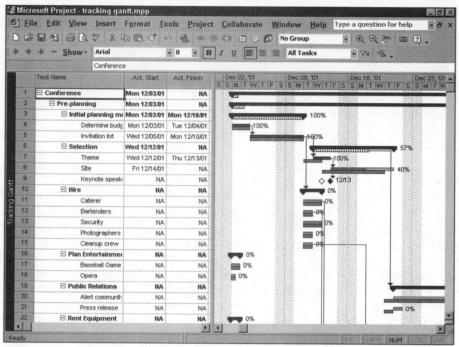

Figure 11-1: Use the Tracking Gantt view to display the progress of your project.

For example, suppose that you estimated that a task would take three days. However, you have already put four days of effort into it, and it's still not complete. Project not only tells you that you're running late but also moves future tasks that depend on this task farther out in the schedule. Project also shows any resource conflicts that result when resources have to put in more work than you estimated in resource views, such as Resource Sheet and Resource Graph. Project shows clearly how one delay ripples through your schedule.

Tip   Project adjusts your project's cost as you track to reflect the effect of higher-than-expected costs.

Project also shows the effect of unanticipated costs on the total budget. If the costs that you track on early tasks are higher than anticipated, Project displays your projected total costs, based on a combination of actual costs and the remaining estimates. Project shows you exactly how much of your budget you have used and how much you have remaining, so you can revise your resource allocations to stay within your overall budget.

How Much Have You Accomplished?

As I describe in Chapter 12, you record activity on a task by entering an estimate of the percentage of the task that's complete, actual resource time spent on the task, or actual costs incurred (such as fees or equipment rentals paid), or by entering the hours of work done per time period. Estimating "the completeness" of a task is not an exact science, and different people use different methods.

With something concrete, such as a building under construction, you can look at the actual building and estimate fairly accurately how far along the project has progressed. Most projects aren't so straightforward, however. How do you estimate how far along you are in more creative tasks, such as coming up with an advertising concept? You can sit in meetings for five weeks and still not find the right concept. Is your project 50 percent complete? Completion is hard to gauge from other, similar projects on which you've worked — perhaps on the last project you came up with the perfect concept in your very first meeting.

Don't fall into the trap of using money or time spent as a gauge. It's (unfortunately) easy to spend $10,000 on a task estimated to cost $8,000 and still be only 25 percent to completion. You probably have to use the same gut instincts that put you in charge of this project to estimate the progress of individual tasks. Hint: If your project has individual deliverables that you can track, document them and use them consistently when you make your estimate.

Using Baselines

You complete the planning phase of your project by setting a baseline. You have seen this term in previous chapters, but take a moment to grasp its significance in the tracking process.

What is a baseline?

A *baseline* is a snapshot of your project when you complete the planning phase, or sometimes at the end of some other critical phase. The baseline is one set of data saved in the same file where you track actual progress data. Project enables you to save up to 11 baselines and up to 10 interim plans during your project. You can show a wide variety of information about your baseline(s), or you can choose not to display baseline information at all.

Some projects, particularly shorter ones that run only a few weeks or even a couple of months, may have one baseline set at the outset and proceed close enough to your estimates that they can run their course against that single baseline. Other projects, especially longer ones, may require you to set several baselines along the way, particularly if the original estimate is so out of line with what has transpired in the project that the original is no longer useful. You can modify the entire baseline if changes are drastic and occur early in the project, or you can modify the baseline estimates only going forward from a particular point in the project.

For example, if your project is put on hold shortly after you complete the schedule and you actually start work three months later than you had planned, you would be wise to set a new baseline schedule before restarting. If, however, you're six months into your project and it is put on hold for three months, you may want to modify the timing of future tasks and reset the baseline only for tasks going forward to help you retain the ability to accurately assess how well you estimated.

Costs can change a baseline, too. For example, what if you save a baseline set to fit within a $50,000 budget and, before you start work, cost-cutting measures hit your company and your budget is cut to $35,000? You'd be wise to make the changes to your resources and costs and then reset your baseline. Setting interim baselines keeps your projects from varying wildly from your estimates when mitigating circumstances come into play.

Setting a baseline

Note Starting in Project 2002, the Planning Wizard no longer appears when you save your project.

In most cases, you need to save the project file — without saving the baseline itself — several times during the planning phase.

New Feature Starting in Project 2002, you can save up to 11 baselines and 10 interim plans for one project.

When you're ready, you can use the Save Baseline dialog box to save up to 11 baselines and 10 interim plans for your project — each baseline is a picture of your project at the time that you save it, and each baseline that you save includes information about tasks, resources, and assignments. For tasks, Project saves duration, start and finish dates, work, timephased work, cost, and timephased cost. For resources, Project saves work, timephased work, cost, and timephased cost information with the baseline. For assignments, Project saves start and finish dates, work, timephased work, costs, and timephased costs.

When you save interim plans, Project saves a set of task start and finish dates that you can compare with another interim plan or with a baseline plan, thus helping you to keep an eye on progress or slippage. Saving baselines and interim plans helps you to compare current information (found in the start and finish fields) with baseline information (found in the baseline fields). The distinction between baselines and interim plans in Project is the amount and type of information that Project saves.

To control the settings when you save a baseline, follow these steps:

1. Choose Tools ➪ Tracking ➪ Save Baseline to open the Save Baseline dialog box, as shown in Figure 11-2.

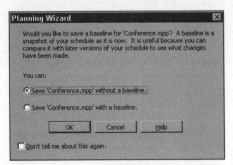

Figure 11-2: Use this dialog box to save a baseline or interim plan.

2. Set up the baseline that you want to save.

3. Open the Save baseline list box and select the baseline that you want to save.

4. Click OK.

When you save baselines for selected tasks, you can now choose to roll up baselines to all summary tasks and from subtasks into their parent summary task(s) — thus helping to maintain accurate baseline information, as shown in Figure 11-3. The relationship between the tasks in the project and the task(s) that you select prior to opening the dialog box determine the effect of these checkboxes.

Figure 11-3: You can control Project's behavior when rolling up baseline information for selected tasks.

For example, suppose you have a project set up like the one shown in Figure 11-4. Further suppose that you select Task 6, a child of Task 1 and the parent of Tasks 7 and 8, before you open the Save Baseline dialog box. If you check only the "From subtasks into selected summary task(s)" checkbox, Project will roll up the information from Tasks 7 and 8 to Task 6. If you check only the "To all summary tasks" checkbox, Project rolls up baseline information from Task 6 without regard to the baseline information stored for Tasks 7 and 8. If you check both checkboxes, Project rolls up baseline information from Tasks 7 and 8 to Task 6 and then rolls up that information to Task 1.

Figure 11-4: Ancestry determines baseline information rollup behavior; in this sample project, Tasks 3 and 6 are children of Task 1, and Task 6 is the parent of Tasks 7 and 8.

Changing the Baseline

Most of the time, you *don't* want to make changes to a baseline. It's a moment frozen in time, a record against which you can compare your progress. If you change a baseline on a regular basis, you are defeating its purpose.

That said — you will encounter some circumstances in which, for strategic reasons, you will need to modify a baseline and resave it, or to save a second or third baseline to document major shifts in the project. However, if you are overriding the original baseline, you must do so in a thoughtful and efficient way. This section discusses some of the times when changes to a baseline are necessary and explains how you can make those changes.

Adding a task to a baseline

It is fairly common to set your baseline plan and then realize that you left out a step, or then decide to break one step into two steps. Perhaps your company institutes a new requirement or process, and you have to modify a task to deal with the change. You don't want to reset your whole project baseline, but you do want to save that one task along with the original baseline. You can make this change after you save the original baseline.

To add a task to your baseline so that you can track its progress, follow these steps:

1. Do one of the following:

   - To add a new task to the schedule and then incorporate it into the baseline, first add the task in the Task Name column on your Gantt Chart and then select it.

   - To save modifications to an existing task, first make the changes and then select the task.

2. Choose Tools ➪ Tracking ➪ Save Baseline. The Save Baseline dialog box appears.

3. Select the baseline that you want to modify from the Save baseline list.

4. Click Selected tasks, as shown in Figure 11-5.

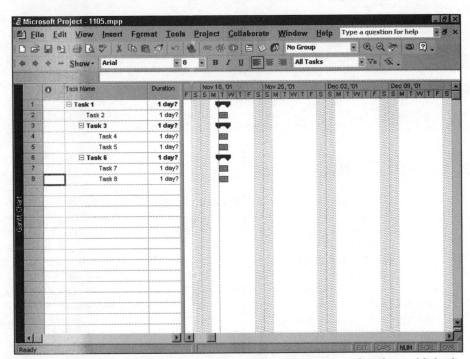

Figure 11-5: Make modifications to tasks and save them in an already established baseline.

5. Choose Roll up settings (see the preceding section for details on these options).

6. Click OK to save the baseline, which now includes the new task.

Note You can add tasks to the baseline by entering them in the Gantt table, using columns such as Baseline Duration and Baseline Start or Finish. However, adding baseline data this way does not enable all baseline calculations. For example, adding a task at the end of the project with this method won't effect a change in the baseline finish date.

Using interim plans

You can use the baseline in different ways. You can refer to it as your original estimate and compare it with actual results at the end of the project to see how well you guessed and to learn to make better guesses on future projects. But the baseline also has an important practical use during the project: It alerts you to shifts so that you can make changes to accommodate them. The second use may prompt you to save interim plans.

The initial baseline(s) may quickly take on more historical rather than practical interest. You should not change the initial baseline(s) because that record of your original planning process is important to retain. However, if timing shifts dramatically away from the baseline plan, all the little warning signs that Project gives you about being off schedule become useless. A project that starts six months later than expected will show every task as late, and every task as critical. To continue generating useful project information, you'll want to revise the schedule to better reflect reality. Only by saving interim plans can you see how well you're meeting your revised goals.

 Note Remember that interim plans contain a set of task start and finish dates that you can compare with another interim plan or with a baseline plan, thus helping you to keep an eye on progress or slippage. A baseline includes much more information — duration, start and finish dates, work, and cost information about tasks, resources, and assignments. Saving baselines and interim plans helps you to compare current information, found in the start and finish fields, with baseline information, found in the baseline fields.

You can set interim plans for all the tasks in the project. However, you will usually want to save an interim plan only for tasks going forward. For example, if a labor strike pushes out a manufacturing project by two months, you keep the baseline intact for all the tasks that were completed at the time the strike started and save an interim plan for all the tasks still to perform when the strike ends.

 Note You also can use interim plans to copy baseline information from one baseline to another.

You can save an interim plan by following these steps:

1. Select various tasks to include in the interim plan.

2. Choose Tools ➪ Tracking ➪ Save Baseline to open the Save Baseline dialog box.

3. Click "Save interim plan." Project makes the Copy and Into fields available.

4. Click the arrow to the right of the Copy field to display the drop-down list. Figure 11-6 shows that I've opened the Into list, which contains the same choices that you'll find in the Copy list.

Figure 11-6: The choices in the Copy and Into lists enable you to save several sets of start and finish dates in interim plans.

5. Select Start/Finish from the Copy drop-down list to copy current start and finish dates.

6. Open the drop-down list for the Into field and select a numbered item, such as Start1/Finish1, to copy the dates into new fields, thus creating an interim plan.

7. Select "Entire project" to create an interim plan for the whole project, or select "Selected tasks" to create an interim plan that retains the original baseline information for any tasks that you didn't select, yet saves new baseline information for the tasks that you have selected.

8. Click OK to save the interim baseline plan.

Remember that you can use the various numbered Start/Finish items to save up to 10 interim plans plus the original, for a total of 11 interim plans over the life of your project.

Clearing a baseline or interim plan

Inevitably, you set a baseline or an interim baseline and then find a reason to clear it. Suppose, for example, that you thought you finished the planning stage of the project. The project hasn't yet started, and you attend a meeting in which you inform everyone that you're "good to go" for next Monday. Naturally, your announcement triggers discussion and — by the time the discussion ends — the scope of the project has expanded (or contracted) considerably. You now need to work again on the planning phase of your schedule — and you really don't want to adjust the baseline. Instead, you want to get rid of it; after you make all your changes, you'll set the correct baseline.

Starting in Project 2000, you can clear baselines. Choose Tools ➪ Tracking ➪ Clear Baseline. Project displays the Clear Baseline dialog box, as shown in Figure 11-7. In this dialog box, you can choose to clear a baseline plan or an interim plan for the entire project or for selected tasks.

Figure 11-7: Set the baseline too soon? Clear it from this dialog box so that you can make adjustments and set the baseline correctly.

Viewing Progress with the Tracking Gantt

Baselines help you to see how your estimates differ from actual activity in the project. Project enables you to see this variance both graphically, with baseline and actual taskbars, and through data displayed in tables in various views. The next section briefly explains how to display a baseline and actual data, and how you can use this feature to understand the status of your project.

Cross-Reference   In Chapter 12, you learn how to enter tracking data.

Interpreting the Tracking Gantt

The Tracking Gantt view is most useful in viewing progress against your baseline estimates. To open the Tracking Gantt view, click its icon in the View bar. This view shows the Tracking table by default. However, you can add or remove fields (columns), or you can display other tables of information. The columns shown in Figure 11-8 include baseline information that I added to the Tracking table.

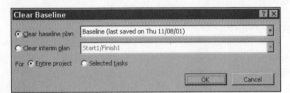

Figure 11-8: The Tracking Gantt table can display a wealth of information.

 Review Chapter 7 for more information about changing and modifying tables.

Notice the Baseline Duration and Baseline Cost, as well as the Actual Duration and the Actual Cost fields, in the Tracking Gantt table. These fields help you to compare estimated versus actual timing and costs.

 You can modify this table so that the Baseline Duration column is next to the Actual Duration column and Baseline Cost is next to Actual Cost.

The Tracking Gantt table also contains the following information:

✦ **% Complete.** This field shows the progress of various tasks in the schedule. Figure 11-9 shows that two tasks are complete.

✦ **Cost Variance.** This field tells you the calculated difference between the baseline and actual information. For example, look at the task "Pour the pool" on Line 3. The Baseline Cost was $210.00, the Actual Cost was $330.00, and the Cost Variance (the difference between the two) is $120.00. Project calculates this amount automatically from baseline and actual data that you enter. You can display other fields that show calculations regarding variances; for example, several fields reflect variance in timing from estimated to actual.

You also can display the taskbars by manipulating the divider between the table and chart areas to get a graphic view of progress on the project. Figure 11-9 uses the Schedule table with the Tracking Gantt and shows the bars of the Tracking Gantt. The various styles of taskbar indicate progress on tasks in the project.

Figure 11-9: Various taskbar styles and color codes display the project's progress and variances.

Notice that various graphic representations indicate progress on different types of tasks. Summary tasks may have a black bar with a black and white bar underneath them. This extra bar indicates the progress (how much is complete) of the summary task. The noncritical tasks are blue and critical tasks are red. The percentage indicator at the edge of a task reflects the percentage complete for that task; the bars of completed tasks are solid in color, while the bars of incomplete tasks are patterned and appear lighter in color. The bars of partially completed tasks are solid on the left and patterned on the right. The baseline bar appears underneath each taskbar.

The Task Variance table

As you change the tables displayed in the Tracking Gantt view, you'll see different information about your progress in the project. The Variance table, for example, highlights the variance in task timing between the baseline and actuals. To display this table, shown in Figure 11-10, right-click the Select Table box in the upper-left corner of the table where the row containing column headings and the task number column meet. Select Variance from the list of tables that appears.

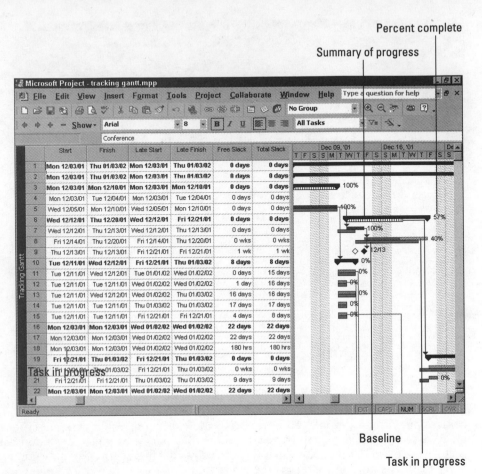

Figure 11-10: If you're behind schedule, you can easily see the awful truth in the Variance table.

You can easily compare the Baseline Start and Finish to the actual Start and Finish columns that show actual data for tasks on which you have tracked progress, as well as baseline data for tasks with no progress. This table also contains fields to show you the Start Variance (how many days late or early the task started) and the Finish Variance (how many days late or early the task ended).

The Task Cost table

The Task Cost table is most useful for pointing out variations in money spent on the project. Figure 11-11 shows a Task Cost table for a project in progress, with some costs incurred and others yet to be expended. At this point, the task "Build the deck" is exceeding its projected cost by $26.66. Project takes the following factors into account when calculating cost variations:

✦ Actual resource time worked

✦ The estimate of days of resource time still to be expended to complete the task

✦ Actual costs (such as fees and permits) that have been tracked on the task

Compared to a baseline estimate of $400.00, this task is over-budget.

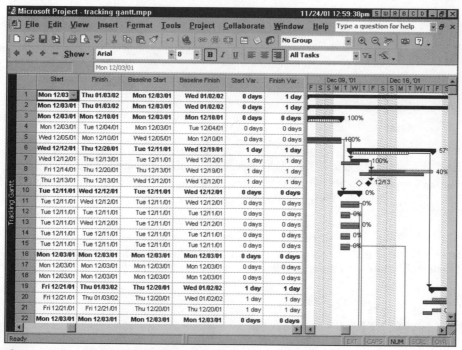

Figure 11-11: The Task Cost table shows where you've spent too much and where you have a lot more money to spend.

The Task Work table

The Task Work table of the Tracking Gantt, as shown in Figure 11-12, focuses on the number of work hours put in by resources working on tasks. For example, the baseline work for the task "Pour the pool" was 16 hours. However, the task is complete and took 62 hours. Therefore, the Variance field (the difference between the baseline hours of work and the actual hours spent) shows a loss of 46 hours. On the other hand, the Baseline estimate for the "Buy lumber for deck" task was 4 hours and the task was completed in 4 hours. The Variance column shows a saving of 2 hours; the negative value indicates fewer hours were used than estimated in the baseline.

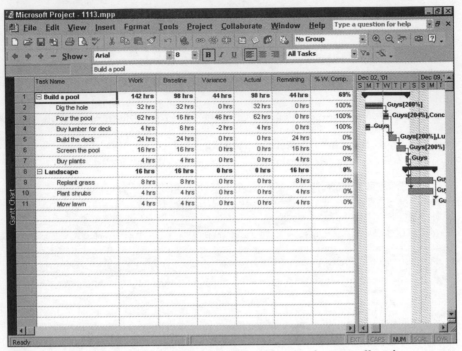

Figure 11-12: To determine whether a task is taking much more effort than you estimated, check the Task Work table.

You'll see many of these tables and more tracking views as you work through the next few chapters. At this point, you should have a good idea of the types of information that you can get by tracking progress on your project.

Tracking Strategies

As you use Microsoft Project on real projects, your tracking skills will improve. However, if you follow certain basic principles of tracking from the start, you can save yourself a lot of aggravation in your first few projects.

Tackling the work of tracking

First, update frequently and at regular intervals. Many people see tracking as a monumental task: All the details of each task's progress and duration, as well as all the resources and costs associated with each task, must be entered one by one. You have to gather that data through resource timecards, reports from other project participants, and vendor invoices. You must type in all the information that you gather. I won't kid you: Tracking can be a big piece of work. The more often you track, the less the tracking data will pile up, and the less likely it is to overwhelm you.

Help yourself with the tracking task by assigning pieces of the updating to various people in your project. If a particular resource is in charge of one phase of the project, have him or her track the activity on just that one phase. You can use various methods of compiling those smaller schedules into a master schedule.

 Part V of this book provides ideas for compiling several schedules and managing schedules with workgroups.

If you have a resource available, such as an administrative assistant who can handle the tracking details — all the better. Make sure that you provide this assistant with appropriate training (and a copy of this book) so that he or she understands the tracking process well enough to be accurate and productive. However, this resource probably does not need to be a Project expert to take on some of the work.

 To help you remember to track, enter tracking as a recurring task, occurring once every week or two, within your project file. And don't forget to include required meetings (such as progress meetings and performance reviews) in your schedule.

Keeping track of tracking

Using task notes to record progress and changes can be another good strategy for effective tracking. If an important change occurs that doesn't merit changing your baseline, use the task notes to record it. When you reach the end of the project, these notes help you to document and justify everything from missed deadlines to cost overruns.

 Try to set some standards for tracking in your organization. For example, how do you determine when a task is complete? How do you measure costs, and what is the source of information on resource time spent on a task? Project becomes a much more effective management tool if each project manager uses identical methods of gauging progress and expenditures, just as your company's accounting department uses standards in tracking costs.

Setting multiple baselines is useful, but how do you decide when to save each iteration? You may want to consider setting a different baseline for each major milestone in your project. Even long projects usually have only four or five significant milestones, and they are likely to occur after you have accomplished a sizeable chunk of work.

Summary

This chapter explored some of the fundamental concepts of tracking activity on a project. You learned the following:

✦ How to set, modify, and clear baselines

✦ How to view your baseline estimates against actual progress

Chapter 12 covers the mechanics of tracking, recording the actuals, and streamlining the entry of this data.

✦   ✦   ✦

Recording Actuals

Actuals represent what has, in fact, occurred during your project. In Microsoft Project, you can record actual information about the cost of a task and about the time spent completing the task. By recording actual information, you accomplish several things:

✦ You let Project automatically reschedule the remainder of your project.

✦ You provide management a way to measure how well your project is going.

✦ You provide yourself with valuable information on your estimating skills — information that you can apply to the remainder of the current project and to your next project.

Organizing the Updating Process

Before you launch into the mechanics of updating a project, you should take a moment to examine the updating process. Updating a project can become complicated, particularly for large projects with many resources assigned to them. You need to establish efficient manual procedures for collecting information in a timely fashion, and then you need to determine the best ways to enter that information into Project.

Individuals working on tasks should answer the following questions regularly:

✦ Is the task on schedule?

✦ How much is done?

✦ Is there a revised estimate on the duration of the task?

✦ Is there a revised estimate on the work required to complete the task?

You may want to create a form for participants to use for their regular reports. Their reports should provide the information you need to update your project plan in Project. You may be able to use one of the reports in Project (or customize one of Project's reports) to provide the necessary information.

Cross-Reference   If you use Project in an e-mail workgroup or you use Project Server, you can take advantage of electronic reporting capabilities. See Chapters 16, 18, and 19 for more information.

You also should decide how often you need to receive the collection forms. If you request the reports too frequently, your staff may spend more time reporting than working. On the other hand, if you don't receive the reports often enough, you won't be able to identify a trouble spot early enough to resolve it before it becomes a major crisis. As the manager, you must decide on the correct frequency for collecting actual information for your project.

Tip   You can use the time-phased fields in Project to track actual work and costs on a daily or weekly basis. Read more about time-phased cost tracking in the "Tracking work or costs regularly" section later in this chapter.

When you receive the reports, you should evaluate them to identify unfinished tasks for which you need to adjust the planned duration, work, and costs. You'll find that these adjustments are easiest to make if you make them before you record a task's actual dates or percentage of completion.

Also, remember that recording actual information enables you to compare estimates to actuals; this comparison often proves to be quite valuable. If you want to make this comparison, make sure you set a baseline for your project.

Cross-Reference   See Chapter 11 for more information on setting baselines.

Understanding Calculation Options

You also need to understand the calculation options that you can set in Project — they affect the "bottom line" of both the project's cost and schedule. You can review and change calculation options on the Calculation tab of the Options dialog box; choose Tools ➪ Options to display the dialog box and then click the Calculation tab, as shown in Figure 12-1.

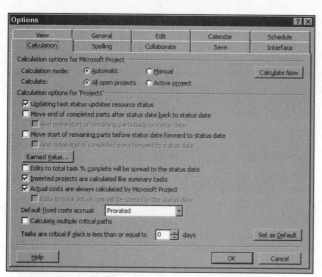

Figure 12-1: Use this dialog box to set the options that Project will use to calculate your project's schedule and cost. In the paragraphs that follow, I describe the various options you see in the figure.

Calculation Mode and Calculate options. You can control when Project calculates changes that you make to the project; if you choose Automatic, Project updates your project as you make changes. If you choose Manual, this dialog box reopens and you can click the Calculate Now button to update your project. You can also choose to apply the calculation mode to all open projects or only to the active project. Automatic calculation is the default, but if your project is very large, calculating can take quite a while; under these circumstances, you may want to switch to manual calculation to save time. When your project is set to manual calculation and you make a change that requires recalculation, you'll see "Calculate" in the status bar — a reminder to calculate the project when you finish making changes.

Updating task status updates resource status checkbox. Place a check in this box to have Project update resource status to correspond with any updated task status. (This option works in reverse, too. If you update a resource's status, Project also updates task status accordingly.) Suppose, for example, that you update the percentage of completion for a task. When you check this box, Project also updates the % Complete field for the resource and the assignment.

New Feature

You can set calculation options that make Project change task start dates and adjust remaining portions of tasks when tasks begin early or late.

Adjusting for late or early starts. By default, when tasks begin late or early, Project doesn't change the task start dates or adjust the remaining portions of tasks. The following four checkboxes are new to Project 2002 and enable you to change this default behavior so that Project updates the tasks in relation to the Status Date:

✦ Move end of completed parts after status date back to status date

✦ And move start of remaining parts back to status date

✦ Move start of remaining parts before status date forward to status date

✦ And move end of completed parts forward to status date

Tip   You can find the project's status date in the Project Information dialog box (choose Project ➪ Project Information). If the status date isn't set, Project uses the current date.

The checkboxes work in pairs; that is, the first two checkboxes work together, and the second two checkboxes work together. To better understand Project's behavior and the first pair of checkboxes, suppose that the Status Date is December 9 and you have a task with a Start Date of December 14 and a duration of four days. Further suppose that the task actually starts on December 7. If you check the first box, Project moves the task start date to 12/7, sets the percent complete to 50%, and schedules the start of the remaining work for 12/16 — thus creating a split task. If you also check the second box, Project makes the changes just described *and* moves the start of the remaining work to 12/9.

Now consider the second pair of checkboxes. Again, suppose that the Status Date is December 9 and you have a task with a Start Date of December 1 and a duration of four days. Further suppose that the task actually starts on December 7. If you check the third box, Project leaves the task start date at 12/1, sets the percent complete to 50%, and schedules the start of the remaining work for 12/9 — again creating a split task. If you also check the fourth box, Project makes the changes just described but also moves the task's actual start to 12/7.

Note that these options don't apply when you record actual information on Summary tasks; these options apply only when you make total actual value edits, including task total actual work, task actual duration, total percent complete, and percent work complete. The settings of these checkboxes won't apply if you use timesheet information from Project Server to update your project.

Earned Value button. Click this button to set Earned Value options for the project.

Cross-Reference   See Chapter 14 for more information about Earned Value.

Edits to total task % complete will be spread to the status date check box. By default, this box is not checked, which makes Project distribute changes to the task percentage of completion to the end of the actual duration of the task. If you check this box, Project will, instead, distribute the changes evenly across the schedule to the project status date.

Inserted projects are calculated like summary tasks check box. When this box is checked (as it is by default) Project treats inserted projects like summary tasks when calculating the project schedule instead of treating them like a separate project.

 See Chapter 15 for more information about inserting projects.

Actual costs are always calculated by Microsoft Project check box. When you check this box, Project calculates actual costs; you can't enter any actual costs until a task is 100% complete — Project will overwrite any costs that you enter prior to 100% completion as it recalculates costs. You also can't import actual cost values

Default fixed costs accrual list box. Use this list box to choose a method for Project to accrue fixed costs for new tasks. You can have Project accrue fixed costs at the start of a task, at the end of a task, or you can prorate the costs throughout the duration of the task.

Calculate multiple critical paths check box. When you check this box, Project calculates and displays separate critical paths in the project — and sets the late finish date for tasks without successors or constraints to their early finish date. By changing the finish dates of these tasks, Project makes these tasks critical. When you *don't* check this box, Project sets the late finish date for these tasks to the project finish date, which leaves these tasks off the critical path.

Tasks are critical if slack is less than or equal to X days box. By default, Project sets this value to 0 — only tasks with no slack appear on the critical path. You can force tasks in your project onto the critical path by increasing this value.

Throughout the rest of this chapter, I use the default settings in Project to demonstrate the effects of updating a project.

Updating Tasks to Reflect Actual Information

You record actual information for a project by filling in the following fields for each task that tracks the progress of your project:

✦ Actual start date

✦ Actual finish date

✦ Actual duration

✦ Remaining duration

✦ Percentage complete

In some cases, when you enter information into one of these fields, Project calculates the values for the other fields. For example, if you enter a percentage complete for a task, Project calculates and supplies a start date, an actual duration, a remaining duration, and an actual work value.

Setting actual start and finish dates

The Gantt Chart view displays projected start and finish dates for tasks. In this section, you learn how to enter and view actual start and finish dates (and compare current, baseline, and actual dates) in the Task Details view, shown in Figure 12-2.

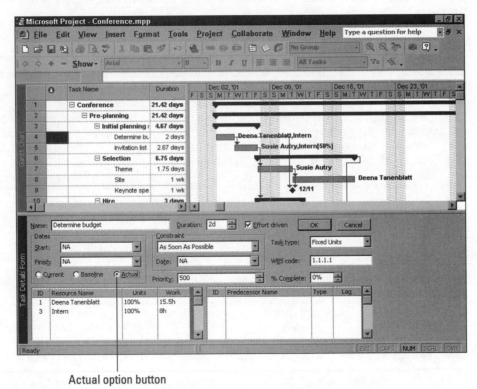

Actual option button

Figure 12-2: Use the Task Details form to enter actual information.

Starting from the Gantt Chart view, follow these steps to set up your screen:

1. Choose Window ➪ Split to display the Task Form view.

2. Click the bottom pane.

3. Choose View ➪ More Views to open the More Views dialog box.

4. Select Task Details Form and click Apply.

5. Select the task (in the top pane) for which you want to record actuals.

6. Click the Actual option button in the bottom pane to identify the type of dates that you want to enter.

   The three option buttons (Current, Baseline, and Actual) refer only to the dates that you can view and set. In other words, you won't see baseline assignments at the bottom of the view if you click Baseline.

7. Record either a Start or a Finish date and click OK.

Project initially sets the Actual Start Date and Actual Finish Date fields to NA to indicate that you have not yet entered a date. When you update your project to provide actual start and finish dates, Project changes the projected start and finish dates to the actual dates that you enter. When you enter an actual start date, Project changes only one other field — the projected start date. However, when you enter an actual finish date, Project changes several other fields: the Percent Complete field, the Actual Duration field, the Remaining Duration field, the Actual Work field, and the Actual Cost field. If you didn't set an actual start date, Project also changes that field.

Recording actual durations

The actual duration of a task is the amount of time that was needed to complete the task. To record an actual duration, you can use the Update Tasks dialog box. Choose Tools ⇨ Tracking ⇨ Update Tasks or click the Update Tasks button on the Tracking toolbar to display the Update Tasks dialog box, as shown in Figure 12-3.

Figure 12-3: Use the Update Tasks dialog box to set the actual duration for a task by filling in the "Actual dur" field.

Tip   You can display the Tracking toolbar by choosing View ⇨ Toolbars ⇨ Tracking.

When you set an actual duration that is less than or equal to the planned duration, Project assumes that the task is progressing on schedule. Therefore, when you click OK, Project sets the actual start date to the planned start date — unless you previously set the actual start date. In that case, Project leaves the actual start date alone. In either case, Project calculates the percentage complete and the remaining duration for the task.

Note   To see the updated remaining duration, reopen the Update Tasks dialog box.

If you set an actual duration that is greater than the planned duration, Project assumes that the task is finished but that it took longer than expected to complete. Project adjusts the planned duration to match the actual duration and changes the Percent Complete field to 100% and the Remaining Duration field to 0%.

You can use the Calculation tab in the Options dialog box (choose Tools ➪ Options) to set Project to update the status of resources when you update a task's status. If you set this option and then supply an actual duration, Project also updates the work and cost figures for the resources.

Cross-Reference   You learn more about this option in the "Overriding resource cost valuations" section later in this chapter.

Note   Don't change the actual duration of a task if you use effort-driven scheduling. Instead, change the number of resource units assigned or the amount of the resource assignment. Remember that the duration of effort-driven tasks is affected by resource assignments.

Setting remaining durations

In the two preceding sections, you saw that you can use the Task Form Details view and the Update Tasks dialog box to record and view actual information. The Task Form Details view provides a limited way to update tasks. Although the Update Tasks dialog box provides a complete way to enter actual information, I find that it's easiest to enter all actual information into Project by using the Tracking Table view, as shown in Figure 12-4.

The Rem. Dur. (Remaining Duration) column shows how much more time you need to complete a task. To display the Tracking Table view, start in the Gantt Chart view and follow these steps:

1. Click the top pane of the Gantt Chart.

2. Choose Window ➪ Remove Split to display the standard Gantt Chart.

3. Right-click the Select All button and choose Tracking. Project displays the Tracking Table view in the left portion of the Gantt Chart view.

Figure showing Microsoft Project - Conference.mpp window with Tracking Table view.

	Task Name	Act. Start	Act. Finish	% Comp.	Physical %	Act. Dur.	Rem. Dur.	Act. Cost	Act. Work
1	⊟ Conference	NA	NA	0%	0%	0 days	21.42 days	$0.00	0 hrs
2	⊟ Pre-planning	NA	NA	0%	0%	0 days	21.42 days	$0.00	0 hrs
3	⊟ Initial planr	NA	NA	0%	0%	0 days	4.67 days	$0.00	0 hrs
4	Determi	NA	NA	0%	0%	0 days	2 days	$0.00	0 hrs
5	Invitatio	NA	NA	0%	0%	0 days	2.67 days	$0.00	0 hrs
6	⊟ Selection	NA	NA	0%	0%	0 days	6.75 days	$0.00	0 hrs
7	Theme	NA	NA	0%	0%	0 days	1.75 days	$0.00	0 hrs
8	Site	NA	NA	0%	0%	0 wks	1 wk	$0.00	0 hrs
9	Keynote	NA	NA	0%	0%	0 wks	1 wk	$0.00	0 hrs
10	⊟ Hire	NA	NA	0%	0%	0 days	3 days	$0.00	0 hrs
11	Caterer	NA	NA	0%	0%	0 days	2 days	$0.00	0 hrs
12	Bartend	NA	NA	0%	0%	0 days	1 day	$0.00	0 hrs
13	Security	NA	NA	0%	0%	0 days	3 days	$0.00	0 hrs
14	Photogr	NA	NA	0%	0%	0 days	1 day	$0.00	0 hrs
15	Cleanup	NA	NA	0%	0%	0 days	1 day	$0.00	0 hrs
16	⊟ Plan Entert	NA	NA	0%	0%	0 days	1 day	$0.00	0 hrs
17	Baseba	NA	NA	0%	0%	0 days	1 day	$0.00	0 hrs
18	Opera	NA	NA	0%	0%	0 hrs	4 hrs	$0.00	0 hrs
19	⊟ Public Rela	NA	NA	0%	0%	0 days	10 days	$0.00	0 hrs
20	Alert co	NA	NA	0%	0%	0 wks	2 wks	$0.00	0 hrs
21	Press re	NA	NA	0%	0%	0 days	1 day	$0.00	0 hrs
22	⊟ Rent Equipr	NA	NA	0%	0%	0 days	1 day	$0.00	0 hrs

Figure 12-4: The Tracking Table view helps you view and enter actual values for tasks.

Tip

To see all the columns available on the Tracking Table view, narrow the chart portion of the window.

If you enter a value into the Rem. Dur. (Remaining Duration) column, Project assumes that the work has begun on the task and will be completed based on the remaining duration value. Therefore, Project sets the Act. Dur. (Actual Duration) and % Comp. (Percent Complete) values based on a combination of the remaining duration value that you supplied and the original planned duration. If necessary, Project also sets the actual start date; if you set Project's options to update the status of resources when you update a task's status, Project updates the work and cost figures for the resources on the task.

Entering 0 in the Rem. Dur. (Remaining Duration) column is the same as entering 100% in the Percent Complete column. For example, suppose that you change the value in the Remaining Duration column so that it is larger than the existing figure. Project assumes that you are changing the planned duration of the task instead of tracking actual progress for the task. In this case, Project adjusts the schedule based on the new planned duration. If the task has already started and you have entered an actual duration when you make the Remaining Duration value larger, Project adds this new estimate to the previously calculated actual duration and adjusts the Percent Complete value.

Setting Percent Complete

You can establish the progress of work performed on a task by assigning a Percent Complete value to the task. Any value less than 100 indicates that the task is not complete. You can set Percent Complete from the Task Details form, from the Update Tasks dialog box, or from the Tracking Table view. Or you can select the task from any task view and use the percentage buttons on the Tracking toolbar, as shown in Figure 12-5. Right-click on any toolbar and choose Tracking to display the toolbar.

Percentage buttons

Figure 12-5: Use these buttons to set a task's actual progress at 0%, 25%, 50%, 75%, or 100% complete.

A value in the Percent Complete column also affects the Actual Duration and Remaining Duration values. If you make an entry into any of these columns, Project automatically updates the others. When you set the Actual Duration value, Project calculates the value for the Percent Complete column by dividing the Actual Duration value by the original planned duration. If, alternatively, you set the Remaining Duration value, Project recalculates (if necessary) the Actual Duration value and the Percent Complete value.

If you change the Percent Complete value, Project assigns an Actual Start Date (unless you had entered one previously). Project also calculates the Actual Duration and Remaining Duration values. If you set your options to update resources when you update tasks, Project also calculates the Actual Cost and Actual Work values. If you enter 100 into the Percent Complete column, Project assigns the planned finish date to the Actual Finish Date column. If this value is not correct, don't enter a Percent Complete; instead, enter an Actual Finish Date.

Setting work completed

Sometimes, you must schedule tasks based on the availability of certain resources. In these cases, tracking progress on a task is easiest if you update the work completed. Updating this value also updates the work that each resource is performing.

In the same way that Project calculates duration information when you fill in a duration field, Project updates the work remaining by subtracting the work performed from the total work scheduled.

Use the Tracking Table view to enter information into the Act. Work column, but start in the Task Usage view so that you can enter actual work performed for specific resources. Choose View ➪ Task Usage, then right-click the Select All button and choose Tracking from the shortcut menu of tables. You'll probably need to drag the divider bar almost completely to the right edge of the screen to reveal the Act. Work column, as shown in Figure 12-6.

	Task Name	Act. Start	Act. Finish	% Comp.	Physical % Complete	Act. Dur.	Rem. Dur.	Act. Cost	Act. Work	Detail
1	☐ Conference	Mon 12/03/01	NA	0%	0%	0 days	22.35 days	$0.00	0 hrs	Work
2	☐ Pre-planning	Mon 12/03/01	NA	0%	0%	0 days	22.35 days	$0.00	0 hrs	Work
3	☐ Initial planning meeting	Tue 12/04/01	NA	0%	0%	0 days	4.6 days	$0.00	0 hrs	Work
4	☐ Determine budget	Tue 12/04/01	NA	0%	0%	0 days	1.94 days	$0.00	0 hrs	Work
	Deena Tanent	*Tue 12/04/01*	*NA*					*$0.00*	*0 hrs*	Work
	Intern	*Tue 12/04/01*	*NA*					*$0.00*	*0 hrs*	Work
5	☐ Invitation list	NA	NA	0%	0%	0 days	2.67 days	$0.00	0 hrs	Work
	Intern	*NA*	*NA*					*$0.00*	*0 hrs*	Work
	Susie Autry	*NA*	*NA*					*$0.00*	*0 hrs*	Work
6	☐ Selection	NA	NA	0%	0%	0 days	6.75 days	$0.00	0 hrs	Work
7	☐ Theme	NA	NA	0%	0%	0 days	1.75 days	$0.00	0 hrs	Work
	Susie Autry	*NA*	*NA*					*$0.00*	*0 hrs*	Work
8	☐ Site	NA	NA	0%	0%	0 wks	1 wk	$0.00	0 hrs	Work
	Deena Tanent	*NA*	*NA*					*$0.00*	*0 hrs*	Work
9	Keynote speaker	NA	NA	0%	0%	0 wks	1 wk	$0.00	0 hrs	Work
10	☐ Hire	NA	NA	0%	0%	0 days	3 days	$0.00	0 hrs	Work
11	Caterer	NA	NA	0%	0%	0 days	2 days	$0.00	0 hrs	Work
12	Bartenders	NA	NA	0%	0%	0 days	1 day	$0.00	0 hrs	Work
13	Security	NA	NA	0%	0%	0 days	3 days	$0.00	0 hrs	Work
14	Photographers	NA	NA	0%	0%	0 days	1 day	$0.00	0 hrs	Work
15	Cleanup crew	NA	NA	0%	0%	0 days	1 day	$0.00	0 hrs	Work
16	☐ Plan Entertainment	NA	NA	0%	0%	0 days	1 day	$0.00	0 hrs	Work

Figure 12-6: The Tracking Table view with resources displayed

Tip

If you are scheduling tasks based on the availability of resources in general, instead of the availability of specific resources, you can still use this technique to record actual work. However, you need to enter the value on the same row as the task, rather than on the individual rows for the resources. Project divides the actual and remaining work among the resources.

Using Actuals and Costs

Except for fixed-cost tasks, Project uses the cost of the resources assigned to the task over the duration of the task to calculate a task's cost. Costs are accrued, and total project costs are the sum of all resource and fixed costs. Therefore, if you previously set up and assigned resources to your tasks, Project has been calculating and accruing the costs for you — all you need to do is review and analyze the costs.

Alternatively, you may have chosen not to assign resources to your tasks, or you may have changed your default options so that Project wouldn't calculate costs. How can you do that? Choose Tools ➪ Options to display the Options dialog box. On the Calculation tab, look at the Calculation options for your project, as shown in Figure 12-7. If you don't see a check in the "Updating task status updates resource status" checkbox, Project has not been calculating your project's costs. Remember, however, that this checkbox contains a check by default, as you see in the figure.

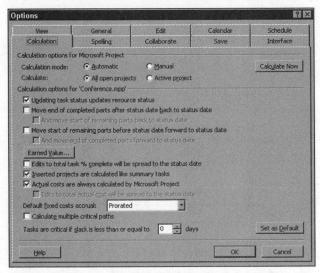

Figure 12-7: From the Calculation tab of the Options dialog box, you can tell whether Project has been calculating your project's costs.

If you did not assign resources or you changed the defaults, Project can't calculate the cost of your project unless you provide additional information after the task is completed. You can review and update your project's costs from one of two cost tables: the Cost table for tasks or the Cost table for resources. You can also override the costs that Project assigns.

Using the Cost table for tasks

The Cost table for tasks shown in Figure 12-8 demonstrates cost information based on each task in your project. This table shows you the baseline cost (the planned cost), the actual cost, the variance between planned and actual costs, and the remaining cost of the task.

If you assign a fixed cost to a task in this table, Project adds the fixed cost to the calculated cost for the task. To display this table, start in the Gantt Chart view. Then right-click the Select All button to display the shortcut menu of tables, and choose Cost. You may also need to slide the chart pane all the way to the right to see all the fields on the Cost table for tasks.

The Cost table for tasks is most useful if you saved a baseline view of your project, because it enables you to compare baseline costs with actual costs.

Figure 12-8: The Cost table for tasks

Using the Cost table for resources

The Cost table for resources is very similar to the Cost table for tasks, with the breakdown of costs being displayed by resource rather than by task, as shown in Figure 12-9.

Figure 12-9: The Cost table for resources

To display this table, begin with a resource view such as the Resource Sheet. Then, right-click the Select All button and choose Cost from the shortcut menu that appears.

Like the Cost table for tasks, the Cost table for resources is useful if you saved a baseline view of your project, because it enables you to compare baseline costs with actual costs.

Overriding resource cost valuations

Project default settings automatically update costs as you record progress on a task. Project uses the accrual method that you selected for the resource when you created the resource.

Cross-Reference For more information about setting a resource's accrual method, see Chapter 5.

Alternatively, you can enter the actual costs for a resource assignment, or track actual costs separately from the actual work on a task. To do so, after the task is completed, you must enter costs manually to override Project's calculated costs. Before you can override the costs that Project calculated, however, you must turn off one of the default options. Follow these steps:

1. Choose Tools ➪ Options to display the Options dialog box.

2. Click the Calculation tab.

3. Click the "Actual costs are always calculated by Microsoft Project" option to clear the checkbox, as shown in Figure 12-10.

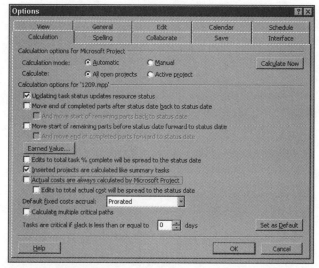

Figure 12-10: Revise the default settings to override Project's calculated costs.

Note The "Edits to total actual cost will be spread to the status date" checkbox becomes available. Place a check in this box if you want Project to distribute the edits that you're going to make through the Status Date. If you leave the box unchecked, Project distributes the edits to the end of the actual duration of the task.

4. Click OK.

5. Choose View ➪ Task Usage.

6. Right-click the Select All button to display the table shortcut menu and choose Tracking. Project displays the Tracking Table view, as shown in Figure 12-11.

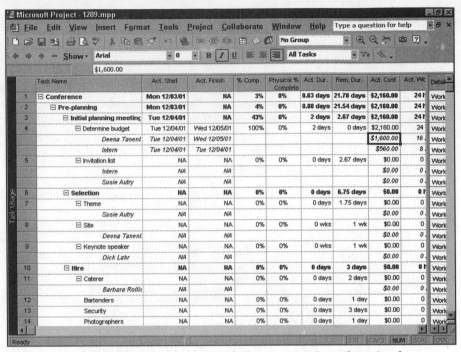

Figure 12-11: The Tracking Table view with the Act. Cost (Actual Cost) column visible

7. Drag the divider bar to the right so that you can see all the columns.

8. Select the task or resource to which you want to assign a cost.

9. Enter the cost in the Act. Cost column.

Tip   If you change your mind and want Project to calculate costs as it originally did, repeat Steps 1, 2, and 3 to restore the default calculation method. Project warns you that it will overwrite any manually entered costs when you click OK.

Techniques and Tips for Updating

Project users can find ways to accelerate the updating process. For example, you can:

✦ Use Project's timephased fields to easily update your project on a regular basis

✦ Update the progress of several tasks simultaneously

✦ Reschedule incomplete work so that it starts on the current date

Tracking work or costs regularly

Project's timephased fields enable you to update the progress on your project on a regular basis, such as daily or weekly. To use timephased fields to record progress information for resources, start by displaying the Resource Usage view (choose View ➪ Resource Usage). Then right-click the Select All button and select Work from the shortcut menu to change the table. Your screen should resemble Figure 12-12.

Figure 12-12: Setting up to use timephased fields

You're going to want to use most of the right side of the view, but on the left side of the view, you really need only the Actual Work column, which is hidden by the right side of the view. You can slide the divider bar over to the right, but then you'd lose the right side of the view. Or, after sliding the divider bar, you can hide all the columns between the Resource Name column and the Actual Work column — to redisplay them, you need to insert each of them.

To set up the left side of the view so that you can see the Actual Work column, insert that column between the Resource Name column and the % Comp. (Percent Complete) column. To insert the column:

1. Click the title of the Percent Complete column to select the entire column.

2. Choose Insert ➪ Column to open the Column Definition dialog box, as shown in Figure 12-13.

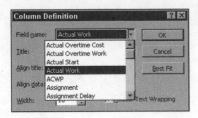

Figure 12-13: Add the Actual Work column from the Column Definition dialog box.

3. Open the Field name drop-down list and select Actual Work.

4. Click OK.

Project inserts the Actual Work column to the left of the % Comp. column and to the right of the Resource Name column.

Next, you should decide how often you want to update your project. If you want to update daily, you don't need to make any changes to the timescale on the right side of the window. But if you want to update weekly (or with some other frequency), you need to change the timescale. To change the timescale, choose Format ➪ Timescale. Project opens the Timescale dialog box, as shown in Figure 12-14. This example doesn't require any timescale changes, but if you want to change the timescale to weekly (for example), choose a tier, open the Units list box, and select Weeks. Then hide the other tiers by checking the Hide tier box on each tier's tab.

When you add a timephased field for Actual Work, you can see the results as you update the schedule. Choose Format ➪ Details ➪ Actual Work. Project adds a row for every task on the right side of the view. To enter hours worked for a particular day, click the letter of the column representing that day to select the entire day, as shown in Figure 12-15. Then enter the hours for the correct resource and task in the Actual Work column that you added on the left side of the view.

Note   Remember, however, that you can't add costs to override Project's automatically calculated costs unless you open the Options dialog box (choose Tools ➪ Options), select the Calculation tab, and remove the check from the "Actual costs are always calculated by Microsoft Project" checkbox.

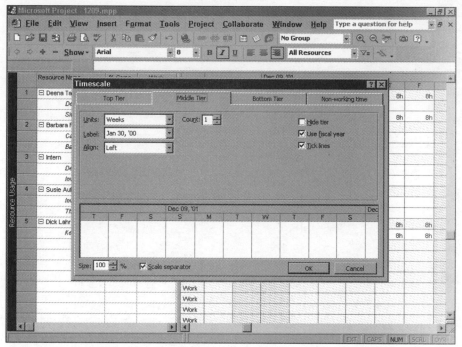

Figure 12-14: Use the Timescale dialog box to change the increments that appear on the right side of the Resource Usage view.

This entire process also works if you are updating costs on a daily basis, with two minor changes:

✦ Begin in the Task Usage view instead of the Resource Usage view.

✦ Add the Tracking table instead of the Work table.

Tip
To hide the Actual Work column that you added to the left side of the view, select the entire column and then choose Edit ➪ Hide Column. The left side of the view returns to its default appearance. To hide the Actual Work row that you added to the right side of the view, choose Format ➪ Details ➪ Actual Work again to remove the check mark.

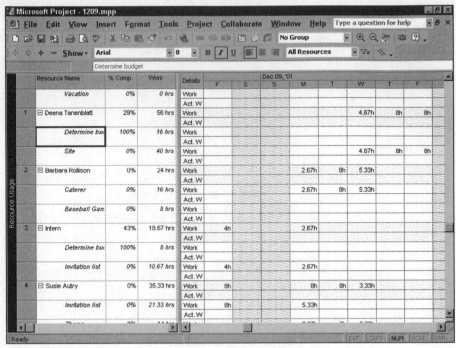

Figure 12-15: Add actual work information for a specific day.

Accelerating the updating process

If you have several tasks that are on schedule or were completed on schedule, you can update these tasks all at once by following these steps:

1. Select the Gantt Chart view.

Tip   If you want to update the entire project, don't select any tasks.

2. In the Task Name column, select the tasks that you want to update. For example, Figure 12-16 shows three tasks selected for updating.

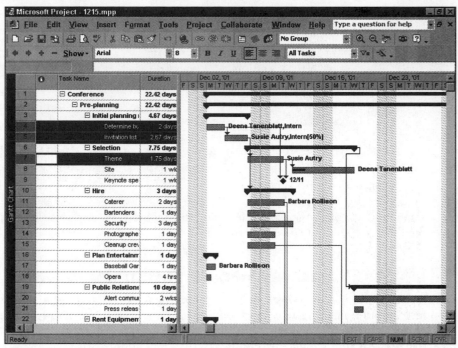

Figure 12-16: Selecting tasks to update

> **Note**
>
> You can select tasks by using the same techniques that you use in Windows Explorer. To select two or more contiguous tasks, click the first task, and then hold down the Shift key and click the last task. To select two or more noncontiguous tasks, hold down the Ctrl key as you click each task that you want to select.

3. Choose Tools ➪ Tracking ➪ Update Project to display the Update Project dialog box, as shown in Figure 12-17.

Figure 12-17: Use the Update Project dialog box to update your project.

4. Make sure that the correct date appears in the box next to the "Update work as complete through" option button.

5. Select one of the following:

   - "Set 0% – 100% complete" if you want Project to calculate the Percent Complete for each task.

   - "Set 0% or 100% complete only" if you want Project to mark completed tasks with 100% and leave incomplete tasks at 0%.

6. Specify whether to update the entire project or selected tasks by selecting the appropriate option.

7. Click OK.

When you update your project by using this method, Project sets the project status date to the date that you selected in Step 4.

Letting Project reschedule uncompleted work

If you updated your project and you had partially completed tasks, you can guarantee that no remaining work is scheduled for dates that have already passed. You can make sure that all remaining work is scheduled for future dates by rescheduling the work to start on the current date.

New Feature

In Project 2000 and earlier, if you rescheduled work by using the technique described in this section, Project would remove task constraints that you applied. For example, suppose that you rescheduled the work of a task that had a Must Finish On constraint, and rescheduling moved the finish date beyond the constraint date. Project 2000 and earlier did not honor the constraint date; instead, it changed the constraint to As Soon As Possible. To preserve a task's constraints, you had to reschedule the remaining work manually.

Project 2002 introduces new behavior; it does not remove constraints and reschedule tasks without progress. However, be aware that this behavior may leave your project in an infeasible situation. Project will display a message if this situation occurs, and you can manually make changes as needed.

Follow these steps to tell Project to reschedule remaining work for future dates:

1. Select the Gantt Chart view.

2. Go to the Task Name column and select the tasks that you want to update. See the previous section for techniques you can use to select tasks.

3. Choose Tools ➪ Tracking ➪ Update Project to open the Update Project dialog box, as shown in Figure 12-18.

Figure 12-18: Use this dialog box to reschedule incomplete work to start today.

4. Click the "Reschedule uncompleted work to start" option button and select the date from which you want to reschedule all unfinished work.

Project 2000 introduced the ability to set a date from which you wanted to reschedule uncompleted work. However, suppose that you rescheduled work *twice*; Project 2000 ignored all dates except the first rescheduling date that you supplied. Project 2002 will reschedule selected tasks or your project each time you change the date.

5. Specify whether to update the entire project or selected tasks by selecting the appropriate option button.

6. Click OK.

When you reschedule partially completed tasks by using the technique just described, Project automatically splits the task between the completed portion and the remaining portion. Therefore, the Gantt Chart may display a split task that has a gap between its two parts because the completed portion may have finished some time before the remaining portion is scheduled to start.

Reviewing Progress

When you start recording actuals, you're going to want to review the progress of your project — and Project can help you.

Using the Tracking Gantt view

The Tracking Gantt view shown in Figure 12-19 uses the Entry table and probably provides the most effective picture of your project's progress. The bottom bar on the chart portion of the view (black hatching on your screen) represents the baseline dates for each task. The top bar spans either the scheduled start and finish dates or (if a task has been completed) the actual start and finish dates for each task.

If a task is finished, a check mark appears in the Indicator column on the left side of the view next to the task.

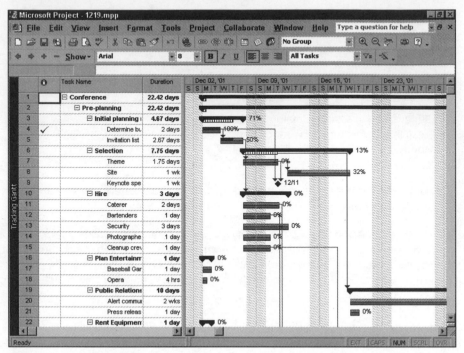

Figure 12-19: The Tracking Gantt view helps you understand the progress of your project.

Project formats the taskbar to indicate the task's status:

✦ If a task is scheduled, but not yet complete, the top bar appears as blue hatching (it appears red if the task is on the critical path).

✦ If the task is completed, the bar appears solid blue (it appears red if the task is on the critical path).

✦ If a task is partially complete, the completed portion appears as solid blue in the top bar, but the unfinished portion appears as blue hatching (red hatching appears if the task is on the critical path).

Using the Work table for tasks

The Work table for tasks shown in Figure 12-20 shows the total time required from all resources to complete the task. Work differs from task duration in the following ways:

✦ Work measures how many person hours are needed to complete a task.

✦ Task duration measures the amount of time (number of days) allotted to the task.

If the total work for a task is 16 hours but the task duration is only one day, you'll either need to add another resource (meaning that two people can complete the task in one day) or extend the task's duration.

Figure 12-20: The Work table for tasks

The Work table for tasks includes baseline information so that you can compare your progress to your original estimate. For this table to be meaningful, therefore, you must have saved a baseline for your project. And as you may have guessed, you can enter information in the Work table for tasks.

You can apply the Work table for tasks to any task sheet view. In Figure 12-19, for example, the Work table for tasks appears on the left side of the Task Usage view. Choose View ➪ Task Usage; then right-click the Select All button and choose Work.

Using the Work table for resources

The Work table for resources shown in Figure 12-21 demonstrates work information for resources. Again, work represents the total time required from all resources to complete the task. The Work table for resources also includes baseline information so that you can compare your progress to your original estimate.

You can apply the Work table for resources to any resource sheet view. In Figure 12-20, for example, the Work table for resources appears on the left side of the Resource Usage view. Select the Resource Usage view from the View bar; then right-click the Select All button and choose Work.

Figure 12-21: The Work table for resources

Viewing progress lines

Project contains another tool that you can use to show the progress that you're making on your project — if you have saved a baseline of your project. If you add progress lines to the Gantt Chart of your project, as shown in Figure 12-22, Project draws a line that connects in-progress tasks. The progress line creates a graph of your project with peaks pointing to the right for work that is ahead of schedule and peaks pointing to the left for work that is behind schedule. The distance between the peaks and the line indicates the degree to which the task is ahead of or behind schedule.

Figure 12-22: A Gantt Chart with a progress line added

To add a progress line, follow these steps:

1. Choose View ➪ Gantt Chart.

2. Choose Tools ➪ Tracking ➪ Progress Lines to open the Progress Lines dialog box and display the Dates and Intervals tab.

3. Place a check in the "Display selected progress lines" checkbox to activate the Progress Line Dates drop-down list.

4. Click once in the Progress Line Dates list. Project displays a list box arrow.

5. Click the list box arrow, and a small calendar appears, as shown in Figure 12-23.

6. Select a date for the progress line.

7. Select either Actual plan or Baseline plan in the "Display progress lines in relation to" box.

8. Click OK. Project adds the progress line to your Gantt Chart, which looks like the progress line shown previously in Figure 12-22.

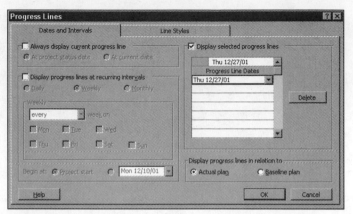

Figure 12-23: The Dates and Intervals tab of the Progress Lines dialog box

As you can imagine, a progress line on a project with a large number of tasks can begin to look messy. But if you decide that you like progress lines, you can display them at varying intervals, as shown previously in Figure 12-23. You also can add specific dates to the Progress Line Dates list on the right side of the Progress Lines dialog box to display multiple progress lines on the Gantt Chart. If you decide to display more than one progress line, you may want to use the Line Styles tab of the Progress Lines dialog box to format the lines so that you can tell them apart (for example, you can change their colors).

To stop displaying progress lines, reopen the Progress Lines dialog box and remove any checks from the boxes on the Dates and Intervals tab.

Summary

In this chapter, you learned how to record actual information about tasks and resources. For example, you learned how to:

✦ Set start and finish dates

✦ Set actual and remaining durations

✦ Set the percent complete for a task

✦ Set the work completed for a task

✦ Use cost tables for tasks and resources

✦ Review the progress of your project

Chapter 13 shows you how to report on a project's progress.

✦   ✦   ✦

Reporting on Progress

As you saw in Chapters 6 and 7, Project contains various views that help you to evaluate the progress of your project, identify areas with problems, and even resolve problems. Although you can print views, sometimes you need to present information in a format that is not available in any view. This chapter examines the use of reports for presenting your Project information.

Reporting Commonalities

All reports in Project have certain common characteristics. For example, you can print any report or you can review the report onscreen.

Note

Project organizes reports into categories of reports related to the same subject; for example, all the cost reports fall into the Costs category.

Here's how to display the reports available in a particular category:

1. Choose View ⇨ Reports to open the Reports dialog box, as shown in Figure 13-1).

Figure 13-1: Select a report category from the Reports dialog box.

2. Click the category of report that you want.

3. Click Select. Project displays the reports available in that category.

4. Select a report.

Note   As you read through this chapter and see the reports available in each category, you can use the Edit button in the Reports dialog box to change the information that appears on the report. You can also use the Edit button to customize the report, which you will learn at the end of this chapter.

5. Click Select. Project displays the report onscreen in Print Preview mode, as shown in Figure 13-2.

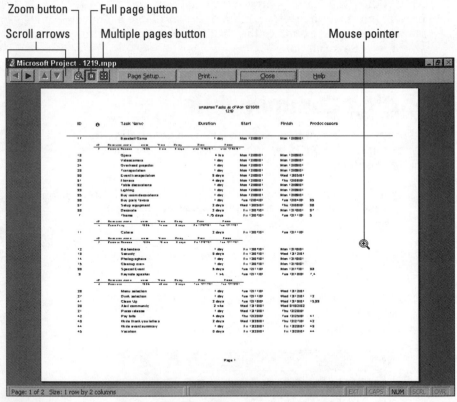

Figure 13-2: A report in Print Preview mode

Use the scroll arrows on the toolbar at the top of the screen to move around the report. The Zoom button enlarges the image so that you can read the report's content onscreen. Or, if you prefer, click the portion of the report that you want to enlarge — the shape of the mouse pointer indicates that it will zoom in on the area that you click. To zoom out again, click the Full Page button or click again on the report. To display more than one page at a time, click the Multiple Pages button.

If you decide to print the report, you can review the page settings first. Click the Page Setup button to display the Page Setup dialog box, as shown in Figure 13-3.

Figure 13-3: Use the Page Setup dialog box to set orientation, scaling, margins, and — if appropriate — header and footer information.

Cross-Reference   Refer to Chapter 6 for a description of the tabs in the Page Setup dialog box.

To print a report, click the Print button. Project displays the Print dialog box, as shown in Figure 13-4. Alternatively, you can return to Project by clicking the Close button.

Figure 13-4: In the Print dialog box, select a print range for the report.

Looking at the Big Picture

When you select Overview in the Reports dialog box, Project displays the top-level, summary-type reports, as shown in Figure 13-5.

Figure 13-5: The reports available in the Overview category

Project Summary

The Project Summary report, as shown in Figure 13-6, shows top-level information about your project. This report presents summarized information about dates, duration, work, costs, task status, and resource status.

newres
Marmel Enterprises, Inc.

as of Mon 12/10/01

Dates

Start:	Fri 10/05/01	Finish:	Fri 11/09/01
Baseline Start:	Fri 10/05/01	Baseline Finish:	Fri 11/09/01
Actual Start:	NA	Actual Finish:	NA
Start Variance:	0 days	Finish Variance:	0 days

Duration

Scheduled:	26 days	Remaining:	26 days
Baseline:	26 days	Actual:	0 days
Variance:	0 days	Percent Complete:	0%

Work

Scheduled:	291 hrs	Remaining:	291 hrs
Baseline:	291 hrs	Actual:	0 hrs
Variance:	0 hrs	Percent Complete:	0%

Costs

Scheduled:	$0.00	Remaining:	$0.00
Baseline:	$0.00	Actual:	$0.00
Variance:	$0.00		

Task Status

		Resource Status	
Tasks not yet started:	21	Work Resources:	7
Tasks in progress:	0	Overallocated Work Resources:	1
Tasks completed:	0	Material Resources:	0
Total Tasks:	21	Total Resources:	8

Figure 13-6: The Project Summary report

Top Level Tasks

The Top Level Tasks report, as shown in Figure 13-7, shows — as of today's date — the summary tasks at the highest level in your project. You can see scheduled start and finish dates, the percentage complete for each task, the cost, and the work required to complete the task.

		Top Level Tasks as of Mon 12/10/01 newres					
ID	Task Name	Duration	Start	Finish	% Comp.	Cost	Work
1	Begin Project	0 days	Fri 10/05/01	Fri 10/05/01	0%	$0.00	0 hrs
2	Product Research	4 days	Fri 10/05/01	Wed 10/10/01	0%	$0.00	60 hrs
7	Brochure Design	11 days	Thu 10/11/01	Thu 10/25/01	0%	$0.00	144 hrs
13	Write Customer Documentation	8.25 days	Wed 10/10/01	Mon 10/22/01	0%	$0.00	87 hrs
14	Press Coverage	8.5 days	Mon 10/29/01	Thu 11/08/01	0%	$0.00	0 hrs
19	Print Collateral	11 days	Fri 11/09/01	Fri 11/09/01	0%	$0.00	0 hrs
20	Advertising	1 day	Fri 11/09/01	Fri 11/09/01	0%	$0.00	0 hrs

Figure 13-7: The Top Level Tasks report

Critical Tasks

The Critical Tasks report, as shown in Figure 13-8, shows the status of the tasks on the critical path of your project — those tasks that make the project late if you don't complete them on time. This report displays each task's planned duration, start and finish dates, the resources assigned to the task, and the predecessors and successors of the task.

ID	❶	Task Name	Duration	Start	Finish	Predecessors	Resource Names
1		Begin Project	0 days	Fri 10/05/01	Fri 10/05/01		
	ID / Successor Name / Type / Lag	2 Product Research FS 0 days / 7 Brochure Design FS 0 days / 13 Write Customer Documentation FS 0 days					
2		**Product Research**	4 days	Fri 10/05/01	Wed 10/10/01	1	
	ID / Successor Name / Type / Lag	7 Brochure Design FS 0 days					
5		Research competition	4 days	Fri 10/05/01	Wed 10/10/01		Alicia Hon
7		**Brochure Design**	11 days	Thu 10/11/01	Thu 10/25/01	2,1	
	ID / Successor Name / Type / Lag	19 Print Collateral FS 0 days					
8		Write copy from overview	3 days	Thu 10/11/01	Mon 10/15/01		Mick Chen
	ID / Successor Name / Type / Lag	9 Storyboard design FS 0 days					
9		Storyboard design	4 days	Tue 10/16/01	Fri 10/19/01	8	Combined Graphics
	ID / Successor Name / Type / Lag	11 Design approval FS 0 days					
11		Design approval	1 day	Mon 10/22/01	Mon 10/22/01	9	Ron Wozniak
	ID / Successor Name / Type / Lag	12 Create final design FS 0 days					
12		Create final design	3 days	Tue 10/23/01	Thu 10/25/01	11	Combined Graphics[300%]
14		**Press Coverage**	8.5 days	Mon 10/29/01	Thu 11/08/01	10	
15		Write press releases	2 days	Mon 10/29/01	Wed 10/31/01		
	ID / Successor Name / Type / Lag	16 Prepare media kit FS 0 days					
16		Prepare media kit	6 days	Wed 10/31/01	Thu 11/08/01	15	
	ID / Successor Name / Type / Lag	17 Press mailing FS 0 days					
17		Press mailing	0.5 days	Thu 11/08/01	Thu 11/08/01	16	
	ID / Successor Name / Type / Lag	18 Press conference FS 0 days					
18		Press conference	0 days	Thu 11/08/01	Thu 11/08/01	17	
	ID / Successor Name / Type / Lag	20 Advertising FS 0 days					
19		Print Collateral	11 days	Fri 10/26/01	Fri 11/09/01	7	
20		**Advertising**	1 day	Fri 11/09/01	Fri 11/09/01	18	
21		Present ad campaign to Board	1 day	Fri 11/09/01	Fri 11/09/01		

Figure 13-8: The Critical Tasks report

Milestones

The Milestones report, as shown in Figure 13-9, shows information about each milestone in your project. If you marked summary tasks to appear as milestones in the Task Information dialog box, summary tasks also appear on this report as milestones. For each milestone or summary task, Project displays the planned duration, start and finish dates, predecessors, and the resources assigned to the milestone.

ID	❶	Task Name	Duration	Start	Finish	Predecessors	Resource Names
				Milestones as of Mon 12/10/01 newres			
1		Begin Project	0 days	Fri 10/05/01	Fri 10/05/01		
14		Press Coverage	8.5 days	Mon 10/29/01	Thu 11/08/01	10	
18		Press conference	0 days	Thu 11/08/01	Thu 11/08/01	17	

Figure 13-9: The Milestones report

Working Days

As Figure 13-10 demonstrates, the Working Days report shows the base calendar information for your project. You can see the name of the base calendar for the project and the working hours established for each day of the week, along with any exceptions that you defined.

BASE CALENDAR:	Standard
Day	Hours
Sunday	Nonworking
Monday	8:00AM - 12:00PM, 1:00PM - 5:00 P
Tuesday	8:00AM - 12:00PM, 1:00PM - 5:00 P
Wednesday	8:00AM - 12:00PM, 1:00PM - 5:00 P
Thursday	8:00AM - 12:00PM, 1:00PM - 5:00 P
Friday	8:00AM - 12:00PM, 1:00PM - 5:00 P
Saturday	Nonworking
Exceptions:	None

Figure 13-10: The Working Days report

Reports on Costs

When you select Costs in the Reports dialog box, Project displays thumbnail sketches of the reports that describe the costs associated with your project, as shown in Figure 13-11.

Figure 13-11: The reports available in the Costs category

Cash Flow

The Cash Flow report, as shown in Figure 13-12, is a tabular report that shows, by task, the costs for weekly time increments.

If you click Cash Flow in the Cost Reports dialog box (previously shown in Figure 13-11) and then select Edit before you choose Select ➪ Project, the Crosstab Report dialog box opens, as shown in Figure 13-13. On the Definition tab, you can change the time increments.

See the section "Customizing Reports" at the end of this chapter for more information about the Crosstab Report dialog box.

	11/25/01	12/02/01	12/09/01	12/16/01	12/23/01	12/30/01	Total
Cash Flow as of Mon 12/10/01 1312							
Conference							
Pre-planning							
Initial planning meeting							
Determine budget		$2,160.00					$2,160.00
Invitation list		$2,453.33					$2,453.33
Selection							
Theme		$213.33	$906.67				$1,120.00
Site			$2,196.18	$2,053.82			$4,250.00
Keynote speaker			$3,583.33	$1,416.67			$5,000.00
Hire							
Caterer		$213.33	$1,066.67				$1,280.00
Bartenders							
Security							
Photographers							
Cleanup crew							
Plan Entertainment							
Baseball Game		$640.00					$640.00
Opera							
Public Relations							
Alert community							
Press release							
Rent Equipment							
Videocamera							
Overhead projector							
Meet with Caterer							
Menu selection							
Drink selection							
Arrangements							
Transportation							
Event transportation							
Flowers							
Table decorations							
Lighting							
Preparation							
Buy room decorations							
Buy party favors							
Setup equipment							
Decorate							
Special Event							
Total		$5,680.00	$7,752.85	$3,470.49			$16,903.33

Figure 13-12: The Cash Flow report

Figure 13-13: Use the Crosstab Report dialog box to change the default settings for the report.

Earned Value

The Earned Value report, as shown in Figure 13-14, shows you the status of each task's costs when you compare planned to actual costs. Some column headings in this report may seem cryptic; see Table 13-1 for translations.

Note Even printed in landscape format, the columns of this report don't fit on one page. The BAC and the VAC columns are missing from the figure; they are printed on Page 2 of the report.

Cross-Reference For more information about Project handling earned value, refer to Chapter 14.

Earned Value as of Mon 12/10/01
1312

ID	Task Name	BCWS	BCWP	ACWP	SV	CV	EAC
4	Determine budget	$2,160.00	$2,160.00	$2,160.00	$0.00	$0.00	$2,160.00
5	Invitation list	$2,453.33	$1,226.67	$1,226.67	($1,226.67)	$0.00	$2,453.33
7	Theme	$853.33	$0.00	$0.00	($853.33)	$0.00	$1,120.00
8	Site	$0.00	$0.00	$0.00	$0.00	$0.00	$4,250.00
9	Keynote speaker	$0.00	$0.00	$0.00	$0.00	$0.00	$5,000.00
11	Caterer	$853.33	$0.00	$0.00	($853.33)	$0.00	$1,280.00
12	Bartenders	$0.00	$0.00	$0.00	$0.00	$0.00	$0.00
13	Security	$0.00	$0.00	$0.00	$0.00	$0.00	$0.00
14	Photographers	$0.00	$0.00	$0.00	$0.00	$0.00	$0.00
15	Cleanup crew	$0.00	$0.00	$0.00	$0.00	$0.00	$0.00
17	Baseball Game	$640.00	$0.00	$0.00	($640.00)	$0.00	$640.00
18	Opera	$0.00	$0.00	$0.00	$0.00	$0.00	$0.00
20	Alert community	$0.00	$0.00	$0.00	$0.00	$0.00	$0.00
21	Press release	$0.00	$0.00	$0.00	$0.00	$0.00	$0.00
23	Videocamera	$0.00	$0.00	$0.00	$0.00	$0.00	$0.00
24	Overhead projector	$0.00	$0.00	$0.00	$0.00	$0.00	$0.00
26	Menu selection	$0.00	$0.00	$0.00	$0.00	$0.00	$0.00
27	Drink selection	$0.00	$0.00	$0.00	$0.00	$0.00	$0.00
29	Transportation	$0.00	$0.00	$0.00	$0.00	$0.00	$0.00
30	Event transportation	$0.00	$0.00	$0.00	$0.00	$0.00	$0.00
31	Flowers	$0.00	$0.00	$0.00	$0.00	$0.00	$0.00
32	Table decorations	$0.00	$0.00	$0.00	$0.00	$0.00	$0.00
33	Lighting	$0.00	$0.00	$0.00	$0.00	$0.00	$0.00
35	Buy room decorations	$0.00	$0.00	$0.00	$0.00	$0.00	$0.00
36	Buy party favors	$0.00	$0.00	$0.00	$0.00	$0.00	$0.00
37	Setup equipment	$0.00	$0.00	$0.00	$0.00	$0.00	$0.00
38	Decorate	$0.00	$0.00	$0.00	$0.00	$0.00	$0.00
39	Special Event	$0.00	$0.00	$0.00	$0.00	$0.00	$0.00
		$6,959.99	$3,386.67	$3,386.67	($3,573.33)	$0.00	

Figure 13-14: The Earned Value report

Table 13-1
Headings in the Earned Value Report

Heading	Translation
BCWS	Budgeted Cost of Work Scheduled
BCWP	Budgeted Cost of Work Performed
ACWP	Actual Cost of Work Performed
SV	Schedule Variance
CV	Cost Variance
BAC	Budgeted at Completion
EAC	Estimate at Completion
VAC	Variance at Completion

Project calculates BCWS, BCWP, ACWP, SV, and CV through the project status date. SV represents the cost difference between current progress and the baseline plan, and Project calculates this value as BCWP minus BCWS. CV represents the cost difference between actual costs and planned costs at the current level of completion, and Project calculates this value as BCWP minus ACWP. EAC shows the planned costs based on costs already incurred plus additional planned costs. VAC represents the variance between the baseline cost and the combination of actual plus planned costs for a task.

Budget

The Budget report, as shown in Figure 13-15, lists all tasks and shows the budgeted costs, as well as the variance between budgeted and actual costs.

Budget Report as of Mon 12/10/01
1312

ID	Task Name	Fixed Cost	Fixed Cost Accrual	Total Cost	Baseline	Variance	Actual
9	Keynote speaker	$0.00	Prorated	$5,000.00	$5,000.00	$0.00	$0.00
8	Site	$250.00	Prorated	$4,250.00	$4,250.00	$0.00	$1,347.00
5	Invitation list	$0.00	Prorated	$2,453.33	$2,453.33	$0.00	$1,226.67
4	Determine budget	$0.00	Prorated	$2,160.00	$2,160.00	$0.00	$2,160.00
11	Caterer	$0.00	Prorated	$1,280.00	$1,280.00	$0.00	$0.00
7	Theme	$0.00	Prorated	$1,120.00	$1,120.00	$0.00	$0.00
17	Baseball Game	$0.00	Prorated	$640.00	$640.00	$0.00	$0.00
12	Bartenders	$0.00	Prorated	$0.00	$0.00	$0.00	$0.00
13	Security	$0.00	Prorated	$0.00	$0.00	$0.00	$0.00
14	Photographers	$0.00	Prorated	$0.00	$0.00	$0.00	$0.00
15	Cleanup crew	$0.00	Prorated	$0.00	$0.00	$0.00	$0.00
18	Opera	$0.00	Prorated	$0.00	$0.00	$0.00	$0.00
20	Alert community	$0.00	Prorated	$0.00	$0.00	$0.00	$0.00
21	Press release	$0.00	Prorated	$0.00	$0.00	$0.00	$0.00
23	Videocamera	$0.00	Prorated	$0.00	$0.00	$0.00	$0.00
24	Overhead projector	$0.00	Prorated	$0.00	$0.00	$0.00	$0.00
26	Menu selection	$0.00	Prorated	$0.00	$0.00	$0.00	$0.00
27	Drink selection	$0.00	Prorated	$0.00	$0.00	$0.00	$0.00
29	Transportation	$0.00	Prorated	$0.00	$0.00	$0.00	$0.00
30	Event transportation	$0.00	Prorated	$0.00	$0.00	$0.00	$0.00
31	Flowers	$0.00	Prorated	$0.00	$0.00	$0.00	$0.00
32	Table decorations	$0.00	Prorated	$0.00	$0.00	$0.00	$0.00
33	Lighting	$0.00	Prorated	$0.00	$0.00	$0.00	$0.00
35	Buy room decorations	$0.00	Prorated	$0.00	$0.00	$0.00	$0.00
36	Buy party favors	$0.00	Prorated	$0.00	$0.00	$0.00	$0.00
37	Setup equipment	$0.00	Prorated	$0.00	$0.00	$0.00	$0.00
38	Decorate	$0.00	Prorated	$0.00	$0.00	$0.00	$0.00
39	Special Event	$0.00	Prorated	$0.00	$0.00	$0.00	$0.00
		$250.00		$16,903.33	$16,903.33	$0.00	$4,733.67

Figure 13-15: The Budget report

Note   This report won't have much meaning unless you have saved a baseline of your project; the values in the variance column change from $0.00 as you complete tasks. Also, the report includes a "Remaining" column that wouldn't fit on the same page as the other columns in the figure.

Overbudget reports

Project contains two Overbudget reports: one for tasks and one for resources. Neither report prints if you haven't yet indicated that some tasks are at least partially completed. Instead, you see the message that appears in Figure 13-16.

Figure 13-16: This message appears when you attempt to print an Overbudget report before you mark any tasks as at least partially complete.

✦ **Overbudget Tasks.** This report, shown in Figure 13-17, shows cost, baseline, variance, and actual information about tasks that exceed their budgeted amounts. In the figure, the "Remaining" column is missing because it wouldn't fit on the first page of the report.

ID	Task Name	Fixed Cost	Fixed Cost Accrual	Total Cost	Baseline	Variance	Actual
			Overbudget Tasks as of Mon 12/10/01 1316				
5	Invitation list	$250.00	Prorated	$2,703.33	$2,453.33	$250.00	$1,351.67
8	Site	$500.00	Prorated	$4,500.00	$4,250.00	$250.00	$1,427.00
7	Theme	$200.00	Prorated	$1,320.00	$1,120.00	$200.00	$0.00
4	Determine budget	$100.00	Prorated	$2,260.00	$2,160.00	$100.00	$2,260.00
		$1,050.00		$10,783.33	$9,983.33	$800.00	$5,038.67

Figure 13-17: The Overbudget Tasks report

✦ **Overbudget Resources.** This report, shown in Figure 13-18, displays resources whose costs are going to exceed baseline estimates, based on the current progress of the project.

ID	Resource Name	Cost	Baseline Cost	Variance	Actual Cost	Remaining
			Overbudget Resources as of Mon 12/10/01 1317			
2	Barbara Rollison	$8,960.00	$1,920.00	$7,040.00	$0.00	$8,960.00
3	Intern	$4,666.67	$1,306.67	$3,360.00	$933.33	$3,733.33
1	Deena Tanenblatt	$7,200.00	$5,600.00	$1,600.00	$2,867.00	$4,333.00
4	Susie Autry	$4,106.67	$2,826.67	$1,280.00	$853.33	$3,253.33
		$24,933.34	$11,653.34	$13,280.00	$4,653.66	$20,279.66

Figure 13-18: The Overbudget Resources report

Reports on Time

By using the Current Activities reporting category, you can produce reports on the timing of your project. Click Current Activities and choose Select to open the Current Activity Reports dialog box, as shown in Figure 13-19, and view the reports available in this category.

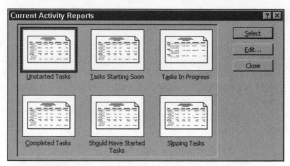

Figure 13-19: The reports available in the Current Activity category

Unstarted Tasks

The Unstarted Tasks report, as shown in Figure 13-20, lists the tasks that have not yet started, sorted by the scheduled start date. For each task, Project displays the duration, predecessor, and resource information (if you assigned resources).

Unstarted Tasks as of Mon 12/10/01
1317

ID	ⓘ	Task Name	Duration	Start	Finish	Predecessors	Resource Names
17		Baseball Game	1 day	Mon 12/03/01	Mon 12/03/01		Barbara Rollison

ID	Resource Name	Units	Work	Delay	Start	Finish
2	Barbara Rollison	100%	8 hrs	0 days	Mon 12/03/01	Mon 12/03/01

ID	ⓘ	Task Name	Duration	Start	Finish	Predecessors	Resource Names
18		Opera	4 hrs	Mon 12/03/01	Mon 12/03/01		
23		Videocamera	1 day	Mon 12/03/01	Mon 12/03/01		Susie Autry

ID	Resource Name	Units	Work	Delay	Start	Finish
4	Susie Autry	100%	8 hrs	0 days	Mon 12/03/01	Mon 12/03/01

ID	ⓘ	Task Name	Duration	Start	Finish	Predecessors	Resource Names
24		Overhead projector	1 day	Mon 12/03/01	Mon 12/03/01		Susie Autry

ID	Resource Name	Units	Work	Delay	Start	Finish
4	Susie Autry	100%	8 hrs	0 days	Mon 12/03/01	Mon 12/03/01

ID	ⓘ	Task Name	Duration	Start	Finish	Predecessors	Resource Names
29		Transportation	1 day	Mon 12/03/01	Mon 12/03/01		
30		Event transportation	3 days	Mon 12/03/01	Wed 12/05/01		
31		Flowers	4 days	Mon 12/03/01	Thu 12/06/01		
32		Table decorations	1 day	Mon 12/03/01	Mon 12/03/01		
33		Lighting	1 day	Mon 12/03/01	Mon 12/03/01		
35		Buy room decorations	1 day	Mon 12/03/01	Mon 12/03/01		
36		Buy party favors	1 day	Tue 12/04/01	Tue 12/04/01	35	
37		Setup equipment	2 days	Wed 12/05/01	Thu 12/06/01	36	
38		Decorate	2 days	Fri 12/07/01	Mon 12/10/01	37	
7		Theme	1.75 days	Fri 12/07/01	Tue 12/11/01	5	Susie Autry

ID	Resource Name	Units	Work	Delay	Start	Finish
4	Susie Autry	100%	14 hrs	0 days	Fri 12/07/01	Tue 12/11/01

ID	ⓘ	Task Name	Duration	Start	Finish	Predecessors	Resource Names
11		Caterer	2 days	Fri 12/07/01	Tue 12/11/01		Barbara Rollison

ID	Resource Name	Units	Work	Delay	Start	Finish
2	Barbara Rollison	100%	16 hrs	0 days	Fri 12/07/01	Tue 12/11/01

ID	ⓘ	Task Name	Duration	Start	Finish	Predecessors	Resource Names
12		Bartenders	1 day	Fri 12/07/01	Mon 12/10/01		Intern

ID	Resource Name	Units	Work	Delay	Start	Finish
3	Intern	100%	8 hrs	0 days	Fri 12/07/01	Mon 12/10/01

ID	ⓘ	Task Name	Duration	Start	Finish	Predecessors	Resource Names
13		Security	3 days	Fri 12/07/01	Wed 12/12/01		Intern

ID	Resource Name	Units	Work	Delay	Start	Finish
3	Intern	100%	24 hrs	0 days	Fri 12/07/01	Wed 12/12/01

ID	ⓘ	Task Name	Duration	Start	Finish	Predecessors	Resource Names
14		Photographers	1 day	Fri 12/07/01	Mon 12/10/01		Intern

ID	Resource Name	Units	Work	Delay	Start	Finish
3	Intern	100%	8 hrs	0 days	Fri 12/07/01	Mon 12/10/01

ID	ⓘ	Task Name	Duration	Start	Finish	Predecessors	Resource Names
15		Cleanup crew	1 day	Fri 12/07/01	Mon 12/10/01		Intern

ID	Resource Name	Units	Work	Delay	Start	Finish
3	Intern	100%	8 hrs	0 days	Fri 12/07/01	Mon 12/10/01

ID	ⓘ	Task Name	Duration	Start	Finish	Predecessors	Resource Names
39		Special Event	5 days	Tue 12/11/01	Mon 12/17/01	38	

Figure 13-20: The Unstarted Tasks report

Tasks Starting Soon

When you print the Tasks Starting Soon report, as shown in Figure 13-21, Project displays the Date Range dialog boxes. The information that you provide in these two dialog boxes tells Project the date range to use when selecting tasks for this report. In the first dialog box, specify the earlier date, and in the second dialog box specify the later date, using the mm/dd/yy format. On the report, Project includes tasks that start or finish between the two dates that you specify.

Figure 13-21: The Tasks Starting Soon report

The information that appears on the report is similar to the information that you find on the Unstarted Tasks report: the duration, start and finish dates, predecessors, and resource information (if you assigned resources). Completed tasks also appear on this report; the check mark that appears in the Indicator column on the report identifies them.

Tasks in Progress

As Figure 13-22 demonstrates, the Tasks in Progress report lists tasks that have started but not yet finished. You see the tasks' duration, start and planned finish dates, predecessors, and resource information (if you assigned resources).

Figure 13-22: The Tasks in Progress report

Completed Tasks

The Completed Tasks report, as shown in Figure 13-23, lists tasks that have completed. You can see the actual duration, the actual start and finish dates, the percent complete (always 100 percent — if a task is only partially complete, it won't appear on this report), the cost, and the work hours.

Figure 13-23: The Completed Tasks report

Should Have Started Tasks

When you print the Should Have Started Tasks report, as shown in Figure 13-24, you must supply a date by which tasks should have started. Project uses this date to determine which tasks appear on the report.

For each task on the report, Project displays planned start and finish dates, baseline start and finish dates, and variances for start and finish dates. Successor task information appears when a task on the report has a successor defined.

Slipping Tasks

The Slipping Tasks report, as shown in Figure 13-25, lists the tasks that have been rescheduled from their baseline start dates.

This report displays the same information as the information you saw on the Should Have Started Tasks report, but the presentation of the information changes the focus of your attention.

Should Have Started Tasks as of Mon 12/10/01
1324

ID	Task Name	Start	Finish	Baseline Start	Baseline Finish	Start Var.	Finish Var.
1	Conference	Mon 12/03/01	Tue 01/01/02	Mon 12/03/01	Wed 01/02/02	0 days	-1 day
2	Pre-planning	Mon 12/03/01	Tue 01/01/02	Mon 12/03/01	Wed 01/02/02	0 days	-1 day
16	Plan Entertainment	Mon 12/03/01	Mon 12/03/01	Mon 12/03/01	Mon 12/03/01	0 days	0 days
17	Baseball Game	Mon 12/03/01	Mon 12/03/01	Mon 12/03/01	Mon 12/03/01	0 days	0 days
18	Opera	Mon 12/03/01	Mon 12/03/01	Mon 12/03/01	Mon 12/03/01	0 days	0 days
22	Rent Equipment	Mon 12/03/01	Mon 12/03/01	Mon 12/03/01	Mon 12/03/01	0 days	0 days
23	Videocamera	Mon 12/03/01	Mon 12/03/01	Mon 12/03/01	Mon 12/03/01	0 days	0 days
24	Overhead projector	Mon 12/03/01	Mon 12/03/01	Mon 12/03/01	Mon 12/03/01	0 days	0 days
28	Arrangements	Mon 12/03/01	Thu 12/06/01	Mon 12/03/01	Thu 12/06/01	0 days	0 days
29	Transportation	Mon 12/03/01	Mon 12/03/01	Mon 12/03/01	Mon 12/03/01	0 days	0 days
30	Event transportation	Mon 12/03/01	Wed 12/05/01	Mon 12/03/01	Wed 12/05/01	0 days	0 days
31	Flowers	Mon 12/03/01	Thu 12/06/01	Mon 12/03/01	Thu 12/06/01	0 days	0 days
32	Table decorations	Mon 12/03/01	Mon 12/03/01	Mon 12/03/01	Mon 12/03/01	0 days	0 days
33	Lighting	Mon 12/03/01	Mon 12/03/01	Mon 12/03/01	Mon 12/03/01	0 days	0 days
34	Preparation	Mon 12/03/01	Mon 12/17/01	Mon 12/03/01	Mon 12/17/01	0 days	0 days
35	Buy room decorations	Mon 12/03/01	Mon 12/03/01	Mon 12/03/01	Mon 12/03/01	0 days	0 days

ID	Successor Name	Type	Lag
36	Buy party favors	FS	0 days

ID	Task Name	Start	Finish	Baseline Start	Baseline Finish	Start Var.	Finish Var.
36	Buy party favors	Tue 12/04/01	Tue 12/04/01	Tue 12/04/01	Tue 12/04/01	0 days	0 days

ID	Successor Name	Type	Lag
37	Setup equipment	FS	0 days

ID	Task Name	Start	Finish	Baseline Start	Baseline Finish	Start Var.	Finish Var.
37	Setup equipment	Wed 12/05/01	Thu 12/06/01	Wed 12/05/01	Thu 12/06/01	0 days	0 days

ID	Successor Name	Type	Lag
38	Decorate	FS	0 days

ID	Task Name	Start	Finish	Baseline Start	Baseline Finish	Start Var.	Finish Var.
38	Decorate	Fri 12/07/01	Mon 12/10/01	Fri 12/07/01	Mon 12/10/01	0 days	0 days

ID	Successor Name	Type	Lag
39	Special Event	FS	0 days

ID	Task Name	Start	Finish	Baseline Start	Baseline Finish	Start Var.	Finish Var.
6	Selection	Fri 12/07/01	Tue 12/18/01	Fri 12/07/01	Wed 12/19/01	0 days	-1 day

ID	Successor Name	Type	Lag
19	Public Relations	FS	0 days

ID	Task Name	Start	Finish	Baseline Start	Baseline Finish	Start Var.	Finish Var.
7	Theme	Fri 12/07/01	Tue 12/11/01	Fri 12/07/01	Tue 12/11/01	0 days	0 days

ID	Successor Name	Type	Lag
8	Site	FS	0 days
9	Keynote speaker	FS	0 days

ID	Task Name	Start	Finish	Baseline Start	Baseline Finish	Start Var.	Finish Var.
10	Hire	Fri 12/07/01	Wed 12/12/01	Fri 12/07/01	Wed 12/12/01	0 days	0 days
11	Caterer	Fri 12/07/01	Tue 12/11/01	Fri 12/07/01	Tue 12/11/01	0 days	0 days

ID	Successor Name	Type	Lag
25	Meet with Caterer	FS	0 days

ID	Task Name	Start	Finish	Baseline Start	Baseline Finish	Start Var.	Finish Var.
12	Bartenders	Fri 12/07/01	Mon 12/10/01	Fri 12/07/01	Mon 12/10/01	0 days	0 days

ID	Successor Name	Type	Lag
27	Drink selection	FS	0 days

Figure 13-24: The Should Have Started Tasks report

Slipping Tasks as of Mon 12/10/01
1325

ID	Task Name	Start	Finish	Baseline Start	Baseline Finish	Start Var.	Finish Var.
1	Conference	Mon 12/03/01	Fri 01/04/02	Mon 12/03/01	Wed 01/02/02	0 days	1.67 days
2	Pre-planning	Mon 12/03/01	Fri 01/04/02	Mon 12/03/01	Wed 01/02/02	0 days	1.67 days
3	Initial planning meeting	Mon 12/03/01	Wed 12/12/01	Mon 12/03/01	Fri 12/07/01	0 days	2.67 days
5	Invitation list	Wed 12/05/01	Wed 12/12/01	Wed 12/05/01	Fri 12/07/01	0 days	2.67 days

ID	Successor Name	Type	Lag
7	Theme	FS	0 days
10	Hire	FS	0 days

ID	Task Name	Start	Finish	Baseline Start	Baseline Finish	Start Var.	Finish Var.
16	Plan Entertainment	Tue 12/11/01	Tue 12/11/01	Mon 12/03/01	Mon 12/03/01	6 days	6 days
17	Baseball Game	Tue 12/11/01	Tue 12/11/01	Mon 12/03/01	Mon 12/03/01	6 days	6 days
18	Opera	Tue 12/11/01	Tue 12/11/01	Mon 12/03/01	Mon 12/03/01	6 days	6 days
22	Rent Equipment	Tue 12/11/01	Tue 12/11/01	Mon 12/03/01	Mon 12/03/01	6 days	6 days
23	Videocamera	Tue 12/11/01	Tue 12/11/01	Mon 12/03/01	Mon 12/03/01	6 days	6 days
24	Overhead projector	Tue 12/11/01	Tue 12/11/01	Mon 12/03/01	Mon 12/03/01	6 days	6 days
28	Arrangements	Tue 12/11/01	Fri 12/14/01	Mon 12/03/01	Thu 12/06/01	6 days	6 days
29	Transportation	Tue 12/11/01	Tue 12/11/01	Mon 12/03/01	Mon 12/03/01	6 days	6 days
30	Event transportation	Tue 12/11/01	Thu 12/13/01	Mon 12/03/01	Wed 12/05/01	6 days	6 days
31	Flowers	Tue 12/11/01	Fri 12/14/01	Mon 12/03/01	Thu 12/06/01	6 days	6 days
32	Table decorations	Tue 12/11/01	Tue 12/11/01	Mon 12/03/01	Mon 12/03/01	6 days	6 days
33	Lighting	Tue 12/11/01	Tue 12/11/01	Mon 12/03/01	Mon 12/03/01	6 days	6 days
34	Preparation	Tue 12/11/01	Tue 12/25/01	Mon 12/03/01	Mon 12/17/01	6 days	6 days
35	Buy room decorations	Tue 12/11/01	Tue 12/11/01	Mon 12/03/01	Mon 12/03/01	6 days	6 days

ID	Successor Name	Type	Lag
36	Buy party favors	FS	0 days

ID	Task Name	Start	Finish	Baseline Start	Baseline Finish	Start Var.	Finish Var.
36	Buy party favors	Wed 12/12/01	Wed 12/12/01	Tue 12/04/01	Tue 12/04/01	6 days	6 days

ID	Successor Name	Type	Lag
37	Setup equipment	FS	0 days

ID	Task Name	Start	Finish	Baseline Start	Baseline Finish	Start Var.	Finish Var.
6	Selection	Wed 12/12/01	Fri 12/21/01	Fri 12/07/01	Wed 12/19/01	2.67 days	1.67 days

ID	Successor Name	Type	Lag
19	Public Relations	FS	0 days

ID	Task Name	Start	Finish	Baseline Start	Baseline Finish	Start Var.	Finish Var.
7	Theme	Wed 12/12/01	Fri 12/14/01	Fri 12/07/01	Tue 12/11/01	2.67 days	2.67 days

ID	Successor Name	Type	Lag
8	Site	FS	0 days
9	Keynote speaker	FS	0 days

ID	Task Name	Start	Finish	Baseline Start	Baseline Finish	Start Var.	Finish Var.
10	Hire	Wed 12/12/01	Mon 12/17/01	Fri 12/07/01	Wed 12/12/01	2.67 days	2.67 days
11	Caterer	Wed 12/12/01	Fri 12/14/01	Fri 12/07/01	Tue 12/11/01	2.67 days	2.67 days

ID	Successor Name	Type	Lag
25	Meet with Caterer	FS	0 days

ID	Task Name	Start	Finish	Baseline Start	Baseline Finish	Start Var.	Finish Var.
12	Bartenders	Wed 12/12/01	Thu 12/13/01	Fri 12/07/01	Mon 12/10/01	2.67 days	2.67 days

ID	Successor Name	Type	Lag
27	Drink selection	FS	0 days

ID	Task Name	Start	Finish	Baseline Start	Baseline Finish	Start Var.	Finish Var.
13	Security	Wed 12/12/01	Mon 12/17/01	Fri 12/07/01	Wed 12/12/01	2.67 days	2.67 days

Figure 13-25: The Slipping Tasks report

Reports on Work Assignments

Using the Assignments reporting category, you can produce reports on the resource assignments in your project. Click the Assignments category and choose Select to open the Assignment Reports dialog box, as shown in Figure 13-26, and view the reports available in this category.

Figure 13-26: The reports available in the Assignments category

Who Does What

The Who Does What report, as shown in Figure 13-27, lists resources and the tasks to which they are assigned, the amount of work planned for each task, the planned start and finish dates, and any resource notes.

Who Does What as of Mon 12/10/01
1325

ID	O	Resource Name			Work		

ID	Task Name	Units	Work	Delay	Start	Finish

1 ◆ Deena Tanenblatt — 72 hrs

ID	Task Name	Units	Work	Delay	Start	Finish
4	Determine budget	100%	16 hrs	0 days	Mon 12/03/01	Tue 12/04/01
8	Site	100%	40 hrs	0 days	Fri 12/21/01	Fri 12/21/01
26	Menu selection	100%	8 hrs	0 days	Fri 12/14/01	Mon 12/17/01
27	Drink selection	100%	8 hrs	0 days	Fri 12/14/01	Mon 12/17/01

2 ◆ Barbara Rollison — 112 hrs

ID	Task Name	Units	Work	Delay	Start	Finish
17	Baseball Game	100%	8 hrs	0 days	Tue 12/11/01	Tue 12/11/01
11	Caterer	100%	16 hrs	0 days	Wed 12/12/01	Fri 12/14/01
20	Alert community	100%	80 hrs	0 days	Fri 12/21/01	Fri 01/04/02
21	Press release	100%	8 hrs	0 days	Fri 12/21/01	Mon 12/24/01

3 ◆ Intern — 66.67 hrs

ID	Task Name	Units	Work	Delay	Start	Finish
4	Determine budget	100%	8 hrs	0 days	Mon 12/03/01	Mon 12/03/01
5	Invitation list	50%	10.67 hrs	0 days	Wed 12/05/01	Wed 12/12/01
12	Bartenders	100%	8 hrs	0 days	Wed 12/12/01	Thu 12/13/01
13	Security	100%	24 hrs	0 days	Wed 12/12/01	Mon 12/17/01
14	Photographers	100%	8 hrs	0 days	Wed 12/12/01	Thu 12/13/01
15	Cleanup crew	100%	8 hrs	0 days	Wed 12/12/01	Thu 12/13/01

4 ◆ Susie Autry — 51.33 hrs

ID	Task Name	Units	Work	Delay	Start	Finish
7	Theme	100%	14 hrs	0 days	Wed 12/12/01	Fri 12/14/01
5	Invitation list	100%	21.33 hrs	0 days	Wed 12/05/01	Wed 12/12/01
23	Videocamera	100%	8 hrs	0 days	Tue 12/11/01	Tue 12/11/01
24	Overhead projector	100%	8 hrs	0 days	Tue 12/11/01	Tue 12/11/01

5 Dick Lahr — 40 hrs

ID	Task Name	Units	Work	Delay	Start	Finish
9	Keynote speaker	100%	40 hrs	0 days	Fri 12/14/01	Fri 12/21/01

Figure 13-27: The Who Does What report

Who Does What When

The Who Does What When report, as shown in Figure 13-28, also lists resources and the tasks to which they are assigned; this report, however, focuses your attention on the daily work scheduled for each resource on each task.

Tip

You can use the Edit button in the Assignment Reports dialog box to change the timescale on the report from daily to some other increment, such as weekly. Also, you may want to change the date format on the Details tab to a wider format (as I did in the figure) if you see pound signs (###) in your report. See the "Customizing Reports" section at the end of this chapter for more information.

	12/01/01	12/02/01	12/03/01	12/04/01	12/05/01	12/06/01	12/07/01	12/08/01	12/09/01	12/10/01	12/11/01	12/12/01	12/13/01	12/14/01
Deena Tanenblatt			8 hrs	8 hrs										5.33 hrs
Determine budget			8 hrs	8 hrs										
Site														
Menu selection														5.33 hrs
Drink selection														
Barbara Rollison											8 hrs	5.33 hrs	8 hrs	2.67 hrs
Caterer												5.33 hrs	8 hrs	2.67 hrs
Baseball Game											8 hrs			
Alert community														
Press release														
Intern			8 hrs		4 hrs	1.33 hrs					4 hrs	6.67 hrs	8 hrs	8 hrs
Determine budget			8 hrs									1.33 hrs		
Invitation list					4 hrs	1.33 hrs					4 hrs	1.33 hrs		
Bartenders												5.33 hrs	2.67 hrs	
Security													5.33 hrs	8 hrs
Photographers														
Cleanup crew														
Susie Autry					8 hrs	2.67 hrs					8 hrs	8 hrs	8 hrs	8 hrs
Invitation list					8 hrs	2.67 hrs					8 hrs	2.67 hrs		
Theme												5.33 hrs	8 hrs	0.67 hrs
Videocamera														7.33 hrs
Overhead projector														
Dick Lahr														7.33 hrs
Keynote speaker														7.33 hrs

Who Does What When as of Mon 12/10/01
1328

Figure 13-28: The Who Does What When report

To Do List

The To Do List report, as shown in Figure 13-29, lists, on a weekly basis, the tasks assigned to a resource that you select. When you are ready to print this report, Project first displays the Using Resource dialog box, which contains the Show tasks using list box. When you open the list box, you see a list of your resources. Select a resource and click OK. The To Do List report shows the task ID number, duration, start and finish dates, predecessors, and a list of all of the resources assigned to each task.

To Do List as of Mon 12/10/01
1325

ID	❶	Task Name	Duration	Start	Finish	Predecessors	Resource Names
Week of December 02							
4	✓	Determine budget	2 days	Mon 12/03/01	Tue 12/04/01		Deena Tanenblatt,Intern
Week of December 09							
8		Site	1 wk	Fri 12/14/01	Fri 12/21/01	7	Deena Tanenblatt
26		Menu selection	1 day	Fri 12/14/01	Mon 12/17/01		Deena Tanenblatt
27		Drink selection	1 day	Fri 12/14/01	Mon 12/17/01	12	Deena Tanenblatt
Week of December 16							
8		Site	1 wk	Fri 12/14/01	Fri 12/21/01	7	Deena Tanenblatt
26		Menu selection	1 day	Fri 12/14/01	Mon 12/17/01		Deena Tanenblatt
27		Drink selection	1 day	Fri 12/14/01	Mon 12/17/01	12	Deena Tanenblatt

Figure 13-29: The To Do List report

Overallocated Resources

The Overallocated Resources report, as shown in Figure 13-30 shows the overallocated resources, the tasks to which they are assigned, and the total hours of work assigned to them. You can also see the details of each task, such as the allocation, the amount of work, any delay, and the start and finish dates.

```
                    Overallocated Resources as of Mon 12/10/01
                                     1325

  ID    ⓘ          Resource Name                    Work


  2     ◈            Barbara Rollison                 112 hrs
         ID   Task Name        Units   Work      Delay    Start          Finish
         17   Baseball Game    100%    8 hrs     0 days   Tue 12/11/01   Tue 12/11/01
         11   Caterer          100%    16 hrs    0 days   Wed 12/12/01   Fri 12/14/01
         20   Alert community  100%    80 hrs    0 days   Fri 12/21/01   Fri 01/04/02
         21   Press release    100%    8 hrs     0 days   Fri 12/21/01   Mon 12/24/01
  1     ◈            Deena Tanenblatt                 72 hrs
         ID   Task Name        Units   Work      Delay    Start          Finish
         4    Determine budget 100%    16 hrs    0 days   Mon 12/03/01   Tue 12/04/01
         8    Site             100%    40 hrs    0 days   Fri 12/14/01   Fri 12/21/01
         26   Menu selection   100%    8 hrs     0 days   Fri 12/14/01   Mon 12/17/01
         27   Drink selection  100%    8 hrs     0 days   Fri 12/14/01   Mon 12/17/01
  3     ◈            Intern                           66.67 hrs
         ID   Task Name        Units   Work      Delay    Start          Finish
         4    Determine budget 100%    8 hrs     0 days   Mon 12/03/01   Mon 12/03/01
         5    Invitation list  50%     10.67 hrs 0 days   Wed 12/05/01   Wed 12/12/01
         12   Bartenders       100%    8 hrs     0 days   Wed 12/12/01   Thu 12/13/01
         13   Security         100%    24 hrs    0 days   Wed 12/12/01   Mon 12/17/01
         14   Photographers    100%    8 hrs     0 days   Wed 12/12/01   Thu 12/13/01
         15   Cleanup crew     100%    8 hrs     0 days   Wed 12/12/01   Thu 12/13/01
  4     ◈            Susie Autry                      51.33 hrs
         ID   Task Name        Units   Work      Delay    Start          Finish
         7    Theme            100%    14 hrs    0 days   Wed 12/12/01   Fri 12/14/01
         5    Invitation list  100%    21.33 hrs 0 days   Wed 12/05/01   Wed 12/12/01
         23   Videocamera      100%    8 hrs     0 days   Tue 12/11/01   Tue 12/11/01
         24   Overhead projector 100%  8 hrs    0 days   Tue 12/11/01   Tue 12/11/01
                                                                  302 hrs
```

Figure 13-30: The Overallocated Resources report

Reports on Workloads

You can use the Workload reporting category to produce reports on task and resource usage in your project. Click Workload in the Reports dialog box and choose Select to open the Workload Reports dialog box, as shown in Figure 13-31.

Figure 13-31: The Workload Reports dialog box

Task Usage

The Task Usage report, as shown in Figure 13-32, lists tasks and resources assigned to each task. It also displays the amount of work assigned to each resource in weekly time increments.

Tip   You can change the time increment by clicking Edit in the Workload Reports dialog box. See the "Customizing Reports" section later in this chapter for more information about editing reports.

	12/02/01	12/09/01	12/16/01	12/23/01	12/30/01	**Total**
Conference						
Pre-planning						
Initial planning meeting						
Determine budget	24 hrs					24 hrs
Deena Tanenblatt	16 hrs					16 hrs
Intern	8 hrs					8 hrs
Invitation list	24 hrs					24 hrs
Intern	8 hrs					8 hrs
Susie Autry	16 hrs					16 hrs
Selection						
Theme		14 hrs				14 hrs
Susie Autry		14 hrs				14 hrs
Site		18 hrs	22 hrs			40 hrs
Deena Tanenblatt		18 hrs	22 hrs			40 hrs
Keynote speaker		18 hrs	22 hrs			40 hrs
Dick Lahr		18 hrs	22 hrs			40 hrs
Hire						
Caterer		16 hrs				16 hrs
Barbara Rollison		16 hrs				16 hrs
Bartenders		8 hrs				8 hrs
Intern		8 hrs				8 hrs
Security		24 hrs				24 hrs
Intern		24 hrs				24 hrs
Photographers		8 hrs				8 hrs
Intern		8 hrs				8 hrs
Cleanup crew		8 hrs				8 hrs
Intern		8 hrs				8 hrs
Plan Entertainment						
Baseball Game		8 hrs				8 hrs
Barbara Rollison		8 hrs				8 hrs
Opera						
Public Relations						
Alert community			18 hrs	40 hrs	22 hrs	80 hrs
Barbara Rollison			18 hrs	40 hrs	22 hrs	80 hrs
Press release			8 hrs			8 hrs
Barbara Rollison			8 hrs			8 hrs
Rent Equipment						
Videocamera		8 hrs				8 hrs

Task Usage as of Mon 12/10/01
1325

Figure 13-32: The Task Usage report

Resource Usage

The Resource Usage report, as shown in Figure 13-33, lists resources and the tasks to which they are assigned. Like the Task Usage report, this report shows the amount of work assigned to each resource for each task in weekly time increments, but this report focuses your attention on the resource.

Note   Project 2000 introduced two variations on the Resource Usage report — the Resource Usage (material) and Resource Usage (work) reports. Both reports look identical to the Resource Usage report but, as you'd expect, one shows only material resources while the other shows only work resources. Both reports are custom reports; to print them, follow the instructions in the next section.

Resource Usage as of Mon 12/10/01
1325

	12/02/01	12/09/01	12/16/01	12/23/01	12/30/01	Total	
Deena Tanenblatt	16 hrs	34 hrs	22 hrs			72 hrs	
Determine budget	16 hrs					16 hrs	
Site		18 hrs	22 hrs			40 hrs	
Menu selection		8 hrs				8 hrs	
Drink selection		8 hrs				8 hrs	
Barbara Rollison		24 hrs	26 hrs	40 hrs	22 hrs	112 hrs	
Caterer		16 hrs				16 hrs	
Baseball Game		8 hrs				8 hrs	
Alert community			18 hrs	40 hrs	22 hrs	80 hrs	
Press release			8 hrs			8 hrs	
Intern	16 hrs	48 hrs				64 hrs	
Determine budget	8 hrs					8 hrs	
Invitation list	8 hrs					8 hrs	
Bartenders		8 hrs				8 hrs	
Security		24 hrs				24 hrs	
Photographers		8 hrs				8 hrs	
Cleanup crew		8 hrs				8 hrs	
Susie Autry	16 hrs	30 hrs				46 hrs	
Invitation list	16 hrs					16 hrs	
Theme		14 hrs				14 hrs	
Videocamera		8 hrs				8 hrs	
Overhead projector		8 hrs				8 hrs	
Dick Lahr		18 hrs	22 hrs			40 hrs	
Keynote speaker		18 hrs	22 hrs			40 hrs	
Total	48 hrs	154 hrs	70 hrs	40 hrs	22 hrs	334 hrs	0 hrs

Figure 13-33: The Resource Usage report

Customizing Reports

Project contains some custom reports; in addition to printing these custom reports, you can customize any of the other reports described in this chapter. Click the Custom category in the Reports dialog box and choose Select to open the Custom Reports dialog box, as shown in Figure 13-34.

Figure 13-34: The Custom Reports dialog box

Not all the reports listed in the Custom Reports dialog box are custom reports. However, you can print any of the standard reports either from this dialog box or as described earlier in this chapter. Remember, though, that you must use this dialog box to print the three custom reports.

Note   You can create your own reports by clicking the New button in the Custom Reports dialog box, as shown in Figure 13-34. When you define a new custom report, Project offers you four formats. Three formats are based on the reports discussed in this section: the Task report format, the Resource report format, and the Crosstab report format. The fourth format is the Monthly Calendar format, and it functions just like the Working Days report that you learned about earlier in this chapter.

Custom reports

Project contains three custom reports:

✦ The Task report

✦ The Resource report

✦ The Crosstab report

Task report

The Task report, as shown in Figure 13-35, shows task information, such as the ID number, the task name, indicator icons, the task duration, planned start and finish dates, predecessors, and (if resources have been assigned) resource names.

ID	❶	Task Name	Duration	Start	Finish	Predecessors	Resource Names
				Task as of Mon 12/10/01			
				1325			
4	✓	Determine budget	2 days	Mon 12/03/01	Tue 12/04/01		Deena Tanenblatt,Intern
5		Invitation list	2 days	Wed 12/05/01	Thu 12/06/01	4	Susie Autry,Intern[50%]
7	▦	Theme	1.75 days	Tue 12/11/01	Wed 12/12/01	5	Susie Autry
8		Site	1 wk	Wed 12/12/01	Wed 12/19/01	7	Deena Tanenblatt
9		Keynote speaker	1 wk	Wed 12/12/01	Wed 12/19/01	7,4	Dick Lahr
11	▦	Caterer	2 days	Tue 12/11/01	Wed 12/12/01		Barbara Rollison
12	▦	Bartenders	1 day	Tue 12/11/01	Tue 12/11/01		Intern
13	▦	Security	3 days	Tue 12/11/01	Thu 12/13/01		Intern
14	▦	Photographers	1 day	Tue 12/11/01	Tue 12/11/01		Intern
15	▦	Cleanup crew	1 day	Tue 12/11/01	Tue 12/11/01		Intern
17	▦	Baseball Game	1 day	Tue 12/11/01	Tue 12/11/01		Barbara Rollison
18	▦	Opera	4 hrs	Tue 12/11/01	Tue 12/11/01		
20		Alert community	2 wks	Wed 12/19/01	Wed 01/02/02		Barbara Rollison
21		Press release	1 day	Wed 12/19/01	Thu 12/20/01		Barbara Rollison
23	▦	Videocamera	1 day	Tue 12/11/01	Tue 12/11/01		Susie Autry
24	▦	Overhead projector	1 day	Tue 12/11/01	Tue 12/11/01		Susie Autry
26		Menu selection	1 day	Thu 12/13/01	Thu 12/13/01		Deena Tanenblatt
27		Drink selection	1 day	Thu 12/13/01	Thu 12/13/01	12	Deena Tanenblatt
29	▦	Transportation	1 day	Tue 12/11/01	Tue 12/11/01		
30	▦	Event transportation	3 days	Tue 12/11/01	Thu 12/13/01		
31	▦	Flowers	4 days	Tue 12/11/01	Fri 12/14/01		
32	▦	Table decorations	1 day	Tue 12/11/01	Tue 12/11/01		
33	▦	Lighting	1 day	Tue 12/11/01	Tue 12/11/01		
35	▦	Buy room decorations	1 day	Tue 12/11/01	Tue 12/11/01		
36	▦	Buy party favors	1 day	Wed 12/12/01	Wed 12/12/01	35	
37	▦	Setup equipment	2 days	Thu 12/13/01	Fri 12/14/01	36	
38	▦	Decorate	2 days	Mon 12/17/01	Tue 12/18/01	37	
39		Special Event	5 days	Wed 12/19/01	Tue 12/25/01	38	

Figure 13-35: The Task report

Resource report

As you can see from the report sample shown in Figure 13-36, the Resource report shows resource information: resource ID numbers; indicator icons; resource names, initials, and groups; maximum units; rate information; accrual information; base calendar information; and code information.

Note

In the figure, you can't see the columns that printed on Page 2 of the report: Overtime Rate, Cost/Use, Accrue At, Base Calendar, and Code.

ID	❶	Resource Name	Type	Material Label	Initials	Group	Max. Units	Std. Rate
				Resource as of Mon 12/10/01				
				1325				
1	✦	Deena Tanenblatt	Work		D		100%	$100.00/hr
2	✦	Barbara Rollison	Work		B		100%	$80.00/hr
3	✦	Intern	Work		I		100%	$70.00/hr
4	✦	Susie Autry	Work		S		100%	$80.00/hr
5		Dick Lahr	Work		D		100%	$125.00/hr

Figure 13-36: The Resource report

Project 2002 contains two variations on the Resource report — the Resource (material) and Resource (work) reports. Both reports look identical to the Resource report but, as you'd expect, one shows only material resources while the other shows only work resources.

Crosstab report

The Crosstab report, as shown in Figure 13-37, is a tabular report that shows task and resource information in rows and time increments in columns.

	12/02	12/09	12/16	12/23	12/30
Conference					
Pre-planning					
Initial planning meeting					
Determine budget	$2,260.00				
Deena Tanenblatt	$1,600.00				
Intern	$560.00				
Invitation list	$2,703.33				
Intern	$746.67				
Susie Autry	$1,706.67				
Selection					
Theme	$251.43	$1,068.57			
Susie Autry	$213.33	$906.67			
Site		$3,225.36	$1,274.64		
Deena Tanenblatt		$2,867.00	$1,133.00		
Keynote speaker		$3,583.33	$1,416.67		
Dick Lahr		$3,583.33	$1,416.67		
Hire					
Caterer	$213.33	$1,066.67			
Barbara Rollison	$213.33	$1,066.67			
Bartenders	$186.67	$373.33			
Intern	$186.67	$373.33			
Security	$186.67	$1,493.33			
Intern	$186.67	$1,493.33			
Photographers	$186.67	$373.33			
Intern	$186.67	$373.33			
Cleanup crew	$186.67	$373.33			
Intern	$186.67	$373.33			
Plan Entertainment					
Baseball Game	$640.00				
Barbara Rollison	$640.00				
Opera					
Public Relations					
Alert community			$2,293.33	$3,200.00	$906.67
Barbara Rollison			$2,293.33	$3,200.00	$906.67
Press release			$640.00		
Barbara Rollison			$640.00		
Rent Equipment					
Videocamera	$640.00				
Susie Autry	$640.00				
Overhead projector	$640.00				
Susie Autry	$640.00				
Meet with Caterer					
Menu selection		$800.00			

Crosstab as of Mon 12/10/01
1324

Figure 13-37: The Crosstab report

Tip   Much of the information on the Crosstab report also appears on the Task Usage report and the Resource Usage report. These reports give you more formatting options, such as the period covered by the report and the table used in the report.

Customizing an existing report

You can customize almost every report that you've seen in this chapter. For a few reports, such as the Working Days report, the only item that you can change is the font information that Project uses to print the report. For other reports, however, you can change the table or the task or resource filter to change the content of the report. Click the Edit button when preparing to print the report to make these changes. When you click the Edit button, Project opens the dialog box that relates to the report you selected. For example, if you select the Working Days report in the Overview Reports dialog box (choose View ➪ Reports ➪ Overview) and then click Edit, Project opens the Report Text dialog box, as shown in Figure 13-38.

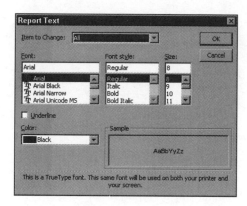

Figure 13-38: Use the Report Text dialog box to change the font report items.

Similarly, if you select the Tasks Starting Soon report from the Current Activities dialog box and then click Edit, Project opens the Definition tab of the Task Report dialog box, as shown in Figure 13-39.

Figure 13-39: Use the Definition tab to change the report's filter or table.

From the Details tab, shown in Figure 13-40, select the information that you want included on the report. You may want to display predecessors for tasks or place a gridline between details.

Note The options on the Details tab change from report to report.

Figure 13-40: Use the Details tab to specify the information that you want to include on the report.

From the Sort tab shown in Figure 13-41, select the sort orders for the report.

Figure 13-41: Select a sort order for the report.

Editing Reports: The Type Determines the Dialog Box

Remember that the type of report that you select initially determines the dialog box that you see when you click Edit in the report's category dialog box (for example, the Overview Reports dialog box or the Cost Reports dialog box). In addition to the dialog boxes that you've seen in this chapter, you may also see the Resource Report dialog box or the Crosstab Report dialog box, both of which contain slightly different options (primarily on the Definitions tab) than the Task Report dialog box.

For example, when you edit the Who Does What report before printing it, Project opens a Resource Report dialog box. On the Definitions tab of this dialog box, you can select filters related to resources, whereas the filters in the Task Report dialog box pertain to tasks. Or, if you edit the Cash Flow report before printing it, Project opens a Crosstab Report dialog box from which you can select the information that you want to appear on each row; the default information is Tasks and Cost.

Summary

In this chapter, you learned how to produce reports in Project, and you examined samples of the reports available in each of Project's six report categories:

✦ Overview

✦ Current Activities

✦ Costs

✦ Assignments

✦ Workload

✦ Custom

In addition, you've learned how to customize any standard report in Project. The next chapter shows you how to analyze your project's progress.

✦　　✦　　✦

CHAPTER

14

◆ ◆ ◆ ◆

In This Chapter

Understanding
earned value

Evaluating cost
information

Making adjustments
during the project

◆ ◆ ◆ ◆

Analyzing Financial Progress

When you analyze the progress of your project, you must measure not only the progress of the schedule but also the progress based on the costs that you incur. In Microsoft Project, you measure the *earned value* of your project.

Understanding Earned Value

Earned value is the measurement that project managers use to evaluate the progress of a project based on the cost of work performed up to the project status date. When Project calculates earned value, by default it compares your original cost estimates to the actual work performed to show whether your project is on budget. You can think of earned value as a measurement that indicates how much of the budget should have been spent in comparison to the cost of the work performed thus far to the baseline cost for the task, resource, or assignment.

 New Feature You can now calculate earned value by manually recording the Physical % Complete instead of letting Project calculate % Complete, which is actual duration divided by total duration. You'll read more about this new method for calculating earned value later in this chapter.

To work with and use earned value information effectively, you must first perform the following tasks:

✦ Save a baseline for your project

✦ Assign resources with costs to tasks in your project

✦ Complete some work on your project

Understanding earned value fields

Remember the Earned Value report from Chapter 12? The fields that appear as headings in that report also appear on various earned value tables. *Earned value fields* are currency fields that measure various aspects of earned value. The following table translates the acronyms that Project uses to represent the earned value fields.

Acronyms	Earned Value Fields
BCWS	Budgeted Cost of Work Scheduled
BCWP	Budgeted Cost of Work Performed
ACWP	Actual Cost of Work Performed
SV	Schedule Variance
CV	Cost Variance
BAC	Budgeted at Completion
EAC	Estimate at Completion
VAC	Variance at Completion

Three of the preceding fields are really at the heart of earned value analysis:

✦ BCWP indicates how much of a task's budget should have been spent given the actual duration of the task. For example, suppose that you have a task budgeted at $100 and work has been performed for one day. You find that, after one day, 40 percent of the work has been completed. You would expect that 40 percent of the cost of the task, or $40, would also be incurred. Therefore, the BCWP for the task is $40.

✦ BCWS measures the budgeted cost of individual tasks based on the resources and fixed costs assigned to the tasks when you schedule them.

✦ ACWP measures the actual cost incurred to complete a task; during the completion process, ACWP represents the actual costs for work performed through the project's status date.

BCWS, BCWP, ACWP, SV, and CV are all calculated through today or through the project status date. SV represents the cost difference between current progress and the baseline plan, and Project calculates this value as BCWP minus BCWS. CV represents the cost difference between actual costs and planned costs at the current level of completion, and Project calculates this value as BCWP minus ACWP. EAC shows the planned costs based on costs already incurred plus additional planned costs. VAC represents the variance between the baseline cost and the combination of actual costs plus planned costs for a task.

Note   Project calculates BCWP at the task level different from how it calculates BCWP at the assignment level; because Project rolls the task-level BCWP values into summary tasks and the project summary task, I suggest that you use the task-level BCWP values.

Project uses BCWS, BCWP, ACWP, SV, and CV as task fields, resource fields, and assignment fields; Project also uses time-phased versions of each field. BAC, EAC, and VAC, however, are task fields only.

New Feature   Project 2002 introduces some new earned value fields.

Project 2002 introduces some new earned value fields; some of these fields will appear by default on earned value tables, and you can add any of these fields to any table.

> ✦ **Physical % Complete.** This field represents your estimate of the progress of a task, regardless of actual work or time, and is not a time-phased field. Project calculates Physical % Complete by rolling up BCWP on subtasks to BCWP on associated summary tasks. You enter Physical % Complete estimates, and Project applies the Physical % Complete to assignment data or Fixed Costs data for the associated summary task. See the next section for details on having Project use Physical % Complete as the method for calculating earned value.

Note   You may be wondering about the difference between % Complete, which is not new to Project 2002, and Physical % Complete. Project calculates % Complete by dividing actual task duration by total duration. Physical % Complete is *your* estimate of where a task stands and has no connection to duration.

> ✦ **CPI.** CPI stands for *Cost Performance Index*, and Project calculates CPI by dividing BCWP by ACWP. This field appears by default in the Earned Value Cost Indicators table and is a time-phased field.

> ✦ **SPI.** SPI stands for *Schedule Performance Index*, and Project calculates SPI by dividing BCWP by BCWS. This field appears by default in the Earned Value Schedule Indicators table and is a time-phased field.

> ✦ **CV%.** CV% stands for *Cost Variance %*, and Project calculates this field by dividing CV by BCWP and multiplying the result by 100. This field appears by default in the Earned Value Cost Indicators table and is a time-phased field.

> ✦ **SV%.** SV% stands for *Schedule Variance %*, and Project calculates this field by dividing SV by BCWS and multiplying the result by 100. This field appears by default in the Earned Value Schedule Indicators table and is a time-phased field.

> ✦ **EAC.** EAC stands for *Estimate at Completion*, and although this field isn't new (it existed in Project 2000), it is improved in Project 2002. Project calculates this field by using the following formula: ACWP + (BAC - BCWP) / CPI. This field appears by default in the Earned Value for Tasks and the Earned Value Cost Indicators tables and is not a time-phased field.

Note   In Project 2000, EAC was simply the cost of the task, because EAC was nothing more than the task's cost, re-titled to "EAC." In Project 2002, the field is a new, separate field with a formula behind it.

✦ **TCPI.** TCPI stands for *To Complete Performance Index*, and Project calculates this field by using the following formula: (BAC - BCWP) / EAC - ACWP). This field appears by default in the Earned Value Cost Indicators table and is not a time-phased field.

Using the Physical % Complete method to calculate earned value

Project can use the % Complete method or the Physical % Complete method to calculate earned value — unless you specify otherwise, Project will use the % Complete method.

You can set Physical % Complete as the default Earned Value Calculation method for your project by following these steps:

1. Choose Tools ⇨ Options.

2. Click the Calculation tab.

3. Click the Earned Value button. You see the Earned Value dialog box, as shown in Figure 14-1.

Figure 14-1: Choose the method of Earned Value Calculation that you want Project to use.

4. Open the Default task Earned Value method list box and choose Physical % Complete.

5. Open the Baseline for Earned Value Calculations list box and choose a baseline (Project will store 11 baselines for Earned Value).

Note   Clearing a baseline *after* entering Physical % Complete values does *not* clear those values.

6. Click OK twice to save the settings.

The preceding steps set the default for all new tasks that you enter in your project; if your project already contains tasks (or if you want to use the Physical % Complete method for some but not all tasks), set the Earned Value Calculation method on a task-by-task basis. Follow these steps:

1. Select the task(s) for which you want to set the Earned Value Calculation method to Physical % Complete.

2. Click the Task Information button on the Standard toolbar.

3. Click the Advanced tab.

4. Open the Earned Value method list box and choose Physical % Complete, as shown in Figure 14-2.

Figure 14-2: Assign the Physical % Complete method as appropriate to tasks in the Task Information dialog box.

To record Physical % Complete, add the field as a column on a table view (in Figure 14-3, I've added it to the Earned Value for Tasks table) and then type in appropriate amounts for tasks. You'll see other earned value fields update accordingly.

Tip To insert a column, click the heading of the column to the right of the column that you are inserting. Then, choose Insert ➪ Column.

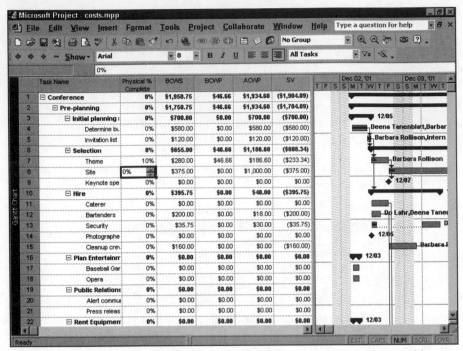

Figure 14-3: Record Physical % Complete values by adding the field to a table and then typing the information.

Setting the date for earned value calculations

By default, Project uses today's date to calculate earned value information. However, you can set a project status date for Project to use instead of today's date when it calculates earned value. From any view, choose Project ➪ Project Information to open the Project Information dialog box, as shown in Figure 14-4.

Open the Status Date list box, select the date that you want Project to use when it calculates earned value, and click OK.

Using Earned Value tables

Project contains four Earned Value tables that you can use to compare your expected costs with your actual costs. The four Earned Value tables — Earned Value for Tasks, Earned Value Cost Indicators, Earned Value Schedule Indicators, and Earned Value for Resources — help you evaluate the relationship between work and costs. You can use the Earned Value tables to forecast whether a task will finish within the budget based on the comparison of the actual costs incurred for the task to date and the baseline cost of the task.

Figure 14-4: Use this dialog box to set a date for Project to use when calculating earned value.

Using the Earned Value table for tasks

When you use the Earned Value table for tasks, you can compare the relationship between work and costs for tasks. This table helps you evaluate your budget to estimate future budget needs and prepare an accounting statement of your project. You can use the information in the table to determine whether sufficient work is getting done for the money you're paying or whether tasks need more money, less money, or perhaps should be cut. That is, the information in the Earned Value table helps you assess whether the money you're spending on a task is enough money, too much money, too little money, or perhaps wasted money.

To display the Earned Value table for tasks, start in any view that contains a table. You can get to the table in Figure 14-5, for example, by starting with the Task Usage view. Right-click the Select All button and choose More Tables from the shortcut menu. In the More Tables dialog box, select Earned Value and click Apply.

All the fields on this sheet are calculated except EAC and BAC. You can type values in those fields to change information in the table.

Using the Earned Value table for resources

When you use the Earned Value table for resources, you can compare the relationship between work and costs for resources. This table also helps you to evaluate your budget in order to estimate future budget needs and prepare an accounting statement of your project. You can use the information in the table to determine whether the work is getting done for the money that you're paying or whether you need more or less of a particular resource.

Figure 14-5: The Earned Value table for tasks

To display the Earned Value table for resources, follow these steps:

1. Start in any resource view, such as the Resource Sheet view.

2. Right-click the Select All button and choose More Tables from the shortcut menu that appears.

3. Select Earned Value in the More Tables dialog box, and click Apply. Your screen will look similar to the one shown in Figure 14-6.

All the fields on this sheet are calculated except BAC. You can type values in this field to change information in the table.

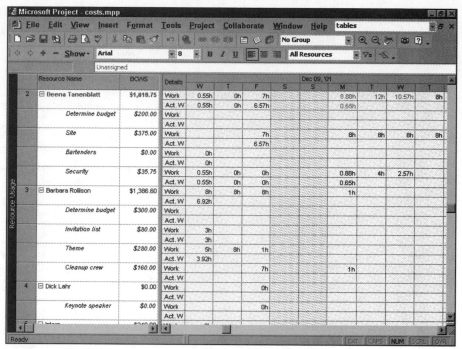

Figure 14-6: The Earned Value table for resources

Using the Earned Value Cost Indicators and Earned Value Schedule Indicators tables

New Feature The Earned Value Cost Indicators and Earned Value Schedule Indicators tables are new to Project 2002.

Project 2002 introduces two new tables that are very similar to their cousin, the Earned Value for Tasks table; the main difference between them is the fields that you find on each table. The Earned Value Cost Indicators table for tasks enables you to compare the various cost factors in your project, as shown in Figure 14-7. The Earned Value Schedule Indicators table for tasks enables you to focus on the effects of scheduling variances on the cost of your project, as shown in Figure 14-8.

Figure 14-7: The Earned Value Cost Indicators table closely resembles the Earned Value for Tasks table, but focuses on different earned value fields.

To display the Earned Value Cost Indicators table for tasks, start in any task view that contains a table. Then, right-click the Select All button and choose More Tables from the shortcut menu. In the More Tables dialog box, select Earned Value Cost Indicators and click Apply.

To display the Earned Value Cost Indicators table for tasks, start in any task view that contains a table. Then, right-click the Select All button and choose More Tables from the shortcut menu. In the More Tables dialog box, select Earned Value Schedule Indicators and click Apply.

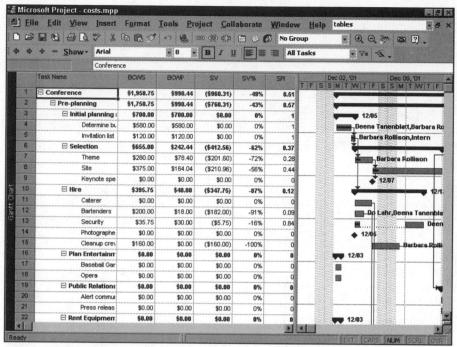

Figure 14-8: The Earned Value Cost Indicators table closely resembles the Earned Value for Tasks table, but focuses on different earned value fields.

Evaluating Cost Information

If you own Microsoft Excel, you can use it for assistance in evaluating cost information. By exporting information to Excel, you can chart earned value, analyze timescaled information, or create pivot tables.

Charting earned value

The saying goes: A picture is worth a thousand words. And when looking at earned value information, you may find it easier to understand the information if you use a picture rather than study Project's Earned Value tables. You can export the earned value information to Microsoft Excel (you must be using Excel version 5.0 or later) and then use Excel's ChartWizard to create charts of earned value information.

Cross-Reference To learn more about Project's capabilities to export and import data, see Chapter 22.

When you export earned values from Project to Excel, you create an Excel workbook that contains a task ID, name, and the various earned values for each task, as shown in Figure 14-9.

Figure 14-9: An Excel workbook created by exporting earned value information from Project to Excel.

To create an Excel workbook like the one shown in Figure 14-9, follow these steps:

1. In the Project file containing the information you want to use in Excel, choose File ➪ Save As to open the Save As dialog box.

2. Type a name for the Excel workbook in the File Name list box. Don't worry about the extension; Project supplies it.

3. Open the Save as type list box and select Microsoft Excel Workbook. The Save As dialog box should resemble the one shown in Figure 14-10.

4. Click Save to start the Export Mapping wizard.

5. Click Next.

6. Choose Selected Data in the next box of the wizard and then click Next.

7. Choose Use existing map in the next box of the wizard and then click Next.

8. Choose Earned Value information from the list of available maps in the Export Wizard, as shown in Figure 14-11, and click Finish.

Figure 14-10: The Save As dialog box as it appears after you choose to save an Excel workbook file.

Figure 14-11: Choose Earned Value information as the map from the Export Wizard Map Selection dialog box.

Note   You can continue clicking Next in the wizard, but to chart earned value in Excel, you usually don't need to make any changes in the remaining dialog boxes that the wizard presents.

Open Microsoft Excel and then choose File ➪ Open to open the workbook that you just created. You can use Excel's ChartWizard to create as many charts from this data as you want. For example, the chart in Figure 14-12 shows all earned values for one task, and the chart in Figure 14-13 shows one earned value for selected tasks.

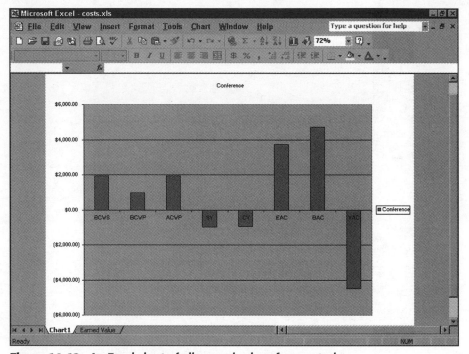

Figure 14-12: An Excel chart of all earned values for one task

Note   If your project is small, you may be able to chart one earned value for all tasks, but if your project is large, Excel may display an error message if you try to chart one earned value for all tasks.

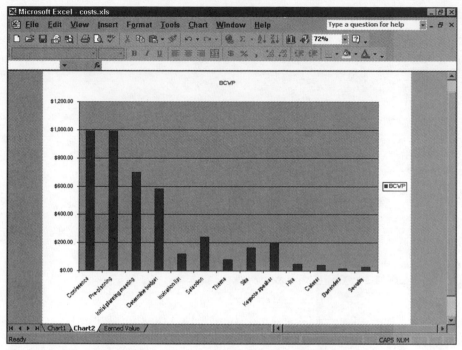

Figure 14-13: An Excel chart of one earned value for selected tasks

To create a chart like the one shown in Figure 14-12, follow these steps:

1. Click the ChartWizard button on the Standard toolbar to start the ChartWizard. In the first ChartWizard dialog box, select the type of chart that you want to create.

2. Click Next to open the second ChartWizard dialog box, as shown in Figure 14-14. In this dialog box, select Rows for the "Series in" option.

3. Click the Collapse Dialog button at the right edge of the Data Range box, which is shown in Figure 14-14, to hide the ChartWizard so you can select the task that you want to chart from the worksheet.

4. Highlight (by dragging) the cells in the row containing the information that you want to chart. Note that I've excluded the ID in Column A in Figure 14-15.

   Your chart will be more meaningful if you omit Column A, which contains the task ID number.

Figure 14-14: Chart the data by rows.

5. Click the Collapse Dialog button to redisplay the ChartWizard.

6. Click the Series tab.

Figure 14-15: Select the cells containing the data that you want to chart.

7. Click the Collapse Dialog button to the right of the "Category (X) axis labels" box.

8. Select the headings in Row 1 that contain the labels for the earned value fields. Your selection will probably include cells C1 through J1.

9. Click the Collapse Dialog button to redisplay the ChartWizard. The Series tab should look similar to the one shown in Figure 14-16.

Figure 14-16: The Series tab after you have selected X-axis labels

10. Click Next and fill in the other dialog boxes for the ChartWizard.

After you finish, your chart should resemble the chart shown in Figure 14-12, which displays all earned values for one task.

To create the chart shown in Figure 14-13, use the ChartWizard again; then in the second ChartWizard dialog box, use the following settings:

✦ On the Data Range tab, select the "Columns" for the Series in option. For the Data Range, select the cells containing the earned value information that you want to chart. In the chart shown in Figure 14-13, I charted only about half of the available tasks in order to keep the chart cleaner.

✦ On the Series tab, remove all series except for one from the Series list (otherwise your chart will be *very* messy). In the "Category (X) axis labels" box, select the cells containing the task names (cells in Column B in the pictured worksheet).

Analyzing timescaled information

Project contains a wizard that helps you chart timescaled earned value data. You can use the Analyze Timescaled Data Wizard to automatically create a chart in Microsoft Excel of earned value information for the entire project. After you complete the wizard, the resulting chart looks similar to the one shown in Figure 14-17.

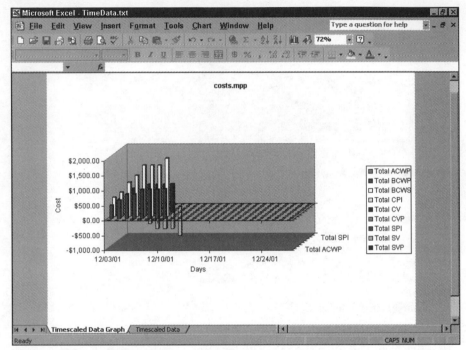

Figure 14-17: A chart of earned values created in Excel by using the Analyze Timescaled Data Wizard in Project

To use the Timescaled Data Wizard in Project, follow these steps:

1. Choose View ⇨ Gantt Chart.

> **Tip** If you want to chart data for selected tasks, select them now.

2. Choose View ⇨ Toolbars ⇨ Analysis. Project displays the Analysis toolbar, as shown in Figure 14-18.

Figure 14-18: The Analysis toolbar

3. Click the Analyze Timescaled Data in Excel button. Project opens the first of five Analyze Timescaled Data Wizard dialog boxes, as shown in Figure 14-19.

Figure 14-19: The first dialog box of the Analyze Timescaled Data Wizard

4. Select either "Entire Project" or "Currently selected tasks" and then click Next to open the Step 2 dialog box.

5. Select the appropriate earned value fields from the Available fields list; click Add to move the fields to the Fields to export list. Highlight the Work field in the Fields to export list, and click the Remove button, as shown in Figure 14-20. Click Next.

Figure 14-20: Select fields to export to Excel.

6. Select the date range and time increments that you want to use. The default time increment is days, which I selected in Figure 14-21. Click Next to open Step 4.

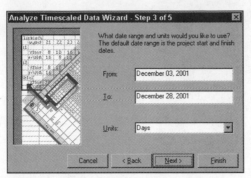

Figure 14-21: Select the date range and time increments for which you want to export data.

7. Select "Yes, please" if you want to graph the data. Otherwise, select "No, thanks," as shown in Figure 14-22. Click Next to open the wizard's final dialog box.

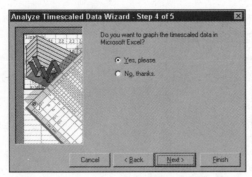

Figure 14-22: Tell Project whether to graph the data.

8. Click Export Data to export the Project data into Microsoft Excel, as shown in Figure 14-23.

Figure 14-23: Finish the process by exporting your data to Excel.

After you finish, the hourglass icon for the mouse pointer appears, indicating that you should wait while action takes place. Excel starts up, processes your data, and then displays a chart similar to the one shown in Figure 14-17 (located at the beginning of this section). Excel also creates a worksheet in the workbook, which you can view by clicking the Timescaled Data tab, as shown in Figure 14-24. The worksheet contains the earned value information that Excel used to create the chart shown in Figure 14-17.

	A B	C	D	E	F	G	H	I	J	K	L	M
1	costs.mpp											
2	Days	12/03/01	12/04/01	12/05/01	12/06/01	12/07/01	12/08/01	12/09/01	12/10/01	12/11/01	12/12/01	12/13/01
3	Conference											
4	ACWP											
5	BCWP											
6	BCWS											
7	CPI											
8	CV											
9	CVP											
10	SPI											
11	SV											
12	SVP											
13	Pre-planning											
14	ACWP											
15	BCWP											
16	BCWS											
17	CPI											
18	CV											
19	CVP											
20	SPI											
21	SV											
22	SVP											
23	Initial planning meeting											
24	ACWP											
25	BCWP											

Timescaled Data Graph | **Timescaled Data**

Figure 14-24: The worksheet that Excel uses to create the chart

Using PivotTables for analysis

Excel PivotTables can be interesting and useful when you want to analyze Project earned value data. The PivotTable is an interactive table that summarizes large amounts of data in a cross-tabular format. When you use Project to create a PivotTable in Excel, you get two PivotTables in the same workbook: a Task PivotTable and a Resource PivotTable. The Task PivotTable shows resources, tasks to which the resources are assigned, and costs for the resource per task. The Resource PivotTable summarizes resources by showing work assigned to each resource and the total cost of each resource. In addition to the PivotTable worksheets, the same Excel workbook also includes two worksheets — Tasks and Resources — that Excel uses to create these two PivotTables.

To export Project information to create PivotTables in Excel, follow these steps:

1. Start in any view of your project.

2. Choose File ➪ Save As to open the File Save dialog box.

3. Type a name for the Excel workbook that you want to create in the File name box. Don't worry about the extension — Project supplies it.

4. Select Microsoft Excel PivotTable from the Save as type list box.

5. Click Save to start the Export Mapping wizard.

6. Click Next.

7. Choose Use existing map and click Next.

8. Select "task and resource PivotTable" and click Finish, as shown in Figure 14-25.

Figure 14-25: The Map Selection dialog box of the Export Wizard

Note You can continue clicking Next in the wizard, but to chart earned value in Excel, you usually don't need to make any changes in the remaining dialog boxes that the wizard presents.

The hourglass icon for the mouse pointer appears, indicating that you should wait while action takes place. You'll also hear action on your hard drive. To view the PivotTables and their source data, start Excel and open the file that you just created. The workbook contains four sheets that should resemble the sheets shown in Figures 14-26, 14-27, 14-28, and 14-29.

Tip You may need to widen columns in Excel to see all the data. Double-click the right border of the column letter.

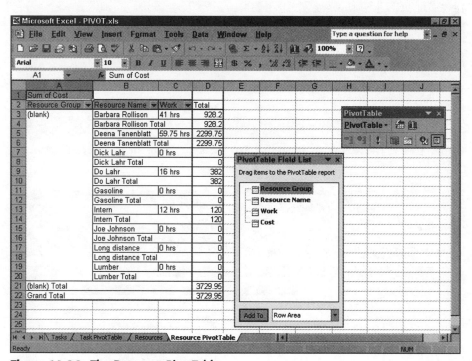

Figure 14-26: The Resource PivotTable

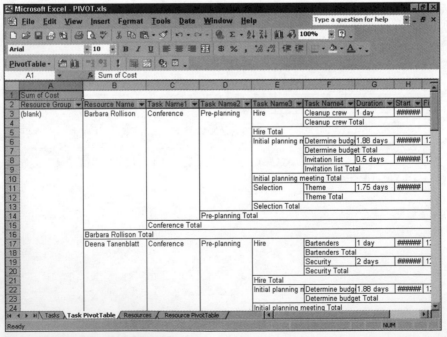

Figure 14-27: The Resources sheet that Excel used to create the Resource PivotTable

Figure 14-28: The Task PivotTable

Figure 14-29: The Tasks sheet that Excel used to create the Task PivotTable

Making Adjustments During the Project

Now that you've seen the various ways you can collect and analyze financial data about your project, you need to use that information to make improvements to your project. You can use many of the techniques that you used to implement changes to your project because of scheduling problems or resource conflicts.

Cross-Reference Learn how to deal with scheduling problems by using techniques discussed in Chapter 9. You'll find help resolving resource problems in Chapter 10.

Changing the schedule

After evaluating earned value information, you may want to change the schedule. For example, you may want to:

✦ Add resources to tasks

✦ Use overtime

✦ Increase task duration

✦ Adjust slack

    ✦ Change task constraints

    ✦ Adjust dependencies

    ✦ Split tasks

    ✦ Adjust the critical path

You may also need to make changes to the baseline project that you saved.

For more information on adjusting the baseline, see Chapter 11.

Modifying resource assignments

Your evaluation of earned value information may prompt you to make changes to resource assignments on your project. For example, you may need to:

    ✦ Change resource allocations

    ✦ Schedule overtime

    ✦ Redefine a resource's calendar

    ✦ Assign part-time work

    ✦ Control when resources start working on a task

    ✦ Level workloads

    ✦ Contour resources

    ✦ Pool resources

When you're working on an unusually large project, you may find it easier to break your project into smaller, more manageable portions called *subprojects*. In Project, you can create subprojects and then consolidate them into the larger project in order to see the bigger picture (see Chapter 15).

Summary

This chapter explained how to analyze the costs in your project. In this chapter, you:

    ✦ Learned how to use Project's Earned Value tables

    ✦ Learned to chart earned value information, to analyze timescaled information, and to use Microsoft Excel PivotTables

    ✦ Reviewed how to make adjustments to your project

In Chapters 15 through 19, you'll learn how Project helps you work in groups.

✦   ✦   ✦

Working in Groups

◆   ◆   ◆   ◆

No man is an island, and in the land of projects, you
rarely work alone. Working in groups presents some
special challenges, and Project provides different ways that
you can meet these challenges. In this part, you'll learn how
to coordinate multiple projects by using only Project and
some of its Web-based tools. You'll also learn how to use
Project in an e-mail workgroup. In addition, you'll learn how
to use Project Professional in conjunction with Project Server,
the Web-based project management database that enables
users without Project Professional to record project information using Project Server's browser-based client, Project Web
Access.

◆   ◆   ◆   ◆

Coordinating Multiple Projects Outside Project Server

✦ ✦ ✦ ✦

In This Chapter

Consolidating
projects

Consolidated projects
and dependencies

Viewing multiple
projects

Using multiple critical
paths

Sharing resources
among projects

✦ ✦ ✦ ✦

Large projects are the most difficult to manage. Organization is a cornerstone to good project management, and in a large project, the sheer number of tasks makes the job more difficult than usual. In Microsoft Project, you can use the concept of consolidated projects to break projects down into smaller, "bite-sized" pieces and then combine the smaller projects to view the bigger picture.

Consolidating Projects

When you're faced with a complex problem, finding the solution typically becomes easier if you can simplify the problem. Similarly, when you need to manage a complex project with many tasks, you may find it easier to organize the process if you deal with a limited number of tasks at one time.

Microsoft Project makes it easy for you to take this approach to planning large, complex projects. By using Project's consolidation features, you can create subprojects, which you can think of as the tasks that constitute one portion of your large project. When you create a subproject, you save it as a separate project file. You can assign resources and set up each subproject with links and constraints — just as if it were the entire project. When you need to view the bigger picture, you can consolidate the subprojects into one large project. When you consolidate, you actually insert one project into another project; therefore, subprojects are also called *inserted projects*.

When you work in a consolidated project, you can focus on just the desired portion of the project. Subprojects appear as summary tasks in the consolidated project, and you can use Project's outlining tools to hide all tasks associated with any subproject.

See Chapter 3 for more information on outlining.

From the consolidated project, you can view, print, and change information for any subproject — just as if you were working with a single project.

If you're a Project Professional user who also uses Project Server, you might be wondering if consolidation applies to you. While views in Project Server can "roll up" project information, you'll still need consolidation techniques if you want to see one critical path across all consolidated projects. Also, I describe resource pooling in this chapter; this concept applies more to Project Standard users than Project Professional users who also use Enterprise Resources in Project Server.

Setting up to use consolidation

Consolidation can help you achieve several objectives. For example:

✦ Tasks in projects managed by different people may be interdependent. Through consolidation, you can create the correct dependencies to accurately display the project's schedule and necessary resources.

✦ A project may be so large that breaking it into smaller pieces can help you to organize it. You can use consolidation to combine the smaller pieces and then view the big picture.

✦ You may be pooling the resources of several projects and find that you need to level the resources; consolidating enables you to link the projects sharing the resources so that you can level the resources.

If you're using Project Standard, you won't be taking advantage of the Enterprise Resource Pool available in Project Server; therefore, the resource pooling techniques described in this chapter apply to you. If you're using Project Professional, you may want to consider using the Enterprise Resource Pool instead of using resource pooling as described in this chapter; if so, see Chapter 19.

When should you decide to use consolidation? It doesn't really matter. You may realize right away that the project is too large to handle in a traditional way, or you may discover that the project is bigger than you originally thought. Suppose, for example, that the marketing department of a software company decides midway through the development cycle to bundle together various products under development. This introduces dependencies where none originally existed — and provides an interesting opportunity for using consolidation.

If you decide to use consolidation before you start your project, simply create separate Microsoft Project files for various portions of the project. These files act as subprojects when you consolidate. You need to set up each subproject file so that it is independently complete, and you need to create links within each subproject file, as necessary. This chapter explains techniques for consolidating the subprojects and linking them.

If you start a project and then decide that you want to use consolidation, you can create subprojects by following these steps:

1. Save your large project file.

2. Select all the tasks that you want to save in your first subproject file and click the Copy button.

3. Click the New button to start a new project and use the Project Information dialog box that appears, as shown in Figure 15-1, to set basic Project information, such as the project's start date and scheduling method.

Figure 15-1: Use the Project Information dialog box to set basic project information.

4. Click the Paste button.

5. Save the subproject and close it.

6. Select all the tasks you want to save in your second subproject file and click the Copy button.

7. Repeat Steps 3 through 6 until you have saved several separate files that contain portions of your larger project.

Edit each subproject file that you create to make it an independently complete project. Then, you can use the techniques explained in the following section to consolidate the subprojects and link them.

Inserting a project

To consolidate project files into one large project, you insert projects into a host project file, often referred to as the *consolidated project file*. Each project you insert appears as a summary task in the consolidated project file, and Project calculates inserted projects like summary tasks. An icon in the Indicator field identifies an inserted project, as shown in Figure 15-2.

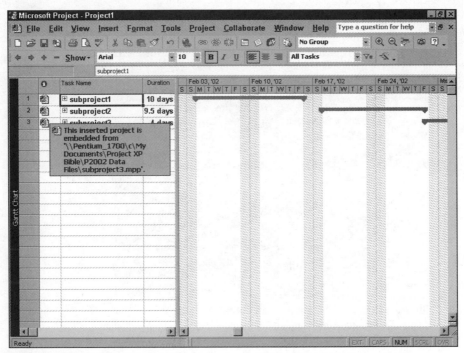

Figure 15-2: A special icon in the Indicator field identifies inserted projects.

You can insert projects at any outline level. The level at which an inserted project appears depends on the outline level that appears at the location where you intend to insert a project. To insert a project, simply select the task you want to appear below the inserted project; Project then inserts the project above the selected task. Typically, an inserted project appears at the same level as the selected task. However, if the task above the selected task is indented further than the selected task, the inserted project will appear at the same level as that indented task. Or, if the task above the selected task is at the same level or out-dented further than the selected task, the inserted project will appear in the outline at the same level as the selected task. Compare Figures 15-3, 15-4, and 15-5.

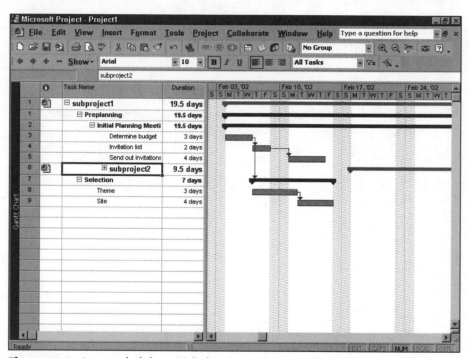

Figure 15-3: I expanded the Initial planning meeting task and then chose the Selection task when I inserted subproject2; it appears at the same outline level as the Invitation list task above it.

Consolidation Concepts

Consolidation changed from Project 95 to Project 98. In Project 95, many project tools, such as copying and pasting, didn't work in consolidated projects. Project 95 used two techniques to work with multiple projects: *consolidation,* and *master projects* and *subprojects*. By using the second technique, you created a link between a placeholder task in the master project and the subproject.

In Project 98, you no longer needed to think about master projects versus subprojects. Subprojects still existed as separate projects, but you included them in a consolidated project. In addition, Project 98 provided much greater flexibility in the consolidated project, but sacrificed performance. Project 2000 and Project 2002 handle consolidation in the same way as Project 98, but Project 2000 considerably improved consolidation performance over Project 98. You can think of the consolidated project as the host project into which you insert subprojects.

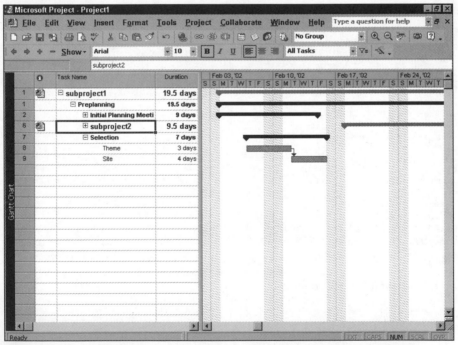

Figure 15-4: I collapsed the Initial planning meeting task and then chose the Selection task when I inserted subproject2; it appears at the same outline level as the Initial planning meeting task.

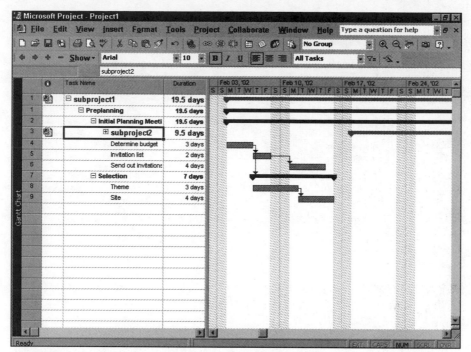

Figure 15-5: I selected the Determine budget task and then inserted subproject2; it appears at the same outline level as Determine budget because the task above — Initial planning meeting — is out-dented further than Determine budget (the selected task).

To produce a consolidated project in which the inserted projects line up at the highest outline level, as is shown in Figure 15-6, make sure that you collapse the preceding inserted project so that you can't see its tasks when you insert the next subproject.

Tip You can hide or show tasks after you insert the project by clicking the summary task's outline symbol — the plus or minus sign next to the task name.

To insert a project, follow these steps:

1. Open the project in which you want to store the consolidated project.

2. Click the Gantt Chart icon in the View bar.

3. Click the Task Name column on the row where you want the inserted project to begin.

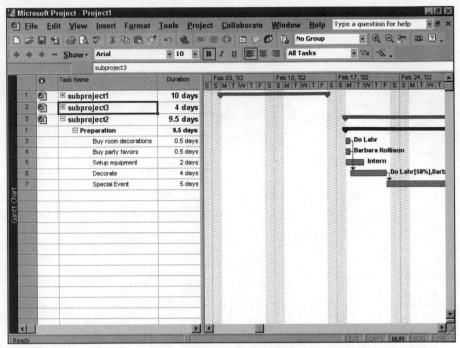

Figure 15-6: When subproject3 was inserted, subproject2 was selected and its subordinate tasks were visible, but the subordinate tasks of subproject1 were not visible.

Note When you insert a project, Project places the project immediately above the selected row. Therefore, if your consolidated project already contains tasks, click the task in the Task Name column that you want to appear below the subproject.

4. Choose Insert ➪ Project to open the Insert Project dialog box, as shown in Figure 15-7.

5. Use the Look in list to navigate to the folder that contains the project you want to insert.

6. Highlight the file you want to insert.

7. Change any insert project options:

   • If you remove the check from the Link to Project checkbox, the inserted project won't be linked to its source project.

   • If you choose Insert Read-Only from the Insert drop-down menu, Project does not change the source project when you change the inserted project.

8. Click Insert (or Insert Read-Only). Project inserts the selected file into the open project. The inserted file appears as a summary task, with its subordinate tasks hidden.

Link to project check box

Figure 15-7: The Insert Project dialog box works like the Open dialog box.

Using inserted projects and their source files

You can link an inserted project to its source file, as was shown in Figure 15-2. If you don't want to link an inserted project to its source file, any changes that you make to the inserted project in the consolidated project file don't affect the source file. Similarly, any changes that you make to the source file don't affect the consolidated project file containing the subproject. Therefore, why wouldn't you want to link the files? You may want to create a consolidated file just so you can generate a report quickly.

In many circumstances, linking the files makes updating easier. Linking ensures that any changes you make in either the consolidated project or the subproject file affect the other file. When you insert a project and link it to its source file, you are creating a link between two files; that link works like any link you create between two files in the Windows environment. For example, if you rename the subproject file or move it to a different folder than the one in which you originally saved it, you need to update the link to the consolidated project; otherwise, the link does not work.

If you do move a file that you have linked, you can update the link on the Advanced tab of the Task Information dialog box for the inserted project, as shown in Figure 15-8.

Figure 15-8: The Advanced tab of the Inserted Project
Information dialog box

Tip You also can unlink subprojects from their source files by using the Advanced tab
of the Inserted Project Information dialog box. Remove the check from the Link to
project checkbox.

Or, you can simply attempt to expand the inserted project; when you click the plus
sign next to the subproject, Project automatically displays a dialog box that looks
like the Open dialog box. Use it to navigate to the new location of the file and click
OK after you finish.

Consolidating all open projects: A shortcut

Follow these steps to consolidate several subprojects at the same time:

1. Open all the subprojects that you want to consolidate.

2. Choose Window ➪ New Window to open the New Window dialog box, as
   shown in Figure 15-9.

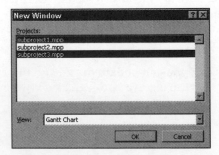

Figure 15-9: Use the New Window dialog
box to quickly consolidate open projects.

3. Press and hold down the Ctrl key and click each project that you want to consolidate.

4. Click OK.

Project creates a new consolidated project that contains the projects that you selected in the New Window dialog box. Project inserts the subprojects into the consolidated project in the order in which the subprojects appear in the New Window dialog box.

Moving subprojects within a consolidated project

You can move subprojects around in the consolidated project by cutting a subproject row to delete it and then pasting the row where you want it to appear. When you select a summary row representing a subproject and click the Cut button on the Standard toolbar, Project opens the Planning Wizard dialog box, as shown in Figure 15-10.

Figure 15-10: The Planning Wizard appears when you try to delete a summary task.

Select the Continue option button and click OK. The summary task representing the subproject and all its subordinate tasks disappears. When you paste the subproject, Project places the subproject immediately above the selected row. Therefore, in the Task Name column, you must click the task that you want to appear below the subproject. Then click the Paste button on the Standard toolbar. Project reinserts the subproject at its new location.

Tip   If you're going to be moving a lot of tasks, you may want to place a check in the "Don't tell me about this again" box to avoid viewing the Planning Wizard box.

Consolidated Projects and Dependencies

In a consolidated project you typically have tasks — either in the consolidated project or in one subproject — that are dependent on tasks in another subproject. You can create links between projects in a consolidated file and, if necessary, you can change the links that you create.

Linking tasks across projects

You can create four different types of dependencies: finish-to-start, start-to-start, finish-to-finish, and start-to finish. In addition, these types support lead and lag time. The process of linking tasks with dependencies across projects is much the same as the process of creating dependencies for tasks within the same project. Starting in the consolidated project file, follow these steps:

1. Click the Gantt Chart on the View bar.

2. Select the tasks that you want to link.

Tip   To select noncontiguous tasks, press and hold down the Ctrl key as you click each task name.

3. Click the Link Tasks button on the Standard toolbar. Project creates a finish-to-start link between the two tasks.

Tip   You can create the link in the consolidated project file by dragging from the Gantt bar of the predecessor task to the Gantt bar of the successor task.

You also can link tasks by typing in the Predecessor field, using the format **project name\ID#**. Project name should include the path to the location of the file, as well as the filename, and ID# should be the ID number of the task in that file. The Buy room decorations task shown in Figure 15-11 is linked to the Site task, which is Task 8 in a Project file called SUBPROJECT1.MPP. You can see the complete path name of a linked task in the Entry bar (just below the toolbars) when you highlight the task.

Figure 15-11: You can type in the Predecessor field to create a link between tasks across Project files.

When you link tasks between projects, the task links look like standard links in the consolidated project. However, when you open either of the subproject files, you'll see that Project has inserted an external link, as shown in Figure 15-12. The name and the Gantt Chart bar of each externally linked task appear gray. If you point at the Gantt Chart bar, Project displays information about the task, including the fact that it is an external task.

If you double-click the task name of the external task, Project opens the subproject containing the task to which the external task is linked.

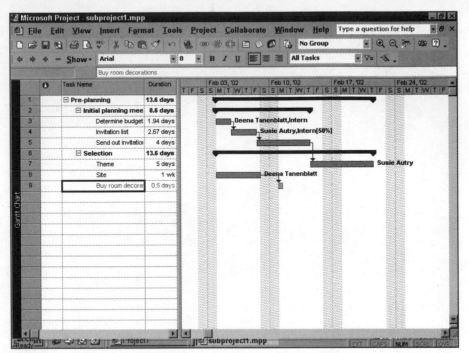

Figure 15-12: When you link tasks across files, Project inserts an external link in the subproject file.

Changing links across projects

After you link tasks across projects, you may need to change information about the link. For example, you may want to change the type of dependency from the default finish-to-start link, or you may want to create lag time.

You can modify a link between tasks in different subprojects from either the subproject or from the consolidated project. In the subproject, double-click the line that links an internal task to the external task, as shown in Figure 15-13. In the consolidated project, double-click the line that links the two tasks, as shown in Figure 15-14. In both cases, Project displays the Task Dependency dialog box.

The two versions of the dialog boxes differ slightly. If you work from within the sub-project, you can update the path of the link and use the Type box to change the type of link and the Lag box to change the amount of lag time between the linked tasks. If you work from within the consolidated project, you can't update the path of the link, but you can change the type of link and the amount of lag time.

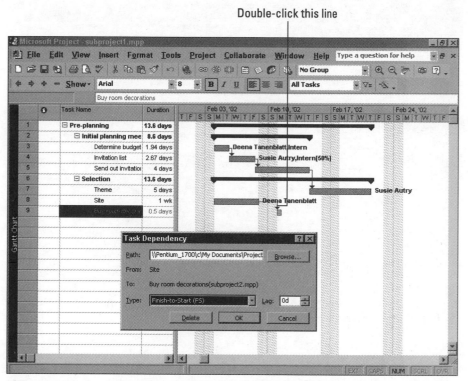

Figure 15-13: In a subproject, double-click the link line between the internal task and the external task to display the Task Dependency dialog box.

Double-click this line

Figure 15-14: In a consolidated project, double-click the line that links the tasks to display the Task Dependency dialog box and change the dependency information about tasks linked across projects.

Consolidated projects — to save or not to save

You don't need to save consolidated project files unless you want them. You can create the consolidated project file by using either the Window ⇨ New Window method or the Insert ⇨ Project method — both are described in this chapter. You can use the consolidated project to create links and maybe even reports, and then close the consolidated project file without saving it. For example, suppose that you created the consolidated project by inserting projects and the inserted projects are not open. When you close the consolidated project, Project first asks if you want to save the consolidated project; your answer does not affect changes that you made to inserted projects, as shown in Figure 15-15.

If you created the consolidated project by using Window ⇨ New Window, Project asks whether you want to save changes to the subprojects as you close them.

If you save the changes to the subprojects — even if you don't save the consolidated project — external tasks, such as the one you saw previously in Figure 15-12, appear in the subproject files when you open them.

Figure 15-15: When you close a consolidated project that you created by inserting projects, Project asks if you want to save changes, including links, that you made to each subproject.

Viewing Multiple Projects

Creating a consolidated project makes your work easier because you can display and hide selected portions of your project. The consolidated project shown in Figure 15-16 contains three inserted projects. As you can tell from the outline symbols, you can't see all the tasks in this consolidated project in the figure; the tasks for subproject3 are hidden.

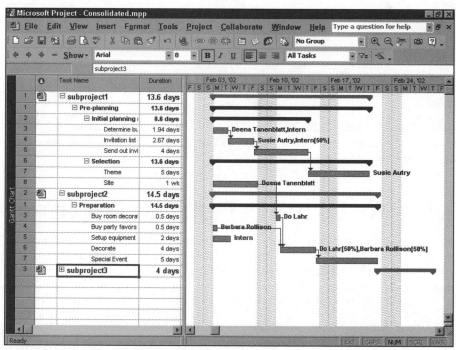

Figure 15-16: This consolidated project contains three inserted projects.

Suppose that you need to focus on the middle portion of the project. As Figure 15-17 demonstrates, you can easily focus on the portion of the project that currently needs your attention by clicking the outline symbols to the left of each summary task to expand only the portion of the project that you want to view.

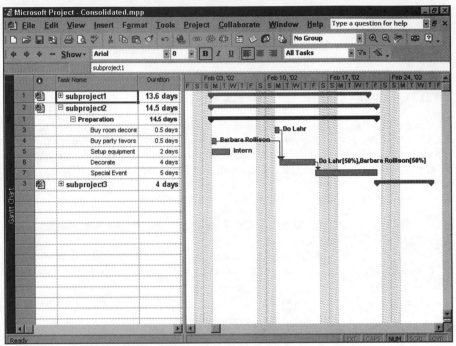

Figure 15-17: Close up inserted projects so that just their summary tasks appear when you want to focus on a portion of a consolidated project.

Viewing the Critical Path Across Projects

When you consolidate projects, by default Project calculates inserted projects like summary tasks, effectively showing you the overall critical path across all the projects by using the late finish date of the master project to make calculations. This behavior can make subprojects within the master project look like they don't have critical paths of their own, as shown in Figure 15-18.

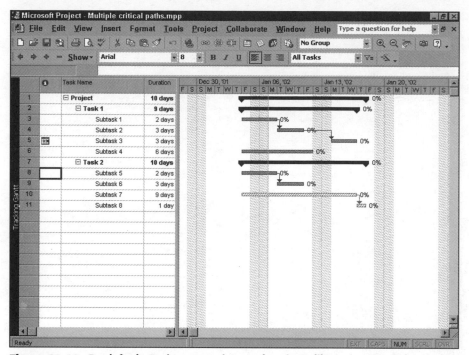

Figure 15-18: By default, Project treats inserted projects like summary tasks, and you won't see an inserted project's critical path.

However, suppose that you want to see each subproject's critical path while viewing the master project. To do so, you turn on multiple critical paths in the master project. Nothing changes, however, because multiple critical paths apply only to tasks owned by the project. In this example, the tasks (Task 1 and Task 2) in Figure 15-18 are owned by subprojects, so turning on multiple critical paths in the master project won't have any effect.

You can, however, tell Project to *stop* treating subprojects as summary tasks; if you do, Project uses the late finish dates that the subprojects pass along to the master project to determine the critical path — and you're likely to see each subproject's critical path, as shown in Figure 15-19. When you turn off this setting, you will see critical paths in the master project as they appear in each subproject.

To change Project's behavior in the master project, choose Tools ➪ Options and click the Calculation tab. Then, remove the check from the "Inserted projects are calculated like summary tasks" checkbox, as shown in Figure 15-20.

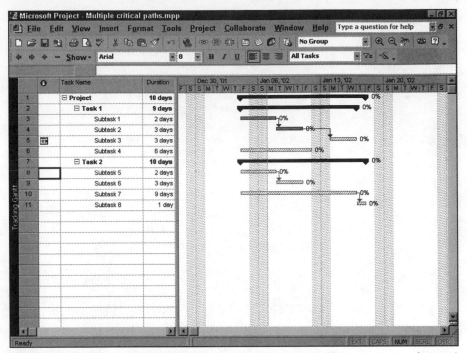

Figure 15-19: When Project doesn't treat inserted projects like summary tasks, you're likely to see multiple critical paths in a master project.

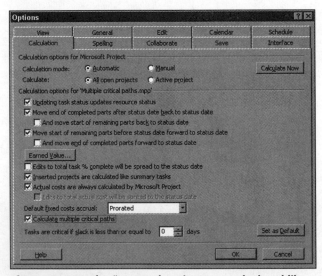

Figure 15-20: The "Inserted projects are calculated like summary tasks" checkbox controls whether Project uses the subprojects' late finish dates or the master project's late finish date for calculations.

Sharing Resources Among Projects

Creating a resource pool can be useful if you don't use Project Server and you work with the same resources on multiple projects. A *resource pool* is a set of resources that are available to any project. You can use resources exclusively on one project, or you can share the resources among several projects.

If you work in an environment in which several project managers use the same set of resources on various projects, consider using a resource pool. Setting up a resource pool in Project can be a good way to schedule resources and resolve resource conflicts.

Cross-
Reference

See Chapter 10 for more information on other techniques that you can employ to resolve resource conflicts. See Chapter 19 for information about using the Enterprise Global Resources feature of Project Server.

Creating a resource pool and sharing the resources

Setting up a resource pool in Project can facilitate resource management, especially for resources shared on several projects. To create a resource pool, you simply set up a project file that contains only resource information.

If you already have a project set up that contains all the resources available, you can use that project as a model. After you identify a project that can serve as the resource pool, you designate it as the resource pool project by using the following steps:

Note

You don't need to delete all of the tasks in the project that will serve as the model for the resource pool. You just need the resource information in the file.

1. Open the project that contains the resources and that will serve as the resource pool file.

2. Open the project that is to use the resource pool (that is, the project on which you want to work).

3. Choose Tools ➪ Resource Sharing ➪ Share Resources. Project displays the Share Resources dialog box, as shown in Figure 15-21.

Figure 15-21: The Share Resources dialog box

4. Click the Use resources option button, then use the From list box to select the resource pool project; this indicates that you want to use the resources defined in that project.

Note

If you open only the project on which you want to work, the "Use own resources" option button is the only choice available, and you won't be able to share resources with the resource pool. The first time you want to enable resource sharing, you must open both the project that you determined would be the resource pool and the project on which you want to work. In addition, if you have any other projects open, they appear as candidates for the resource pool project when you open the From list box because Project enables you to select from any open project when you identify the resource pool.

5. Tell Project how to handle calendar conflicts. If you select "Pool takes precedence," the resource calendars in the resource pool file will take precedence when conflicts arise. If, however, you select "Sharer takes precedence," the resource calendars in the file you're updating will take precedence over the resource calendars in the resource pool file when conflicts arise.

6. Click OK.

If you switch to the Resource Sheet view of the file that you want to update, Project displays all the resources contained in the resource pool file, along with any resources that you may have set up in your project file.

You can now continue working in your project, or you can save your project and close it. You can also close the resource pool file.

Opening a project that uses a resource pool

At some point, you will save and close your file and then come back to work on it a second time. You don't need to open the resource pool file at that time. Instead, when you open your file after you have set it up to share resources, a dialog box appears, as shown in Figure 15-22.

Figure 15-22: The Open Resource Pool Information dialog box

When you select the first option, Project opens your file and the resource pool. If you select the second option, Project opens only your file; Project does not transfer any changes that you make to the resources in your file to the resource pool because the resource pool file won't be open.

Note

When you select the first option, Project automatically opens the resource pool file as a read-only file. This action enables you to make changes to your project without tying up the resource pool file; therefore, multiple users can simultaneously use the resource pool.

Updating information in the resource pool

If you make any changes to resource information while you're working on your project, you must update the resource pool file so that others using the resource pool have the most up-to-date information. To update the resource pool, make sure that the resource pool file is open, even in read-only mode. Then choose Tools ➪ Resource Sharing ➪ Update Resource Pool, as shown in Figure 15-23.

Figure 15-23: The Update Resource Pool command is available if you set up resource sharing and you make a change in your project while the resource pool file is open.

If you opened only your project and made changes to the resources, this command is not available while working in your project. Furthermore, if you opened only your project, saved and closed your project, and then opened the resource pool file, this command is still not available. To ensure that Project incorporates the changes you make to resources in your project in the resource pool, be sure to open the resource pool file when you open your file.

Tip   To ensure consistency and avoid arguments in the workplace, it's best to make one group or person responsible for updating the resource pool.

If you forget to update the resource pool after you make a change in your project that affects the resource pool, Project displays a message, shown in Figure 15-24, when you close your project and save it.

Figure 15-24: If you forget to update the resource pool, Project alerts you when you close and save your project.

Note   Starting with Project 2000, Project stores the relative path to projects linked to resource pools; if you move one or the other, Project will still be able to open the files.

Quit sharing resources

Suppose you decide that you no longer want to use the resource pool file. Follow these steps to disable the resource pool for a specific project:

1. Open that project.

2. Choose Tools ➪ Resource Sharing ➪ Share Resources.

3. Select the "Use own resources" option button in the Share Resources dialog box (refer back to Figure 15-21).

However, suppose you decide that you want to disable the resource pool in general for all files sharing the resources of one resource pool. Do you need to open each file and disable resource sharing? No. Follow these steps to disable the resource pool file in general:

1. Open the resource pool file in read-write mode by using the Open dialog box — the same way you'd open any file. Project displays a dialog box, shown in Figure 15-25. Choose the middle option or the last option — either option will enable you to disable the pool because both open the file as a read-write file.

Figure 15-25: Use this dialog box to determine whether you open the resource pool file as a read-only file or a read-write file.

2. Choose Tools ⇨ Resource Sharing ⇨ Share Resources. Project displays the Share Resources dialog box, as shown in Figure 15-26.

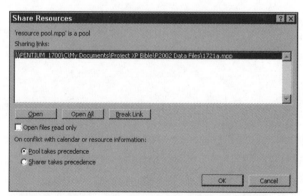

Figure 15-26: The Share Resources dialog box

3. Select the project(s) that you want to exclude from the resource pool. You can select multiple noncontiguous projects by pressing and holding down the Ctrl key when you click the mouse, or you can select contiguous projects by pressing and holding down the Shift key when you click the mouse.

4. Click Break Link.

Summary

This chapter described how to consolidate projects and pool resources. You learned how to

✦ Insert projects

✦ Understand and work with consolidated projects and dependencies

✦ Manage the view of a consolidated project

✦ Display multiple critical paths

✦ Share resources

In Chapter 16, you'll read about using Project in an e-mail workgroup.

✦   ✦   ✦

Using Project in an E-mail Workgroup

To paraphrase John Donne, no project manager is an island. Most projects involve you and at least one other person. The people involved in your project constitute your *workgroup*, and the project manager is the *workgroup manager*. Workgroups can vary in their structure. For example, on one project, you may manage it and coordinate activities of all its resources; on another project, you simply may be a member of a workgroup team that someone else is managing. In either case, you'll be interacting with many people over the days, weeks, or months that it takes to reach your goal — and you need tools to make that interaction a success.

Project has many workgroup features to help you manage and work with other members of a project team, and Project permits you to collaborate by using either e-mail or the Internet. This chapter explores workgroup tools that you can use when collaborating via e-mail:

♦ For communication

♦ To make task assignments

♦ To keep your schedule up-to-date

Note Because Project Server is the preferred method of collaborating and users of Project Server use many of the same dialog boxes as e-mail collaborators, you'll see references to Project Server in many of the screens that appear throughout this chapter.

Cross-Reference In Chapters 18 and 19, you learn about using Project Server, Project's Web-based project management tool, to update and manage projects.

You can use a combination of e-mail collaboration and Project Server to meet the needs of all users involved in the project. The two methods share one common feature — the project manager publishes assignments directly from Project. The two methods differ in the way you receive updates and status information. If you're using Project Server, you receive updates and status information in Project Web Access, the browser-based client for Project Server. If you're using e-mail to communicate, you receive updates and status information in your e-mail program's inbox.

> **Note**   If you've used versions of Project prior to Project 2002, you'll notice a significant change in Microsoft's strategy for handling project management for workgroups via e-mail and for workgroups using the Web that started in Project 2000. In Project 98, Project combined techniques for workgroup project management; in other words, you basically employed the same techniques whether you used e-mail or the Web. Beginning with Project 2000, Microsoft completely separated the Web-based strategy from the e-mail strategy — and the techniques changed completely. This chapter focuses on using e-mail to manage projects in workgroups from the perspective of people using Microsoft Exchange Server and Microsoft Outlook as their tools.

Setting Up an E-mail Workgroup

To use an e-mail-based workgroup, the manager and workgroup members must have access to a Messaging Application Programming Interface (MAPI)–compliant, 32-bit e-mail setup. MAPI is a standard e-mail interface that Microsoft supports with products such as Outlook, Microsoft Exchange, and Microsoft Mail, but it is common to other major e-mail products as well.

Within Project, you set up a workgroup by establishing a workgroup manager and the members of the workgroup. You can then exchange workgroup messages via e-mail. This exchange of information enables the workgroup manager to alert workgroup members to task assignments by using commands on Project's Publish menu. Workgroup members then can return information to the workgroup manager via e-mail, which the manager can use for tracking progress throughout the life of the project. Finally, managers can use commands on the Publish menu to notify workgroup members about shifts in the schedule or other project parameters.

The workgroup manager builds and maintains the project schedule and makes task assignments. (In most cases, the workgroup manager is also the project manager.) The "boss" creates the schedule, makes assignments, and uses communications from workgroup members to track their activities.

As the workgroup manager, you must first install and set up Project to enable work-group management on your computer. Although workgroup members can also install Project on their computers, this step isn't absolutely necessary. On your computer, complete the following steps to set up a particular project to exchange information via e-mail:

1. Choose Tools ➪ Options.

2. Click the Collaborate tab to select it, as shown in Figure 16-1.

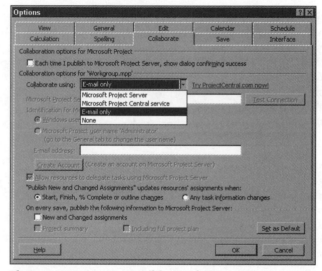

Figure 16-1: To use e-mail for workgroup management, set the collaboration options to E-mail only.

3. Open the Collaborate using list box and choose E-mail only.

Cross-Reference See Chapters 18 and 19 for more information about setting up Project for work-group management by using your company's intranet or the Internet.

4. Click the General tab.

5. In the User name box, fill in the workgroup manager's e-mail address, as shown in Figure 16-2, so that workgroup members who receive e-mail from the manager can respond to that e-mail.

6. Click OK to save your settings.

Figure 16-2: Fill in the e-mail address of the workgroup manager.

To use e-mail for workgroups, all workgroup members (including the workgroup manager) must run an executable file called `Wgsetup.exe`, which is located on the Project CD-ROM, to send and receive messages.

Note Some members of your team won't have Project on their computers — and that's okay. By running `Wgsetup.exe`, they will have everything that they need to communicate via e-mail.

To run `Wgsetup.exe`, you can copy the entire WGSETUP folder from the Project CD-ROM to a network drive or you can move from workstation to workstation with the Project CD-ROM. You'll find the WGSETUP folder in the FILES\SUPPORT folder on the CD-ROM. Run `Wgsetup.exe` and follow the prompts onscreen to install the Project Workgroup Message Handler.

Building a Resource Workgroup

To use Project's workgroup collaboration features, you first must assign resources to your project and designate them as belonging to your workgroup. When you create these resources, you enter an online address so Project can communicate with them. Follow these steps to create a resource group:

1. Choose View ➪ Resource Sheet.

2. Enter a resource name and any other pertinent information about the resource in the columns of the Resource Sheet.

3. Double-click the resource name to open the Resource Information dialog box, as shown in Figure 16-3.

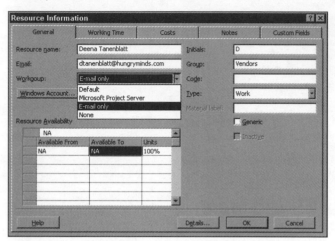

Figure 16-3: Enter a group name and e-mail address for every resource that you want in your workgroup communication circle.

4. Enter an e-mail address in the E-mail field.

5. Enter a group name in the Group field; this entry is required to use the workgroup features with this resource.

6. Select a workgroup from the Workgroup drop-down list. This choice should match the messaging method that you chose when you set up the workgroup manager's connection.

7. Click OK to save the resource, which is now part of the workgroup and is set up for workgroup communications.

Tip   If you need to enter many e-mail addresses, you may find that editing is faster if you add a column to the Resource Sheet view for the e-mail address and the Workgroup. See Chapter 7 to learn how to insert columns.

Communicating via E-mail

After a manager sets up a workgroup, both the manager and the workgroup members can use Project's workgroup collaboration features. The manager uses Project's collaboration commands on the Collaborate menu, as shown in Figure 16-4, to notify workgroup members of project-related information. In particular, the manager uses three of the commands — All Information, New and Changed Assignments, and

Republish Assignments — that appear on the Publish submenu as well as the Request Progress Information command on the Collaborate menu.

Figure 16-4: Use the Publish submenu when collaborating in an e-mail workgroup.

Publishing all information

After you (the workgroup manager) have set up the project, made assignments, and established a workgroup, you can automatically generate e-mail messages notifying resources of assignments. Choose Collaborate ➪ Publish ➪ All Information. Project indicates that it will save your project after sending e-mail messages. When you click OK, Project generates the messages and displays a dialog box, stating that the process has completed successfully. In your project, you'll see indicators next to each task showing that an e-mail was sent but no reply has been received, as shown in Figure 16-5.

Whenever you choose the All Information command, Project will generate an e-mail message to all resources who have not yet responded to their assignments. Although there are other ways, workgroup managers *can* use the All Information command to nag resources if necessary.

In Project Server, the All Information command sends project schedule information to Project Server, as well as notifications to resources.

Team members receive an e-mail that contains an attachment with an extension of .MTM. When the team member opens the attachment, he or she sees the Publish All Information reply dialog box, as shown in Figure 16-6. To accept an assignment received through e-mail, the team member leaves the Yes in the Accept? column. To decline the assignment, the recipient double-clicks in the Accept? column to change Yes to No, or the recipient can type an N in the Accept? column. If appropriate, the recipient can enter a message and click Reply.

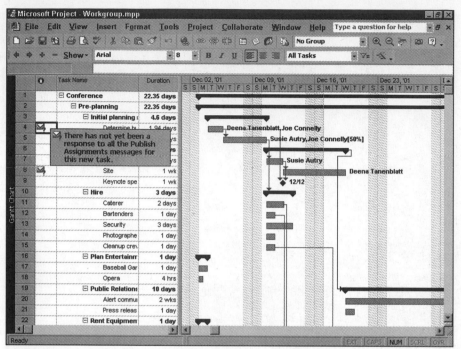

Figure 16-5: Indicators in your project let you know that you sent e-mail messages to each resource.

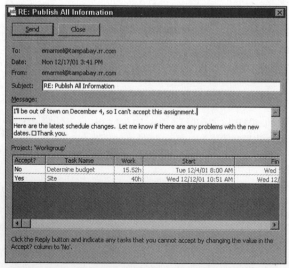

Figure 16-6: Use this dialog box to respond to an assignment.

After the workgroup member sends a reply, the workgroup manager will receive an e-mail with the .MTM extension. When the workgroup manager opens the attachment, a dialog box containing an Update Project button appears, as shown in Figure 16-7. The workgroup manager can click this button to transfer the changes to the project schedule. Project opens and applies the changes.

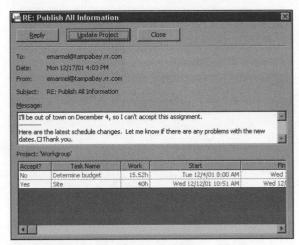

Figure 16-7: The response that the workgroup manager receives contains an Update Project button that transfers changes automatically to Project.

Publishing new and changed assignments

As the project progresses, you may need to make assignment changes. You can update resources about new and changed assignments by choosing Collaborate ➪ Publish ➪ New and Changed Assignments. Project displays the Publish New and Changed Assignments dialog box, as shown in Figure 16-8.

If you select only one task in the project, Project shows (by default) that everyone in the project will receive an e-mail assignment update. You can limit the e-mail update by selecting tasks prior to opening the dialog box; in this case, Project will show only resources assigned to the selected tasks.

Note The All Information command sends out messages to all resources about assignments — without showing the workgroup manager who will receive messages. If you want more control, use the Publish New and Changed Assignments dialog box and choose Entire project in the Publish new and changed assignments for list.

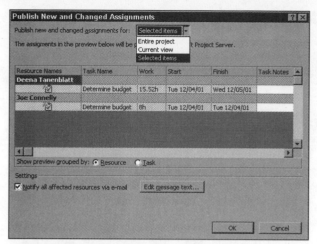

Figure 16-8: In this dialog box, you can see who will receive an e-mail message.

Project lists the task(s) to which the resource is assigned in a table below your message, indicating:

✦ The name of the task

✦ The amount of work time that you expect from the resource on the task

✦ The task start and finish dates

✦ Any comments that you entered into the Comments column of the Gantt table

You can choose to view the information either by resource or by task by clicking the appropriate option button toward the bottom of the dialog box.

Project automatically generates a message that asks the recipient to indicate his or her acceptance of the assignment. If you want to view or change the message that each resource will receive, click the Edit message text button to display the Edit message text dialog box, as shown in Figure 16-9.

Tip   You can modify the information in this table, as explained in the "Customizing Your Workgroup" section, later in this chapter.

When the information in the Publish New and Changed Assignments dialog box is correct, click the OK button to send the message. Project indicates that it will save your project after sending e-mail messages. After generating the messages, Project places indicator icons next to the tasks included in the message, just like the indicator icons you saw previously in Figure 16-5. Project also places messages that you'll need to send in the outbox of your e-mail application.

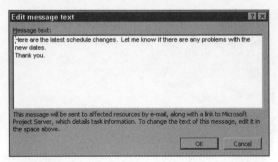

Figure 16-9: In this dialog box, you can change the message that resources will receive, along with their assignments.

Team members receive an e-mail that contains an attachment with an extension of .MTM. When the team member opens the attachment, he or she sees the Publish and Changed Assignments reply dialog box, as shown in Figure 16-10. To accept an assignment received through e-mail, the team member leaves the Yes in the Accept? column. To decline the assignment, the recipient double-clicks in the Accept? column to change Yes to No, or the recipient can type an N in the Accept? column. If appropriate, the recipient can enter a message and click Reply.

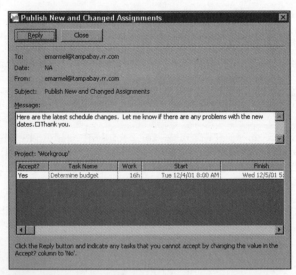

Figure 16-10: Use this dialog box to respond to an assignment.

After the workgroup member sends a reply, the workgroup manager will receive an e-mail with the .MTM extension. When the workgroup manager opens the attachment, a dialog box containing an Update Project button appears (as shown previously in Figure 16-7). The workgroup manager can click this button to transfer the changes to the project schedule. Project opens and applies the changes.

Republishing assignments

As the workgroup manager, you may feel the need to periodically republish assignments, even if they haven't changed. You can republish all or selected assignments by choosing Collaborate ➪ Publish ➪ Republish Assignments. Project displays the Republish Assignments dialog box, as shown in Figure 16-11, which closely resembles the Publish New and Changed Assignments dialog box. When you choose this command, Project will create e-mail messages for all resources — even if you previously sent messages to and received replies from them.

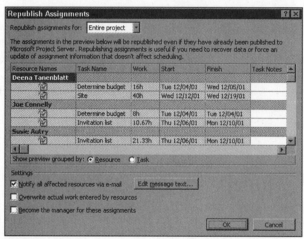

Figure 16-11: Use this dialog box to republish assignments.

Team members receive an e-mail that contains an attachment with the .MTM extension. When the team member opens the attachment, he or she sees the Publish and Changed Assignments reply dialog box, as shown in Figure 16-12. To accept an assignment received through e-mail, the team member leaves the Yes in the Accept? column. To decline the assignment, the recipient double-clicks in the Accept? column to change Yes to No, or the recipient can type an N in the Accept? column. If appropriate, the recipient can enter a message and click Reply.

Note   The check boxes at the bottom of the Republish Assignments dialog box apply to Project Server.

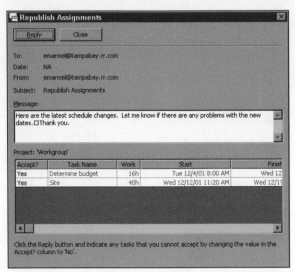

Figure 16-12: Use this dialog box to respond to an assignment.

After the workgroup member sends a reply, the workgroup manager will receive an e-mail with the .MTM extension. When the workgroup manager opens the attachment, a dialog box containing an Update Project button appears (as shown previously in Figure 16-7). The workgroup manager can click this button to transfer the changes to the project schedule. Project opens and applies the changes.

Requesting a status update

As the workgroup manager, you may periodically want to request a status report from your team members; to do so, choose Collaborate ➪ Request Progress Information. Project displays the usual message about saving your project and then displays the Request Progress Information dialog box, as shown in Figure 16-13. You can select tasks prior to opening this dialog box to request status updates for the selected items.

You can view information in this dialog box either by resource or by task, as shown in Figure 16-13. As with the other dialog boxes in this chapter, you can edit the message text and specify a time frame for which you want to receive status information.

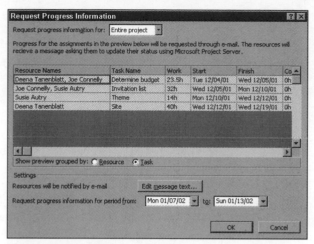

Figure 16-13: Use this dialog box to request status updates from some or all resources for some or all tasks.

The team member receives an e-mail message containing an attachment with the .MTM extension, as shown in Figure 16-14.

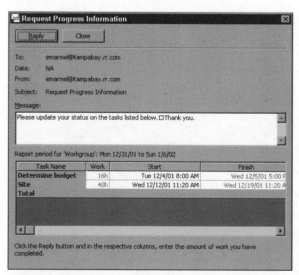

Figure 16-14: To respond to the Progress Information request, the recipient clicks the Reply button — and the Reply button changes to the Send button.

While not visible in the figure, team members can scroll to the right in the Report period for section and edit the task information fields for Start, Remaining Work, and the days of the week. The team member enters information in the Remaining Work field reflecting actual work progress, optionally adds a return message about the status of the tasks, and then clicks Send to return the message to the workgroup manager. When the manager receives the response and clicks the Update Project button at the top of the message, Project uses the team member's entries to automatically update the tasks in the actual schedule.

Customizing Your Workgroup

You can modify the task information that appears in your workgroup messages by using the customizing feature of Project. This feature enables you to add or delete items that appear in the task information fields, rearrange the fields, or request more detailed breakdowns of task timing.

Follow these steps to customize your messages:

1. Choose Tools ➪ Customize ➪ Published Fields to open the Customize Published Fields dialog box, as shown in Figure 16-15.

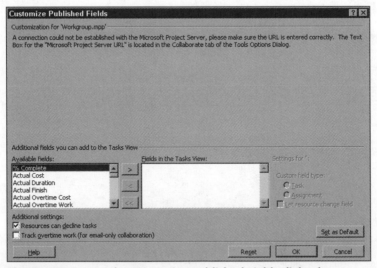

Figure 16-15: Use the Customize Published Fields dialog box to include the information most relevant to your project in your workgroup messages.

2. To add a field, highlight the field in the Available Fields list on the left side of the dialog box and click the button containing the arrow button that points to the right. If you add more than one new field, each new field appears above whatever field was highlighted when you clicked the Add button.

Note You can remove a field that you previously added. Click the name of the field that you want to remove in the Fields in Tasks View list on the right side of the dialog box and then click the arrow button that points to the left.

Tip If you have made several changes and want to return to Project's standard settings for workgroup messages, click the Reset button in the Customize Workgroup dialog box.

3. Click OK to save the new settings.

Establishing Management Procedures

If you are responsible for managing a workgroup, your job involves more than just setting up your group to send and receive workgroup messages. You also need to orchestrate those communications and manage project files efficiently to get the most out of the workgroup structure. Use the following suggestions to guide you:

✦ Make sure that all workgroup members understand how Project's workgroup features function. You (the workgroup manager) may be the only person in the workgroup to have a copy of Project on your computer. Help your team to understand not only how to use the workgroup features that are available to them but also why these features are important to using Project effectively.

✦ Set up a communication schedule with your workgroup. Make assignments and status requests on a regular basis, perhaps allowing a week or two of activity to occur before you perform updates. If workgroup members know that they will receive requests for updates and status reports every Friday, for example, and that they must respond by end of day every Tuesday, they can establish a routine to deliver the information in a timely way.

✦ Check your mailbox on a regular basis. If you aren't being responsive to your workgroup's input, they'll stop being responsive to your requests.

Sending Notes and Routing Files

Project has two other tools that are helpful in communicating with various resources assigned to a project — regardless of whether they are part of your designated workgroup. First, you can send a project schedule note to selected resources assigned to the project. Second, you can route a project file from one resource to another. The ability to route notes and files can be useful if you want each resource to add information to the file or note and then forward it to the next person for his or her comments.

Sending Project notes

You can send a copy of your Project file, and perhaps a note to all resources or a subset of resources on a project, even if the resources are not part of your regular workgroup. Before beginning this procedure, select a specific task if you want to send a note concerning the resources assigned to that task only. Otherwise, don't select any specific task. To send a message through your MAPI-compliant e-mail system, follow these steps:

1. Choose File ➪ Send to ➪ Mail Recipient (as Schedule Note).

2. Select the people to whom you want to send the note in the Address message to field in the Send Schedule Note dialog box, as shown in Figure 16-16. Your choices include the Project manager, resources for the selected task or entire project, or contacts. Then select the appropriate options:

Figure 16-16: This dialog box gives you some flexibility for designating who should get this note: resources, the project manager, or various contacts for the project, such as a vendor.

- **Address message to.** If you want everyone on the project to get this message, choose Entire project. If you want only the resources assigned to the task that you selected before opening this dialog box, choose Selected tasks.

- **Attach.** If you want to attach the currently open Project file to your message, place a check in the File checkbox. Remember, only those people who have Project installed on their computers can open the Project file.

3. Click OK. A new e-mail message form appears, with a copy of the Project file attached.

4. Type your message in the large, blank message area.

5. Use your e-mail addressing method to send the message to anyone other than the designated resources assigned to tasks, who were automatically addressed when you created the message.

6. Send the message.

Routing a Project file

Routing a Project file to a group of people is another good way to keep workgroup members informed and involved in the project. Each person can add information that the next person on the route can build or comment on. Routing a file is a simple process. Follow these steps:

1. Choose File ➪ Send To ➪ Routing Recipient to open the Routing Slip dialog box, as shown in Figure 16-17.

Figure 16-17: The Routing Slip dialog box enables you to track your message as it moves along its route by clicking the Track status checkbox.

2. Click the Address button to display the address book for your e-mail software program. Select as many addressees as you want by using this method and then click OK to return to the Routing Slip dialog box.

3. Enter information for the Subject of the message.

4. Type your message in the Message text box.

5. Select one of the option buttons in the Route to recipients box, choosing to route sequentially or all at once.

6. Place a check in the Return when done checkbox if you want Project to return the file to you at the end of the route.

7. Place a check in the Track status checkbox if you want Project to notify you each time the file moves to the next person on the routing list.

8. Click Route to send the message.

Tip If you're the last recipient of the routing, you can remove the routing slip from the Project file. Click the Remove All button in the Routing Slip dialog box.

Summary

Because most projects are team efforts and because successful teams communicate effectively, establishing good workgroup procedures in your projects is key. In this chapter, you learned how to

✦ Set up the workgroup manager and workgroup members to send and receive project information via e-mail

✦ Use commands on the Collaborate menu to keep members informed and update the project file

✦ Route messages and files among team members

In addition to knowing how to use these features, you must know how to set up effective, consistent procedures for their use among your workgroup members.

Chapter 17 introduces you to Internet basics in Project.

✦   ✦   ✦

Project and the World Wide Web

As you may have found with other software packages, Project contains tools to facilitate interfacing with the Internet. The *Internet* is a large network of computers that you can use to send and retrieve information, images, and messages around the globe. The World Wide Web is perhaps the biggest success story on the Internet: This graphical Internet service enables you to move around the Web by using a programming language called *Hypertext Markup Language* (HTML). With HTML, you can jump between Web locations by clicking images or text linked to a specific online address. These links are *hyperlinks*.

Connectivity helps you to manage projects more effectively, and Project includes a few useful tools that help you access and use the World Wide Web, including the following:

✦ **You can use Project's Web capabilities to navigate the Internet by using the Web toolbar.** Rather than embedding a link to a site in your schedule, you can save lists of your favorite Web locations and go quickly to a site on that list by using the Web toolbar. Your favorite sites may include your company's Web page, a newsgroup related to your industry, or a data source, such as a university library, that you search often for information related to your project.

✦ **You can insert hyperlinks to Internet addresses within your project file.** This way, you or someone using your schedule can move instantly to an area on the Web that contains related information or images. For example, if your project involves the design of a network for your company, you can insert a hyperlink in your schedule to the network software vendor's home page so that you can find answers to technical questions or order software.

Cross-Reference You can also use the Internet to communicate with your workgroup via e-mail. Chapter 16 covers this feature in more detail.

Using the Web Toolbar

Project has a special set of tools specifically designed for navigating the World Wide Web. You can display this toolbar by right-clicking anyplace on the Standard toolbar and choosing Web from the shortcut menu that appears; or, you can choose View ➪ Toolbars ➪ Web. The tools that are available on the Web toolbar are shown in Figure 17-1.

Figure 17-1: The Web toolbar appears just below the Formatting toolbar, though you can drag it away to be a floating toolbar if you prefer.

The tools on the Web toolbar work with your Web browser to help you to navigate either an organizational intranet or the Web. Table 17-1 briefly describes each tool.

Table 17-1 The Project Web Toolbar	
Tool	**Function**
Back	Takes you back to the last site visited during the current online session.
Forward	Moves you one site ahead in the list of sites visited during the current online session.
Stop Current Jump	Becomes active if you initiate a jump to a site; clicking this button when it's active stops the hyperlink jump that's in progress.
Refresh Current Page	Refreshes or updates the contents of a currently displayed page, incorporating any changes made by the author as you read the page.
Start Page	Takes you to the home page that you have set your Web browser to access by default.
Search the Web	Takes you to whatever search engine page that you have set your Web browser to use.

Tool	Function
Favorites	Opens a list of favorite sites that you have saved into a Favorites folder. Click any site name in this list to go directly to that site.
Go	Displays a menu of common Web navigation commands.
Show Web Toolbar Only	Hides any other currently displayed toolbars, leaving only the Web toolbar visible onscreen.
Address	Shows the address of the current site and, when opened by clicking the arrow on the right, displays a drop-down list of recently visited sites.

To use these tools on the World Wide Web, you need an Internet connection and a Web browser. After you have all the elements in place, click the Search tool button (for example); Project connects with the Internet and opens the search page that you have set up in your browser. After you are connected, you can use the Back and Forward buttons to move through the Web pages. You can use your browser's Favorites feature to save addresses of sites that you like to visit often; Project also saves these addresses in its own Favorites list.

You also can use the Web toolbar to open Project files that are located on a server or on your own hard drive; simply fill in the correct address in the Address box of the Web toolbar.

Working with Hyperlinks

A hyperlink is a mechanism that enables you to jump from the currently displayed document to another document on your hard drive or on a computer network, or to an Internet address (referred to as a *Uniform Resource Locator*, or URL).

For example, suppose that your company is planning to move into a new manufacturing facility, and the Finance department has placed the budget for the move in an Excel spreadsheet on your company's network. You, on the other hand, must manage the move and have created a project schedule that deals with moving all equipment into your new manufacturing facility. You can place a hyperlink in the project schedule that connects to the Excel file that contains the budget for the move to the new facility. The hyperlink appears as an icon in the Indicator field of the Gantt Chart. When you open the project file and click that hyperlink, the Excel file appears so that you can check on the budgeted dollars for each aspect of the move.

You also can insert a hyperlink to an Internet address, for example, to link a research task to the Internet site where most of the research is performed.

Inserting a hyperlink

To insert a hyperlink in your project, follow these steps:

1. Select the task for which you want to create a hyperlink. (After you finish inserting the hyperlink, a link icon appears in the Indicator column for the selected task.)

2. Choose Insert ➪ Hyperlink or click the Insert Hyperlink button on the Standard toolbar. The Insert Hyperlink dialog box appears, as shown in Figure 17-2.

Figure 17-2: Enter a file path and name, or a URL, to set up the hyperlink.

3. Use the Look In list to perform one of the following tasks:

   • To link to an Internet address, type the URL (for example, www. microsoft.com) or browse for a URL by clicking the Web Page button.

   • To link to a file on your hard drive or a network, type the path or browse for the file by clicking the File button.

4. In the Text to Display box, type the text that you want to appear in your Project schedule to represent the hyperlink.

5. Click OK to insert the hyperlink. A hyperlink icon, like the one shown in Figure 17-3, appears in the Indicator field to the left of the selected task.

Note To remove a hyperlink, right-click the task for which you created the link and then choose Hyperlink ➪ Remove Hyperlink. No warning appears; Project simply removes the hyperlink.

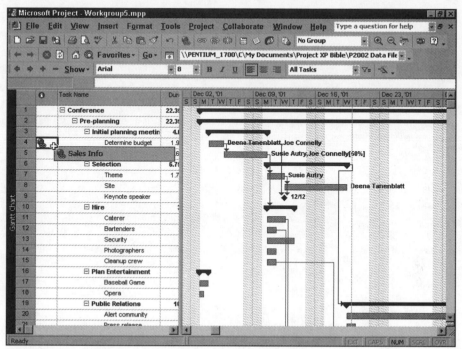

Figure 17-3: To go to a URL or file, click the hyperlink icon.

Editing hyperlinks

If you create a lot of hyperlinks, identifying them can be a tedious chore if you rely on the ScreenTip that you see when you point at each link. You can, however, display the links in one of Project's built-in tables. Begin in any view that includes a table, such as the Gantt Chart view. Choose View ➪ Table ➪ Hyperlink. The hyperlink table shown in Figure 17-4 displays columns of information relevant to any links that you've created for your project.

To edit the hyperlink, its address, or its sub-address, click the task name of the task for which you created the hyperlink. Then, use the right-arrow key to move to the cell that you want to edit and make the changes that you want to make. You also can press F2 to make changes directly in the cell, or you can edit the cell contents in the Formula bar that appears below the toolbars in Project. If you prefer to work in the Hyperlink dialog box, right-click the link and choose Hyperlink ➪ Edit Hyperlink to reopen the dialog box and make changes.

Note

Because the cells in this table contain hypertext, clicking the cell itself activates the link.

When Hyperlinks Don't Work

After you establish a hyperlink, some things can happen to cause the link to not work. This condition usually involves a change in the location of the linked file. On a network or hard drive, a file simply may have been deleted or moved to another directory. Similarly, a Web site may have been moved to a new URL, or perhaps it no longer exists.

Or, you may have mapped your hyperlink to a file on a network that is in a location to which you don't have access. Or perhaps you gave a copy of your schedule to a coworker, and she doesn't have access to that location from her computer.

The best way to work around this problem is to use relative addressing whenever possible when you create the hyperlink. For example, `f:\budget.xls` is an absolute address. If your server drive changes from F:, the link won't work. However, if you use `\\server\share\budget.xls`, a relative address, your server drive can change from F: to G:, and the relative address to your server will still work. For more help with hyperlink problems, check out the topic, "hyperlink troubleshooting" in Project's Help feature.

Moving or copying hyperlinks

You can also use the hyperlink table to move or copy a hyperlink by following these steps:

1. Select the hyperlink cell by clicking its task name and then by using the right-arrow key to select the hyperlink cell.

2. Press the Shift key and the right-arrow key to also select the address of the hyperlink.

3. Do one of the following:

   - **To move the link:** Click the Cut button on the Standard toolbar, then click the hyperlink cell next to the task where you want to move the link, and then click the Paste button.

   - **To copy the link:** Select the link, click the Copy button, click the hyperlink cell next to the task where you want to place a copy of the link, and then click the Paste button.

Figure 17-4: The hyperlink address and representation are two fields available here.

Summary

Project's Web capabilities enable you to link files or to create links from a file to an Internet address. These simple Web features can help you to communicate project information to coworkers or clients in an effective, high-tech way.

In this chapter, you learned to

✦ Use the Web toolbar

✦ Insert hyperlinks

✦ Edit hyperlinks

✦ Move or copy hyperlinks

In Chapter 18, you'll learn about Project Server, which is a Web-based way of working with Project and schedules.

✦   ✦   ✦

Managing Projects on the Web

At this point in the book, you have probably realized that the world of project management has moved beyond the traditional pencil-and-ruler war room and into the world of technology. Nowhere is this shift more evident than in the many ways project managers can take advantage of the Internet to communicate with others, present information, and gather data.

The Internet is a large network of computers that you can use to send and retrieve information, images, and messages from around the globe. If you're using Project Professional, you can purchase Project Server, which is a tool that makes Web-based project management possible. The project manager creates the project in Microsoft Project Professional and saves it to the Project Server database; at that point, any team member with Internet Explorer and the address to the Project Server database can view and update the project. In other words, everyone in the workgroup doesn't need to have a copy of Project. Those who don't have Project can use Project Web Access — the browser-based interface that connects to the Project Server database — to view the tasks that they need to accomplish, update the schedule with work completed, and even enter new tasks that may arise.

Project Server moves well beyond the capabilities of Project Central, its predecessor in Project 2000. In this chapter, you'll read about the basics of Project Server, and you'll learn how the average team member can connect to the Web database, update task status, and report to the project manager. In Chapter 19, you'll learn how the project manager can utilize the Enterprise functions of Project Professional and Project Server.

The information in this chapter and in Chapter 19 applies to Project Professional. If you are using Project Standard, you can't use Project Server and Project Web Access. You can, however, use the Internet to communicate with your workgroup via e-mail. Chapter 16 covers this feature in more detail.

Understanding Project Server and Project Web Access

Project Server enables you to manage projects on your company's intranet or on the Internet — and only the manager must actually install and use Project. All other resources on the project use Project Web Access, the Web-based product that connects to the Project Server database, which contains your project data. Without using Microsoft Project, resources can:

✦ View a project's Gantt Chart

✦ Receive, refuse, and delegate work assignments

✦ Update assignments with progress and completion information

✦ Attach supporting documentation, such as budget estimates or feasibility studies to a project

✦ Receive notices about task status

✦ Send status reports to the project manager

Project managers can do much more than the actions listed in the preceding list. See Chapter 19 for details.

Here's how the process works in a general fashion. The network administrator installs Project Server on a Web server or the company's server. The project manager creates a project in Project Professional that is "Web-based." When the project manager is ready to store the project in the Project Server database, s/he publishes the project information. At this point, anyone with Internet Explorer 5.5 (or a later version) and access to the Project Server database can view the project information as it appears in Project Professional by using Project Web Access, the Web-based client side of Project Server.

Using a variety of tools, the project manager can assign resources to the project from the Enterprise Global, which you can think of as a company-wide source of available resources. Resource personnel can see, in Project Web Access, the assignments that they have received. Team members use Project Web Access to update work assignments and send status reports to the project manager.

See Chapter 19 for more information about the tools used by project managers to assign resources to projects from Enterprise Global.

Setting up a Web-based project involves the following actions:

✦ A network administrator installs Project Server on a Web server or on your company's server.

✦ The project manager creates a project in Microsoft Project, with or without the resources the project will need, and publishes the project to the Web-based database.

✦ Resources and the project manager use Project Web Access (the client side of Project Server) to update the project.

Note The project manager uses both Project Professional and Project Web Access, but other project resources use only Project Web Access.

You'll need a network administrator (or someone of similar knowledge and expertise) to set up Project Server on a Web server or on the company's server. (On the client side, the project manager needs Project, but other resources need only Internet Explorer 5.5 or a later version.)

This server should have Windows 2000 Server with Service Pack 2 or above, and Microsoft Internet Information Server (also called IIS) 5.0. (When you install Project Server, it installs and sets up a connection between your database engine and IIS.)

You'll also need SQL Server 2000. If you want to use the Portfolio Modeling features that are available in Project Web Access, you'll need SQL Server Analysis Services, which is included with SQL Server. If you want to use the Documents and Issues feature, you'll need Microsoft SharePoint Team Services. You'll find Microsoft SharePoint Team Services on the Microsoft Project Server CD.

In addition, each person in the workgroup must be able to access either your organization's network or a TCP/IP network.

Project Server for the Day-to-Day User

Project Server and Project Web Access actually are used by three different types of Project users: the Administrator, the project manager, and the day-to-day user. In this section, I'll focus on the day-to-day user's interaction with Project Web Access. Typically, the day-to-day user doesn't really interact with the Project Server.

Logging on to Project Web Access

To log on to Project Server by using Project Web Access, a resource needs to know the URL for the Web database. The project manager should notify the resource of the URL in an e-mail message or through some other form of communication. To log on to Project Server, open Internet Explorer and, in the Address box, type the URL of the Web database.

Tip

Save the URL in your Favorites list or, if you use Project Web Access more than any other Web page, set it up as your home page, which will appear when you open Internet Explorer. To set Project Web Access as your home page, type the address into the Address box. Then, choose Tools ➪ Internet Options. On the first page, click the Use Current button in the Home Page section, and click OK.

The window that appears next depends on the method that you use to log on to Project Server. If you aren't using Windows user accounts, you'll see a Web page similar to the one shown in Figure 18-1.

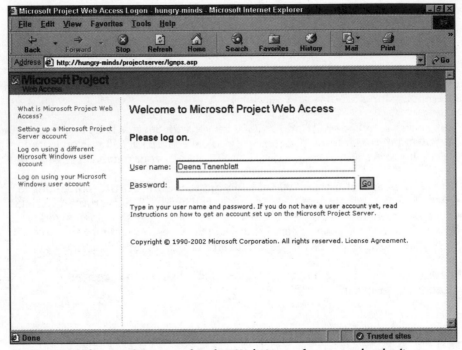

Figure 18-1: The opening page of Project Web Access for users who don't use Windows user account logon information

Note

If you're using Windows user account logons, you won't see the Log on page; instead, you'll bypass this page and see your home page, which is discussed in the next section.

Select your name from the User name list. If you're not using Windows user account logons, then initially your password is blank, so you don't need to enter anything in the Password box. Simply click Enter.

Note The first time you log on, you'll need to type your user name; from that point on, you can select it from the list. And, if you set a password by using the techniques described later in this chapter, you'll need to supply that password in the Password box if you see the Logon page of Project Web Access.

Reviewing the Home page

The Project Web Access Home page serves the same function as most home pages on the Web; it introduces you to Project Web Access, displays summary information, such as the number of new tasks that you have, and provides you with links to navigate to other areas of Project Web Access. Your Home page in Project Web Access looks similar to the page shown in Figure 18-2. In the center of the page, you'll see notices of new events.

Tip If you need to work away from the office (for example, suppose that you use a notebook computer while traveling), you can keep track of the time you work by working offline. Click the Go offline link in the Actions Pane, as shown in Figure 18-2. When you reconnect in the office, you can upload information.

Click here to hide the Actions Pane

Figure 18-2: A typical Project Web Access Home page, from which you can navigate to other areas of Project Web Access

The tabs (Home, Tasks, Projects, Status Reports, Documents, Issues, Logout, and Help) that are located across the top of Project Web Access remain visible at all times, and you can click them to move to different areas within Project Web Access. The Actions Pane that runs down the left side of the screen contains links that enable you to view pages within a particular area. To navigate in Project Web Access, you click a link or a tab.

Tip   You can hide the Actions Pane by clicking the small arrow at the top of the pane.

Implementing security

When you begin to pass around plans for a project, you may run into issues of security. For example, you may have resource rate information that you don't want everyone to see, or perhaps you want messages that you receive on project status to be for your eyes only. You can protect the contents available for viewing in Microsoft Project Web Access by assigning a password to it.

If you aren't using Windows user account logon information, your password is initially blank. As long as your password remains blank, Project Web Access will prompt you to change your password each time you use Project Web Access. You'll see a dialog box similar to the one shown in Figure 18-3.

Figure 18-3: As long as your password remains blank, Project Web Access prompts you to create a password.

A word about passwords and security

The password is the basic method of protecting project data. However, setting a password does not guarantee safety; the procedures that you use to devise an effective password and keep it from being discovered are vital to project security.

Cross-Reference   For information on setting passwords for individual files in Project, see Chapter 2.

Whether they have criminal motives, such as industrial espionage, or just simple workplace curiosity, people may try to peek at your project information. The computer world has spawned a whole subculture of people, known as *hackers*, who have made an art out of breaking into supposedly secure files.

Here are some guidelines for working with passwords:

✦ Don't use an easy-to-guess password. A clever hacker can find out your spouse's name, your middle name, your phone extension, and your date of birth in no time.

✦ Use the longest password that Project allows (up to 17 characters); the longer the password, the harder it is to crack.

✦ Don't give your password to anybody. If you have to give it out (for example, if you are away from the office and someone else must access data to keep the project going), be sure to change your password as soon as you return.

✦ Create a password that is a random combination of letters and numbers. For example, T2J773N is a good password; MyFile isn't.

✦ Change your password on a regular basis, even if you never give it to anyone. Hackers break passwords by using software that randomly generates and tries out different options and combinations. Hackers may need a few sessions to break your code, but they *can* break your code. The more often you change your password, the more times someone else will have to start from scratch to break it.

Setting your password

When you haven't set a password, Project Web Access prompts you to set one each time you log in, as was shown previously in Figure 18-3. If you click Yes, you'll see the page shown in Figure 18-4, where you enter a password and confirm it.

You can display this page at any time by clicking the Change Password link on the left side of the Project Web Access Home page.

If you had no password at all, leave the Old Password box blank. Type your new password twice — first in the New Password box, and then in the Confirm Password box. If you make a mistake, Project asks you to enter the password again. Click Change Password to save the password; the next time you log on to Project Web Access, you'll need to supply this password.

You can change your password at any time by clicking the Change password link in the Actions Pane on the left side of the Project Web Access Home page. If you previously assigned a password, type it in the Old password field.

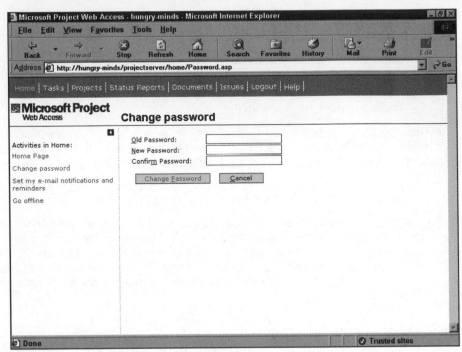

Figure 18-4: After you set a password, you must enter it in the Password box to log on to Project Web Access.

Working with your tasks

Note   If you previously worked with Project Central, you know about the Inbox. Project Server and Project Web Access don't use an inbox like Project Central did; instead, work assignments go from Project Professional to team members via Project Web Access. If your organization chooses, the Project Server Administrator can set up e-mail notifications so that Project Server will generate e-mail notices and reminders of events, such as past due tasks; these e-mail notices and reminders will appear in your regular e-mail client inbox. See Chapter 19 for more information on e-mail notifications and reminders.

Click the Tasks tab at the top of Project Web Access or the Tasks link on the Home Page to view tasks, as shown in Figure 18-5. By default, you see all tasks in the Gantt Chart view (notice the small boxes next to Gantt Chart and All tasks in the Actions Pane), but you can use the timesheet view to record and report any work that you've performed, as shown in Figure 18-6.

Tip   In the Timesheet view, you can use the Current Tasks link in the Actions Pane to filter out completed tasks and tasks that are far ahead in the future.

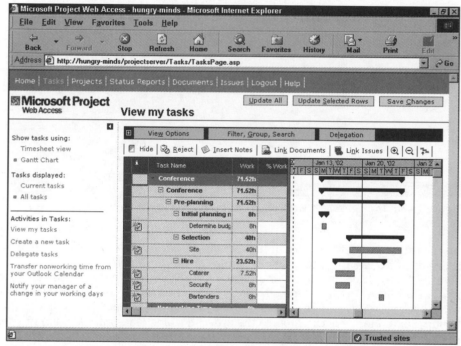

Figure 18-5: The Gantt Chart view of the Task page in Project Web Access

Figure 18-6: The Timesheet view of the Task page in Project Web Access

Above the timesheet, you see three tabs: View Options; Filter, Group, Search; and Delegation. To use these tabs, click the plus sign (+) at the left edge of the tabs. In Figure 18-7, you see the View Options tab of the Timesheet page; when you click either the Filter, Group, Search tab or the Delegation tab, the Tasks page redisplays with different options appearing above the tasks. For example, by using the Filter, Group, Search tab, you can change the order in which tasks appear from the default (by project) to start date, work, or task name. From the Delegation tab, you can choose to show only delegated tasks, only your own tasks, or both; you also can delegate tasks from this tab.

Click here to display the settings you can establish for each of these tabs

Figure 18-7: Use the information below each tab to customize the view of your tasks.

Entering time on tasks

The Timesheet view is actually divided in half — notice two scroll bars running across the bottom of the view, as shown in Figure 18-8. What you see in either half of the Timesheet view depends on the options that your manager chose for you to record updates, and you can enter information into any field on either side of the timesheet that is light gray. The Timesheet view works like a spreadsheet; you click in the cell that you want to update, and then you type. At the right edge of the view, you see a set of dates with arrows pointing either direction; click the arrows to display the time frame that you want to update. Then, click in the cell that represents the intersection of the day that you worked and the task on which you worked, type the appropriate number, and then click the Save Changes button at the top of the Project Web Access page.

Note The numbers that you can enter depend on the settings your project manager has selected. You may be able to fill in the % Work and Remaining Work fields, the Total Actual Work and Remaining Work fields, or the Actual Work and Remaining Work fields.

Click here to add a note to the selected tasks   Change the date using these arrows

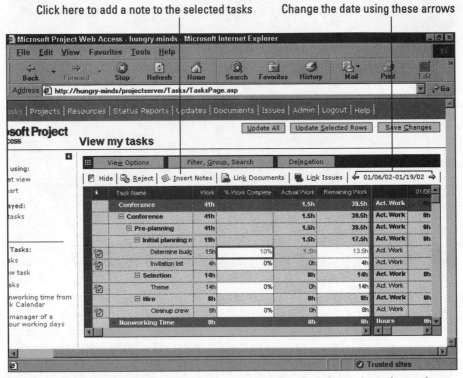

Figure 18-8: Enter information on the left side of the Timesheet view; the updates appear on the right side of the view.

The information that you save updates the Project Server database, but it doesn't automatically update the manager's information stored in the Project file. To let your manager know that you've completed some work, click the Update All button or the Update Selected Rows button. Project Web Access sends an e-mail message to your manager.

Tip

If necessary, you can add a note to a task by clicking the Insert Note button while the task is selected. Project Web Access displays a dialog box in which you can type; the Note is included in updates to the project manager and the text becomes read-only as soon as Project Server does an update. If you add more than one note to a task, Project Web Access appends notes so that the Project Manager isn't deluged with notes.

Adding tasks

As a team member, you may realize that what you're doing will require more work than the manager anticipated — and may even call for tasks that the manager didn't assign to you. You can enter the tasks in Project Web Access and notify your manager about the additional work.

To create a new task, click the Create a new task link in the Actions pane. Project Web Access displays a page similar to the one shown in Figure 18-9.

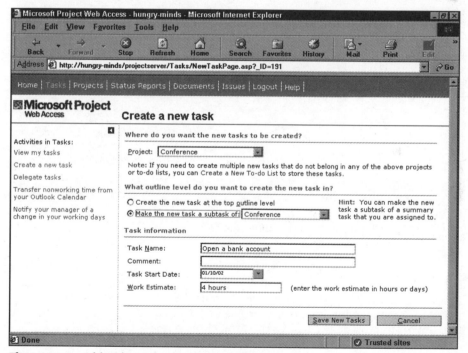

Figure 18-9: Add tasks to the project from this page.

Select the project to which you need to add the task from the Project drop-down list, and then select the task's level in the outline. For the Task Information, supply a task name, a comment about the task (optional), a start date, and the amount of work that you estimate the task will require. Click the Save New Tasks button, and Project Web Access adds the task to your Timesheet, along with an icon in the Remarks column on your Timesheet (see Figure 18-10).

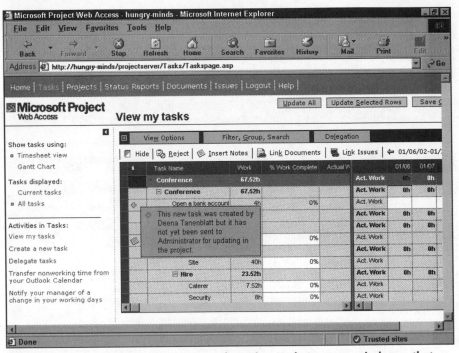

Figure 18-10: After you create a new task, Project Web Access reminds you that you haven't notified your manager about the task.

To notify your manager of the new task, click the Update All button or the Update Selected Rows button. Project Web Access sends the notice of the new task to the manager and changes the icon to reflect the task's new status — that you've noti-fied your manager, but your manager hasn't yet updated the project. Your manager has the option to add the task to the project or to reject the task.

Transferring information from Microsoft Outlook

Do you use Outlook? Would you like to be able to get a better handle on *all* the things you need to do by viewing them all in one place? Transfer nonworking time from your Outlook Calendar into Project Web Access so that you can view your entire schedule in one place.

Note If you want Project Web Access to display in Outlook, then you need Outlook 2000 or a later version. If you want to transfer Outlook information into Project Web Access, then you can use Outlook 98 or a later version.

Click the View Options tab and place a check in the Show Outlook tasks box. Then, click the Get from Outlook button. Project Web Access adds Outlook tasks at the bottom of the view, as shown in Figure 18-11.

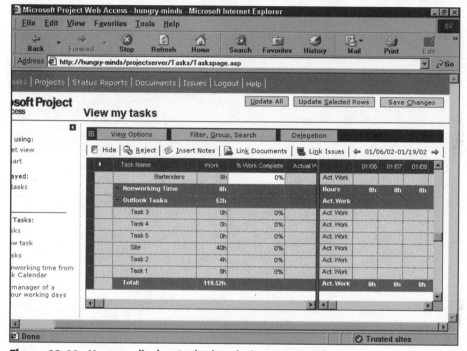

Figure 18-11: You can display Outlook tasks in Project Web Access.

Tip If you *don't* want to see Outlook tasks anymore, simply remove the check on the View Options tab.

Notifying managers of workday changes

Suppose that you were just selected for jury duty. And, of course, you're scheduled to work on a project at the same time. It happens — something comes up and you are not available to work during the time that you had previously been scheduled to work. Or, you are now available to work when you thought you wouldn't be available. For example, the case you were hearing wrapped up earlier than expected and the jury's been dismissed.

You can use a wizard in Project Web Access to notify your manager of changes to your workday from Project Web Access. Click the Notify your manager of a change in your working days link in the Actions pane. Project Web Access displays the page shown in Figure 18-12. Choose the appropriate option and click Next to enable the wizard to walk you through the process.

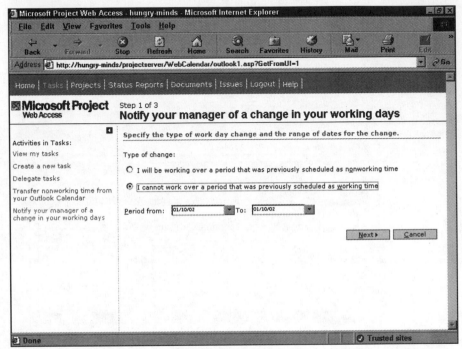

Figure 18-12: Enable this wizard to walk you through the process of notifying your manager about a change in your work schedule.

Delegating a task

You're overloaded with work and can't possibly complete everything that you've been assigned. But, lucky for you, they just approved your request to hire an intern to help you. Now you need to delegate some tasks — and keep your project manager informed of the change in assignment.

To delegate tasks, simply click the Delegation tab. Select the tasks that you want to delegate and click the Delegate Task button. A new page appears — and a wizard walks you through the delegation process, as shown in Figure 18-13. Click Next after you fill in the information for Step 1.

Tip   If you select a summary task, Project Web Access will delegate all subtasks.

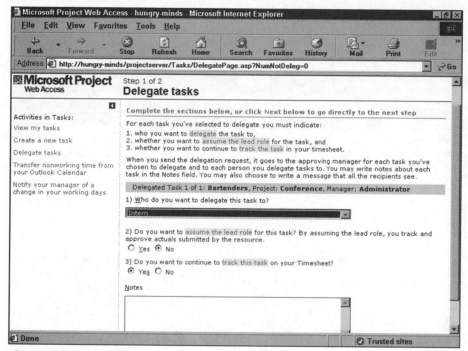

Figure 18-13: Identify to whom you want to delegate the tasks and what role you want to continue to play.

In Step 2 of the wizard, send a message to the delegate and to your project manager to notify them of the action, as shown in Figure 18-14.

Click Send to complete the process; new tasks will appear in the Microsoft Project Web Access Task view of each affected recipient and the Project Manager. The person to whom you delegated can refuse the assignment by selecting the task and clicking the Reject button.

Note that you may not be able to delegate certain tasks because of the following:

✦ Your manager doesn't permit tasks to be delegated.

✦ Your manager has deleted the task.

✦ The task is a tracking copy of a delegated task or is a nonworking time entry.

✦ A resource created the task, or actual work has been performed and the manager's approval is still pending.

Figure 18-14: To complete the delegation process, notify everyone affected by the delegation.

Using the task list

Suppose that you're using Project Web Access and you find that you really need a "to-do list." If the Project Server Administrator has enabled this feature, you can use the To-Do List feature in Project Web Access to start the list, and you can maintain the list in Project Web Access or you can upload it to Project Professional.

Note You can create as many to-do lists as you want. Think of each list as the task list for a potential new project.

Click the Projects tab in Project Web Access to view the Project Center. In the Activities Pane, click the Create a new personal or shared to-do list link to display the page shown in Figure 18-15.

Note You may not have security rights to view projects in the Project Center, but you can still create a to-do list.

Figure 18-15: Creating a to-do list

After you complete the first page and click Next, you'll see a page like the one shown in Figure 18-16, where you can create tasks. Any task that you assign to a resource appears immediately on that resource's Task page. Resources can update progress, delegate, or reject tasks that you created on a to-do list.

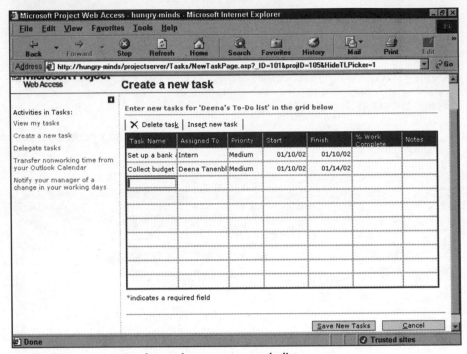

Figure 18-16: Create tasks to place on your to-do list.

After you complete the second page, click the Save New Tasks button. You'll see the Manage my to-do lists page, which lists your tasks in a Gantt Chart view, as shown in Figure 18-17. You can add new tasks by clicking the New Task(s) button in this window.

Figure 18-17: You manage to-do lists from this view.

If you click the To-do list options link in the Actions Pane, you'll see the To-do list options screen, as shown in Figure 18-18. From this screen, you can rename a to-do list, transfer the list to someone else, send the tasks in the list to Project Professional, delete the list, or change the viewing permissions of the list.

Figure 18-18: The To-do list options screen controls the behavior of your to-do list.

Attach supporting documents to projects

By using this feature, you can link supporting documents to a project, a task, or a to-do list. This feature comes in handy when you have a budget justification or a feasibility study or some other supporting document that you want to be able to "grab" whenever the need arises.

You can post documents in the Shared Documents folder, which is a public, company-wide space that anyone in the organization can access, or you can store them in a project-specific space, where only those with access to the project plan will also have access to the documents.

Note   To use this feature, you must install and set up SharePoint Team Services.

To work with documents, click the Documents tab in Project Web Access. You'll see a page similar to the one shown in Figure 18-19, which shows all the projects to which you have access.

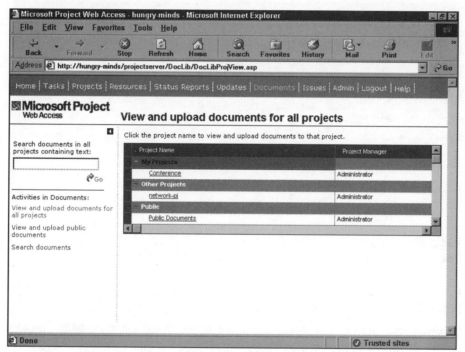

Figure 18-19: The projects to which you have access and for which you can view documents.

Viewing documents

To view the documents for a particular project, click the link for that project. You'll see a page similar to the one shown in Figure 18-20. Notice that each project has a Shared Documents folder; the project can also have libraries of its own. Click the Shared Documents link to view any documents that are shared by the team. You'll see the contents of the Shared Documents library, as shown in Figure 18-21.

To view a document, click its link; you'll be prompted to save the file to your local drive or view it from its current location. After you make a choice, click OK and you'll see the contents of the document.

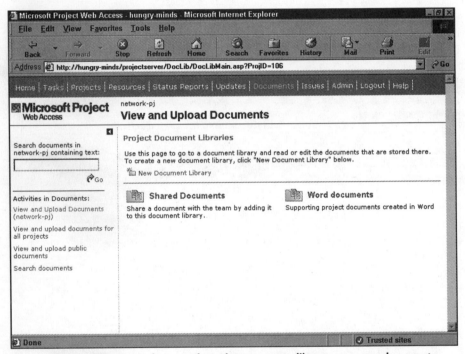

Figure 18-20: All projects have a Shared Documents library; you can also create special libraries for your project that are visible only to team members who have access to your project.

Figure 18-21: The contents of the Shared Documents library.

Posting a document

You can add a document to a document library. From the main Documents page, which was previously shown in Figure 18-19, select the project for which you want to add a document. On the next screen, which was previously shown in Figure 18-20, select the library to which you want to upload a document. You can now create a new document by clicking the New Document button or by clicking the Upload Document button (as I did) to upload a document from your hard drive or the network server to one of your project's document libraries. When you upload, you see a screen like the one shown in Figure 18-22.

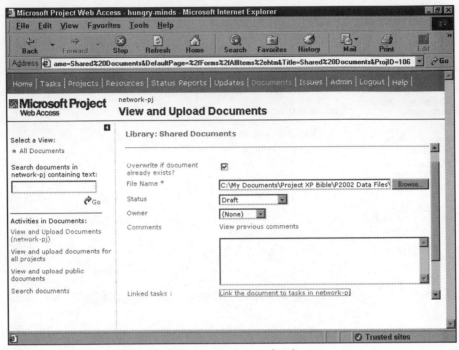

Figure 18-22: Locate the file that you want to upload.

After you locate the file that you want to upload, you can link the file to a particular task by clicking the Link the document to tasks in *project name* link. If you choose to link, you'll see a list of tasks in the project. Place a check in the checkbox next to the task to which you want to link the document.

Creating a document library

You can create libraries specifically for your project; any documents that you place in those libraries will be visible *only* to team members who have access to your project.

From the main Documents page, which was previously shown in Figure 18-19, select the project for which you want to add a document. On the next screen, which was previously shown in Figure 18-20, click on New Document Library. You'll see a screen like the one shown in Figure 18-23.

Figure 18-23: Fill in this screen to create a document library for your project.

Supply a name for the library and then choose the format for the document: Word, FrontPage, Excel, or PowerPoint. After you finish, click the Create button. Your new library will appear on the same page where you previously saw the Shared Documents library.

Viewing information

As life would have it, you may not work on only one project at a time. To help you manage your time, the Project Center in Project Web Access enables you to view tasks from more than one project at a time. In the Project Center, you will see individual projects or you may see *Project Center views*, which are collections of projects. The administrator creates Project Center views and then identifies the team members who can view each Project Center view.

Note   In Project Central, Project Center views were called *Portfolio views*. For example, the administrator may create a Project Center view for a collection of projects that share common budget management or resource management.

Cross-Reference   In Chapter 19, you'll see how the administrator creates a Project Center view.

When you click the Projects tab in Project Web Access to view the Project Center, you see line item entries that represent Web-based projects, as shown in Figure 18-24. Typically, you see entries for projects for which you have work assigned, but what you actually see depends on your security setting. On each line, you see a Gantt bar showing you the duration of the project and any progress that's been made on the project so far.

Figure 18-24: In the Project Center, you'll see one-line entries representing Web-based projects.

You can organize the projects by using the list boxes that appear on the Filter, Group, Search tab, as shown in Figure 18-25, and you can open a particular project in Project Web Access by clicking the link that appears in the Project Name column.

Figure 18-25: Organize the projects that appear in the Project Center by using the choices on the Filter, Group, Search tab.

When you open a project, you choose a view; in Figure 18-26, you see the Task Tracking view. Again, you can organize the tasks in the project, or you can zoom in or out or go to a particular task. If the Administrator has defined multiple views for you, you can change the view by using the Choose a view list box at the top of the page.

Figure 18-26: When you open a project, you can choose the view of that project that you want to see.

You can also view your assignments from the Resource Center, as shown in Figure 18-27. Click the Resources tab and then click View resource assignments in the Actions Pane. You'll be able to see the assignments that the Administrator has defined in the view available to you; for example, in Figure 18-27, Deena Tanenblatt can see only her own assignments. You can use the tab above the chart to organize and set options for the view.

Figure 18-27: Viewing your assignments

Reporting status

Project Web Access provides you with a few different ways to report to your project manager. You can use status reports and you can establish an *issue*. An issue is exactly what it sounds like — you've run into something unexpected that you want to report, and other team members can see and comment on the issue.

Status reports

You've already seen how Project Web Access enables you to send updates from the Tasks view. But you also can send both solicited and unsolicited status reports to your project manager. Click the Status Reports tab and click the Submit a status report link in the Actions Pane. If your project manager has not requested a status report, you'll see a page like the one shown in Figure 18-28; if your project manager has set up status reports due on certain dates, you'll see a notice on your home page like the one shown in Figure 18-29.

Note   You may only be able to send solicited status reports, depending on your security settings.

Figure 18-28: Use this page to submit an unsolicited status report or to simply communicate with other members of your team.

Figure 18-29: Use this page to display the status report layout as requested by your project manager.

You can click the link on your home page to open the status report or you can go to the Status Reports page, where you'll see a link to the status report that your manager has requested. When you click either link, you see a page similar to the one shown in Figure 18-30. The actual page that you see depends on the status report your manager sets up. Fill in the report; if you need to include information that doesn't fit into any of the existing sections, you can add a section at the bottom of the report. When you're ready to submit the report, click the Send button at the bottom of the page.

Figure 18-30: A typical status report page

Tracking issues

Issues are unexpected things that occur on projects. They may be problems, or they may be opportunities. When they arise, you have the opportunity to create an issue, let others on the team review the issue, assign the issue to someone to address, and monitor the progress of the issue.

Note The Project Server Administrator must give you rights to work with issues.

To set up an issue for tracking, click the Issues tab. Project Web Access displays an overview screen like the one shown in Figure 18-31, which shows the overall number of Active, Postponed, and Closed issues for each project that you have security rights to view.

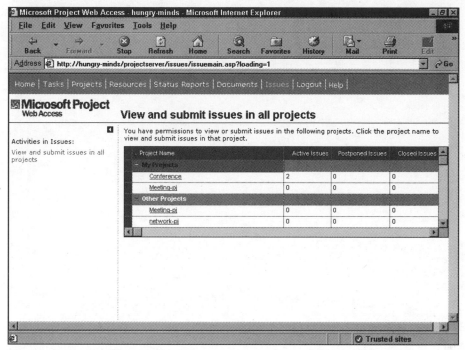

Figure 18-31: On this overview page, you get a sense of the number and status of issues.

Click a project to view the issues for it and set up a new issue, as shown in Figure 18-32.

Figure 18-32: On this page, you see outstanding issues for the selected project.

Click the New issue button to create a new issue; Project Web Access displays the Create a New issue page. In Figure 18-33, you see the top half of the page, where you assign a title, status, and priority to the issue, assign the issue to someone, identify the issue owner, set a due date, describe the issue, and (if possible) provide a resolution for it.

Note You save an issue by clicking Save Changes at the top of the Create a New Issue page.

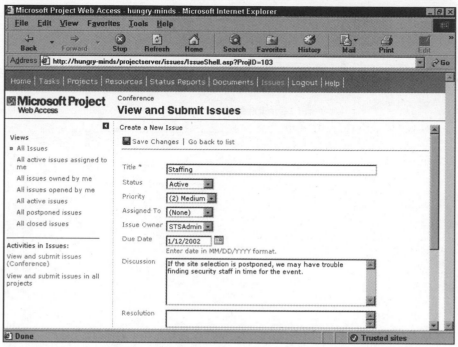

Figure 18-33: You describe basic identifying information on the top half of the Create a New Issue page.

When you scroll down the page, as shown in Figure 18-34, you have the opportunity to identify affected tasks, tasks that will help resolve the issue, other linked tasks, linked issues, and linked documents.

Figure 18-34: On the bottom of the page, you identify tasks, documents, and other issues related to the current issue.

Note   You edit an issue by clicking its link; you can filter issues using the links in the Action Pane.

Logging off

When you finish working in Project Web Access, click the Logoff tab to complete your session. You don't need to worry about saving before logging off; Project Server saves every action you take while logged on.

Summary

In this chapter, you learned how the day-to-day user interacts with Project Server using Project Web Access. The user can view and update tasks and provide status reports. If the features are enabled, the user can create a personal "to-do" list and can establish and view documents pertinent to projects.

In Chapter 19, you'll see how the Project Manager and the Project Server Administrator use Project, Project Web Access, and Project Server.

✦   ✦   ✦

Managing Project Server

In Chapter 18, you saw how the day-to-day user uses Project Web Access to record time and update the project manager. In the first half of this chapter, you'll see how the project manager interacts with Project Server and Project Web Access and uses tools supplied by Project Server and information from day-to-day users to manage projects. In the second half of the chapter, you'll learn about the elements of Project Server and Project Web Access that the Project Server Administrator can control for your organization.

Project Web Access for the Project Manager

Project Server offers a wide variety of tools to project managers to help them manage projects more effectively. In this section, you'll learn how to connect to Project Server, create a Web-based project, use the Enterprise Resource Pool to assign resources to your project, track project progress, and take advantage of Project Server's management tools to more effectively utilize resources and manage projects.

Note   The information in this chapter and in Chapter 18 applies to Project Professional. If you are using Project Standard, you can't use Project Server and Project Web Access. You can, however, use the Internet to communicate with your workgroup via e-mail. Chapter 16 covers this feature in more detail.

Connecting to Project Server

If you're going to use Project with Project Server (as opposed to using Project in a standalone environment), you'll need a Project Server account, which enables you to log on to Project Server.

Creating a Project Server logon account

You can easily create your own Project Server account from within Project after you know the URL for your Project Server database — your Project Server Administrator will most likely give you this URL.

To create a Project Server Account, follow these steps:

1. Choose Tools ➪ Enterprise Options ➪ Microsoft Project Server Accounts. You'll see the Microsoft Project Server Accounts dialog box, as shown in Figure 19-1.

Figure 19-1: Use this dialog box to add a Project Server logon account and specify connection state detection options.

2. Click the Add button. You'll see the Account Properties dialog box, as shown in Figure 19-2.

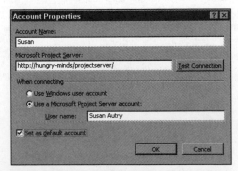

Figure 19-2: Use this dialog box to create a new Project Server account.

3. In the Account Name box, type a name for the account; you must use a name that no other user is already using.

4. In the Microsoft Project Server box, type the URL for the location of your Project Server database.

To ensure that you type the URL correctly, click the Test Connection button; if you've typed it correctly, you'll see a dialog box telling you that Project has successfully connected to the server you specified.

5. In the When connecting section, choose the type of connection that your organization uses:

   • Use your Windows 2000 login information by choosing Windows user account.

   • Use your Microsoft Project Server account, which uses Project Server authentication. In the user name box, type your name.

Windows 2000 user account authentication is generally more stringent than Project Server authentication.

6. (Optional) If you intend to create more than one account and you want the current account to be your default logon account, check the Set as default account box.

7. Click OK. You'll see the Microsoft Project Server Accounts box again.

8. At the bottom of the box, choose whether you want to log on automatically or manually control the connection state. If you choose to automatically detect the connection state, you won't see the dialog box that is shown in Figure 19-3, in which you choose the account that you want to use to log on; instead, Project will simply attempt to detect the Project Server.

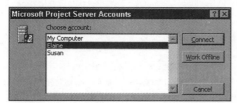

Figure 19-3: You'll see this box if you choose to manually control the connection state.

You may also see the Microsoft Project Server Accounts box if you've lost your connection with the Project Server.

Logging on to Project Server

You have the option of working with a project while connected to Project Server or working with the project in a standalone environment — and you make that choice when you start Project Professional.

For example, suppose that you use Project from a notebook computer while traveling. During your time away from the office, you want to keep track of the time that you spend working. If you manually control the connection state, which was discussed in the previous section, click the My Computer icon in the Microsoft Project Server Accounts box (shown previously in Figure 19-3), and then click the Work Offline button. If you chose to automatically detect the connection state, you won't connect to Project Server when you start Project.

If your organization chose to use Project Server authentication, you'll see the dialog box shown in Figure 19-4.

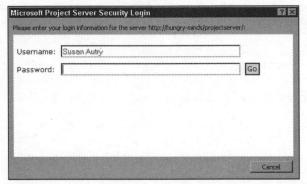

Figure 19-4: Supply your password and click Go to finish opening Project and logging on to Project Server.

Creating a Web-based project

The project manager is the person who builds and maintains the project schedule and makes task assignments. The "boss" uses Project to create the schedule and make assignments to team members to track their activities. When setting up the project schedule, the project manager must set up the project so that it appears in the Project Server database. To successfully establish a Web-based project, the project manager should complete the following tasks in Project:

- ✦ Set the project's options to use Web communications
- ✦ Store the project in the Project Server database
- ✦ Publish project information to the Project Server database

Setting a project's Web-based options

Follow these steps to set the options of a project schedule to use Web communications:

1. Choose Tools ➪ Options.

2. Click the Collaborate tab, as shown in Figure 19-5.

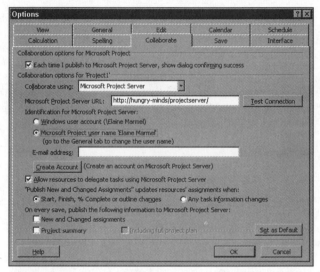

Figure 19-5: To set a project's options for Web communication, use the Collaborate tab of the Options dialog box.

3. In the Collaborate using drop-down list, select Microsoft Project Server.

Cross-Reference

See Chapter 16 for more information about setting up a project schedule to collaborate using e-mail.

4. In the Microsoft Project Server URL box, enter the URL that resources should use in their Web browsers to display Project Web Access. This Internet address points to a Web server or your organizational server and a folder that contains the Project Server database. It is the same URL that you supplied when you created your Project Server logon account.

5. For the method of identification, you can specify one of two methods:

   • Use Windows 2000 login information by choosing Windows user account.

   • Use Microsoft Project user names, which you can set on the General tab of the Options dialog box.

Note The name on the General tab is grayed out and can't be changed when you are logged on to Project Server. You must open Project Professional without logging on to Project Server to be able to change the user name on the General tab.

6. In the E-mail address box, type in the e-mail address of the person who should receive notifications about assignment updates; typically, this is the project manager.

7. As the project manager, you may not be assigning yourself any tasks. However, you'll need access to Project Web Access on the Web to interact with your team members electronically. To provide access for yourself to Project Web Access, click the Create Account button.

8. At the bottom of the tab, choose whether resources can delegate tasks in Project Web Access, and what updated information is sent to the Project Server database when you save your project. You can also choose the types of changes that will cause resources' assignments to be updated.

9. Click OK to save your settings.

Storing a project in the Project Server database

At this point in the book, you've probably set up a project schedule on your local hard drive that you're ready to store in the Project Server database. After you've set the project's options to define it as a Web-based project, you need to log on to Project Server and then save the project into the Project Server database.

Open Project Professional and log on to Project Server (refer to "Logging on to Project Server" earlier in this chapter). Then, open the project that you want to store on the Project Server and choose File ➪ Save As. You'll see the Save to Microsoft Project Server box that is shown in Figure 19-6.

Tip If you prefer wizards, you can use the Import Project wizard to save your project to the Project Server database. Don't open your project; instead, choose Tools ➪ Enterprise Options ➪ Import Project to Enterprise. Then, follow the wizard's steps.

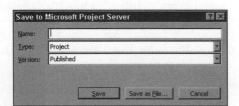

Figure 19-6: When you save your project by using this dialog box, you save the project to the Project Server database.

After saving your project, Project changes the name of your project in the title bar so you know that you're viewing the version you saved to the Project Server database. The name of the published version includes the word *Published*; for example, if your original project name was *network*, the published version would be named `network.Published`.

Opening a project stored in the Project Server database

Even if you're connected to the Project Server database, you have the option of opening in Project Professional either the original project schedule or the version that's been published to Project Server. Click the Open button on the Standard toolbar. You'll see the Open from Microsoft Project Server box, as shown in Figure 19-7.

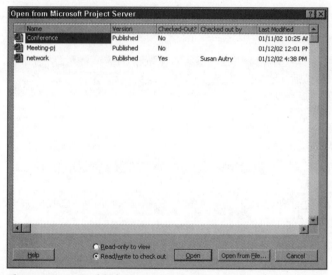

Name	Version	Checked-Out?	Checked out by	Last Modified
Conference	Published	No		01/11/02 10:25 AI
Meeting-pj	Published	No		01/12/02 12:01 Pt
network	Published	Yes	Susan Autry	01/12/02 4:38 PM

○ Read-only to view
⊙ Read/write to check out

Help   Open   Open from File...   Cancel

Figure 19-7: In this box, open a project in the Project Server database or open it from the original .mpp file.

Select the project that you want to open and then click the Open button to open the version stored in the Project Server database; to open the original Project .mpp file, click the Open from File button.

Tip

When do you use the Open from File button? Suppose that you publish a project and then discover that you want to make major changes to it; for example, the project start date has changed. Open the original file instead of the version stored in the Project Server database. Make the necessary changes to the original file and then publish it again.

You'll see the ".published" version of your project in Project Professional. At this point, Project Server views this project as *checked out* — that is, nobody else can open the project in Project Professional and save changes to it. You can see the status of the project from the Open from Microsoft Project Server dialog box (previously shown in Figure 19-7); for each checked-out project, you can see who has opened it.

Viewing Project Server pages in Project Professional

One of the neat features available in Project 2002 is the ability to display Project Server pages in Project. Choose Collaborate ➭ Project Center to see the Project Center, as shown in Figure 19-8, or Collaborate ➭ Resource Center to see the Resource Center, as shown in Figure 19-9. To return to Project, click the Click here to close this view link in the upper-right corner of the page.

Click this link to return to Project

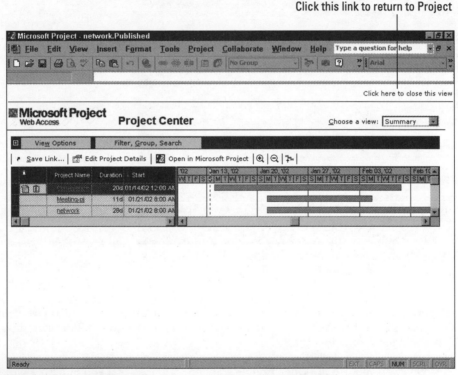

Figure 19-8: View the Project Center while working in Project.

Note   You'll be able to see the Project Center and Resource Center views only if the Project Server Administrator has given you the proper security permissions.

Figure 19-9: View the Resource Center while working in Project.

Publishing project information

Saving the project to the Project Server database (which you did previously in this chapter in "Storing a project in the Project Server database") doesn't send any of the scheduling or summary information; it simply puts a placeholder in the Project Server database for the project. To view the details of the project, you need to publish information; use the commands on the Collaborate menu to publish information.

Choose Collaborate ➪ Publish to see the menu of commands that you can use to update the Project Server database with information from Project:

✦ **All Information:** Publishes both new and changed assignments and a project plan (either complete or summary — see Project Plan for more details).

✦ **New and Changed Assignments:** Publishes changes to tasks, such as new start or finish dates. Resources receive notification in Project Web Access and via e-mail if your organization has set up Project Server to provide e-mail notifications and reminders.

✦ **Project Plan:** When you choose this command, you are given the option to publish the entire plan or a summary of the plan. The summary includes only task and scheduling information, and the complete plan includes assignments. If you publish the summary only, you'll see the project in the Project Center, but you won't be able to drill down and see details because they won't be there.

✦ **Republish Assignments:** Use this command to force Project to publish assignments — even if they've been published previously. You can choose to republish all or only some assignments.

Assigning resources to projects

If your organization opts to use Project Server, you have some additional powerful tools at your disposal to assign resources and manage resource utilization. In all probability, your organization will use the global resource pool that's available in Project Server, which provides a list of all resources owned by your organization. As the project manager, you can use the Team Builder feature and the resource pool to select resources appropriate for your project. You also can assign generic resources to your project and then use the Team Builder to help you replace the generic resources with real resources.

In addition, if you manage more than one project at a time, you can take advantage of the Resource Substitution Wizard to identify the best possible utilization of limited resources.

Cross-Reference   You can assign resources to Web-based projects the same way that you assign them to standalone projects — see Chapter 5 for details.

Adding enterprise resources to your project

You can use the Team Builder dialog box to view the resources in the Enterprise Resource Pool and assign them to your project. Choose Tools ➪ Build Team from Enterprise. Project displays the dialog box shown in Figure 19-10.

By default, you see all resources, but you can limit the resources that you see by applying filters. Use the Existing filters list and click the plus sign (+) that appears next to Customize filters to choose fields by which to filter. In Figure 19-10, I've already clicked the plus sign, so it appears as a minus sign (-), but you can see the additional space for specifying filters. You also can filter by available hours to work for a given time period.

After you select resources and click OK, the resources appear on the Resource Sheet of your project, and you can assign tasks to them. When you republish your project, the Enterprise Resource Pool is updated to reflect the assignments.

Replacing generic resources with real resources

If your organization uses generic resources, you can use the Team Builder to match a generic resource in your project to a real resource that has the same skill set that you defined for the generic resource. Project matches generic resources to real resources by using Resource Breakdown Structure (RBS) codes assigned to both types of resources.

Figure 19-10: Use this dialog box to select resources to assign to your project.

 Note

The Project Server Administrator typically creates the RBS code in Project Server; anyone who has security rights to update the Enterprise Resource Pool can assign the appropriate RBS code to each resource. To see how to set up and assign the RBS code, see the "Creating custom fields" and "Editing resources in the Enterprise Resource Pool" sections, later in this chapter.

Use the following two-part process to use the Team Builder to replace generic resources with real resources. First, filter the Enterprise Resource Pool so that it displays only resources with the appropriate RBS code:

1. In Project, open the published version of the project containing generic resources that you want to replace.

2. Choose Tools ➪ Build Team from Enterprise. Project opens the Enterprise Resource Pool in the background and displays the Build Team for dialog box.

3. At the top of the box, click the plus sign to open the Customize filters area.

4. Create a filter where you set the RBS code equal to the appropriate RBS code you need in your project.

5. Click the Apply Filter button. Project filters the Enterprise Resource list on the left to show you only those Enterprise resources with the RBS code you specified, as shown in Figure 19-11.

Figure 19-11: Find Enterprise resources with a specified skill set.

Second, replace a generic resource in your project with a resource from the Enterprise pool:

1. Click the resource that you want to use in your project from the list on the left.

2. Click the generic resource that you want to replace in the list on the right, as shown in Figure 19-12.

3. Click the Replace button. Project replaces the resource in the Team Resource list with the Enterprise resource that you selected.

Notifying resources of assignments

The project manager assigns work to resources. To notify the resources of the work assignments, the project manager publishes the assignments. At a minimum, the team members will receive notifications in Project Web Access of new or updated assignments; if your organization chooses, team members may also receive e-mail notifications.

Figure 19-12: Select a resource from the filtered Enterprise Resource list on the left to replace a generic resource in your project.

After making assignments in Project, follow these steps to send work assignments to resources:

1. (Optional) Select the tasks about which to notify resources of work assignments.

2. Choose Collaborate ➪ Publish. At this point, you have two choices:

   • You can choose New and Changed Assignments to send notifications only about those assignments.

   • You can choose Republish Assignments to force Project to update all assignments.

   When you choose Republish Assignments, Project displays the Republish Assignments dialog box, as shown in Figure 19-13, from which you can set options for updating assignments. Before you click OK, you can choose to

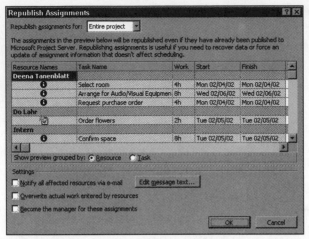

Figure 19-13: Use this window to send notice of work assignments to resources.

- Send e-mail messages to all affected resources. The e-mail message is sent in addition to the notification that the resource sees in Project Web Access. In Figure 19-14, you see a typical e-mail notification sent via Outlook Express.

- Tell Project to overwrite actual work entered by resources.

- Become the manager for the assignments.

Tip   If you want, you can edit the message or the subject line by clicking the Edit message text button.

New Feature   Project Server in Project 2002 now supports multiple managers. You can be the manager of one or more assignments without being the overall project manager. You become a manager not by publishing the project plan, but by publishing an assignment for a task or assuming responsibility upon republishing assignments. You can only view and process resource updates on assignments for which you are the manager.

Using the Resource Substitution Wizard

Suppose that you manage multiple projects with the same set of resources and you want to try to smooth work assignments and reduce overallocations across one or more projects. You can use the Resource Substitution Wizard to help you find resources that will fill your needs.

New Feature   The Resource Substitution Wizard is new in Project 2002.

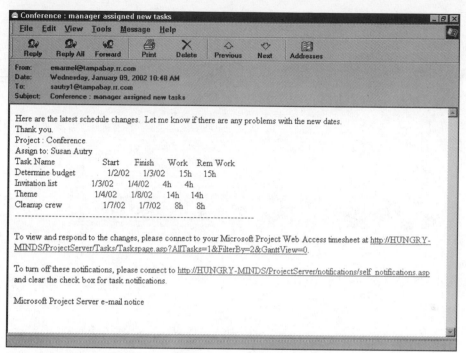

Figure 19-14: An e-mail notification sent via Outlook Express

The Resource Substitution Wizard can use different criteria to substitute resources. For example, the Resource Substitution Wizard can simply consider the resources in the projects that you select and reallocate them to better utilize their time. Or, the Resource Substitution Wizard can use the RBS (Resource Breakdown Structure) code assigned to resources to match skills required by resources that are already assigned to tasks and then substitute other resources with the same RBS code.

Note
The Project Server Administrator typically creates the RBS code; the creator of the resource (often the Project Server Administrator) also assigns the code to the resource. To see how to set up and assign the RBS code, see the "Creating custom resource fields" and "Editing resources in the Enterprise Resource Pool" sections later in this chapter.

Here's how to run the Resource Substitution Wizard:

1. Open the project(s) for which you want to substitute resources.

2. Choose Tools ➪ Substitute Resources. The first screen of the Resource Substitution Wizard appears. Click Next.

3. Check the project(s) that you want the wizard to consider while substituting resources, as shown in Figure 19-15. Click Next.

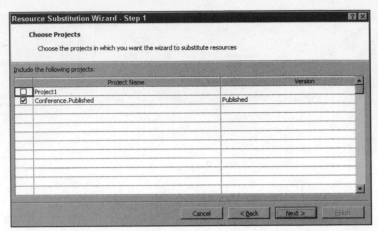

Figure 19-15: Each project that you have open will be listed and selected.

4. Choose resources for the wizard to consider when rescheduling projects, as shown in Figure 19-16. Click Next.

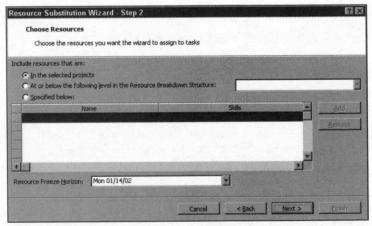

Figure 19-16: Use this screen to identify the resources that the wizard should consider when making substitutions.

5. Choose related projects to consider when rescheduling. Click Next.

6. Specify options for the wizard to use when rescheduling, as shown in Figure 19-17. You can set the priority or choose to use resources from the pool or from the project. Click Next.

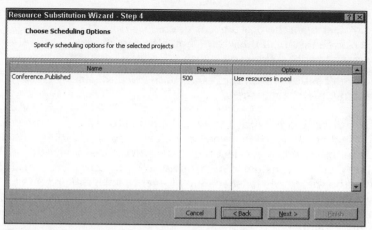

Figure 19-17: Specify options for rescheduling.

7. You'll see a summary of the options that you've selected. Click Run to run the wizard with the options that you've selected.

8. Click Next. The wizard displays a grid of assignments that it has changed, as shown in Figure 19-18, so that you can:

- Review the results

- Back up and change the wizard's options to try again.

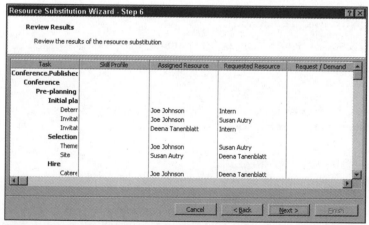

Figure 19-18: The wizard's suggested changes

After you make your decision(s), click Next.

9. You see the Update Options screen of the wizard, where you can choose to have Project open the projects considered by the wizard and update them based on the results of the wizard. You also can choose to save the results of the wizard to a file. When you click Next, a final page appears.

10. If you aren't satisfied with the results of the wizard, simply close the affected projects without saving them.

The Resource Substitution Wizard can also help you to select resources for more than one project at a time, so that you can quickly develop staffing models. As Step 3 demonstrated, you can select the open projects that you want the Resource Substitution Wizard to consider; simply open each project before you start the wizard. After the wizard has finished, don't forget to level the projects to see how the wizard's resource assignments change project finish dates and resource utilization. If you aren't satisfied with the results of the wizard, simply close the affected projects without saving them.

Note   Project Web Access contains another tool that can help you with resource allocation: the Portfolio Modeler. By using the Portfolio Modeler, you can select projects to include in the model and then interactively change tasks or staffing to view the impact on a project portfolio. Although you can save the models, you can't automatically transfer changes that you make in models to actual projects.

Tracking Progress

After you've set up a project and uploaded it to Project Server, you'll need to track the progress on your project. To effectively track progress, you need to

✦ Establish a tracking method

✦ Set up a status report form for team members to complete

✦ Receive updates from team members as they update the project in Project Web Access.

Cross-Reference   You also can track issues and assign them for review and resolution. See Chapter 18 for more information about creating and tracking issues.

Establishing a tracking method

Project offers three possible ways for users to record actual work in Project Server, and each has its advantages and disadvantages:

✦ **Percent of Work Complete:** This method is the fastest way for resources to record time, but it is also the least accurate because it is based on the resource's estimate of the total amount of work to be done, along with the amount actually completed. Resources enter the percentage amount.

✦ **Actual Work Done and Work Remaining:** This method is the "middle of the road" method. It is both moderately accurate and moderately fast. Resources enter in the hours, days, weeks, etc., of the amount of work done and the amount of work remaining to complete.

✦ **Hours of Work Done per Time Period:** This method is the most accurate method but also the most time-consuming. Resources enter the actual hours worked on each task for a specified time — typically, a day.

Your organization may have selected a tracking method for you — if so, you won't be able to select a tracking method. To check the tracking method (and possibly change it), choose Tools ➪ Customize ➪ Published Fields. Project displays the Customize Published Fields dialog box, as shown in Figure 19-19.

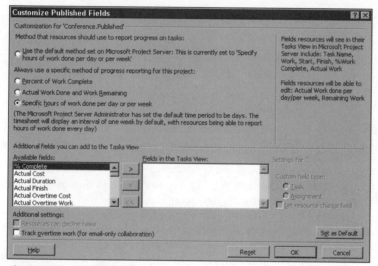

Figure 19-19: Use this dialog box to check the tracking method and, if possible, change it.

If your organization has locked down the tracking method in Project Server, the first option shown in Figure 19-19 will be selected and the next three options will be grayed out and unavailable. If the options are available, you can choose to use the Project Server method or select a method for the current project.

Setting up status reports

As a manager, you can create the layout for the status report that you want to view from your team members — and you can specify how often you want status reports.

The project manager's status report page looks a little bit different than the team member's page, as shown in Figure 19-20.

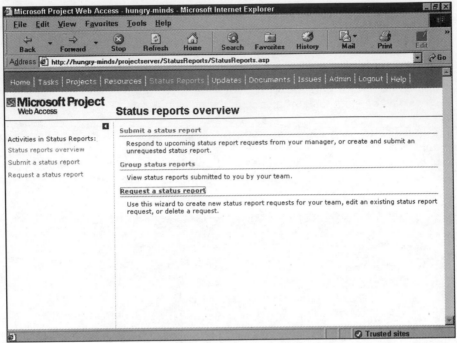

Figure 19-20: The project manager can create a status report format for use by the team.

Note   By using the Group Status Reports feature, managers can combine the status reports of team members into one overall status report.

To create a standard layout for a status report, click the Request a Status Report link in the Actions pane or on the page to start a wizard that walks you through the process. On the first screen of the wizard, you can choose to create a new status report, edit an existing status report, or delete a status report. After you click Set up a new status report for your team to respond to and click OK, Project Web Access displays the first of four screens, on which you provide titles and information about how often you want the report, as shown in Figure 19-21.

Fill in the page and click Next. You'll see a page where you can identify who should report, as shown in Figure 19-22.

Decide who should submit status reports and click Next. Project displays a page like the one shown in Figure 19-23, where you can identify the topics that you want covered in the status report and click Next.

Figure 19-21: Provide overview information for the status report layout that you're creating.

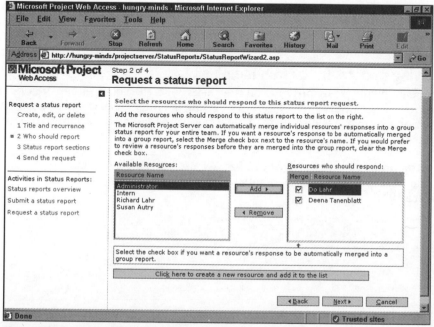

Figure 19-22: Select resources to submit status reports.

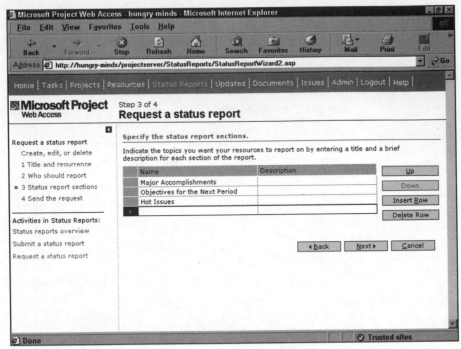

Figure 19-23: List the topics that you want included in the status report.

On the last page of the wizard, as shown in Figure 19-24, click the Send button to send a skeleton of the status report to the selected team members. The team members can then use the skeleton to fill in the information that you want to see.

Receiving updates from team members

When team members record time on the Tasks page, they click either the Update All button or the Update Selected Rows button; in either case, they see a message like the one shown in Figure 19-25, indicating that an update was sent to the project manager for approval.

When the project manager logs onto Project Web Access, the home page contains a link that isn't found on a team member's home page — the Updates link, as shown in Figure 19-26.

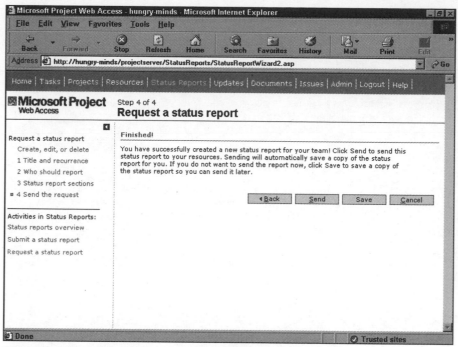

Figure 19-24: Send the layout to the selected team members.

Figure 19-25: Project team members see notices that their project managers will be notified of actual work that they've recorded.

When the project manager clicks the Update link, Project Web Access displays the View task changes submitted by resources page, as shown in Figure 19-27. Or, if resources submit calendar changes, the View changes to resource calendars page.

Figure 19-26: The project manager's home page contains an Updates section with information about pending updates.

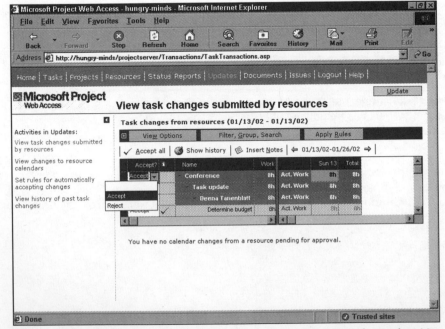

Figure 19-27: The project manager views and accepts or rejects the update(s).

The project manager can accept or reject any update by clicking in the Accept column to display the drop-down list. If, after reviewing updates, the project manager wants to accept all updates received, the project manager can click the Accept All button. After accepting or rejecting task updates, the project manager clicks the Update button in the upper-right corner of the window. If Project isn't already running, Project Web Access launches it, opens the project from the server in Project, and updates it. After updating has completed, you'll see a message indicating that you need to save your project. If you click Yes, Project will save the project.

Note   If you don't save the Project file, updates will remain in Project Web Access until you do.

In Project Web Access, you'll see a message telling you that approved task changes have been updated in Project and resources have been notified by e-mail of rejected tasks.

Tip   The project manager can set up rules for automatically accepting changes from selected users for selected projects. Click the Set rules for automatically accepting changes link in the Actions Pane.

Using Versions

New Feature   Versions are new to Project 2002.

Project Server comes with a few tools to help you manage the Enterprise project. When you use the Versions feature, you can compare variations of the same project. For example, you can compare versions that include added and deleted tasks that were not saved in baselines. Making comparisons between snapshots of a project taken at different times can help you with trend analysis.

Before you can use the Versions feature, the Project Server administrator must define the available versions. After the Project Server administrator makes versions available for use, you create a version by doing nothing more than saving your previously published project to Project Server as a type of version. Choose File ➪ Save As. In the Save to Microsoft Project Server dialog box, as shown in Figure 19-28, select a version.

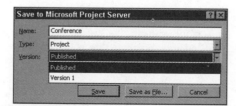

Figure 19-28: Save a version of your project.

To open a version, click the Open button in Project; you'll see the version in the Open from Microsoft Project Server dialog box, along with other projects that you can open, as shown in Figure 19-29.

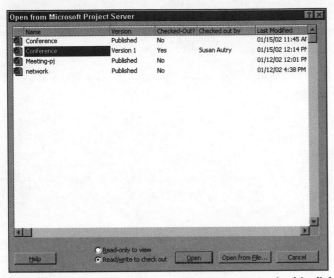

Figure 19-29: Versions that you can open appear in this dialog box, along with published versions of projects.

Note   You may also want to take a look at the Portfolio Analyzer feature in project. This feature provides graphic representations of project and resource information that give you a fast and powerful way to analyze information. After the Project Server Administrator sets up the technology needed to generate the views, Project Web Access users with appropriate security rights can use the Portfolio Analyzer from either the Project Center or the Resource Center.

Administering Project Web Access and Project Server

Prior to this point in the chapter, you've seen how team members and the project manager use Project Web Access. And, along the way, I've referred to the administrator role involved in Project Web Access. The administrator manages the information in the Project Server database.

The administrator can update Project Server in a variety of ways by using Project Professional. In the following sections, you'll see how to

✦ Create custom fields that are stored in the Enterprise Global

✦ Set up enterprise resources

✦ Edit enterprise resources

Creating custom fields

Custom fields can be used for many purposes. For example, if your organization opts to use generic resources and wants to be able to match the skills of a generic resource with a real resource that possesses those skills, you'll need to set up a code scheme where each code represents a set of skills. You can then assign the appropriate code to each resource by creating a custom field for the code. Conceptually, you can compare this code for resources to a WBS code for tasks; the staff at Microsoft pre-named one of the custom outline codes as RBS. Project Server uses the RBS codes that you establish to match skills required by generic resources with skills possessed by real people when project managers run the Team Builder.

To set up the RBS code, follow these steps in Project Professional:

1. Choose Tools ➪ Enterprise Options ➪ Open Enterprise Global to open the Enterprise Global template code. Project displays the Check-out Enterprise Global template.

2. Choose Tools ➪ Customize ➪ Enterprise Custom Fields. You'll see the Customize Enterprise Fields dialog box, as shown in Figure 19-30.

Figure 19-30: Instead of Enterprise Resource Outline Code30, you'll see RBS.

3. Click the Custom Outline Codes tab.

4. Click the Resource option button.

5. Scroll down to the bottom of the list of Enterprise Resource Outline codes.

6. Click RBS and then click the Define Code Mask button to open the Outline Code Definition for RBS dialog box, as shown in Figure 19-31.

Figure 19-31: Define the structure for your RBS code here.

7. In the Sequence column, define the type of values that will be acceptable in your company's RBS code. In the Length column, provide a number (or choose Any) for the length of the RBS code. If your RBS code is composed of parts, choose a separator character to distinguish the first part of the code from the second part of the code.

Cross-
Reference

See Chapter 20 for more details about creating custom fields.

8. Click the Edit Lookup Table button to display the Edit Lookup Table for RBS window, as shown in Figure 19-32.

9. Enter the RBS codes for your organization and click Close.

10. Click OK twice.

11. Click the Save button to save the Enterprise Global and your new RBS code.

If you've already stored resources in the Enterprise Resource Pool, you'll need to edit the resources to assign an RBS code to each of them. Follow the steps in the preceding section to assign RBS codes to resources stored in the Enterprise Resource Pool.

If you have not yet stored resources in the Enterprise Resource Pool, edit the resources in the usual way; when you import the resources to the Enterprise Resource Pool, you have the option of including the custom fields.

Figure 19-32: In the Lookup table, define the codes that you want to use.

Setting up and editing Enterprise resources

As the Project Server administrator, you may be asked to set up the Enterprise resource pool, a single repository that project managers will use when assigning resources to their projects. The Enterprise Resource Pool includes summary resource assignments, resource base calendars, and any Enterprise resource fields that you defined in the Enterprise Global. Project managers "check out" resources from the Enterprise Resource Pool to assign them to a project. As the Project Server administrator, you can set the permissions for others to add, edit, and delete resources from the Enterprise Resource Pool. Project Server manages the check-out/ check-in operations.

Creating the Enterprise Resource Pool

You'll find it easiest to create the Enterprise Resource Pool if you use a project that contains the resources that you want to store in the Enterprise Resource Pool. Then, a wizard can walk you through setting up the Enterprise Resource Pool. Make sure that the project containing the resources is closed or checked-in, and then follow these steps in Project Professional:

1. Choose Tools ➪ Options ➪ Import Resources to Enterprise. The Import Resources Wizard starts. On the first screen of the wizard, click Next.

2. If you've set up any custom fields for resources, complete the next screen of the wizard, as shown in Figure 19-33. Map custom fields that you've set up for resources to enterprise resource fields.

Note Custom fields and values for resources won't appear in the Enterprise Resource Pool unless you map them to enterprise resource fields.

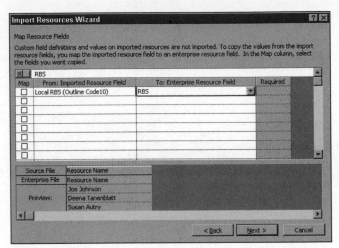

Figure 19-33: Map custom resource fields to enterprise resource fields.

3. Click Next and identify the resources that you want to upload to the Enterprise Resource Pool by placing a check next to their names, as shown in Figure 19-34.

Tip You can view and change the information for any displayed resource by selecting that resource and clicking the Resource Information button. Project will display the Resource Information dialog box for the selected resource. Errors will appear in red.

4. Click Next. Project sends the resources to the Enterprise Resource Pool in the Project Server database.

Editing resources in the Enterprise Resource Pool

After you have stored a resource in the Enterprise Resource Pool, what happens if you find out that you need to make a change to that resource? You can edit the resource by checking it out, making the change, and then checking it back in. While resources are checked out, others can't make and save changes to them.

Figure 19-34: Identify resources to store in the Enterprise Resource Pool.

Follow these steps to check out resources from the Enterprise Resource Pool:

1. Choose Tools ➪ Enterprise Options ➪ Open Enterprise Resource Pool. Project displays the Open Enterprise Resources box, as shown in Figure 19-35.

Figure 19-35: Use this box to check out enterprise resources.

2. Place a check next to the resource(s) that you want to edit.

3. Click Open/Add. Project opens a temporary project called Checked-out Enterprise Resources and lists the resources that you checked on the resource sheet of that project.

As long as you have checked out the resource, nobody in your company can assign work to the resource. Make changes to the resource by using the Resource Information dialog box. After you have finished, check the resource back in by clicking the Save button. At that time, Project Server will update the resource information in the Enterprise Resource Pool.

Using Project Web Access for administration

For several activities, such as creating custom fields and setting up and editing enterprise resources, the Administrator uses Project Professional. For most other administrative activities, however, the administrator uses Project Web Access, which you can launch by starting Internet Explorer and entering the URL for the Web database. If your organization uses Project Server authentication, the administrator selects Administrator and clicks Go. The administrator sees the Project Web Access Home page for the administrator, which contains an additional tab: The Admin tab. From the Admin tab, the administrator can manage and customize the Web-based database and Project Web Access by using the links shown in Figure 19-36.

Figure 19-36: From the Admin tab, the administrator can manage and customize the Project Server database and Project Web Access.

Note Unless otherwise specified, all tasks described in the following sections assume that you begin by logging on to Project Web Access as administrator and clicking the Admin tab.

Managing users

From the Users page, as shown in Figure 19-37, the administrator can add, modify, or delete users from the Web-based database; in addition, the administrator can merge two user names into one account if a user appears twice in the Log On list under two different names. Display this page by clicking the Manage users and groups link in the Action Pane of the Admin tab.

Figure 19-37: Use the Users page to make changes to user accounts in Project Web Access.

When you add or modify a user, you specify the type of authentication to use (Windows Authentication or Project Server authentication), the user's e-mail address, the groups to which the user belongs, the categories of information that the user can access, and the user's global permissions — all of which determine the actions that the user can take. For example, the administrator controls whether team members or the manager can delegate tasks to other team members.

Note   Unlike Project Central, in Project Web Access, you can turn on delegation for some team members while turning it off for other team members.

You can control what users see in Project Web Access. In the middle of the page, you specify the categories to which a user belongs and (if you want) model the user's permissions for these categories on the permissions of an available group, as shown in Figure 19-38.

Figure 19-38: Select categories for the user.

In the bottom section of the page, as shown in Figure 19-39, you can specify the global permissions for the user — and again model the permissions on the permissions of a Project Server group.

Note   You also can add or change the properties of groups; in the Actions Pane, click Groups of users. Then, select a group and click the Add Group or Modify Group buttons.

Figure 19-39: Set or modify user global permissions here.

Setting security options

From the Security Options page, the administrator controls the categories and groups defined in the Project Server database and in Project Web Access. The administrator also controls the types of authentication used to log on to the Project Server database.

Working with categories

Categories enable you to map users to projects and views. In other words, in a category, you identify the users, projects, project views, portfolio views, and assignment views to include in the category.

To create a new category, click the Manage security link in the Action Pane of the Admin tab. Then, click the Specify security on collections of projects, resources, and assignments link in the Actions Pane. On the Categories page that appears, as shown in Figure 19-40, click Add Category. Project Web Access displays the page shown in Figure 19-41.

Figure 19-40: Use this page to create a new category or modify or delete an existing category.

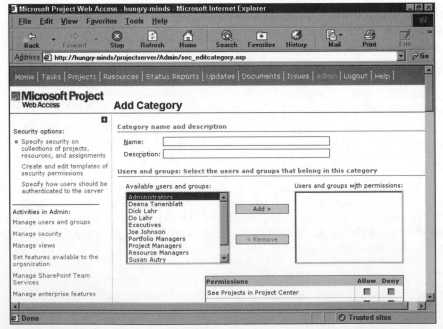

Figure 19-41: Use this page to define the users that you want to include in the category.

At the top of the page, provide a name and, optionally, a description for the category. Select the users that you want to include in this category and the permissions that you want assigned. In the next section of the page, as shown in Figure 19-42, specify the projects that you want to include in the category and the views and options that you want to apply to the projects.

Figure 19-42: Specify the projects that you want to include in the category.

In the next section of the page, as shown in Figure 19-43, add the resources whose information will be visible by users of the category and the assignment views that you want included in the category.

In the last portion of the page, as shown in Figure 19-44, add the Project Center views, Portfolio Analyzer views, and the Portfolio Modeler views that you want to include in the category.

Click OK to save the category.

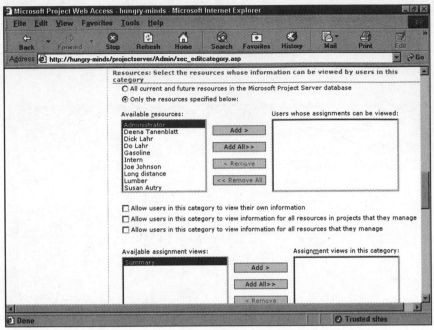

Figure 19-43: Add resources to the category.

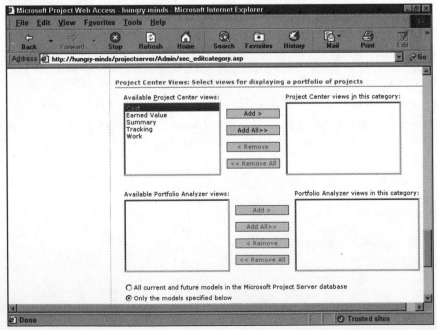

Figure 19-44: Add the project-related views that you want to include in the category.

Managing security templates

The default Project Server database contains some security templates, which are collections of permissions that may be used by certain groups of users. You can modify the default security templates or create your own. As you can see on the Modify Template page, as shown in Figure 19-45, security templates can contain a long list of information; you include or exclude permissions in a template by checking the Allow or Deny box for that right.

Display this page by clicking the Manage Security link in the Action Pane of the Admin tab. Then click the Create and edit templates of security permissions link in the Action Pane and, on the Security templates page that appears, click Add Template or select a template and click Modify Template.

Figure 19-45: Permit or deny rights to groups of users by using security templates.

Managing user authentication options

On the Authentication options page, as shown in Figure 19-46, the administrator decides how the Project Web Access server should authenticate users who try to log onto Project Web Access. From this page, the administrator can also determine the minimum length to which users must set their passwords and the type of authentication required for publishing a project. Display this page by clicking the Manage security link in the Action Pane of the Admin tab and then clicking the Specify how users should be authenticated to the server link in the Action Pane.

Figure 19-46: Control authentication and password issues from this page.

Working with views

A view contains a set of fields and filters that Project Web Access uses when displaying project information. Through views, the administrator controls what you see in Project Web Access. The administrator establishes views that enable users to examine project information in different ways. The administrator uses the Specify Views page, as shown in Figure 19-47, to create new views, modify or delete existing views, and manage DSNs for Project 2000 project drilldown views. Display this page by clicking the Manage views link in the Action Pane of the Admin tab.

Creating or modifying a view

Determine whether the view is a project view, a Project Center view, an Assignment view, a Resource Center view, or a Portfolio Analyzer view. The type of view that you select determines the choices that you see when you create the view. For example, on project views, you'll be able to choose a Gantt Chart format that won't be available for resource views.

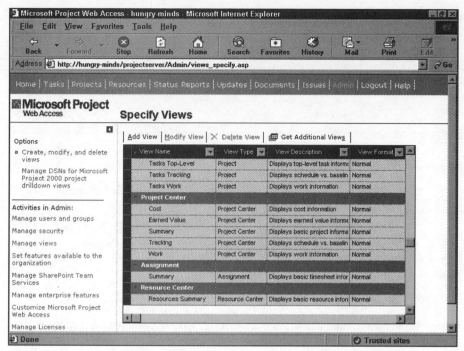

Figure 19-47: Begin on this page to create a new view or modify or delete an existing view.

The Project Server database contains, by default, only one resource-related view — the Resource Summary view. If you want to do any resource management from Project Web Access, you need to create additional resource views. Figures 19-48 and 19-49 demonstrate how I created a Resource Center view. You specify the fields that should appear in the view. At the bottom of the page, select the Gantt Chart format (Gantt, Detail Gantt, Leveling Gantt, Tracking Gantt, and so on), grouping, any filters for the view, and the categories to which this view belongs. You read about categories earlier in this chapter. Click the Save Changes button to save the view.

Controlling data sources for views

From the Data Sources for Views page, as shown in Figure 19-50, the administrator can establish connections to external databases that contain project information. For example, suppose that project information isn't stored in a Microsoft Project file. In this case, the administrator can establish a "shortcut" that defines the location of the source of the project information, thus enabling team members to access that information from Project Web Access. Display this page by clicking the Manage views link in the Action Pane of the Admin tab. Then, click the Manage DSNs for Microsoft Project 2000 project drill down views link in the Action Pane.

Figure 19-48: At the top of the page, specify the type of view, the view name, and the fields that you want to appear on the view.

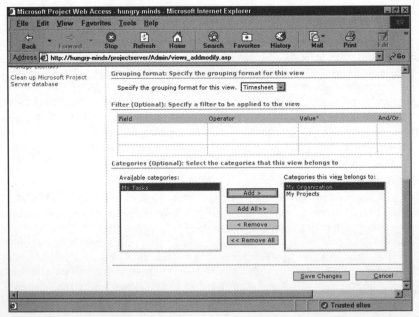

Figure 19-49: At the bottom of the page, specify the grouping format, and optionally, any filters and categories for the view.

Figure 19-50: Use this page to establish data sources for projects that aren't stored in an MPP file.

Setting features for your organization

The Project Server administrator can set features available to the organization in two ways:

✦ By establishing features available on the server

✦ By defining the menus displayed in Project Web Access

Specifying Project Server features for your organization

On the Organization page, as shown in Figure 19-51, the administrator places a check in the Allow box or in the Deny box for each Project Server feature. Display this page by clicking the Set features available to the organization in the Actions Pane of the Admin tab. Then, click the Specify the features available on your server link in the Actions Pane.

Note

For the curious, yes, you *can* (although I can't think when you'd really want to) check both the Allow and Deny boxes. And, although the visual effect is that you have both allowed and denied permission, you haven't. Deny takes precedence over Allow.

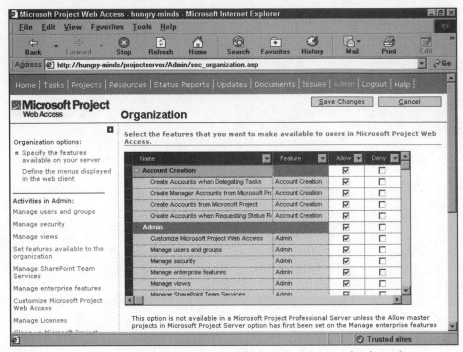

Figure 19-51: Choose to use or not use various Project Server database features.

Establishing Project Web Access menus

On the Set features available to the organization page, as shown in Figure 19-52, the administrator can modify the appearance of all pages in Project Web Access. From this page, the administrator can set the order of the links on each page, move links to different pages, change a link's name, add custom menus (tabs), and provide custom ToolTips for links. Display this page by clicking the Set features available to the organization link in the Action Pane of the Admin tab. Then, click the Define the menus displayed in the Web client link in the Actions Pane.

Managing SharePoint Team Services

Project Web Access uses SharePoint Team Services technology to manage documents and issues. If your organization chooses to use these features, the administrator can manage SharePoint Team Services by clicking the Manage SharePoint Team Services link in the Actions Pane of the Admin tab.

On the Connect to servers page, the administrator can set up, modify, and remove connection information for SharePoint servers, as shown in Figure 19-53.

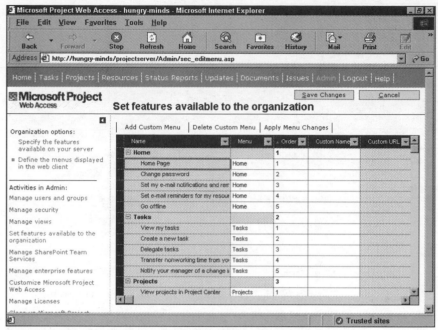

Figure 19-52: Use this page to customize the appearance of menus and pages in Project Web Access.

Figure 19-53: From this page, add, modify, or delete SharePoint server connections.

On the Default settings for provisioning SharePoint subwebs page, the administrator can control whether subwebs are created automatically or manually and then choose whether to grant users access to project subwebs automatically or manually, as shown in Figure 19-54.

Figure 19-54: From this page, establish the behavior for project subwebs.

On the Manage SharePoint Team Services subwebs for Microsoft Project Server page, as shown in Figure 19-55, the administrator can create a subweb, change the address of a subweb, delete a subweb, and update the list of users who have access to a subweb.

On the Synchronize Administrators with Servers Running SharePoint Team Services page as shown in Figure 19-56, the Project Server administrator can add Project Server users who have permission to manage SharePoint Team Services via Project Web Access to the administrator (Microsoft Project Server) role on the root of each web and on each project subweb of each SharePoint Team Services server to which the Project Server is connected.

Figure 19-55: Use this page to make changes to subwebs.

Figure 19-56: Synchronize administrators from this page.

Managing enterprise features

From the Manage enterprise features link in the Actions Pane, the administrator can

✦ Enable or disable enterprise features

✦ Manage the updating process

✦ Check in enterprise projects and resources

✦ Manage enterprise project versions

Enabling or disabling features

On the Enterprise mode page, as shown in Figure 19-57, you determine whether your organization will

✦ Use enterprise features (if you don't check this box, nobody in the organization has access to any Project Server features)

✦ Allow master projects in the Project Server database

✦ Allow projects to use the local base calendar instead of the Enterprise base calendar

✦ Enforce a uniform, single currency in the Project Server database (you specify the currency in the Enterprise global template)

Figure 19-57: The features on this page control some basic enterprise features in the Project Server database.

Display this page by clicking the Manage enterprise features link in the Action Pane of the Admin tab. Then, click the Enable or disable enterprise features link in the Action Pane.

Managing the updating process

On the Updates to Resource Tables and OLAP Cube page, as shown in Figure 19-58, the administrator can build an OLAP cube for use with the Portfolio Analyzer feature of Project Server and update resource tables that contain resource availability data. You have two more options not shown in the figure: When you choose to update resource tables, you control the date range for the information retrieved during the process, as well as the frequency with which the updating process occurs.

Note

Both building an OLAP cube and updating resource tables work the machine housing the Project Server database extensively because they gather lots of information for reporting purposes. You should schedule these operations at a time when most people are *not* using the Project Server database.

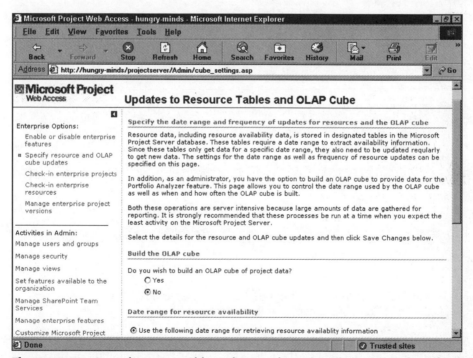

Figure 19-58: Control resource table updates and creation of an OLAP cube of project data from this page.

Display this page by clicking the Manage enterprise features link in the Action Pane of the Admin tab. Then click the Specify resources and OLAP cube updates link in the Action Pane.

Checking in enterprise projects and resources

Occasionally, as administrator, you may want or need to check in projects or resources. For example, after hours, you may be planning maintenance to the Project Server database, and somebody left work without closing a project.

Instead of hunting down the machine of the person who checked out the project, you can use the Manage Project Check-In/Out page, as shown in Figure 19-59, to check the project back in. Simply highlight the project and click the Check-In button.

Figure 19-59: Check in projects from this page.

> **Note** The Manage Resource Check-In/Out page looks just like the Manage Project Check-In/Out page except that it lists resources instead of projects.

Display this page by clicking the Manage enterprise features link in the Action Pane of the Admin tab. Then click the Check-in enterprise projects link or the Check-in enterprise resources link in the Action Pane.

Managing enterprise project versions

After your organization decides what versions they want available, you must create those versions in the Project Server database to make them accessible to the organization. Follow these steps:

1. Click the Admin tab.

2. Click Manage Enterprise Features.

3. Click Manage Enterprise Project Versions from the Actions Pane. Project Web Access displays any available versions on the Versions page, as shown in Figure 19-60.

Note   The "Published" version is a protected version that is created automatically when Project Server is installed and will always appear on the Versions page.

Figure 19-60: From this page, add, modify, or delete versions.

4. Click the Add Version button. You'll see the Add Version page, as shown in Figure 19-61.

5. Supply a version name.

6. Decide if the version should be archived. When a user opens an archived project version, it won't be updated with any enterprise global or enterprise resource pool information; instead, it will be a snapshot of the project at the time it was saved.

Figure 19-61: Create a version on this page.

7. Choose a Gantt Bar Name; by default, you can choose Project Summary or Project Summary Version 1, Project Summary Version 2, Project Summary Version 3, Project Summary Version 4, or Project Summary Version 5.

> **Tip** The Project Server Administrator can create other Gantt bar formats, based on the organization's needs, from the Customize Microsoft Project Web Access link in the Actions Pane under Admin.

8. Click Save Changes.

Customizing Project Web Access

The administrator can customize Project Web Access in a number of ways:

✦ Establish tracking settings

✦ Control the formatting of Gantt bar styles and the timescale

✦ Establish grouping formats for the timesheet and views in the Project Center and the Resource Center

✦ Set up nonworking time categories

✦ Modify the default home page appearance

✦ Set up defaults for the e-mail server and messages used in the Notifications and Reminders features

Establishing Tracking Settings

By using the Tracking settings page, as shown in Figure 19-62, the administrator can set the default tracking method for projects published to the Project Server database and permit project managers to select different tracking methods when creating their projects. Display this page by clicking the Customize Project Web Access link in the Actions Pane of the Admin tab. Then click the Tracking Settings link.

Figure 19-62: The administrator can select a default tracking method for published projects and allow managers to choose a different method.

Selecting the Gantt bar styles and timescales

Using the Gantt Bar Styles and Timescale page, as shown in Figure 19-63, the administrator can control the appearance of Gantt bars and the timescale on Gantt Charts for some or all Gantt Charts that team members and managers view in Project Web Access. To select specific Gantt Charts to change, use the Gantt Chart list box on the page. Display this page by clicking the Customize Project Web Access link in the Actions Pane of the Admin tab. Then click the Gantt Chart formats link in the Action Pane.

Figure 19-63: The administrator can modify the appearance of Gantt bars and timescales in Project Web Access.

Selecting Grouping formats

Using the Grouping formats page, as shown in Figure 19-64, the administrator can format the appearance of grouped information on the timesheet shown on the Tasks tab. The administrator can also define the appearance of up to ten groups for views in the Projects Center and the Resource Center. Display this page by clicking the Customize Project Web Access link in the Actions Pane of the Admin tab. Then, click the Grouping formats link in the Action Pane.

Setting up nonworking time categories

By default, Project Web Access contains categories that team members can use to record time spent not working. You can establish additional non-working time categories for time spent on work other than projects. By letting users record non-project time, you can use Project Web Access to account for all time that a user spends working. This non-project time appears in the Timesheet view, where users can record the time spent on tasks not involving projects.

Figure 19-64: Establish grouping formats for the timesheet shown on the Task tab and for views shown in the Project Center and the Resource Center.

From the Nonworking Time Categories page, as shown in Figure 19-65, the administrator can change the default categories, add new categories, or delete old categories. Display this page by clicking the Customize Project Web Access link in the Actions Pane of the Admin tab. Then click the Reporting nonworking time link in the Action Pane.

Setting the default Home page appearance

Using the Add to Home page, as shown in Figure 19-66, the administrator can add links or content to the Project Web Access Home page. Links may jump team members to other places on the company server or on the Internet. Content may include important information or an announcement that you want users of Project Web Access to see when they log on.

Figure 19-65: Establish or modify nonworking time categories.

Figure 19-66: Use this page to add links or content to the Project Web Access Home Page.

Links will appear in a special Links section at the bottom of each user's Home Page; for links, the administrator must supply the URL (the full path, including "http" or the file prefix) for the link. The content from each file will appear in its own section on the Home Page. For content, the administrator must specify the height (in pixels) that the content will occupy on the home page and provide the full URL, including "http" or the file prefix to the file that contains the content.

Display the Add to Home page by clicking the Customize Project Web Access link in the Actions Pane of the Admin tab. Then, click the Default Home page appearance link in the Action Pane.

Establishing Notifications and reminders options

Using the Customize e-mail notifications and reminders page, as shown in Figure 19-67, the administrator can set up the SMTP mail server used in the Notifications and Reminder feature and customize the default e-mail message sent. Display this page by clicking the Customize Project Web Access link in the Actions Pane of the Admin tab. Then, click the Notifications and reminders link in the Action Pane.

Figure 19-67: Establish the e-mail server and default e-mail message from this page.

Managing Project Server licenses

Using the License Management page, as shown in Figure 19-68, you can track the number of licensed copies of Project Web Access and compare that number to the number of Project Web Access users to help ensure that you are in compliance with your licensing agreement. Display this page by clicking the Manage Licenses link in the Action Pane of the Admin tab.

Figure 19-68: Use this page to manage the number of licensed copies of Project Web Access.

Managing information in the Project Server database

The administrator can (and should) periodically delete old information from the Project Server database because response time from the database will slow down as the database grows in size. To help maintain some semblance of speed for team members when they use the database, the administrator can delete old, unnecessary information by using the Delete Items from Database page, as shown in Figure 19-69. Display this page by clicking the Clean up Microsoft Project Server database link in the Action Pane of the Admin tab.

Click the option button next to the types of items that you want to delete; note that you can "selectively delete" information. And, although you can't see these options in Figure 19-69, from the bottom of the Delete Items from Database page, you can delete task, resource task updates, and status report information for specified users. After setting up the page, click the Delete button to delete information.

Figure 19-69: Use this page to reduce the size of the database and speed up the processing in the database.

Summary

Both Project managers and the Project Server database administrators can use a combination of Project Professional and Project Web Access to manage projects on the Web. Typically, the Project Server database administrator uses Project Web Access more than Project Professional, and the Project manager will still rely largely on Project Professional.

In this chapter, you learned to

✦ Use Project Web Access as a manager

✦ Use Project Web Access as the Project Server database administrator

✦   ✦   ✦

Advanced Microsoft Project

I n this final section of the book, you'll look at some of the tools that are of interest especially to advanced users. You'll learn how to customize Project's interface to suit your working needs and to create custom fields that can store information you want users to provide. You'll learn how to record macros and how to import and export information into and out of Project to and from other sources, such as Excel, Access, or Outlook. Finally, you can review some real-life situations where Project was used to solve problems — these may give you some ideas.

Customizing Microsoft Project

You can customize the Project working environment in several ways. For example, you can use custom fields to store and manipulate custom data in a project file. And you can change the way various elements appear onscreen and how you use Project's tools and commands. Suppose that you use a particular command for sharing resources all the time — you can perform that action quickly if you could access it from a tool on the standard toolbar. Or, maybe you never use the Task Note tool and prefer to get it off the toolbar and place its command on a menu. Perhaps none of Project's built-in views or tables contains quite the combination of information that you use most often.

Microsoft Project enables you to customize most of its elements. This chapter shows you how to create and use custom fields, make changes to the behavior of the Project interface, and create and modify toolbars and menus to make Project work the way that's best for you.

Cross-Reference This chapter focuses on customizing Project. See Chapter 19 for information about customizing Project Server.

Using Custom Fields

In Chapter 7, you read about Outline codes, which are custom fields in Project. In previous versions, you've had the ability to store custom data in a project file. However, you haven't been able to manipulate that data. Starting in Project 2000, custom fields enable you to create pick lists to use to ensure accurate data entry, create formulas to perform calculations on custom data, and insert icons that indicate graphically that a field contains custom data.

Customizing data entry

Suppose that your boss wants your best guess about whether you'll keep to the schedule on a task-by-task basis. You can set up a custom field and provide the information on any sheet view of Project. I'll show you this process in two phases. In the first phase, I'll create the custom field and, in the second phase, I'll show you how to use it.

To create a custom field, follow these steps:

1. Choose Tools ➪ Customize ➪ Fields. Project displays the Customize Fields dialog box, as shown in Figure 20-1.

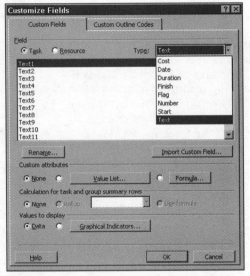

Figure 20-1: Select a custom field type.

2. Select either Task or Resource. Then, open the Type list box and choose the type of field that you want to customize. The type that you choose determines the values you can include in the pick list. Choose Text to include only alphanumeric characters in the pick list. If you choose Date, Start, or Finish, you must include date-formatted numbers in the pick list. If you choose Number or Cost, you can include only numbers in the pick list. If you choose Flag, you can include only Yes or No in the Value List. For the example, I chose Text because I want to set up a value list that contains Yes, No, and Maybe.

3. To provide a meaningful name for the code, click the Rename button and type the new name. You can't use any name that Project already is using. In the example, I named the field "Best Guess." Then, click OK to redisplay the Customize Fields dialog box.

4. Click the Value List button to display the value list for Field Name dialog box, as shown in Figure 20-2.

Figure 20-2: Use this dialog box to define the values that you want Project to display in the pick list during data entry.

5. In the Value column, type the first value that you want to appear in the list. The values that Project lets you include in the value list depend on the field type that you chose in Step 2. If you chose Text, you can include only combinations of letters and numbers. If you chose Date, Start, or Finish, you must include date-formatted entries. If you chose Number or Cost, you can include only numbers in the value list. If you chose Flag, you can include only Yes or No in the value list.

Note   If you chose Flag, you'll need to substitute Yes or No for standard flag choices, such as True and False, or On and Off.

6. (Optional) In the Description column, provide a description of the value.

7. Repeat Steps 5 and 6 for each level that you want to define.

8. If you want, you can set a default value to appear as the entry for the field by placing a check in the "Use a value from the list as the default entry for the field" box. If you choose this option, highlight a value in the light and click the Set Default button to select the value as the default.

9. In the Data Entry options section of the dialog box, you can restrict data entry so that the user can enter only values in the value list, or you can permit the user to enter values other than those in the list and add those values to the value list.

10. You can specify the order for the value list in the last section of the dialog box.

11. Click OK to save the value list and redisplay the Customize Fields dialog box.

Note   If you left the "Restrict field to items in the value list" option selected as I did, Project will display a message explaining that *only* the values you created will be accepted during data entry.

12. Click OK again to redisplay your project.

Steps 1 through 12 comprise Phase 1. In Phase 2, you use the custom field that you defined. To use it, you need to display it on a sheet view. If you defined a task field, then you can use any task sheet view; if you defined a resource field, use any resource sheet view.

To display the column, right-click the title of the column that you want to appear to the left of the custom field. Project selects the column and displays a shortcut menu from which you can choose Insert Column. In the Column Definition dialog box, as shown in Figure 20-3, open the Field Name list box and select the custom field that you defined, using the name that you supplied when you defined the field. Optionally, change the rest of the information in the dialog box and click OK. The custom field appears onscreen.

Figure 20-3: Select the custom field that you created.

When you click in the field, a list box arrow appears; when you open the list box, the value list that you established appears, as shown in Figure 20-4. Select values from the list or simply type them; in my example, if you try to enter a value that doesn't exist in the list, Project displays an error message instructing you to use a value from the list.

Caution   You can't use custom fields to create value lists for regular Project fields. For example, suppose that you've decided that you don't want to use all 1,000 of Project's priorities; in fact, you want your people to use only five possible priorities: 100, 200, 300, 400, and 500 (100 being the lowest priority and 500 being the highest priority). You can create a Number custom field (called Priority Lvl, for example) that only allows the entry of these five values on a sheet view. However, users can open the Task Information dialog box and assign any priority value in the Priority field — and Project will permit the assignment. The custom field Priority Lvl is not substituting for the actual field Priority, and users can circumvent the custom value list.

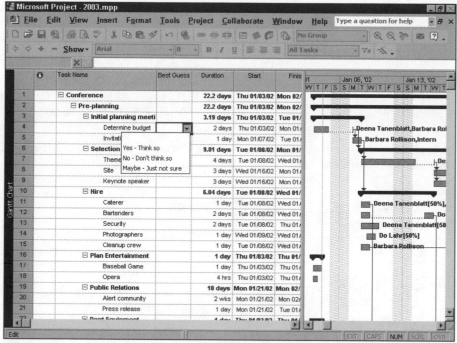

Figure 20-4: As you fill in the field, select from the pick list.

Using formulas in custom fields

Suppose that your manager tells you that part of your evaluation in project management will depend on the accuracy of your cost estimates. Under these circumstances, you may want to monitor the tasks for which actual cost exceeds baseline cost. You can set up a custom field to help you easily identify those tasks.

1. Choose Tools ➪ Customize ➪ Fields. Project displays the Customize Fields dialog box shown previously in Figure 20-1.

2. Select either Task or Resource and then open the Type list box and choose the type of field that you want to customize. For this example, I'll choose Task and Cost because I want to compare task cost values.

Tip

The type of field that you select from the Type list matters in a different way when you're creating a formula instead of a value list. If you select the wrong type when creating a value list, you won't be able to set up the appropriate values for the list. However, if you select a type that doesn't match what you're trying to calculate in a formula, Project lets you create the formula but displays "ERROR" in the custom field column on the sheet. For example, suppose that you want to calculate a cost and you select Date from the Type list. Project still permits you to create the formula but, because the formula really doesn't make sense, you'll see "ERROR" when you display the custom field column.

3. To provide a meaningful name for the code, click the Rename button and type the new name. You can't use any name that Project already is using; in the example, I named the field "Difference." Then, click OK to redisplay the Customize Fields dialog box.

4. Click the Formula button to display the "Formula for" dialog box. Figure 20-5 shows the formula I set up for this example.

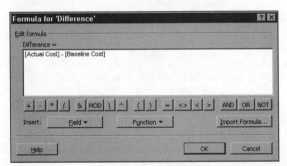

Figure 20-5: This dialog box lets you define the values that you want Project to display in the pick list during data entry.

5. Create a formula in the text box by selecting fields or functions. To select a field, click the Field button; Project displays a list of field categories. Select the appropriate field category, and Project displays a list of the available fields, as shown in Figure 20-6. To select a function, follow the same process by clicking the Function button.

Cross-Reference

In Appendix C, you'll find three tables. Table C-1 contains a list of all available Task fields, and Table C-2 contains the same information for Resource fields. Table C-3 lists the functions that you can include in a formula, as well as a description of each function's purpose.

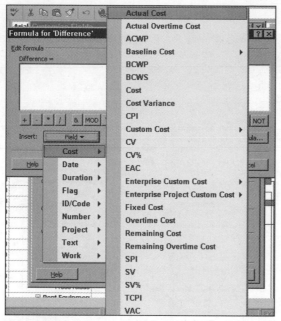

Figure 20-6: Select a field or a function to include in the formula.

6. To make a calculation, use the operators that appear above the Field and Function buttons.

> **Tip** If you've created this formula in another project, you can import the formula from the Global template (assuming that you save the formula in the Global template), or you can open the project that contains the formula before you create the formula in the new project. When you click the Import Formula button, Project displays a list of available templates or open Project files. Select the appropriate location, field type, and field name. Then click OK.

7. Click OK. Project warns you that it will discard any information previously stored in the custom field and replace the information with the calculated values based on the formula.

8. Click OK to save the formula and redisplay the Customize Fields dialog box.

9. (Optional) Assign the formula to summary rows.

If you click OK at this point, Project calculates a value for the formula. You can see the value if you display the column for the custom field, as shown in Figure 20-7. Based on the formula that I created, positive values represent tasks where Actual Cost exceeded Baseline Cost — and technically, my Difference column is nothing more than the Variance column of the Cost table.

Custom field

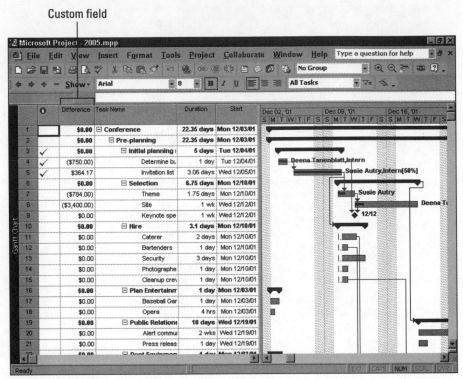

Figure 20-7: When you display the column for the custom field, you see the result of the formula.

Suppose that you don't want to eyeball figures to find the problem tasks. You can insert icons to represent positive and negative values (and make the job of identifying the problem tasks much easier) by following these steps:

1. In the Custom Fields dialog box, highlight the custom field that you created and click the Graphical Indicators button, as shown in Figure 20-8.

2. Choose the type of row to which you want to assign an indicator: Nonsummary, Summary, or Project summary.

3. In the Test for section, set up the test that Project should use. In each column, you can choose from lists; in the Value(s) column, you can compare the formula result to the value of another field or to a numeric value, as shown in Figure 20-9. In my example, if the result of the formula is greater than zero, I want to see a red flag, because the actual cost of the task exceeds the baseline cost. If, however, the actual cost is less than or equal to the baseline cost, things are fine, so I want to see a happy face (you'll find other indicator choices in the Image list).

Graphical Indicators button

Figure 20-8: Click this button to assign icons to custom fields.

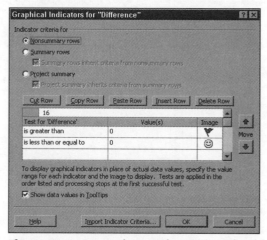

Figure 20-9: Set up the test that Project should perform on the formula's result and the indicator to display, based on the test results.

Tip If you've set up graphical indicators in another project, you can import the criteria from either the Global template (assuming that you saved the formula in the Global template) or from another open project. When you click the Import Graphical Indicator Criteria button, Project displays a list of available templates or open Project files. Select the appropriate location, field type, and field name. Then click OK.

4. If you want to see the mathematical results of the formula in a ToolTip when you point the mouse at the indicator, place a check in the "Show data values in ToolTips" checkbox.

5. Click OK to redisplay the Customize Fields dialog box.

6. Click OK again to redisplay your project.

If necessary, display the column for the custom field; right-click the column that you want to appear to the right of the custom field, and choose Insert Column. Then, select the custom field. When Project displays the column, it will contain an indicator, as shown in Figure 20-10. If you placed a check in the "Show data values in ToolTips" checkbox, you can point the mouse at an indicator to see the results of the formula (the ToolTip hides the icon onscreen; otherwise, I'd show you the ToolTip).

Figure 20-10: The custom field column contains an indicator.

Customizing the Interface

In addition to using custom fields to customize data entry and make calculations, you can customize Project's interface. For example, you can control the number of icons that appear in the Windows taskbar when you open multiple projects. Use Project's Organizer to move tables and views between project files. And, you can modify toolbars and customize menus to make them work the way that you work.

Windows taskbar icons

In Project 98 and earlier versions of Project, you saw only one icon on the Windows taskbar while Project was open — regardless of the number of Project files that you opened. Starting in Project 2000, you see an icon by default on the Windows taskbar for every open Project file, as shown in Figure 20-11.

Figure 20-11: By default, you'll see multiple icons for Project on the Windows taskbar when you open multiple projects.

Although you can't necessarily identify the file from the icon on the Windows taskbar, you can see a few letters of the filename on the icon; in addition, if you point the mouse at the icon, you'll see a ToolTip showing the entire path and filename.

Suppose that you belong to the school of users who don't *want* individual icons on the Windows taskbar for each open file — you believe that makes working harder, not easier. You can reinstate the behavior of Project 98 and earlier by removing the check from the "Windows in taskbar" box on the View tab of the Options dialog box, as shown in Figure 20-12.

Remove the check from this box

Figure 20-12: To reintroduce the behavior of Project 98 and earlier versions, remove the check from the Windows in Taskbar checkbox.

Note   Regardless of the behavior you choose, all open Project files will appear at the bottom of the Windows menu. You can switch between Project files by using the Windows menu in Project or the Windows taskbar.

Saving Project files

Using the Save tab of the Options dialog box, as shown in Figure 20-13, you can set several defaults:

✦ Using the "Save Microsoft Project files as" list box, you can specify the file format for each new Project file that you save. For example, you can save all Project 2002 files in Project 98 format if you regularly share files with someone who uses Project 98.

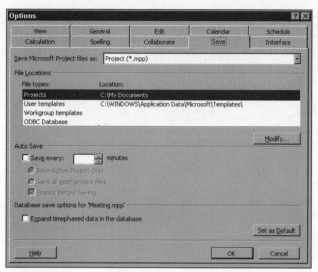

Figure 20-13: Project has several features associated with saving files.

Caution If you save files created in Project 2002 in the format of Project 98 or earlier, you may lose information. For example, WBS and outline codes don't exist in any version of Project prior to Project 2000. If you use them in a file and then save the file in Project 98 format, you'll lose them.

Note Because Project 2002 and Project 2000 share the same file format, you can't (and don't need to) select Project 2000 as a file format in the Save Microsoft Project files as list box.

✦ You can set a default file location to save all files, user templates, and workgroup templates. By setting this location, you won't need to navigate to the correct folder each time you want to save a new file.

✦ Use the Auto Save feature to save project files on a regular basis. The Auto Save feature is particularly valuable to people who tend to work extensively, forget to save regularly, and become victims of power failures or server crashes. If you use Auto Save, you'll be able to open your file as of the last automatic save.

✦ You can choose to expand timephased data in the database. If you check this box, you'll be able to see the contents of timephased fields in your Project file, but you'll also slow down Project's functioning. If you leave this box unchecked (the default), Project stores timephased data in binary format, which you can't read (unless you're a computer guru), but using binary format for this data speeds up Project's reading and writing.

Using the Organizer

Project uses the Organizer to help you share views, tables, forms, reports, and more between projects. To display the Organizer dialog box, choose View ➪ More Views. Project displays the More Views dialog box, as shown in Figure 20-14. Click the Organizer button to display the Organizer dialog box, as shown in Figure 20-15.

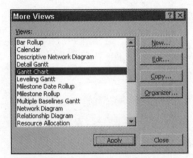

Figure 20-14: You display the Organizer by clicking the Organizer button in the More Views dialog box.

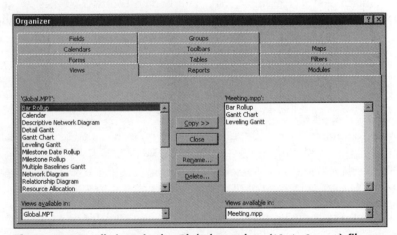

Figure 20-15: All views in the Global template (`Global.mpt`) file are available to every file based on the `Global.mpt` file.

Use the various tabs in the Organizer dialog box to copy elements from the Global template (`Global.mpt`) to the current project. You also can copy elements from the current project to the Global template or simply between projects. Use the views available in list boxes at the bottom of the Organizer to select files to use when copying elements.

Note   When you copy an element to the Global template, that element becomes available to all files created with your copy of Project.

Making changes to toolbars

Toolbars are to Windows software what remote controls are to television: effortless, hi-tech ways to take action. Toolbars are easy to use and always right at hand. However, you and Microsoft may not agree on which tools you use most often.

You can easily modify the arrangement of tools in Project. You can add or remove tools from a toolbar, change the function of a tool, create your own set of tools, or even edit the look of tools.

Note   You can make changes to your Project environment effective for your copy of Project alone, for those in a group, or across your company. Project saves your changes to a file named Global.mpt and opens new projects based on the Global file by default; consequently, your changes remain intact. You can use the Organizer to make the changed Global file available to others.

Combining or separating toolbars

Throughout this book, you've seen the Standard toolbar on a separate row from the Formatting toolbar — much like they appeared in Project 98 and earlier versions. If screen real estate is vital to you, consider placing the toolbars on the same row, as shown in Figure 20-16. When you use this feature, Project initially displays the tools that Microsoft thinks users use most often. If you need a tool that you don't see, click the Toolbar Options button to display a hidden palette of additional available buttons, as shown in Figure 20-17. After you select a tool from the hidden palette, that tool appears on the toolbar, replacing the least used tool, if necessary. As you work, the toolbars become personalized to your work habits, displaying the tools that you use most often.

Note   Starting in Project 2000, the Standard and Formatting toolbars can share the same row onscreen, increasing the screen "real estate" available for your project information. Also, menus can show only the most recently used commands.

In a similar fashion, you can personalize the menus in Project to display the commands that you use most frequently. When you enable this behavior and open a menu, you see a limited set of commands. At the bottom of the menu, you see the Expand arrows pointing down, as shown in Figure 20-18. When you click the Expand arrows, the rest of the commands on the menu appear. The gray bar that runs down the left side of the menu is lighter for hidden commands than for the more frequently used commands, as shown in Figure 20-19. Like the tools on the toolbars, if you select a "hidden" command, it becomes a "frequently used" command and appears on the abbreviated menu the next time that you open the menu.

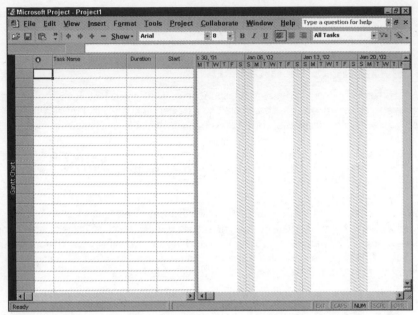

Figure 20-16: You can make the Standard and Formatting toolbars share a row on-screen.

Toolbar Options button

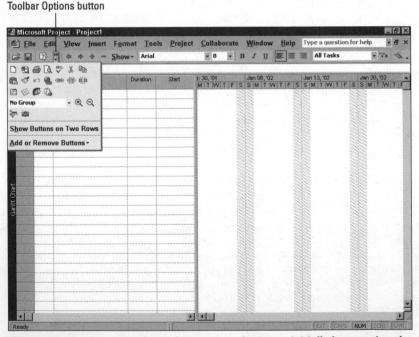

Figure 20-17: You can select a button you don't see initially by opening the hidden palette.

Tip   You can tell Project to automatically show all commands on the menu after a short delay so that you don't have to click the Expand arrows.

Figure 20-18: Initially, only some commands appear on the menu.

You control this toolbar and menu behavior by using the first three checkboxes on the Options tab of the Customize dialog box, as shown in Figure 20-20.

Adding and deleting tools from a toolbar

Although toolbars include many commonly used functions, they aren't all-inclusive. For example, the Formatting toolbar includes commands to change the font and font size; apply bold, italic, and underline effects; and align tasks. But it doesn't include tools for modifying the timescale, gridlines, or bar styles. If you use those features often, you may want to add them. Alternatively, you may prefer to have a tool that appears on one toolbar by default appear on the Standard toolbar instead.

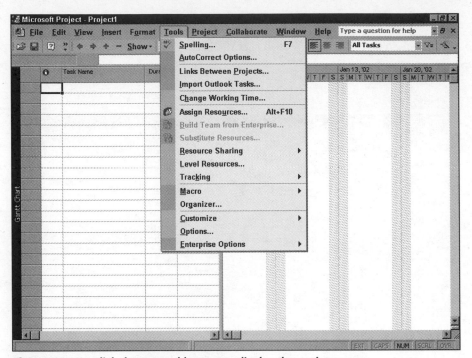

Figure 20-19: Click the Expand button to display the entire menu.

Figure 20-20: Use the Personalized Menus and Toolbars section to control the behavior of Project's menus and toolbars.

To add tools to any toolbar, locate the tool in the appropriate category and then drag it onto the toolbar where you want it to appear. Follow these steps to add a tool to a toolbar:

1. Choose View ➪ Toolbars ➪ Customize to open the Customize dialog box, as shown in Figure 20-21, and click the Toolbars tab.

Figure 20-21: The toolbars that have a check mark here are currently displayed onscreen.

2. Click the checkbox for the toolbar on which you want to place the tool so that Project displays that toolbar. For example, if you want to add the Paste as Hyperlink button to the Web toolbar, make sure that the Web toolbar is displayed.

3. Click the Commands tab, as shown in Figure 20-22.

Figure 20-22: These categories of commands contain all the possible tools built into Project.

4. Click the category of command that contains the tool that you want to add to a toolbar. For example, the Paste as Hyperlink tool appears in the Edit category because that category is where cutting, copying, and pasting tools typically reside.

Tip

If you don't know the category to which a tool command belongs, use the scroll bar in the Categories list and select All Commands at the bottom of the list. The Commands list displays every available command in alphabetical order.

5. Click the item in the Commands list, drag it from the dialog box onto your screen, and place it on the toolbar of your choice.

You also can easily remove a tool from a toolbar. With the Customize dialog box open, display the toolbar that contains the tool that you want to remove and drag the tool off the toolbar.

Note

To restore a toolbar's original settings, open the Customize dialog box, select the Toolbars tab, click the toolbar name in the list of toolbars, and click Reset. Project restores the default tools.

Creating custom toolbars

Rather than modifying some of Project's toolbars, you may prefer to create a custom toolbar that contains all the tools that you use most often. You create custom toolbars from the Customize dialog box by following these steps:

1. Display the Toolbars tab of the Customize dialog box.

2. Click the New button. The New Toolbar dialog box appears, as shown in Figure 20-23.

Figure 20-23: Name your toolbar anything you like — perhaps after your spouse, your pet, or your favorite movie star.

3. Type a toolbar name and click OK. A small toolbar, devoid of tools at the moment, appears. You can drag this floating toolbar to any location on the screen that's convenient for you.

4. Click the Commands tab to select it.

5. Click tools in any category and drag them onto the new toolbar. Figure 20-24 shows the new toolbar that I created.

Figure 20-24: Place tools in any order you like. If you want to move a tool, drag it to its new position on the toolbar.

6. Add dividers (thin gray lines) to separate groups of tools on your new toolbar. Select the tool that you want to place to the right of the divider and click the Modify Selection button on the Commands tab. The menu shown in Figure 20-25 appears.

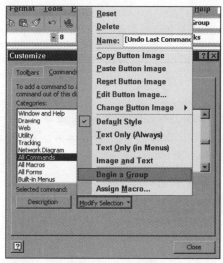

Figure 20-25: This menu offers options to work with button images, as well as options to modify other toolbar features.

7. Select the Begin a Group command from this menu to insert a divider in your toolbar, as shown in Figure 20-26.

Divider

Figure 20-26: Place a divider on a toolbar to make logical groupings of tools that perform certain types of functions.

To delete a divider, select the tool to its right and, using the Modify Selection pop-up menu, select Begin a Group again to remove the check next to that command.

Changing and editing button images

Don't like the little pictures Microsoft assigned to its tools? Feeling creative? Project enables you to select from a whole set of other button designs, from smiling faces to musical notes, or to edit a button image yourself with picture and color tools.

Caution   If anyone else uses your copy of Project, be cautious about changing tool images. Someone accustomed to Project's standard tool images may press a button and, unaware of its true function, do damage, or simply not be able to function with your copy of Project. And you aren't immune from forgetting the changes you made.

To change the images that appear on tools, follow these steps:

1. Choose Views ➪ Toolbars ➪ Customize to open the Customize dialog box.

2. Click the Commands tab to select it.

3. Click a tool on any toolbar that you have displayed. (If you need to display a toolbar, you can select it on the Toolbars tab of this dialog box.)

4. Click the Modify Selection button and select Change Button Image. The pop-up palette of images appears, as shown in Figure 20-27.

Figure 20-27: From an hourglass to an eight ball, these images are both clever and descriptive.

5. Click an image that you want to use.

 Note   To return an image to its original setting, choose Modify Selection ➪ Reset Button Image.

6. Click Close to close the Customize dialog box after you finish.

 Tip   ToolTips still work with modified buttons and are a great help in remembering what function a button performs. Just pass your mouse pointer over any tool, and its original name appears.

If you prefer — rather than replacing the button image with a predefined picture — you can edit the existing picture by modifying the pattern and colors on it. For example, if two tools seem similar to you, help yourself differentiate them by applying a bright red color to either one. Button images comprise many tiny squares called *pixels*. By coloring in the pixels, you can form an image. You can use a color palette and the individual pixels to modify button images or even draw an entirely new image.

To edit a button image, follow these steps, starting from the Customize dialog box Commands tab:

1. Click a tool on any displayed toolbar and then click Modify Selection.

2. Select the Edit Button Image command to open the Button Editor dialog box, as shown in Figure 20-28.

Figure 20-28: The small Preview helps you see how changes to individual picture pixels will appear on the button image.

3. Try the following techniques:

   • To make changes to an image, click a color block in the Colors palette and then click an individual pixel.

   • To remove color from a pixel, click the Erase block in the Colors palette and then click the pixel.

Tip   To color in or erase a large area of pixels, click a color in the palette or the Erase block, click a pixel, and then drag your cursor in any direction to color or erase multiple pixels in one motion. Release your cursor to stop painting or erasing the pixels.

   • To see more of a large button that doesn't fit in the Picture box, use the Move arrows to move from side to side or up and down to display the image's edges.

4. Click OK to save your changes and to return to the Customize dialog box. Click Close to return to your Project screen.

Customizing project menus

Toolbars aren't the only way to get things done in Project, and they aren't the only elements in Project that you can customize. You also can create new menus and modify existing menus to your heart's content. For example, you can add a command to the File menu that changes the current view to the Network Diagram view and prints a report. You can add these functions because menu commands are actually *macros*, that is, recorded series of keystrokes or programming commands.

Note   Macros are really a form of computer program. Visual Basic is the macro-programming language that you use in Microsoft products. In a macro, you save a string of commands that instruct the software to perform one or more actions. Project provides an easy method for selecting commands to associate with a macro and for saving the macro as a custom menu command. See Chapter 21 for more on macros.

When you select a menu command, you are really running a macro, telling Project to repeat the sequence of events that copies a selected piece of text, causes a dialog box to appear, and so on.

You can use your own macros and Project's built-in commands to customize Project by building new menus and changing the function of existing commands. Or, you can delete menus or commands on menus that you don't need.

Adding menus

To add a new menu to your Project menu bar, you follow a process similar to that used to add a new toolbar. First, you drag a new, blank menu to the menu bar, then you assign it a name, and finally, you drag commands onto it.

Note   As with toolbars, Project adds new menus to your Global file, the default file on which all project files are based. Therefore, changes you make to menus or the menu bar are, in effect, for all files you create with this copy of Project.

Follow these steps to add a new menu to Project:

1. Choose View ➪ Toolbars ➪ Customize to open the Customize dialog box.

2. Make sure that the menu bar is showing on your screen; if it's not, click the menu bar item on the Toolbars tab of the Customize dialog box.

3. Click the Commands tab to select it.

4. Scroll to the bottom of the list of Categories and click the category named "New Menu." The single selection, New Menu, appears in the list of Commands, as shown in Figure 20-29.

Figure 20-29: The New Menu category has only one command in it.

5. Click the New Menu item in the Commands list and drag it up to the menu bar. When the dark vertical line of your mouse pointer appears where you want to place the new menu, release the mouse button. Project places a New Menu item on the menu bar.

6. Select the New Menu and then click the Modify Selection button. From the new pop-up menu, as shown in Figure 20-30, highlight New Menu and type a specific menu name. Then click outside the Modify Selection menu to close it.

7. Select a category of command that you want to place on the new menu. If you have created a macro and want to place it on the menu, select the category All Macros, which includes standard menu command macros, as well as macros you've created.

8. Drag an item in the Commands list up to the New Menu on the menu bar. A small, blank box appears under the menu heading.

9. Place the mouse pointer in that blank area and release the mouse button to place the command on the menu.

10. Click Close to close the Customize dialog box.

You can repeat Steps 7 through 9 to build the new menu. To divide the menu into groups of commands, you can use Modify Selection ⇨ Begin a Group to add dividing lines.

Assigning new commands

You may also want to modify the function of an existing menu command. For example, if you create a macro that invokes the Print command and accepts all the Print dialog box defaults for you, you can assign that macro to the Print command. That way, you don't have the extra step of clicking OK to accept print defaults every time you print. As always, be careful about replacing the function of one command with another if other people will be using your copy of Project.

Figure 20-30: The menu name should help you remember what commands it contains.

Tip

You can reinstate all the menu defaults by opening the Toolbars tab in the Customize dialog box, clicking the Menu Bar item, and clicking Reset.

To change the macro associated with a command, follow these steps:

1. Display the Customize dialog box (View ➪ Toolbars ➪ Customize).

2. Open the menu on which you want to edit a command.

3. Right-click the command you want to change; the menu shown in Figure 20-31 appears.

4. Select the Assign Macro command from this menu to open the Customize Tool dialog box, as shown in Figure 20-32.

5. Click the Command drop-down list and select the command that you want to associate with the menu item.

6. (Optional) Type a description of what this command does.

7. Click OK to return to the Customize dialog box and then click Close to save the new command with the menu item.

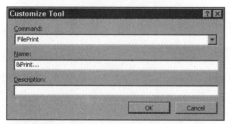

Figure 20-31: You can use this menu to add a button image next to a menu command.

Figure 20-32: The Name entry in the Customize Tool dialog box is the name of the macro it invokes.

Deleting commands and menus

Is your screen getting cluttered with custom commands and menus? To remove a particular command or a whole menu without resetting all the menu changes that you've made, follow these steps:

1. Open the Customize dialog box.

2. Click a menu name, or open the menu and click a particular command.

3. Drag the item off the menu bar and close the Customize dialog box.

That's all there is to it!

Summary

In this chapter, you learned how to:

✦ Work with custom fields to create data entry value lists and formulas

✦ Modify Project's behavior to display only one icon on the Windows taskbar or to display an icon for each open project

✦ Take advantage of the new features for saving your projects

✦ Display the Standard and Formatting toolbars on the same row or on separate rows

✦ Customize the features (toolbars and menus) that you use to get things done

In the next chapter, you learn details about creating your own macros, which can form the basis for new tools and menus and streamline the repetitive tasks that you perform to create and track a schedule.

✦　　✦　　✦

Using Macros to Speed Your Work

Macros are small programs that carry out repetitive tasks that you perform frequently. You may have used macros in a word processing program; macros work the same way in Project as they do in your word processor.

Don't let the word *program* in the preceding paragraph deter you from learning about macros. Although you can actually work with the macro programming code, Project provides an easier way for you to write a macro, which you will learn in this chapter.

Why Use Macros?

Macros are most useful when you need to perform any repetitive task. In particular, you can use Project macros to

✦ Display or hide frequently used toolbars

✦ Display frequently used tables

✦ Display frequently used views

✦ Switch to a custom view

✦ Generate standard reports

As you learn to use Project, you'll identify the steps that you take over and over again; these tasks are excellent candidates for macros.

Recording Macros

Project stores macros in the Visual Basic for Applications programming language. And, if you're adept at programming, you can write your macro directly in the Visual Basic for Applications programming language. Figure 21-1 shows a sample of the instructions stored in a macro in Visual Basic.

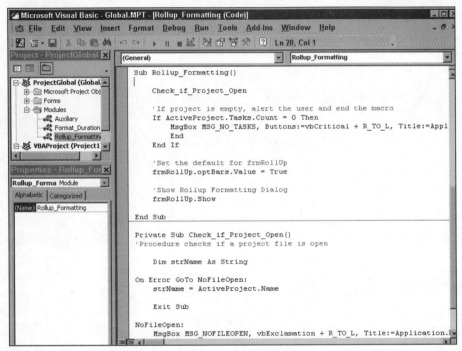

Figure 21-1: A sample set of instructions stored in a macro

Most people prefer to record a macro. When you record a macro, you have Project memorize the steps that you want to take and store those steps. That is, you do whatever it is you want Project to do; Project then converts those actions into Visual Basic statements and stores the statements in a macro. Later, when you want to take that action again, you run your macro, which you learn how to do in the next section.

Before you record a macro, you should run through the steps that you want to take. You may even want to write down the steps. That way, you are less likely to make (and record) mistakes.

Suppose that you want to create a macro that displays the Task Details Form in the bottom pane when you display the Gantt Chart view. Here are the steps that you need to record for this macro:

1. Open the View menu and click Gantt Chart.

By selecting the view first, you force Project to start your macro from the Gantt Chart view, regardless of the view that you were using before you ran your macro.

2. Use the split bar (or choose Window ➪ Split) to open the bottom pane that shows, by default, the Task Form view.

3. Click the bottom pane and choose View ➪ More Views to open the More Views dialog box.

4. Select the Task Details Form.

5. Click Apply.

Now that you know what you're going to record, use the following steps to record the macro:

1. Choose Tools ➪ Macro ➪ Record New Macro to open the Record Macro dialog box, as shown in Figure 21-2.

Figure 21-2: The Record Macro dialog box

2. Enter a name for the macro in the Macro name box.

The first character of the macro name must be a letter, but the other characters can be letters, numbers, or underscore characters. You can't include a space in a macro name, so try using an underscore character as a word separator or capitalize the first letter of each word.

3. (Optional) To assign the macro to a keyboard shortcut, type a letter in the Shortcut key box. The letter that you assign can be any letter key on your keyboard, but it can't be a number or a special character. You also can't assign a key combination that is already used by Microsoft Project; if you select a reserved letter, Project displays the warning message shown in Figure 21-3 when you click OK.

Figure 21-3: Project displays this warning message if you select a keyboard shortcut already in use.

Note   Keyboard shortcuts are only one of the ways that you can run a macro. Later in this chapter, you learn the other methods to play back a macro, as well as how to assign a keyboard shortcut after you've recorded and stored your macro.

4. Open the "Store macro in" list box and click the location where you want to store the macro. You can store the macro in the Global File or in the current project. To make a macro available to all projects, select Global File.

Note   The Global File is also called the *Global template*, and it acts like the Normal template in Word or the Book1 template in Excel. Any customized features (such as macros, toolbars, or menus) that you store in the Global File are available to any project file. On the other hand, customized features that you store in an individual project file are available only to that file.

5. Type a description of the purpose of the macro or the function that it performs in the Description box. This description appears whenever you run the macro from the Macro dialog box.

6. Use the options in the Row references and Column references boxes to control the way that the macro selects rows and columns if you select cells while running a macro. For rows, the macro always selects rows — regardless of the position of the active cell — because it records relative references to rows. If you want a macro to always select the same row, regardless of which cell is first selected, select Absolute (ID).

Note   For columns, the macro always selects the same column each time that it is run — regardless of which cell is first selected — because it records absolute references to columns. If you want a macro to select columns, regardless of the position of the active cell when you run the macro, select Relative.

7. Click OK. Project redisplays your project, and you won't notice any differences, but Project is now recording each action that you take.

8. Take all the actions that you want to record.

9. Choose Tools ➪ Macro ➪ Stop Recorder, as shown in Figure 21-4, to stop recording.

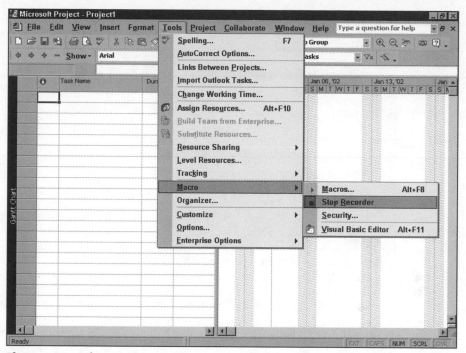

Figure 21-4: When you're recording a macro, the Stop Recorder command is available.

Running Macros

To use a macro that you have recorded, simply run the macro. Some people refer to this action as "playing back" the macro because they associate recording and playing back with the process of recording a TV program on a VCR and then playing back the recording.

If your macro makes substantial changes to your project, you should save the project before you run the macro. You can't undo the effects of a macro easily. To run a macro, follow these steps:

1. Open the project that contains the macro; if you stored the macro in the Global file, you can open any project.

2. Choose Tools ➪ Macro ➪ Macros to open the Macros dialog box, as shown in Figure 21-5.

3. Select the macro that you want to run from the Macro name list.

Figure 21-5: The Macros dialog box

4. Click Run. Project performs the steps that you recorded in the macro.

Tip   If your macro is long and you want to stop it while it's still running, press Ctrl+Break. If your macro is short, it will probably finish before you can stop it.

Using Shortcuts to Run Macros

Although you can run macros by selecting them from the Macro dialog box, if you use a macro on a regular basis, you may want to shorten the method for running the macro. You can create one of the following:

✦ A toolbar button that runs the macro

✦ A menu command that runs the macro

✦ A keyboard shortcut that runs the macro

Assigning a macro to a toolbar button

Suppose you're a fan of toolbar buttons, and you create a macro that you use a lot. You find yourself wanting a toolbar button that you can click to make your macro run. Well, you can get your wish by adding a button to a toolbar and assigning your macro to that button.

Caution   Adding buttons to the toolbars that come with Project isn't always a good idea. If you add a toolbar button to one of the toolbars that comes with Project and you reset that toolbar, the button you added disappears.

The following steps explain how to add a button assigned to a macro to the Standard toolbar, but you can also add toolbar buttons for macros to a custom toolbar you create.

Cross-Reference

Chapter 20 explains how to create a custom toolbar.

1. Check to see whether the toolbar to which you want to add a button appears on screen. If it does, go to Step 2. Otherwise, display the toolbar by right-clicking any toolbar button and choosing the toolbar from the shortcut menu that appears.

2. Choose View ⇨ Toolbars ⇨ Customize to open the Customize dialog box.

Tip

You can also open the Customize dialog box by choosing Tools ⇨ Customize ⇨ Toolbars.

3. Choose Commands to display the Commands tab, as shown in Figure 21-6.

Figure 21-6: From the Commands tab of the Customize dialog box, you can add macros as buttons to toolbars.

4. Scroll down the Categories list and select All Macros. Project displays a list of macros in the Commands list on the right side of the dialog box.

5. Drag the macro you want to add onto the desired toolbar, as shown in Figure 21-7. As you drag, the mouse pointer image changes to include a small button and a plus sign. As you move the mouse pointer over a toolbar, a large insertion point marks the location where the button appears when you release the mouse button.

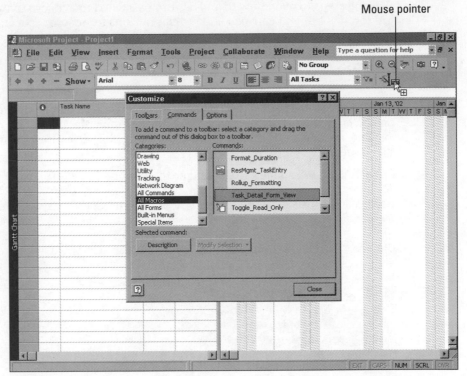

Figure 21-7: The image of the mouse pointer icon changes as you drag a macro onto the Standard toolbar.

6. Release the mouse button and a new button appears on the toolbar, as shown in Figure 21-8. The name of the button is so long that Project wrapped the Standard toolbar onto a second row.

Tip   If you're concerned about using excessive screen real estate, you may want to take advantage of the feature in Project that permits the Standard toolbar and the Formatting toolbar to share the same row. Buttons not used frequently reside on a hidden palette. See Chapter 20 for more information about customizing Project.

7. To change the name on the toolbar button, click Modify Selection in the Customize dialog box to open the pop-up menu, as shown in Figure 21-9.

8. Type the name, exactly as you want it to appear on the toolbar button, into the Name box. You can include spaces.

9. Press Enter. The pop-up menu disappears, and Project renames the macro toolbar button, as shown in Figure 21-10.

New macro button

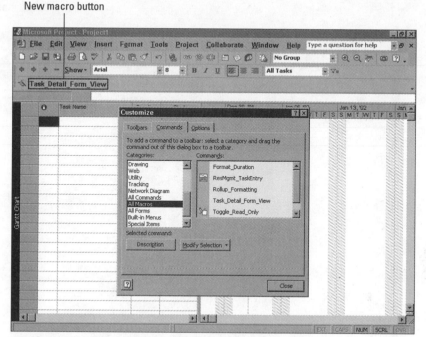

Figure 21-8: The new button after dropping it on the toolbar

Figure 21-9: The menu that appears when you click the Modify Selection button to change a macro button's name

The renamed macro button

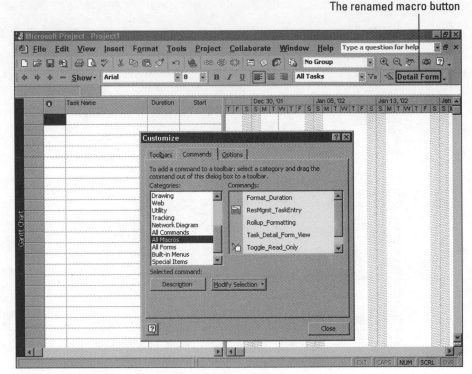

Figure 21-10: The toolbar button after renaming it

10. Close the Customize dialog box.

When you add a toolbar button to an existing toolbar, Project saves it in your Global file. Any other project files that you open on your computer using that Global file contain the new toolbar button.

Tip   If you change your mind and don't want the button on the toolbar, you can remove it by opening the Customize dialog box and then simply dragging the button off the toolbar and dropping it anywhere on your project. The button disappears, but the macro is still available.

Assigning a macro to a menu command

Maybe you're not a toolbar person, or maybe you just prefer to use menu commands. This section shows you how to add a command assigned to a macro to the Tools menu.

Caution   As with toolbars, be aware that adding commands to the menus that come with Project isn't always a good idea. If you add a command to one of the standard menus and you reset that menu, the command that you added will disappear.

You can also add commands for macros to custom menus that you create, and if you don't want your custom menu to appear all the time, you can create a custom toolbar and drag menus onto it. Then you can hide or display the toolbar as needed.

Cross-Reference See Chapter 20 for more information about creating custom menus and toolbars.

Follow these steps to add a command that runs your macro from a menu:

1. Choose View ➪ Toolbars ➪ Customize to open the Customize dialog box.

Tip You also can open the Customize dialog box by choosing Tools ➪ Customize ➪ Toolbars.

2. Click the Commands tab, as shown in Figure 21-11.

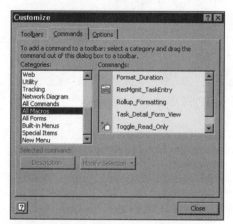

Figure 21-11: You can add macros as commands on menus by using the Commands tab of the Customize dialog box.

3. Scroll down the Categories list and select All Macros. Project displays a list of macros in the Commands list on the right.

4. Drag the macro that you want to add to the desired menu, as shown in Figure 21-12. As you drag, the mouse pointer image changes to include a small button and a plus sign (+). As you move the mouse pointer over a menu, the menu opens; a large horizontal insertion point marks the location where the button appears when you release the mouse button.

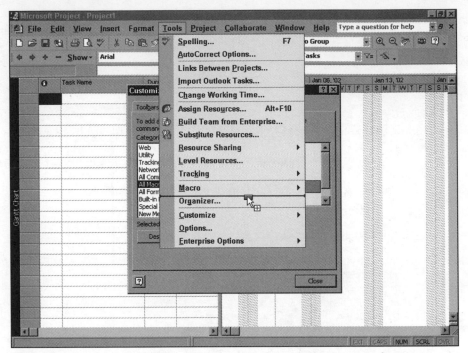

Figure 21-12: The image of the mouse pointer icon changes as you drag a macro onto a menu.

5. Release the mouse button. The macro appears on the menu, as shown in Figure 21-13.

6. To change the name on the menu, click Modify Selection in the Customize dialog box to open the pop-up menu, as shown in Figure 21-14.

7. Type the name (including spaces) in the Name box, exactly as you want it to appear on the toolbar button.

Note

To provide a hotkey for your macro name, place an ampersand (&) immediately before the character that you want to be the hotkey — as I did before the D of Detail in Figure 21-14. Make sure that the letter you select is not already in use by some other command on the same menu. When the command appears on the menu, the hotkey letter will be underscored, enabling you to choose it from the menu by using the hotkey letter. For example, I can choose the Detail Form command by pressing Alt+T+D.

8. Press Enter. The pop-up menu disappears, and Project renames the menu command. As Figure 21-15 shows, the command includes your hotkey if you added an ampersand.

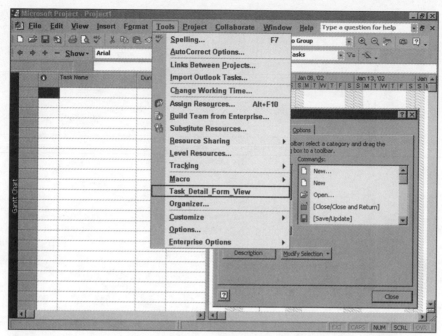

Figure 21-13: A macro placed on the Tools menu

Figure 21-14: Modifying the command name on the menu

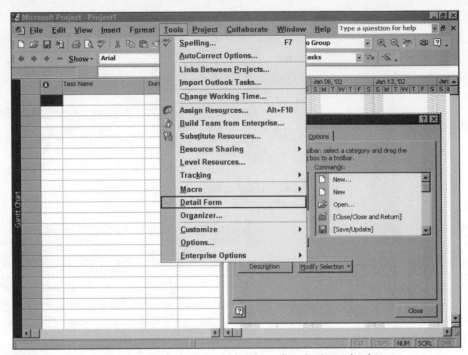

Figure 21-15: The command after renaming it and assigning a hotkey

9. Close the Customize dialog box.

When you add a command to one of the default menus, Microsoft Project saves the command and the menu in your Global file. Any other project file that you open on your computer using that Global file contains the new menu command.

Tip   If you change your mind and don't want the command on the menu, you can remove it by opening the Customize dialog box and then simply dragging the command off the menu and dropping it anywhere on your project or even in the Customize dialog box. The command disappears, but the macro is still available.

Assigning a keyboard shortcut to a macro

Suppose that after you experiment, you decide that you really want to run your macro from a keyboard shortcut. Further suppose that you didn't set a shortcut when you created the macro. Follow these steps to add a keyboard shortcut to the macro after you create it:

1. Open the project containing the macro.

2. Choose Tools ⇨ Macro ⇨ Macros to open the Macros dialog box, as shown in Figure 21-16.

Figure 21-16: The Macros dialog box

Tip

You can also press Alt+F8 to display the Macros dialog box.

3. Highlight the macro to which you want to add a keyboard shortcut.

4. Click Options to open the Macro Options dialog box that appears in Figure 21-17.

Figure 21-17: Set a keyboard shortcut
for a macro from the Macro Options
dialog box.

5. Place the insertion point in the Shortcut key box and type a letter.

6. Click OK. If the combination that you selected (Ctrl plus the letter you typed) is not in use by Project, Project displays the Macros dialog box again. If Project is using the combination you selected, even for another macro, Project asks you to try a different combination.

7. Close the Macros dialog box.

To run your macro, press the keyboard combination you assigned. If you decide that you don't want to run your macro by using this keyboard combination, you can change the combination by using the preceding steps, or you can remove the keyboard combination you assigned completely by reopening the Macro Options dialog box and deleting the letter from the Shortcut key box.

Summary

In this chapter, you learned about using macros in Project. You learned how to

✦ Create macros

✦ Use macros

✦ Assign shortcuts to macros to make them easy to run

Chapter 22 explains how to import and export Project data.

✦　✦　✦

Importing and Exporting Project Information

CHAPTER

22

♦ ♦ ♦ ♦

In This Chapter

General importing and exporting concepts

Exporting information

Importing information

Troubleshooting

♦ ♦ ♦ ♦

Sometimes, you need to move information in and out of Project. Although you can do this by copying and pasting the information, you'll find that you make these moves primarily by using Project's import and export functions. You can import and export information using various file formats; for example, you can export a Project schedule as a graphic image to use in a graphics program, on a Web page, or to print on a plotter.

New Feature You can now import tasks from Outlook into Project, and you'll find that importing Excel workbook information is easier in Project 2002.

Occasionally, you may find it convenient to start a project in an Excel workbook or Outlook's Task List. Although you've been able to import information from Excel for quite some time, Project 2002 includes a template to make the importing process easier. And, new to Project 2002, you can import tasks from Outlook into Project.

General Importing and Exporting Concepts

Importing is the process of bringing information into a Project file from another program; exporting is the process of sending information from Project to another program. When you import or export information, you use an import/export map. Project comes with a series of useful import/export maps that you can edit if necessary, or you can create a custom map. To view, copy, or edit any of the predefined import/export maps, or to create your own map, you use the Import/Export Wizard.

New Feature   The Export Wizard is new to Project 2002.

Think of an import/export map as a template that Project uses to correctly translate information from one program to another. An import/export map defines the information that you want to import or export and enables you to describe how to match the information in the Project file with the information in the other program's file. For example, when you charted earned value in Excel in Chapter 14, you selected the Earned Value Information export map to send the data to Excel. This mapping information told Project what data to send to Excel for charting and how to identify the information in Excel. Whenever you import or export, you can use one of the predefined maps that come with Project, or you can create a new map. Because the Wizard walks you through the process, creating a new map really is fairly easy to do.

Exporting Information

You can export information to Microsoft Office products, such as Excel workbooks, Access databases, or Word documents. You also can export some Project information to graphic images that you can use in any graphics program or as an image on a Web page. And you can export information to any program that can read text (TXT) files or comma-separated value (CSV) files.

Note   Although the steps for each file type vary slightly, the process for importing or exporting is generally the same.

Exporting to Office files

You can export information to Excel workbooks or to Access databases. You also can include Project information in Word, but you won't use the export process.

Sending Project data to Excel

Using the Import/Export Wizard, you can easily send information to Excel. The Wizard gives you the choice of creating a new map or using an existing map. Follow these steps to start the process.

1. Open the Project file containing the information you want to export.

2. Choose File ➪ Save As to open the File Save dialog box.

3. Type a name in the File name list box for the file you want to export.

4. Open the Save as type list box and select Microsoft Excel Workbook or Microsoft Excel PivotTable.

Note   When you create an Excel PivotTable file, Project creates two sheets in the workbook for each type of data that you export. One sheet contains the data used in the PivotTable, and the other sheet contains the PivotTable. Project uses the last field in each map as the default field for the PivotTable, and all the other fields appear as rows in the PivotTable.

5. Click Save. Project starts the Export Wizard. Click Next.

6. Choose Selected Data and click Next.

Note   When you choose Project Excel Template, Project exports the entire Project file to Excel.

7. Choose New map or Use existing map.

If you choose Use an existing map, you'll see the Map Selection dialog box shown in Figure 22-1.

Note   If you choose New map, you won't see the Map Selection dialog box; instead, when you click Next, you'll see the Map Options dialog box.

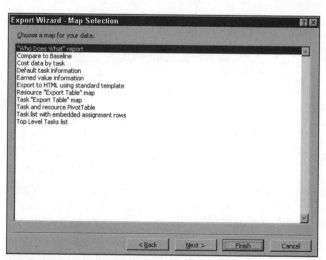

Figure 22-1: Use this dialog box to select the map that you want to use to export your data.

8. Select a map and click Next. The Export Wizard displays the Map Options dialog box.

9. Select the type of data to export, as shown in Figure 22-2. The boxes that you check determine which Wizard screens will subsequently appear when you click Next.

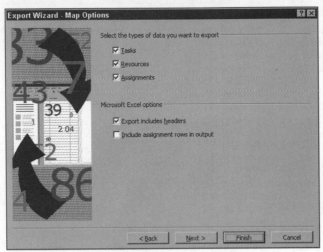

Figure 22-2: Select the type of data to export on the Map Options screen.

Tip If you want your Excel workbook to contain assignments listed under tasks or resources, similar to the Task Usage or Resource Usage views, place a check in the "Include assignment rows in output" checkbox.

10. When you click Next, you see one of the mapping dialog boxes. In the example, I checked Tasks on the Map Options dialog box. The Task Mapping dialog box appears, as shown in Figure 22-3, and functions as follows:

- **Destination worksheet name.** This box contains the name that Excel will assign to the sheet in the workbook. You can change this name.

- **Export filter.** Use this list box to select the tasks that you want to export. By default, Project assumes that you want to export all tasks, but you can export, for example, only completed tasks.

- **From: Microsoft Project Field.** Under this column, click "(Click here to map a phrase)" to add fields to export one at a time. After you click, you can use the list box arrow that appears to view a list of the fields available for exporting and to select a field.

- **To: Excel Field.** Select a field to export and click the column next to the field that you added. Project suggests a column heading for the field in the Excel worksheet; you can change this heading.

- **Data Type.** You can't change the data type for the field in the destination program, which appears in this column.

- **Add All.** To quickly add all the fields in the Project file, click the Add All button.

- **Clear All.** To remove all the fields you added, click the Clear All button.

- **Insert Row.** If you decide to add a field between two existing fields, click the row that you want to appear below the new field. Then click the Insert Row button, and Project inserts a blank row above the selected row.

- **Delete Row.** To delete a field, click anywhere in the row containing the field and click the Delete Row button.

- **Base on Table.** To add all the fields in a particular Project table, such as the Entry table or the Cost table, click the Base on Table button. Project displays the Select Base Table for Field Mapping dialog box, from which you can select a table. When you click OK, Project adds all fields contained in that table to the list of fields that you want to export.

- **Move.** You can use the Move buttons on the right side of the dialog box to reorder fields. Click the field that you want to move and then click either the Move up arrow or the Move down arrow.

Note If you selected Resources and Assignments as well as Task fields on the Map Options dialog box (shown previously in Figure 22-2), when you click Next, the Export Wizard displays additional boxes almost identical to the Task Mapping dialog box but for each of these data types.

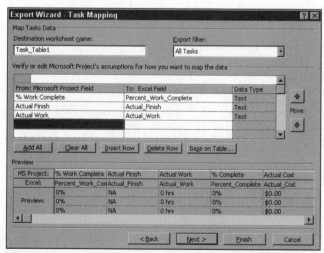

Figure 22-3: As you add fields in the Task Mapping dialog box, a preview of the Excel worksheet that you're creating appears at the bottom of the Task Mapping dialog box.

11. After you finish defining your map, you'll see the final box of the Export Wizard, as shown in Figure 22-4. If you elect to save your map by clicking the Save Map button, Project displays the Save Map dialog box, as shown in Figure 22-5. Provide a name for the new map in the "Map name" text box.

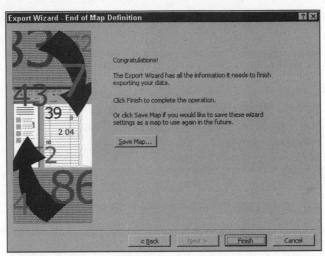

Figure 22-4: In the final dialog box of the Export Wizard, choose whether to save the map you've defined.

Figure 22-5: If you decide to save the map, provide a name for it in the Save Map dialog box, which displays a list of all existing maps.

Sending Project data to an Access database

You can export some or all of the information in a Project file to an Access 97 or later database file using the Export Wizard and an export map. If none of the existing maps can export data into the proper fields in your Access database, you may need to create a new map.

Note   Because Access tables are conceptually the same as Excel worksheets — both consist of data organized in rows and columns — you will notice that the process for exporting Project information to Access sounds suspiciously like the process for exporting Project information to Excel. You're not imagining it.

When you export to any database format, Project makes the following changes to the names of some fields in the database to ensure compatibility with database field naming conventions:

✦ Underscores replace spaces and forward slashes (/).

✦ The string "Percent" replaces the percent sign (%).

✦ Periods are deleted.

✦ Start changes to Start_Date.

✦ Finish changes to Finish_Date.

✦ Group changes to Group_Name.

✦ Work changes to Scheduled_Work.

Note   You can append Project information to an existing Access database. However, you should make sure you have a backup copy of the database, just in case the information doesn't appear the way you expect in Access. You may even want to create a test copy of your database and use the copy to ensure that Project information appears in the correct fields.

Follow these steps to export Project information to a file in Microsoft Access database format:

1. Open the Project file containing the data you want to export.

2. Choose File ➪ Save As to open the File Save dialog box.

3. Open the Save as type list box and select Microsoft Access Database.

4. Type a name in the File name box for the file that you are exporting.

5. Click Save. Project starts the Export Wizard.

Note   If you selected an existing Access database, Project displays the Existing database screen of the Wizard, where you can choose to append information to an existing database or overwrite that database.

6. On the Data screen of the Export Wizard, choose to export "A full project" or "Only selected data" and click Next.

   If you choose "A full project" in Step 6, the Project Definition screen appears, as shown in Figure 22-6. Type a name for the project in the Project Name box and click Finish.

Figure 22-6: When you export your entire project to Access, you supply a name for the project in this dialog box.

If you choose "Only selected data," the Map screen of the Export Wizard appears, where you can choose to create a new map or use an existing map.

7. If you choose to use an existing map, you'll see the Map Selection dialog box shown in Figure 22-7. After you select a map and click Next, the Export Wizard displays the Map Options dialog box.

   If you choose to create a new map, you won't see the Map Selection dialog box; instead, when you click Next, you'll see the Map Options dialog box, as shown in Figure 22-8.

8. Select the type of data to export. (The boxes that you check determine which Wizard screens will appear when you click Next.)

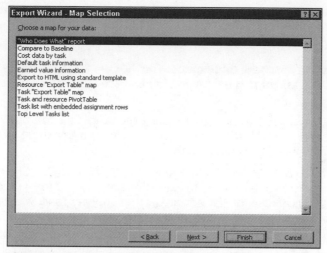

Figure 22-7: Use this dialog box to select the map that you want to use to export your data.

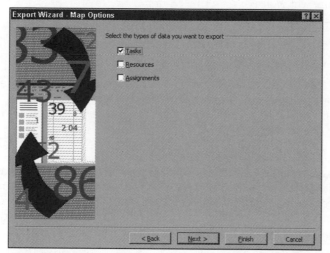

Figure 22-8: Select the type of data to export on the Map Options screen.

9. When you click Next, you see one of the mapping dialog boxes; in the example, I checked Tasks on the Map Options dialog box. The Task Mapping dialog box appears, as shown in Figure 22-9, and functions as follows:

- **Destination database table name.** This box contains the name that Access will assign to the table in the database. You can change this name.

- **Export filter.** Use this list box to select the tasks that you want to export. By default, Project assumes that you want to export all tasks, but you can export, for example, only completed tasks.

- **From: Microsoft Project Field.** Under this column, click "(Click here to map a phrase)" to add fields to export one at a time. After you click this option, you can use the list box arrow that appears to view a list of fields available for exporting and to select a field.

- **To: Database Field.** Select a field to export and click the column next to the field that you added. Project suggests a column heading for the field in the Access table; you can change this heading.

- **Data Type.** You can't change the data type for the field in the destination program, which appears in this column.

- **Add All.** To quickly add all the fields in the Project file, click the Add All button.

- **Clear All.** To remove all the fields you added, click the Clear All button.

- **Insert Row.** If you decide to add a field between two existing fields, click the row that you want to appear below the new field. Click the Insert Row button, and Project inserts a blank row above the selected row.

- **Delete Row.** To delete a field, click anywhere in the row containing the field and click the Delete Row button.

- **Base on Table.** To add all the fields in a particular Project table, such as the Entry table or the Cost table, click the Base on Table button. Project displays the Select Base Table for Field Mapping dialog box, from which you can select a table. When you click OK, Project adds all fields contained in that table to the list of fields that you want to export.

- **Move.** You can use the Move buttons on the right side of the dialog box to reorder fields. Click the field that you want to move and then click either the Move up arrow or the Move down arrow.

If you selected Resources and Assignments as well as Task fields on the Map Options dialog box (shown previously in Figure 22-8), then, when you click Next, the Export Wizard displays additional boxes almost identical to the Task Mapping dialog box but for each of these data types.

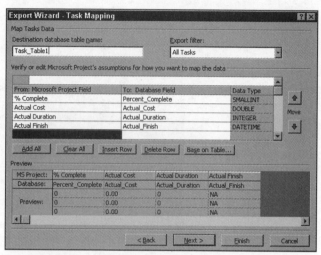

Figure 22-9: As you add fields in the Task Mapping dialog box, a preview of the Access database that you're creating appears at the bottom of the Task Mapping dialog box.

After you finish defining your map, you'll see the final box of the Export Wizard in which you can elect to save the map that you just defined. If you elect to save your map by clicking the Save Map button, Project redisplays the Save Map dialog box. Provide a name for the new map in the "Map name" text box.

Sending Project data to Microsoft Word

Although you can't export Project data directly to Word, you can use the Windows Copy and Paste commands to incorporate Project text or table data in a Word file. For example, you can copy the columns in any table to a Word document. Start in Project and follow these steps:

1. Open the file containing the information you want to incorporate in a Word document.

2. Select the information; you can copy text information from the Notes tab of either the Task Information dialog box or the Resource Information dialog box. In addition, as shown in Figure 22-10, you can copy table columns.

3. Click the Copy button on the Standard toolbar.

4. Open or switch to Word.

5. Position the insertion point where you want the Project information to begin.

6. Click Paste. The Project information appears in Word.

Figure 22-10: Select information to copy to Word.

As shown in Figure 22-11, table information appears in Word as tab-separated columns. Using Word's Convert Text to Table feature (select the data, choose Table, point at Convert, and choose Text to Table), you can convert the information into a Word table.

Figure 22-11: Project table information as it appears when you copy it into Word.

Exporting Project information to a graphic image

You can create a picture from your Project information and view the picture in any graphics program or save the picture in a Web-compatible file format. When you use the following technique, you copy Project information to the Windows Clipboard; you can copy all or part of any view except the Task PERT, Task Form, and Resource Form views.

1. Select the view of which you want a picture.

2. Tell Project how much of your plan to copy. To copy only a portion of your plan, select the information that you want to copy. To copy all visible portions of your plan, click the Copy Picture button on the Standard toolbar. The Copy Picture dialog box appears, as shown in Figure 22-12.

Copy Picture button

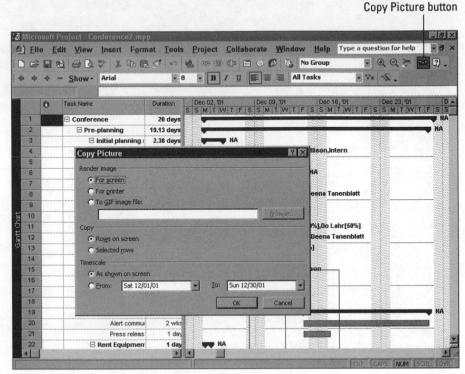

Figure 22-12: Use the Copy Picture dialog box to describe how you want to copy the picture.

3. Select an option button to specify how you want Project to copy the picture:

   - **For screen** — Select this to copy the information for display on a computer screen.

   - **For printer** — Select this to copy the information for a printer to use.

   - **To GIF image file** — Select this to save the information as an image that you can use on a Web page and in other programs. Be sure to specify the path and filename in the box below this option.

4. (Optional) If you selected rows before you started this process because you want to copy only those rows, select Selected rows.

5. (Optional) If you want to copy information for a range of dates other than those currently displayed, click the Date option button and then enter From and To dates.

6. Click OK.

To view an image that you copied as a screen or printer image, switch to the program in which you want to display the Microsoft Project information and then paste the picture by using the program's Paste command. A copied image in Microsoft Paint appears in Figure 22-13.

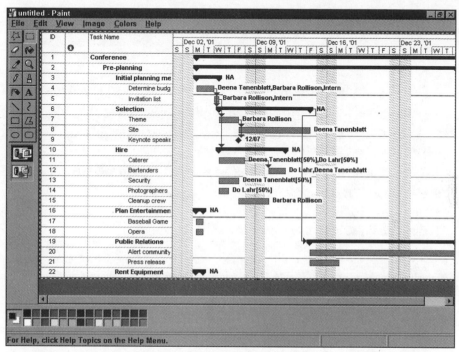

Figure 22-13: A Project image pasted into Microsoft Paint

Exporting to other formats

If you want to export information to a program that can read either text files or Microsoft Project Exchange Files, you can create an export file that the receiving program can read. Text files are a common format and are also called *comma-separated value files* (CSV). Microsoft Project Exchange format (MPX) is an ASCII, record-based file format.

Tip   If the program to which you want to export information supports the Microsoft Access database format (MDB), you should use that format for the best results when you import the information that you exported from Project.

Exporting to text files

If you have a program that can read either a text file or a CSV file, you can export information from Project to that program. You need to save the information that you want to export as either a text file or a CSV file (also called an *ASCII, comma-delimited file*) in Project.

Note This process uses the Export Wizard and closely resembles exporting information to Excel or Access.

Follow these steps to export information to a text file:

1. Open the Project file containing the information that you want to export.

2. Choose File ➪ Save As to open the File Save dialog box.

3. Select Text or CSV, whichever format works best in the program to which you're exporting, in the Save as type box.

4. Type a name in the File name box for the file that you are exporting.

5. Click Save. The Export Wizard begins. Click Next.

6. Choose to create a new map and click Next. Project displays the Map Options dialog box, as shown in Figure 22-14.

Note If you choose to use an existing map, Project displays a list of available maps; choose one and click Next to display the Map Options dialog box. If you choose to create a new map, you won't see the list of available maps.

Figure 22-14: Select the options for the export map.

7. Select the options for the export map and click Next. You'll see one of the mapping dialog boxes; the one(s) that you see depends on the information that you chose to export. Refer back to the sections "Sending Project data to Excel" or "Sending Project data to an Access database" in this chapter for details on completing this dialog box.

8. Click Next and complete additional mapping dialog boxes as appropriate.

You can click the Save Map button to save the map that you created.

Exporting to other project management software

You can use the MPD file format to export Project 2002 information to older versions of Project. Some other project management software packages also support MPD, so if you need to export Project information to another project management software package, you can save it as an MPD file.

To export information in MPD format:

1. Choose File ➪ Save As.

2. In the File Save dialog box, open the Files of type list box and select MPD.

3. In the File name box, supply a name for the file that you want to export.

4. Click Save, and Project displays the Project Definition dialog box, which suggests a name for the Project.

5. Click Finish.

The Microsoft Project database (MPD) format has replaced the MPX format. You can use the MPD format with any program that supports either the MPD format or Microsoft Access database formats.

Saving Project files as Web pages

Suppose that you want to include information from your schedule within an HTML document — for example, as a page on a company intranet or a corporate Web site. To do so, you have to save the project file in HTML format. This process uses the Export Wizard and closely resembles exporting Project information to Excel, Access, or a text file.

To save project information in HTML format, follow these steps:

1. Choose File ➪ Save As Web Page to open the Save As dialog box.

2. Type a new filename or accept the default of your project filename with the .html extension. Click Save. Project starts the Export Wizard.

3. Choose to create a new map. Project displays the Map Options dialog box, as shown in Figure 22-15.

If you choose to use an existing map, Project displays a list of available maps; choose one and click Next to display the Map Options dialog box. If you choose to create a new map, you won't see the list of available maps.

Figure 22-15: Select the options for the export map.

4. Select the options for the export map and click any of the HTML options checkboxes. Here's what they do:

- **Export header row** — Includes the row of field titles in the HTML file

- **Include assignment rows in output** — Includes rows that contain information about resource assignments in the file

- **Base export on HTML template** — Enables you to use a template that applies a predesigned look to the HTML document

- **Include image file in HTML page** — Enables you to include a graphic file on the HTML document

5. Click Next. You'll see one of the mapping dialog boxes; the one(s) that you see depends on the information that you chose to export. Refer back to the sections "Sending Project data to Excel" or "Sending Project data to an Access database" in this chapter for details on completing this dialog box.

6. Click Next and complete additional mapping dialog boxes as appropriate.

You can click the Save Map button to save the map you create.

Figure 22-16 shows a Project file in HTML format. When you save a file in this format, you can publish the file as a Web page by using any Web page design and management software.

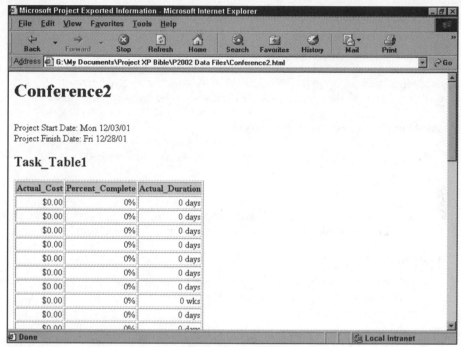

Figure 22-16: Your Web browser displays Project data saved in HTML format in columns across the page.

Importing Information

You can bring information into Project from another Project file or from Microsoft Excel, Microsoft Access, or Microsoft Word. You also can import information created in any program that can save text (TXT) files or comma-separated value (CSV) files. When you import a Project file, you actually consolidate two Project files. When you import non-Project files, you use an import/export map to define the data that you want to import.

Inserting another project

When you import one project file into another, you don't use an import/export map. Instead, importing one Project file into another Project file is the same as consolidating Project files, which you learned about in Chapter 15.

Importing Office files

You can import information from Excel workbooks, Access databases, or your Outlook Task List by using the Import Wizard and maps that define the way the information should be viewed by Project. You also can include information from Word, but you won't use the import process.

Bringing Excel workbook information into Project

Want to start your project in Excel? You can use the Excel template and then easily transfer the information from Microsoft Excel workbooks to Microsoft Project files. The Excel template automatically installs to the Office template folder (`drive:\Program Files\MicrosoftOffice\Templates\1033`) and will be available in the Templates dialog box in Excel.

New Feature   The Excel template is a new template provided with Project 2002.

Note   You can use any of the existing import/export maps to either import to or export from an Excel workbook, but you can't import an Excel PivotTable into Project.

1. Open Excel and choose File ➪ New.

2. From the New Workbook task pane, click General Templates. Excel displays the Templates dialog box shown in Figure 22-17.

Figure 22-17: You'll find the Excel template on the Spreadsheet Solutions tab of the Templates dialog box.

3. Click the Spreadsheet Solutions tab.

4. Choose Microsoft Project Task List Import Template. The workbook that you see looks like the one shown in Figure 22-18.

Figure 22-18: An Excel workbook based on the Microsoft Project Task List Import Template

Note   The first time that you use the template, you'll be prompted for your Project CD so that the template can be installed.

If you already started your project in Excel without using the template, you can still use the Import Wizard to bring your Excel data into Project. Follow these steps.

1. In Project, choose File ➪ Open or click the Open button on the Standard toolbar.

2. Open the Files of type list box and select Microsoft Excel Workbooks, as shown in Figure 22-19.

Figure 22-19: Set the type of file that you want to import to Microsoft Excel Workbooks.

3. Use the Look in list box to navigate to the folder containing the Excel workbook that you want to import.

4. Highlight the workbook and click Open. Project starts the Import Wizard.

5. Click Next. In the Data Type dialog box, click "Only selected data."

If you choose Project Excel Template, Project will ask how you want to import the file — as a new project, appended to the active project, or merged with the active project. After you make your selection, Project will import the data.

6. Click Next. In the Map dialog box, choose New map.

If you choose Use existing map, Project will display the list of maps from which you can choose. After you select a map, Project will import your data.

7. Click Next. In the Import Mode dialog box, choose "As a new project."

If you select "Append the data to the active project," Project will import the data and place it after any existing tasks in the Project file. If you select "Merge the data into the active project," you'll complete Steps 8 and 9, but in the Task Mapping dialog box, you'll click the Set Merge Key button to identify the field found in both the Excel file and the Project.

8. Click Next. In the Map Options dialog box, select the types of data that you want to import, as shown in Figure 22-20.

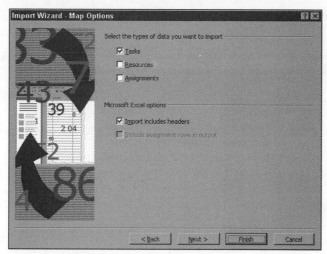

Figure 22-20: Select the types of data that you want to import.

9. Click Next. If necessary, make changes to the Task Mapping dialog box, as shown in Figure 22-21.

Figure 22-21: The Task Mapping dialog box shows the fields that Project expects to import from your workbook.

For a complete list of the function of each field in this dialog box, see the "Sending Project data to Excel" section earlier in this chapter.

10. Click Next. You'll see the final box of the Export Wizard, in which you can elect to save the map that you just defined.

If you selected Resources and Assignments as well as Task fields on the Map Options dialog box (shown previously in Figure 22-20), when you click Next, the Export Wizard displays additional boxes almost identical to the Task Mapping dialog box but for each of these data types.

11. If you elect to save your map by clicking the Save Map button, Project displays the Save Map dialog box. Provide a name for the new map in the "Map name" text box.

Bringing Access database information into Project

Importing Access databases into Project is similar to importing Excel workbooks except that you can import all or part of an Access database into a Project file. Again, you use an import/export map to describe to Project the type of data that you're importing. If the map that you need doesn't exist, you must create it; earlier in this chapter, you learned how to create maps.

To import some or all of an Access database into Project, follow these steps:

1. Choose File ➪ Open or click the Open button on the Standard toolbar.

2. Open the Files of type list box and select Microsoft Access Databases.

3. Use the Look in list box to navigate to the folder containing the Access database you want to import.

4. Highlight the database and click Open. Project starts the Import Wizard.

5. Click Next. In the Map dialog box, choose New Map.

If you choose Use existing map, Project displays a list of available maps from which you can choose; after you select a map, Project imports the Access file.

6. Click Next. In the Import Mode dialog box, choose "As a new project."

If you select "Append the data to the active project," Project will import the data and place it after any existing tasks in the Project file. If you select "Merge the data into the active project," you'll complete Steps 7 and 8, but in the Task Mapping dialog box, you'll click the Set Merge Key button to identify the field found in both the Excel file and the Project.

7. Click Next. In the Map Options dialog box, select the types of data that you want to import.

8. Click Next. If necessary, make changes to the Task Mapping dialog box as shown in Figure 22-22.

Figure 22-22: The Task Mapping dialog box shows the fields that Project expects to import from your workbook.

Cross-Reference

For a complete list of the function of each field in this dialog box, see the "Sending Project data to Excel" section earlier in this chapter.

9. Click Next. You'll see the final box of the Export Wizard, in which you can elect to save the map that you just defined.

Note

If you selected Resources and Assignments as well as Task fields on the Map Options dialog box, then, when you click Next, the Export Wizard displays additional boxes almost identical to the Task Mapping dialog box but for each of these data types.

10. If you elect to save your map by clicking the Save Map button, Project displays the Save Map dialog box. Provide a name for the new map in the "Map name" text box.

Bringing Outlook task lists into Project

Perhaps you started a task list in Outlook's Task List, and now you realize that your list of tasks is really a project and you need the scheduling and cost features in Project. You don't need to start over — you can import the Outlook Task List into Project. Follow these steps:

1. In Project, choose Tools ➪ Import Outlook Tasks. Project displays the Import Outlook Tasks dialog box, as shown in Figure 22-23.

2. Check the tasks that you want to import and click OK. The tasks appear in Project. If the open project already contains tasks, the Outlook tasks will be appended to the task list.

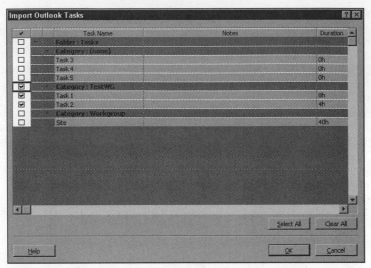

Figure 22-23: In this dialog box, mark the tasks that you want to import into Project.

Bringing Word document information into Project

Unlike other types of files, you can't import Word files directly into Project. You can, however, include information in Word documents in a Project file by using one of two techniques:

✦ You can paste information.

✦ You can link or embed information.

Pasting information from Word into Project

When you use the paste method, you can paste the information either into a table view or into a note in Project. Pasting eliminates the extra step of retyping information.

If you paste text into blank rows, Microsoft Project treats the information as new tasks or resources. If you paste information into fields that already contain information, Microsoft Project replaces the information in those fields with the pasted information. However, you can't paste information into Project fields that contain calculated values, such as some of the fields in a cost table.

Note

You can use the following technique to paste information from an Excel workbook into a Project table view, but first you must organize the information in your workbook to match the organization of a Microsoft Project table. For example, suppose that you want to paste information into a resource sheet with the Entry table applied. Your workbook has 3 columns, but the resource sheet has 12 columns; and you want to paste the information into Columns 2, 5, and 8. To paste this information, you need to create and apply a table in Project that displays only the fields that you intend to paste from your workbook. Make sure that the order and type of columns in the Project table match the order and type of information in the Excel table that you're pasting.

To paste information from Word into a Project table, follow these steps:

1. Open the Word document from which you want to copy information and then copy the information to the Windows Clipboard, as shown in Figure 22-24.

2. Switch to Microsoft Project.

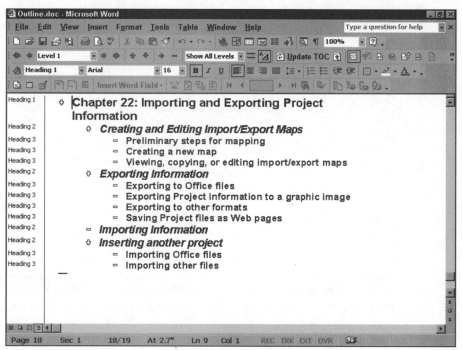

Figure 22-24: A Word document that you can paste into a Project table

3. Switch to the view into which you want to paste the information. If necessary, use the View bar to click More Views. From the More Views dialog box that appears, select the view that you need and then click Apply.

4. Pick the table into which you want to paste information by choosing View ⇨ Table ⇨ More Tables. Select the table that you want from the More Tables dialog box and then click Apply.

5. (Optional) If the table you select has columns you don't need or is missing columns you do need, then add or hide columns. Also add rows if necessary.

6. Click the first field in which you want information to appear after you paste.

7. Click the Paste button on the Standard toolbar. The information stored on the Windows Clipboard appears in the Project table, as shown in Figure 22-25.

Figure 22-25: The information from the Word document appears in Project.

You can paste information from a Word document into a note in Project by using the same technique. Copy the information in Word to the Windows Clipboard. Switch to Project and double-click either the task or the resource to which you want to add a note. In the Task Information or Resource Information dialog box that appears, click the Notes tab. Then right-click the Notes area to display a shortcut menu, shown in Figure 22-26, and choose Paste. The information from Word appears in the Notes area.

Figure 22-26: You can use a shortcut menu to paste information from the Windows Clipboard into a task or resource note.

Linking or embedding a Word document in Project

When you link or embed a Word document in Project, you actually insert the document as an object in your Project schedule:

✦ When you link a Word document to a Project file, the Project file reflects any changes that you make to the Word document.

✦ When you embed a Word document in a Project file, the Project file does not reflect subsequent updates to the Word document.

Project views objects that you insert as graphics; therefore, you can link or embed a Word document as a graphic element in any *graphics area* of a Project file. A graphics area is any area in Project that can display picture information, including task, resource, or assignment notes; headers, footers, and legends in views; headers and footers in reports; the chart portion of the Gantt view; and the Objects box in a task or resource form.

To insert a Word document as a linked or embedded object, follow these steps:

1. Open a Microsoft Project file and display the graphics area into which you want to insert a document.

2. Open the Insert Object dialog box, as shown in Figure 22-27.

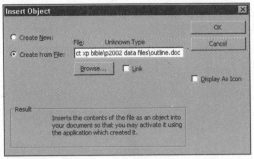

Figure 22-27: Use the Insert Object dialog box to link or embed a Word document in a Project file.

To open the Insert Object dialog box in a task, resource, or assignment note, right-click to display a shortcut menu and choose Object. To open the Insert Object dialog box in the Gantt Chart view or Objects box, choose Insert ⇨ Object.

3. Select the Create from File option.

4. Type in the path and filename of the document that you want to insert, or click Browse to locate and select the file.

5. Do one of the following:

   • To link the object to the source document, place a check in the Link checkbox.

   • To embed the object, leave the Link checkbox unselected.

6. Click OK. Project displays a graphic image of your file, as shown in Figure 22-28.

   You can use the handles around the image in the Task Information dialog box to move or resize the image.

By default, Project displays the contents of the file you insert rather than an icon representing the file. To display the object as an icon, place a check mark next to Display As Icon.

You can delete the object by making sure that you see the handles surrounding it and pressing the Delete key on your keyboard.

Figure 22-28: A Word document inserted as a graphic image in a task note

After you click OK, an icon appears in the Indicator column. When you slide the mouse over that icon, however, you won't see the contents of the note because it is a graphic image. Instead, you see a pair of single quotation marks, as shown in Figure 22-29.

Figure 22-29: When you link or embed an object in the note of a task or resource, you can't reveal the contents of the note with the mouse pointer.

Importing other files

If the information that you want to import comes from a program that can produce either text files or Microsoft Project Exchange Files, you can import that information. Text files are a common format and are also called comma-separated value files (CSV). Microsoft Project Exchange format (MPX) is an ASCII, record-based file format.

Importing Microsoft Project Exchange Files

You can use the MPX file format to import information from older versions of Project into Project 2000. Some other project management software packages also support MPX, so if you need to import information from another project management software package, you can save it as an MPX file and import it into Project.

Importing an MPX file is similar to importing an Excel workbook or an Access database.

1. Choose File ➪ Open.

2. In the Open dialog box, open the Files of type list box and choose MPX.

3. Use the Look in list box to navigate to the file and click Open.

Importing text files

If you have a program that can create either a text file or a comma-separated value file, you can import information from that program into Project. You need to save the information that you want to import as either a text file or a CSV file in the native program. The Import Wizard will walk you through the process; if the map that you need doesn't exist, you need to create it.

Follow these steps in Project to import the information:

1. Choose File ➪ Open or click the Open button on the Standard toolbar.

2. Open the Files of type list box and choose Text (*.txt) or CSV (*.csv).

3. Use the Look in list box to navigate to the folder containing the file you want to import.

4. Highlight the file and click Open. Project starts the Import Wizard.

5. Choose an existing map or create a new one. See the "Bringing Excel Workbook information into Project" section earlier in this chapter for details.

Troubleshooting

Importing and exporting can be tricky operations. Little things go wrong that cause these operations to fail. This section suggests ways to solve some of the problems you may encounter while importing or exporting.

Project imports incorrect times in data from Microsoft Excel

In Excel, when you assign a date to a cell, Excel assigns a default time to the cell of 12:00 a.m. You may not see that time, but Excel has attached it to the cell. If the data you import from Microsoft Excel to Microsoft Project contains dates without specific times, Project automatically uses Excel's default time of 12:00 a.m.

Linked or embedded objects don't import or export

You're not imagining things; Project does not import or export linked or embedded objects when exchanging data with Microsoft Excel, Microsoft Access, HTML, MPX, or text files. You need to re-link or re-embed the objects again after you complete the import or export operation.

The export file contains more or less information than expected

The information you find in your exported file depends on the import/export map you select, the table you choose, and the filter you apply. If you export more or less information than you expect, check the map, table, and filter. Choose File ➪ Save As and specify a filename and file type to display the Export Format dialog box. Highlight the map that you want to use and click Edit. Click the appropriate mapping tab; then use the map to inspect the fields you selected for export, the table you selected, and the filter you applied.

Project imports invalid information

Project checks data that you import to ensure that the data types for each field are valid. If necessary, Project may modify the values of some fields to handle inconsistencies.

If Project warns that you are trying to import invalid data, check the import/export map you've selected to make sure you are importing the correct type of information into a Project field. Also check the data in the import file and make sure that the field values are valid and within the acceptable range for the Project field into which you intend to import the data.

The values of imported information change

This situation is similar to the previous one, where Project determines that the information you're trying to import is invalid. Project checks (and changes, if necessary) the data that you import to ensure that the data types and the values for each field are valid. Project may also change data to make sure that it falls within ranges valid for Project fields and won't create inconsistencies between fields that depend on each other. Project also overrides values you attempt to import into calculated fields by replacing the imported data with the calculated value.

The imported project is empty

As you know, importing depends on the import/export map that you select. If you choose the wrong map, no data may import. Also, make sure that you're looking at the correct view after importing. If you import task information, you may not see it if you're looking at a resource view.

Project displays imported information in the wrong fields

When imported information appears in the wrong Project field, you should check the import/export map. Make sure that you select the correct map and that the table you used contains the correct fields. Finally, check the mapping of the fields between the import file and your Project file.

Summary

In this chapter, you learned how to import and export information in Microsoft Project. You learned to

✦ Create and edit import/export maps

✦ Export information to Excel, Access, and Word

✦ Export information to graphics files, text files, HTML files, and other project management software files

✦ Import information from another project; from Excel, Access, or Word; or from text files

✦ Solve common problems that occur when you export or import information

✦   ✦   ✦

Project Case Studies

In this chapter, I provide nine case studies featuring the use of Project 2000 — sometimes in conjunction with an add-on product — to solve real-life problems. Also, I deliberately included cases that run the gamut from small businesses to large corporations. For example, in one case you'll read about a non-profit organization that used Project to solve a problem.

Note　Although Project 2000 was used (Project 2002 wasn't available when these cases were written), the subject matter will still apply to Project 2002 — and in some cases, Project 2002 will provide ways to enhance some of these solutions.

Case 1

The challenge that faced this Fortune 100 company was met jointly by Ray Coker and Neal Boring of The Southern Project Group.

Problem statement

One division within a major Fortune 100 company in the aerospace industry made the corporate decision to use Microsoft Project to support widely adopted project management practices. After a close look at Microsoft Project, they found that it didn't calculate certain factors the way that the company needed. Specifically, the company wanted to report on progress on a summary level, have progress bars drawn on the summary task bars, and calculate the SPI (Schedule Performance Index) metric to support the green light/yellow light/red light–reporting model that they use.

When calculating Percent Complete duration on a Summary Task, Microsoft Project weighs and averages durations of detail tasks below summary task without considering the effort (work) involved. For example, Project weighs a 3-day task that takes 5 hours of effort as heavily as a 3-day task that takes 50 hours when calculating Percent Complete on a Summary Task.

The company preferred to view Percent Progress rather than Percent Complete on Gantt Charts. In the mathematical model that the company developed, Percent Progress considers both the duration of a task and the effort involved, and calculates SPI, the Budgeted Cost of Work Performed (BCWP)/Budgeted Cost of Work Scheduled (BCWS). Project contains the information to calculate SPI but doesn't calculate it.

Problem solution

Figure 23-1 demonstrates Microsoft Project's method for displaying Percent Complete, and Figure 23-2 shows the solution created for the company by Ray Coker of Project Direct and Neal Boring of The Southern Project Group. As you can see from the figures, there is a significant difference between Percent Complete and Percent Progress.

The solution that Ray and Neil produced was a collection of menus and toolbars that managed the process for updating and reporting in Microsoft Project and the actual analysis or math in Excel. In other words, updated Project data was mapped to Excel, where formulas that calculate SPI, supplied by the company, are applied to the data. Finally, the data calculated in Excel is brought back into Project, updating the project for the company's reporting criteria.

Figure 23-1: Microsoft Project's method for displaying Percent Complete shows that 63 percent of the project is complete.

Figure 23-2: The solution created for Lockheed shows a significant different between Percent Complete and Percent of Progress.

An official for the company comments on the solution: "Microsoft Project, customized with our Schedule Tracking Tool, has provided our company with valuable tools that are used weekly to report progress against plan."

Problem solvers

Ray Coker
Project Direct
4523 Azeele Street West
Tampa, FL 33609
Phone: 813-282-8246
Email: ray@projectdirect.com

Neal Boring
Southern Project Group
11206 Big Canoe*461 Chestnut Rise Trail
Jasper, GA. 30143
Phone: 706-268-2154
Email: rneal@mindspring.com

Case 2

The challenge that faced the Nebraska Arts Council was met by Barbee Davis of Davis Consulting.

Problem statement

Education budget cuts have, for the most part, been felt most strongly in the arts programs of most schools. Many schools have lost their music or art programs entirely or those programs have been cut back significantly. The Nebraska Arts Council received substantial grant money to be used to find a way to make arts basic to education through teacher education and school reform. The Nebraska Arts Council decided to use the money to re-educate classroom teachers at six schools to include the arts as part of the typical classroom curriculum — as opposed to relying on schools to provide separate arts programs. Initially, the Nebraska Arts Council ran into some challenges while trying to organize an effective approach to meet all of the requirements of the various grant providers. So, Barbee Davis of Davis Consulting was hired as a project consultant to help the Nebraska Arts Council clarify and meet their goals.

Problem solution

Using the process in Microsoft Project for planning a project, Davis Consulting met with the Nebraska Arts Council, and together they clarified the charge of the Nebraska Arts Council: to aid teachers in producing curriculum units that included visual arts selections, and to help produce a plan to sustain the production and use of curriculum units in the coming years when the funding was no longer available. In particular, they decided that they had to deal with four distinct issues:

✦ Ensure that the teachers finished the curriculum units as their final product to meet the grant requirements.

✦ Motivate the teachers.

✦ Get administrators to buy in and support the project.

✦ Create a plan for sustaining the project.

To meet the first goal, the Nebraska Arts Council chose a curriculum writing process and set up a "teach the teacher" program, in which several "mentor" teachers were trained. Then, the teachers attended a series of four classes/workshops where they learned a formal curriculum process and actually began to write their units under the supervision of their mentors.

To meet the second goal, the Nebraska Arts Council kicked the year off by offering up to ten people at each school a $400 trip to London to view the actual art pieces that the teachers were using in their curriculum units. The teachers paid $200 at the beginning of the year and signed a contract in which they agreed to produce the curriculum units. The terms of the contract stated that, if the teachers met a series of performance goals during the year, they would pay the balance of the money due — (another $200) and the grant money would fund the rest of the trip.

To meet the third goal, the Nebraska Arts Council decided to allow each school involved in the program to send up to eight teachers and two administrators to London. The administrators had their own series of activities to complete to qualify for the trip.

To meet the fourth goal, the teachers put their units on a Web site for all Nebraska teachers and agreed to mentor other teachers to help develop additional curriculum units. They agreed to teach their curriculum units throughout the upcoming school year.

Davis Consulting and the Nebraska Arts Council created a plan in Microsoft Project and tracked and reported on the progress systematically. It was a great success: Every goal was met and the morale for the year was higher than it had ever been. Teachers who had been bored and some who had never really understood what the project was all about were awakened and involved.

Figure 23-3 shows a portion of the Gantt Chart that was used for this project. Each teacher was set up as a subproject within the overall project and most of the dates had "Must Finish On" constraints — the final date was the trip to London. Each teacher's requirements were listed separately and not merged to an entire project, because the successful completion of the project didn't depend on each person completing his or her individual activities. If a teacher fell behind or dropped out of the program, other teachers signed up as alternates and stepped in.

In this case, Project wasn't used in the traditional way — to set up task dependencies and determine a critical path to figure out when the project would end. Instead, Project was used to track tasks that needed to be completed by each teacher and by specified dates; if a teacher didn't complete the tasks, he or she was dropped from the program, but the project continued along.

This example is an important one because users of Microsoft Project often narrow their thinking to believe that it is only useful for construction, architecture, and manufacturing. In fact, it also is an extremely powerful software tool for organizing more esoteric projects and keeping them on track. Microsoft Project's feedback reports have credibility, whereas mere progress updates are soon forgotten.

Microsoft Project helped to boost enthusiasm and buy-in for the project, which is critical to the success of any project. This case, which can also be used in any business environment, demonstrates a very effective use of Microsoft Project as a model for change management.

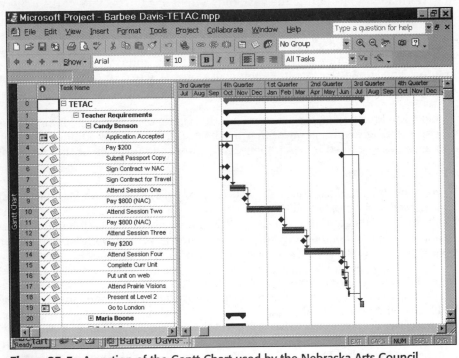

Figure 23-3: A portion of the Gantt Chart used by the Nebraska Arts Council

Problem solver

Barbee Davis
Davis Consulting
9524 Hascall
Omaha, NE 68124
Phone: (402) 397-4716
Cell: (402) 690-7066
Fax: (402) 397-1551
Email: barbeedavis@home.com

Case 3

The challenge that faced this young Webcasting services company was met by Bluewater Project Management Services, LLC.

Problem statement

In 2000, a young company that offers Webcasting services 24 hours a day, 7 days a week for radio, television, and Internet-only programming found themselves facing a new challenge. Their client base and Webcasting services had grown to such a degree that they needed to increase their Webcasting ability. To meet this need, they began constructing the largest and most advanced Webcasting facility in the Seattle area, working with proprietary hardware suppliers and installation contractors. Because they needed to complete the facility rapidly to satisfy work contracts and customers' needs, the project required in-depth management and some customized tools.

In developing their hardware and software systems, the Webcasting company chose a hardware supplier who competed on the supply side with their integration contractor. This situation required management diligence and help in understanding how to communicate project information through all parties. The integration contractor provided a schedule that described when parts would be needed, based on their integration schedule. The Webcasting company internally managed the P.O. process to get hardware on site in time for integration and at or below the budgeted price through the integration contractor. The Webcasting company began this process using a Microsoft Excel 2000 spreadsheet, listing all of the parts required, the budgeted cost, and supplier names in separate columns.

Based on the spreadsheet information, the Webcasting company used a manual process to determine when orders needed to be placed and when they would arrive on site. There were several drawbacks to this approach:

✦ The manual process was very labor-intensive and required continuous phone calls between the Webcasting company staffers, the integration contractor, and the hardware supplier.

✦ This solution required that the spreadsheet be passed around among team members to add information, thus calling into question versioning and data integrity issues.

✦ The Webcasting company staffers also lacked the time to work through the estimations to determine when P.O.s needed to be placed.

As a result, several of the first integration parts were ordered too late to be on site in time to meet the integration schedule established by the integration contractor. To help them better manage the procurement process, the Webcasting company hired Bluewater Project Management Services, LLC, to develop a custom software solution using Microsoft Project 2000, Project Central, and Microsoft Excel 2000.

Problem solution

The Webcasting company requested a system that used a familiar interface that would do the following:

✦ Give them an understanding of the hardware and software orders that needed to be completed

✦ Identify when the orders would be on site

✦ Report on this process based on the role that the individual played in the process — supplier, integration contractor, the Webcasting company employee, and project stakeholder

Bluewater worked with the Webcasting company to understand their internal and external P.O. process constraints and developed a software solution based upon these discussions. Using the Microsoft Excel spreadsheet that the Webcasting company had created, Bluewater estimated the date that each P.O. needed to be submitted for a particular part to arrive at the dock on time. After the P.O. was placed, the spreadsheet rolled forward through the process, detailing when certain activities in the process needed to be completed, and providing a more solid estimate of the delivery and testing date.

All of the information in this workbook was processed through Microsoft Project automatically and forwarded to Microsoft Project Central for reporting. This information was then customized using the Microsoft Project fields that are forwarded into Project Central, providing these users with graphical indicators of the procurement process for each part in the integration process. Each user, according to their role in the project, sees reports of project status down to the hardware part level, with the supplier seeing cost and schedule information, the integration contractor seeing schedule information only, and the Webcasting company seeing all procurement-related information.

This solution gave the Webcasting company the ability to make hardware purchasing decisions easily and in a timely manner based upon the integration schedule. The use of Microsoft Project Central allowed the Webcasting company to give information to and receive information from outside contractors and suppliers, and allows internal project participants to have a deep understanding of what is happening within the procurement process to ensure that the project, and any future projects, is on time and on budget. Through the integration of Microsoft Project 2000, Project Central, and Microsoft Excel 2000, Bluewater Project Management Services, LLC, was able to help the Webcasting company control the supply chain in their largest project to date.

Several key factors influenced the use of Microsoft Project and Project Central:

✦ **Support for Collaboration.** The Webcasting company hardware procurement solution put in place by Bluewater Project Management Services, LLC, relies on the integration of Microsoft Excel front end; Microsoft Project 2000 capabilities of OLE linking and embedding, customized fields, and graphical indicators; and Microsoft Project Central for role-based security and Web-based project reporting of delivery procurement process information to company project participants, suppliers, and contractors in an easily interpretable format. The solution also maintains the integrity of the data by allowing a single copy to be maintained and controlled by a single individual of the project team. The value of getting information out easily and quickly helps everyone stay up to date on where the project is and what needs to be done, thus giving people a better idea of where changes need to be made and when things need to be done.

✦ **Portfolio View.** With the Portfolio View, the Webcasting company employees and external participants can view rollup project information and drill down to see where individual part issues are slowing the integration project. This allows them to see how their contributions to the project affect the end date of the integration.

✦ **Field Linking.** By linking information from Microsoft Excel with Microsoft Project and Project Central, the Webcasting company staffers are able to use their familiar Microsoft Excel interface and formulas to enter and maintain information, while relying on Microsoft Project and Project Central to display this information based upon their role in the process. Microsoft Project's membership in the Microsoft Office group provides interactivity between it and other popular office productivity software pieces to aid in customizing solutions and meeting customer needs.

The solution offered the following benefits:

✦ **Quicker information dispersal.** By providing a Web-based interface with connectivity to the Webcasting company's spreadsheet, current project information can be published with the push of a button, thus making the information immediately available to all participants in the project. Changes can be made and distributed much more quickly than through previous methods.

✦ **Project status from anywhere.** Because Project Central uses a Web interface, team participants can check status information from supplier and contractor offices, on site, or on the road.

✦ **More control over data access and integrity.** Placing the project information into a single source document means that only one version of the document can exist — and no one needs to ask, "Is this the latest information?" Project Central's role-based security ensures that the appropriate people can see the information that they are meant to see, and have the appropriate rights (viewing or modifying), so change order processes are better managed.

With their hardware procurement solution, developed by Bluewater Project Management Services, LLC, on Microsoft Project 2000, Microsoft Project Central, and Microsoft Excel 2000, the Webcasting company employees have more control over the procurement process and are able to share their vital information with those who need it while still maintaining control over who has access to that data. All team members can stay informed about what is happening on the project and have a communication mechanism to share that information and maintain a rigid change control process. The Webcasting company can focus on delivering Webcasting and broadcasting solutions and know that they will have the infrastructure to meet their customers' needs.

Problem solver

Bluewater Project Management Services, LLC
S. 336th Ave., Ste. 204
Federal Way, WA 98003
Phone: (253) 874-8884
Fax: (253) 838-1798
Web: www.bluwtr.com
E-mail: bluewater@bluwtr.com

Case 4

The challenge faced by a large Asian conglomerate that needed a unique software application was met by John D. Callos of IdeaBridge — an international strategy and management consulting firm. Callos used Microsoft Project and Project KickStart — a Project add-on developed by Experience in Software.

Problem statement

An IdeaBridge client was in negotiations to sell their e-commerce company with a unique software application to a large Asian conglomerate that needed to use and integrate the IdeaBridge client's application in order to quickly establish a new market position. This project was a high-profile initiative, and it was vital that the solution/technology be integrated, checked, marketed, promoted, and launched within a three-month period.

The conglomerate's team called John Callos, Managing Director of IdeaBridge Consulting Group, to say that they were coming over in a few days to try to close a deal with his client, but that they wanted to meet him to gauge his ability to assist the integration team. They wanted Callos to be involved because of his familiarity with the product and the target market. They gave him a few scant details and asked him to have a proposed project plan and integration timeline mapped-out by the time their flight touched down in Los Angeles.

For this multi-million-dollar project, John had to be able to use Microsoft Project, which concerned him greatly; at the time, he was just a novice user of Microsoft Project.

John used the Internet to research project management approaches for a project of this magnitude and to look for some templates available for download to hit the ground running, but he wasn't able to find any that would have been viewed as an impressive platform from which to launch the project.

Problem solution

John found a program called Project KickStart that turned out to be perfect for what he needed. The program was instantly intuitive. John answered the series of questions that Project KickStart asked him, and the program then logically and simply walked him through all the project phases. The simplicity of Project KickStart was vital, because John had no time to learn anything from scratch. John's job was made even easier, because he could merge Project KickStart information instantly into Microsoft Project, which was a requirement of the project.

Within a few hours, John had a *very* detailed outline of the project plan. With this outline in hand, John augmented the plan with some bullet points he found on the Microsoft Project portion of the Microsoft Web site and other project management sites. By the time the prospective buyers had arrived, John was able to present them with an extremely detailed plan that took just a few hours to complete.

The prospective buyers were impressed with the detail of the plan and began negotiating for a role far beyond what they had initially envisioned, ultimately leading to John's full time, on-site management of the entire project team in Asia. During this time, John used Project KickStart's link to Microsoft Project to transfer his project plan to Microsoft Project and to e-mail the particulars to the team in Asia.

Using a full-time person to keep the project plan constantly updated, the project team integrated the various project plans of the technology development firm, the advertising and marketing firms, the business partners, the media people, and the opening day kick-off event planners. They developed an incredibly useful document that kept everyone on task and prevented things from falling through the cracks. The client was thrilled that they could focus on other pressing matters, knowing that the project was 100 percent under control because John had a detailed project plan that included well over 500 distinct items. Anytime this company has a similar project, they can refer to this plan and use it as a template to ensure that they have thought of everything that should be included in a project plan.

In this case, Project KickStart enabled John's firm to land a large international project with a well-known Asian conglomerate because Project KickStart helped John put together a project plan outline quickly — even before he learned Microsoft Project. And none of John's efforts were wasted because of Project KickStart's seamless integration with Microsoft Project.

Problem solvers

John D. Callos, Managing Director
IdeaBridge Consulting Group
5300 East El Prado Avenue, Suite B
Long Beach, CA 90815
Phone: (562) 986-1223
Web: www.IdeaBridge.com
Email: info@IdeaBridge.com

Experience in Software
2000 Hearst Ave.
Berkeley, CA 94709-2176
Phone: (510) 644-0694
Web: www.projectkickstart.com

Case 5

EDS provides strategy, implementation, and hosting for clients managing the business and technology complexities of the digital economy. The challenge faced by EDS was met by Tenrox, Inc. — a Quebec-based developer of business-optimization software products — using Microsoft Project and Projeca.

Problem statement

EDS, based in the United Kingdom (UK), had to track all the resources and work for the largest IT project in Europe. This project consisted of building a whole new suite of applications for a department of the British government.

During this crucial and long-term project, the most pivotal area was the need to track detailed time entries and hourly costs for 1,000 users. The reporting of these entries needed to be presented in detailed fashion on a weekly basis with minimum error and in real-time.

Problem solution

After careful considerations and evaluation of several options, Projeca, from Tenrox, was selected for four reasons: its complete, fast and live integration with Microsoft Project, it required no installation on the part of the client, it has an intuitive user interface, and it can be rapidly launched. Projeca enabled EDS to better control budgets and estimates through the life cycle at various phases of this exceptionally sizeable project. This was a key point for EDS — the decision had just been made to proceed with the use of Microsoft Project 2000 as a planning tool.

Currently, 1,000 active users are benefiting from this system. The staff is spread across six sites in the UK and others across Europe. EDS is the general contractor, but the project involves several market leaders in the IT industry.

Projeca is used to track all work — including time, labor costs, and related notes for the entire labor costs of the project. The timesheet management process has been streamlined due to Projeca's intuitive and powerful features. Projeca includes

✦ Work submission

✦ Validation and approval

✦ Compliance reporting

✦ Supervisory controls

✦ Automatic approval

✦ Notes

✦ Document attachments

✦ Work assignment

✦ Regional holiday

✦ Overtime and administrative tasks processing

✦ Constraints

✦ Validations

✦ Usage rules with full compliance for the European Time Directives

The cost and revenue accounting engine has provided the flexibility required to support rate dependencies and history (defined for general conditions and overridden for special cases). EDS can define rate rules for fixed, hourly, daily, and custom rates, as defined at various Work Breakdown Structure (WBS) and Organization Breakdown Structure (OBS) levels.

The benefits have been tremendous: The software was rolled out completely in a matter of weeks, and the entire project staff now consists of just two people who have no difficulties managing over 150 project plans — each produced by individual managers. The previous full-time and temporary staff consisted of approximately ten people who would manually enter all the time and related information into a Microsoft Project plan or a high-level Excel spreadsheet. Their entire cost and time reporting, which used to take roughly four working days to fully compile, now takes approximately 14 seconds in precisely the same format that EDS was using previously. The software runs with 100 percent uptime.

Problem solver

Tenrox, Inc.
600 Boulevard Armand-Frappier
Laval, Quebec
Canada, H7V-4B4
Web: www.tenrox.com/
Phone: (450) 688-3444
Fax: (450) 688-7862

Case 6

The challenge faced by this Fortune 100 company was met by Project Assistants, Inc. — a Microsoft Project Certified Partner based out of Wilmington, Delaware.

Problem statement

The IT division within a major Fortune 100 company was looking for a way to collect project management metrics data in a more consistent, accurate, and automated fashion. This data would be used to support trend analysis across all the projects within the organization. The company had initiated other programs previously to collect project management metrics, but these programs were always very time-consuming and created a lot of additional work for the project managers.

Project Assistants convinced the company to standardize on the use of Microsoft Project by demonstrating how the company would be able to collect the project management metric data directly from within Microsoft Project — without changing the current process used by the project managers. In this way, current work processes in Microsoft Project wouldn't be interrupted.

In particular, the company wanted to

✦ Collect metric data on schedule and work variances throughout the life of a project. This data would allow management to identify why some projects finish behind schedule or over budget and in turn improve the estimating accuracy over time.

✦ Collect methodology compliance data to determine whether a correlation existed between overall project quality, when project managers closely followed the standard methodology tools, and procedures that the organization had invested heavily in developing.

Problem solution

To solve these problems, Project Assistants developed a COM add-in to collect key metric data directly from within Microsoft Project, as shown in Figure 23-4. To address the company's first business requirement, the COM add-in collects metric data on schedule and work variances throughout the life of a project. The system calculates the finish variance and work variance at key stages of a project, and if the variance exceeds the allowed tolerance (e.g., 10 percent), the project manager must enter the reason for the variance being out of tolerance.

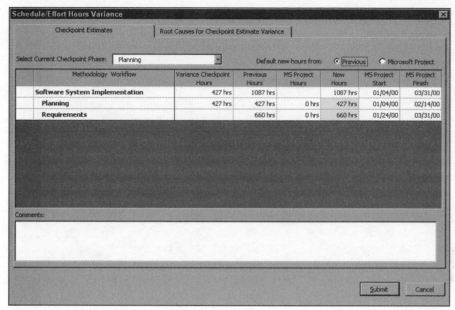

Figure 23-4: The COM add-in developed by Project Assistants collects metric data on schedule and work variances.

To address the company's second requirement, the COM add-in collects methodology compliance information, thus allowing project managers to map their project to one of the approved methodologies and in turn associate the required deliverables for the methodology to their corresponding tasks in the Microsoft Project plan. For example, the "Conceptual Data Model" deliverable would be mapped to the task "Create Conceptual Data Model" in the project plan, as shown in Figure 23-5. The metrics collection tool allows the project manager to report the status of these required deliverables to management, as well as provide a reason why the project manager may have chosen not to follow an approved methodology at certain points in the project.

The COM add-in also includes an automated status-reporting module that allows project managers to complete a questionnaire that focuses on key project management factors, such as scope, budget, and risk. Based on the answers to the questions, the project manager receives a "red light," "yellow light," or "green light" for his or her project, as shown in Figure 23-6. In this way, the company can measure the "health" of a project in a consistent and standard way throughout the organization.

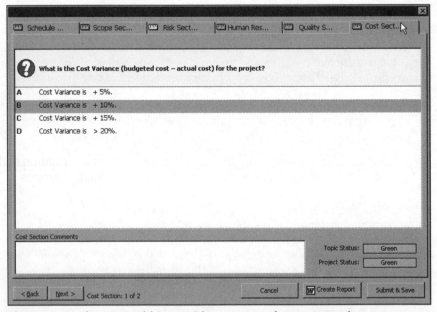

Figure 23-5: The same COM add-in collects methodology compliance information.

Figure 23-6: The COM add-in provides automated status reporting.

Problem solver

Project Assistants, Inc.
1409 Foulk Road, Suite 200
Wilmington, DE 19803
Phone: (302) 477-9711
Fax: (302) 477-9712
Web: www.projectassistants.com
E-mail: ibrown@projectassistants.com

Case 7

BCE Emergis caters to a client list that includes leading banks, insurance companies, and healthcare companies across North America, developing sophisticated
transaction-based Web applications to transform their customers' business processes and provide them with a competitive edge in the global economy. The challenge faced by BCE Emergis was met by Tenrox, Inc. — a Quebec-based developer
of business-optimization software products — using Projeca and Microsoft Project.

Project statement

BCE Emergis has enjoyed tremendous success in quickly growing its business to
2,000 employees, but this growth has been accompanied by challenges. After several company acquisitions and offices in Montreal, Toronto and Greensboro, North
Carolina, BCE Emergis quickly found itself with a mixture of multilingual reporting
systems being used by its project managers. Because the company did not have a
standardized bilingual management system in place to measure each project's time
allocation and budget cost center, reporting results had to be manually combined
and analyzed — a time-intensive and tedious effort.

Upper management found it very difficult to consolidate project information and
track profitability. Management had no tools or metrics to reorganize groups
according to workload and to improve productivity. Additionally, project managers
were only able to track the amount of time spent on a project — as opposed to
being able differentiate overtime hours.

BCE Emergis sought an affordable and easy-to-use turnkey solution that was
designed to handle time management and expense management and would be
compatible with all leading ERP, CRM, Project Management, Payroll, and accounting
systems.

Project solution

Projeca — an out-of-the-box, pure HTML system developed by Montreal-based Microsoft Certified Partner, Tenrox — automates, optimizes, and helps standardize paper-intensive and time-consuming administrative tasks. Designed for integration with Microsoft Project (used by the majority of BCE Emergis project managers), Visual Basic, C++, SAP, and other popular systems, Projeca's deployment and implementation was painless and saved the company countless hours of training and replicating data. It also provides 250 reports that can be modified by using other software and allows users to create new reports with ease.

Problem solver

Tenrox, Inc.
600 Boulevard Armand-Frappier
Laval, Quebec
Canada, H7V-4B4
Web: www.tenrox.com/
Phone: (450) 688-3444
Fax: (450) 688-7862

Case 8

The challenge facing Longs Drug Stores was met by Sicun Management Group, Inc., using Microsoft Project and Project KickStart.

Problem statement

Longs Drug Stores' Human Resources Department had to implement a new Human Resources Information and Payroll System (HRIS) while going through an acquisition and conducting business as usual. For Longs, a delay in deploying the HRIS system was not an option for two primary reasons:

✦ The system was linked to a massive HR re-engineering effort that would bring a new information system to the $3 billion company and its 16,000 employees.

✦ The existing HR/payroll system was almost 30 years old, had no additional capacity, and had year 2000 problems that couldn't be fixed, thus placing the majority of the burden for human resources on individual operating managers.

Problem solution

To ensure the success of this massive project, skeptical operating managers had to buy in to the transformation. Input from all participants involved in the project plan was paramount; with this concept in mind, a steering committee and a working staff group — both composed of representatives of operations and Human Resources — were established, and brainstorming sessions began.

Sally Cabbell of Sicun Management Group, Inc., used Project KickStart — a project planning tool that links to Microsoft Project — in order to capture ideas during brainstorming sessions. Project KickStart is ideal to use when a group is providing input; it allows for easy and rapid entry of Phases, Tasks, Resources, Notes, and some timing.

During the dynamic brainstorming sessions, Sally projected Project KickStart on a screen so that the task forces could see their ideas being captured. When the group was satisfied with their work each day, Sally printed the Project KickStart plan and each member of the group took away a beginning project plan. In this way, project-management discipline was introduced into a segment of the organization where project plans had never before been used.

Sally then dumped the Project KickStart data into Microsoft Project, where the more sophisticated project planning of resources, timing, dependencies, and baselines can be captured. Project KickStart fed beautifully into a Microsoft Project plan.

Microsoft Project was then used throughout the project, which lasted about 18 months. At the end of the project, the HR functional operations were completely transformed, including reassigned responsibilities and staffing the key jobs with new, internal operations people who were taught HR during the long transformation process.

The success of this project proved to the participants that managing change is a logical, methodical, carefully planned activity; and when done well, everyone benefits and no one loses — even when sweeping changes are implemented. Careful planning and rigorous management of the plan does not have to be disruptive, but can actually improve productivity without the pain of an unproductive period due to the change.

Problem solvers

Sicun Management Group, Inc.
2255 Morello Ave., Suite 166
Pleasant Hill, CA 94523
Phone: (925) 288-8755
Fax: (925) 735-8071
E-mail: scabbell@sicun.com

Experience in Software
2000 Hearst Ave.
Berkeley, CA 94709-2176
Phone: (510) 644-0694
Web: www.projectkickstart.com

Case 9

The challenge faced by a North American services group of a major Fortune 500 technology company was met by Joe Kovacs of Ciber, Inc., using Project and WBS Chart Pro — created for use with Microsoft Project by Critical Tools of Austin, TX.

Problem statement

The services group of a major Fortune 500 technology company found themselves facing a weakened financial position due to a downturn in both the economy and their competitive position in the marketplace. Cash flow was critical to keep them afloat through the implementation of an aggressive turnaround strategy — it had been determined that millions of dollars in revenue were going unbilled due to a lack of process capability and inadequate systems. The financial process improvement program team was challenged with redefining the billing process and implementing systems enhancements to improve the company's ability to identify and bill previously unbilled revenue.

The team analyzed the root causes of the billing problems and identified a number of countermeasures to address them, including process improvements, training, and systems enhancements. The challenge was to develop and implement a program in which multiple teams and organizations within the company would execute the countermeasures in a coordinated fashion. To further complicate matters, a project of this scope and magnitude would have taken 12 to 18 months to implement, but the team was given only 6 months to complete the task. Initial planning was haphazard at best, and the need for an experienced program manager with the right project management tools quickly became apparent.

Problem solution

Joe Kovacs of Ciber, Inc., was called in as a consultant to manage the project across the United States. Prior to his arrival, the client company's team had begun entering hundreds of tasks related to the various countermeasures into Microsoft Project. Joe's first step was to produce a work breakdown structure. It was difficult to comb through hundreds of tasks in Microsoft Project, but with WBS Chart Pro, he was able to look at the tasks entered in Project in a graphical view. Items such as duplicate tasks, task dependencies, and incorrect hierarchical organization were easier to spot and correct. Using the highly customizable graphical views offered by WBS Chart Pro, he was able to utilize the previously entered tasks along with newly identified tasks to create 99 percent of the work breakdown structure much more quickly than by using Microsoft Project alone.

Joe's solution was to organize the project into countermeasure groups, such as Process, Training, and System Enhancements. He rearranged the tasks that the team had entered into Microsoft Project, deleting any duplicates, and then he updated dependencies and hierarchical organization. After he had a fairly complete WBS, he was able to take subsets of it to each team leader for validation and negotiation of his or her commitments. He was also able to use the graphical views in WBS Chart Pro to communicate the complexity of the project to the client company's senior leadership. Joe then used Microsoft Project to track and report project progress.

Problem solvers

Joe Kovacs
Ciber, Inc.
345 Woodcliff Drive
Fairport, NY 14450
Voice: (716) 385-7710
Web: www.ciber.com
E-mail: jkovacs@ciber.com

Jim Spiller
Critical Tools
8004 Bottlebrush Dr.
Austin, TX 78750
Voice: (512) 342-2232
Web: www.criticaltools.com

Summary

In this chapter, you've had an opportunity to read about some real-life situations in which Project helped provide a solution. The cases covered a variety of industries, including some where you wouldn't expect Project to be used.

✦　　✦　　✦

What's on the CD-ROM

The CD-ROM that accompanies this book contains demos or demonstration/trial versions of several popular add-on products for use with Microsoft Project. In addition, this CD-ROM includes sample files for three of the most common types of projects that you can use as time-savers when you begin building similar schedules. You'll also find this book in Adobe Acrobat Reader (.PDF) format — along with Adobe Acrobat Reader — and a Web page of links to some Project partners.

If you have AutoRun enabled on your computer, the CD should load automatically; you'll see an HTML interface with hot links to view various components on the CD. If you don't have AutoRun enabled (or if you prefer to navigate on your own), you can view the contents of the CD manually; and you'll find the contents of the CD organized into folders.

Software on the CD-ROM

This appendix describes the contents of the CD-ROM and, where necessary, gives instructions for installing programs on your computer. You can use the demo versions of these products to see how they fit your needs. Each listing includes contact information so that you can buy the software directly from the vendor.

Note   In some cases, these vendors did not have the fully updated version of their software for Project 2002 prepared in time for this book's publication. If you have access to Project 2000, you can test the early version and then order the Project 2002 version. If you no longer have access to Project 2000, you can contact the companies to get an updated demo or more product information.

PDF

You'll find a .PDF file of this book on the CD. You can use this file to electronically search for topics in the book. You'll also find a .PDF file of the forms in Appendix B of this book, which you can use to help you plan your project. You can read .PDF files with Adobe Acrobat Reader, which you'll also find on the CD-ROM. If you open either file in Adobe Acrobat Reader, you can easily search for topics or print the forms.

Project 2002 Bible Web page

Last, but certainly not least, you'll find the Project 2002 Bible Web page. This is a Web page of links to the sites of Microsoft Project partners who offer software that enhances Microsoft Project and assistance in using Microsoft Project, as shown in Figure A-1. At several of the Web sites, you'll find Web-based demo products.

Figure A-1: A sample of my Web page that you'll find on the CD-ROM of this book

Empire TIME

The Windows Support Group, Inc.
150 West 22nd St.
New York, NY 10011
Phone: (212) 675-2500
Web: www.wsg.com

Installation instructions: On the main screen of the Microsoft Project 2002 Bible CD, click the Empire TIME. Follow the onscreen prompts to install the demo version of the program. Installation creates a Demo folder on your hard drive and an Empire TIME Demo group on the Programs menu. You can uninstall the demo by running unInstallSHIELD from the same Empire TIME Demo group.

Running the program: To run Empire TIME from the Windows Start menu, choose Programs ➪ Empire TIME Demo ➪ ETDemo.

You can use Empire TIME, a multicurrency project time and expense accounting system, for internal chargebacks or external billing. Empire TIME is a high-performance, Windows-based client/server system that integrates with Microsoft Project, allowing managers to analyze time, staff assignments, costs, and revenue on their projects. Empire TIME is distinguished by its robust accounting capabilities for tracking and invoicing actual cost and revenue for time, expenses, services, and materials.

Innate Info

Innate, Inc.
Saracens House, 25 St. Margarets Green
Ipswich, Suffolk
England IP4 2BN
E-mail: mikew@innate.co.uk
Phone: +44 1473 251550

Running the demonstration: On the main screen of the Microsoft Project 2002 Bible CD, click Innate Info. The demo will run correctly in Internet Explorer 4 or Netscape 4 or later. Follow the onscreen links and prompts to see the demonstration and more information.

Innate Info works with Innate products to publish your data for staff and managers to view as a web of information (via browsers or via printers). Exception reports and progress reports, from top-level views to the finest level of detail, can all be produced automatically.

Innate Timesheets

Innate, Inc.
Three First National Plaza
70 W. Madison, Ste. 1400
Chicago, IL 60602
Phone: (312) 781-9674
E-mail: sales@innateus.com
Web: www.innateus.com

Running the demonstration: On the main screen of the Microsoft Project 2002 Bible CD, click Innate Timesheets. The demo will run correctly in Internet Explorer 4 or Netscape 4 or later versions. Follow the onscreen links and prompts to see the demonstration and more information.

Innate Timesheets is a simple-to-use application for use with the Web or Microsoft Windows. You record time, effort, and progress into a central open database, and Innate Timesheets gives you a wide range of reports and options to link to other corporate systems. You can automatically incorporate and update Microsoft Project plans.

Milestones Professional 2002

Kidasa Software
1114 Lost Creek Blvd., Ste. 300
Austin, TX 78746
Phone: (800) 765-0167
E-mail: sales@kidasa.com

Installation instructions: On the main screen of the Microsoft Project 2002 Bible CD, click Milestones Professional 2002. Follow the onscreen prompts to install the trial version of the program. (Note that no serial number is required to install this trial version.) When you are asked to enter this number, remove any characters from the Program Key field and type **Eval** to proceed.

Running the program: Milestones Professional 2002 trial version is Project 2002–compatible. To run Milestones Professional 2002 from the Windows Start menu, choose Programs ➪ Milestones Professional 2002.

Milestones Professional 2002 is a front end for Microsoft Project. You can enter and manage project data in Milestones and then move (export) it into Project. You can also import Project data to Milestones. This approach enables you to better control the display of some Project data because you can make settings for the number of tasks per page, column and page layout, and OLE linking and embedding.

You also can use Milestones Professional 2002 as a stand-alone scheduler for creating and updating simple Gantt or timeline schedules without using the resource management features of Project.

PERT Chart EXPERT

Critical Tools
8004 Bottlebrush Dr.
Austin, TX 78750
Phone: (512) 342-2232
Web: www.criticaltools.com

Installation instructions: Connect to the Internet. Then, on the main screen of the Microsoft Project 2002 Bible CD, click PERT Chart EXPERT. You will be prompted to download another file; after the download completes (the file is approximately 2MB and the length of time needed for the download depends on the speed of your Internet connection), click the Open button to install PERT Chart Expert.

Running the program: When you install this program, you can opt to add a toolbar to Project. Then simply open a Microsoft Project file and either select the PERT Chart EXPERT menu or click the toolbar button to automatically generate a PERT chart. Alternatively, you can open the program from the Windows Start menu. Choose Programs ⇨ PERT Chart EXPERT ⇨ PERT. When the program window opens, choose Tools ⇨ Microsoft Project ⇨ Project to open Project 2002.

PERT Chart Expert is a Windows-based application that enables you to create PERT charts from existing Project schedules, text files, or spreadsheets. As an add-on to Microsoft Project, PERT Chart EXPERT integrates with Project to generate presentation-quality PERT chart diagrams.

MPX Translator

Bluewater Project Management Services, LLC
S. 336th Ave., Ste. 204
Federal Way, WA 98003
Phone: (253) 874-8884
Web: www.bluwtr.com

Installation instructions: On the main screen of the Microsoft Project 2002 Bible CD, click MPX Translator. When you are prompted for a password, type **BrownsPoint** — capitalizing the *B* and *P* and leaving the rest of the letters lowercase.

Running the program: MPX Translator adds a toolbar, two export tables, and a macro to Project. After installing MPX Translator, open Project and simply use the new tools.

MPX Translator is a new product of Bluewater Project Management. Current users of Microsoft Project already know the importance of using MPX. The MPX Translator permits Microsoft Project 2000 and 2002 users to create an MPX file format to interface with other software applications.

ProjectCommander

Project Assistants, Inc.
2503 Silverside Rd., Ste. 200
Wilmington, DE 19810
Phone: (800) 642-9259
Web: www.projectassistants.com
E-mail: info@projectassistants.com

Installation instructions: On the main screen of the Microsoft Project 2002 Bible CD, click ProjectCommander.

Running the program: This self-running demo requires Windows Media Player or another similar product.

ProjectCommander combines Microsoft Project's powerful project management engine with a comprehensive and easy-to-use set of functions that make planning, tracking, analyzing, and reporting a snap. Project Commander is the first project management software product that provides a step-by-step approach to project management — leading the user down an intuitive, flexible, and reliable path. With Project Commander, you can expect to

+ Increase speed to initiate a project

+ Increase productivity as projects are managed

+ Flatten the learning curve for the users

+ Automate entry of metrics data for improved availability and accuracy

Project KickStart

Experience in Software
2000 Hearst Ave.
Berkeley, CA 94709-2176
Phone: (510) 644-0694
Web: www.experienceware.com

Installation instructions: On the main screen of the Microsoft Project 2002 Bible CD, click Project KickStart. Follow the prompts onscreen to complete the installation.

Running the program: This trial version of Project KickStart is compatible with Project 2002. Double-click the icon placed on your desktop during installation or click Start ➪ Program Files ➪ Project KickStart 3 ➪ Project KickStart 3. The first screen of this 20-day trial version gives you the option of purchasing the full program or running the trial version. From the main screen, you can start to build a project outline with Project Kickstart's easy-to-use tools.

Project KickStart is the fast, easy way to plan and organize your projects. The software's seven-step icons quickly guide you through the process of building a strategic plan. You'll consider project goals, obstacles, resources, and other "big picture" issues. Use the Project KickStart "hot-link" icon to transfer your plan into Microsoft Project. Project data will appear in MS Project's Task column, ready for scheduling.

Project Kickstart is a front-end planning tool for project managers. With Project Kickstart, you can outline your objectives, list things to do, and anticipate major project issues. The software has features to help you brainstorm, strategize, and organize the details of your project before you start to build your project schedule. An online planning Advisor and templates for project planning help you to formulate your approach to your project. Then you can seamlessly output your data to Microsoft Project.

Knowledge Central

Ira Brown
Project Assistants, Inc.
2503 Silverside Road, Suite 200
Wilmington, DE 19810
Phone: (302) 529-5700
Fax: (302) 529-7035
Web: www.projectassistants.com

Installation instructions: On the main screen of the Microsoft Project 2002 Bible CD, click Knowledge Central.

Running the Program: This self-running demo requires Windows Media Player or another similar product.

Knowledge Central delivers all the information that you need to complete a project task: the suggested inputs required to perform a task, the procedures that suggest the best practices for completing the task, and the finished outputs or project deliverables from the task. Knowledge Central is seamlessly integrated with and accessed through Microsoft Project Central's Web-based interface.

StatusReporter

Project Assistants, Inc.
2503 Silverside Rd., Ste. 200
Wilmington, DE 19810
Phone: (800) 642-9259
E-mail: info@projectassistants.com

Installation instructions: On the main screen of the Microsoft Project 2002 Bible CD, click StatusReporter.

Running the Program: This self-running demo requires Windows Media Player or another similar product.

StatusReporter is a Microsoft Project companion product from Project Assistants, which runs within the standard Microsoft Project environment. It automates the creation of status reports by extracting data directly from fields within Microsoft Project plans and dynamically building your project status report in Microsoft Word. Furthermore, through customization of the tool from Project Assistants, you can generate the status reports by using your organization's standard status reporting templates. Typical content includes issues, scope changes, risks, tasks that started or completed or should have started or completed, key tasks and milestones, schedule summary, and schedule and/or cost variance. StatusReportercan be customized to a client's specific status reporting needs and is available as an unlimited-user CPU license.

TimeSheet Professional

Best U.S. Holdings Inc.
17950 Preston Rd., Ste. 800
Dallas, TX 75252
Phone: (972) 818-3900
E-mail: tspsales@sageus.com

Installation instructions: On the main screen of the Microsoft Project 2002 Bible CD, click Timesheet Professional.

Running the program: This single-user version of TimeSheet Professional is Project 2000–compatible, but should work with Project 2002 as well. To review the program using the sample supplied data, click Start ⇨ Programs. Then click the Timesheet Professional for Windows folder. A group of icons appears; double-click Timesheet Sample Data. To use Project 2002 data with Timesheet Professional, open the Online User Guide, also found in the Timesheet Professional Folder. Click the Help Topics button and, on the Contents tab, double-click Exchanging Data.

TimeSheet Professional is an easy-to-use front end for tracking of resource time in Microsoft Project. If people working on your project don't have a copy of Microsoft Project, they can enter the time that they have spent on various tasks in TimeSheet Professional's simple calendar-like interface. The project manager can then import this information into a Project file, thus automatically updating resource effort expended on a task-by-task basis. You can also export TimeSheet information on resource time and expenses to a payroll system.

WBS Chart Pro

Critical Tools
8004 Bottlebrush Dr.
Austin, TX 78750
Phone: (512) 342-2232
Web: www.criticaltools.com

Installation instructions: On the main screen of the Microsoft Project 2002 Bible CD, click WBS Chart for Project. You will be prompted to download a file. After the download completes (the file is approximately 2MB and the length of time needed for the download depends on the speed of your Internet connection), click the Open button to install WBS Chart for Project.

> **Note**   This setup program needs access to Microsoft Project. If you are accessing Project through a network, you may not have Read/Write access to the `Global.mpt` file.

Running the program: When you install the program, you can choose to add a toolbar to Project 2002. Then open Project and simply use the toolbar to run WBS Chart. Alternatively, you can open WBS Chart from the Windows Start menu. Choose Programs ➪ WBS Chart Pro ➪ WBS Chart Pro. From the program window, choose Tools ➪ Microsoft Project ➪ Project to open Project 2002.

> **Note**   Depending on your hardware configuration, you may see messages about setup failure. However, because this is a demo, click OK or Continue; the program should install correctly. If you continue to have problems, call the tech support number that appears onscreen.

WBS Chart for Project is a planning tool that enables you to create projects by using a WBS (work breakdown structure) Chart. You can use this method to plan, manage, and display projects with a tree-style diagram. With WBS Chart for Project, you can sketch a project quickly and easily by dragging your mouse on the screen. You can then transfer the plans that you create in WBS Chart for Project directly to Microsoft Project or to any program that can read a Microsoft Project file format (*.mpp). You can also use WBS Chart for Project to automatically generate presentation-quality WBS charts from existing Microsoft Project files.

Project Sample Files

The CD-ROM also contains three sample files that give you a head start on typical projects. Copy these sample files to your hard drive, open them, save them with your own project name, and then add, delete, and change settings for the various tasks included here.

You need to create your own resources and assign them to tasks and add timing and dependency relationships between tasks. The three sample files are as follows:

✦ Publication sample file (Publish.mpp). This sample file, as shown in Figure A-2, is useful for any kind of publishing project, from a simple brochure to a product documentation manual. Phases for writing and editing content, design, layout, printing, and distribution give you the basis for your own publishing project.

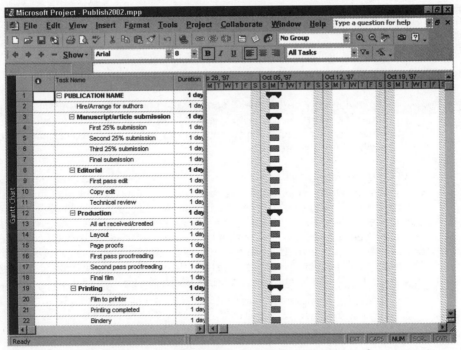

Figure A-2: Whether you're publishing product documentation or the company newsletter, many of these tasks will prove useful.

✦ Meeting sample file (`Meeting.mpp`). Everybody plans meetings. Whether it's a regular weekly staff meeting or your company's annual meeting, this sample file, as shown in Figure A-3, provides the tasks that you need to arrange for location, transportation and lodging, invitations, catering, equipment, and speakers.

Tip

Project 2002 comes with some predefined templates on which you can base projects. To use a template, choose File ➪ New and click the Project Templates tab. Like my sample files, the templates provide a starting place for projects that you enter into Project.

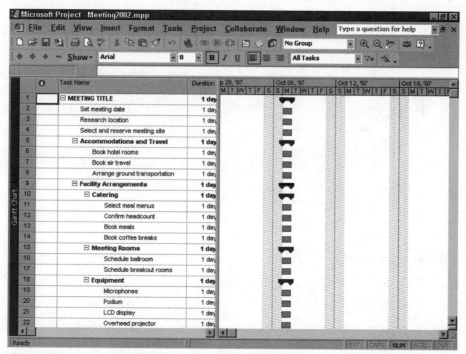

Figure A-3: All the details of arranging for meeting space, catering, equipment, and participant transportation and lodging are included here to give you a head start on planning your next meeting.

✦ Facility sample file (`Facility.mpp`). You can use this sample file, as shown in Figure A-4, to set up a new facility or to move to a new space. Tasks include planning space, coordinating movers, managing utilities, and setting up computer networks.

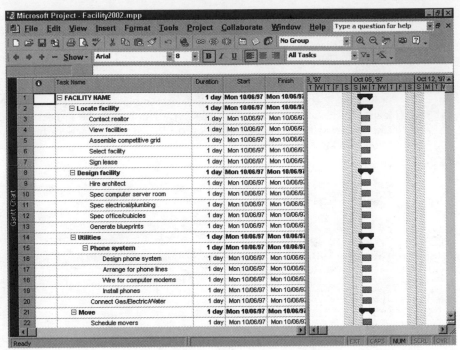

Figure A-4: Moving to a new facility or expanding an existing facility is a complex project. This sample file provides the basics.

Troubleshooting

If you have difficulty installing or using any of the materials on the companion CD, try the following solutions:

+ **Turn off any anti-virus software that you may have running.** Installers sometimes mimic virus activity and can make your computer incorrectly believe that it is being infected by a virus. (Be sure to turn the anti-virus software back on later.)

+ **Close all running programs.** The more programs you're running, the less memory is available to other programs. Installers also typically update files and programs; if you keep other programs running, installation may not work properly.

If you still have trouble with the CD, please call the Hungry Minds Customer Care phone number: (800) 762-2974. Outside the United States, call 1 (317) 572-3994. You can also contact Hungry Minds Customer Service by e-mail at techsupdum@ wiley.com. Hungry Minds will provide technical support only for installation and other general quality control items; for technical support on the applications themselves, consult the program's vendor or author.

✦   ✦   ✦

Project Management Worksheet

◆　　◆　　◆　　◆

In This Appendix

Researching your project

Planning your project

Creating your project schedule

Tracking your project

Preparing for the next project

◆　　◆　　◆　　◆

This appendix provides worksheets that allow you to plan every phase of a project. Feel free to make copies of these pages and fill them in as you work through your project to be sure you've covered all the bases.

 You can find a copy of this appendix in the *Microsoft Project 2002 Bible* Forms folder on the CD-ROM of this book in .PDF (Adobe Acrobat) format to help you print and use these forms. You'll also find a copy of Adobe Acrobat Reader.

Phase I: Research

In this phase, you gather information about the scope and goals of your project; you determine parameters, such as dates, resources, and money available for your project; and finally, you specify deliverables.

1. Ask the following people or groups of people to define the goal of this project. Note any discrepancies in their goal statements and resolve them before you begin planning your project:

   - Your manager.

   - Your staff.

   - The manager of finance.

   - The person who manages the product or service that pertains to your project. For example, if you are setting up a new manufacturing unit, contact the production line supervisor. If you are organizing the move to a new facility, contact the office or facilities manager.

Write their responses here:

_____

_____

_____

_____

2. In the space provided, sketch the organizational chart of those who will implement your project. Indicate who reports to whom within your general organization and then specifically for this project (these two hierarchies may differ slightly). Who will expect to receive reports, communications, and deliverables?

3. To help you begin to build a project team, list the resources you may have available for your project in the following table, noting each resource's department, expertise, and availability.

Project Resources Table		
Resource Department	*Expertise*	*Availability*

4. Research timing for this project and answer the following questions:

- How long have similar projects taken in your organization or your experience?

  _____

- Are any of the dates related to your project unchangeable, such as a yearly inspection by an outside organization or the end of your fiscal year? List them here. Also make note of holidays and vacation times.

  _____

  _____

  _____

  _____

- Rank the priority of the three major areas that typically affect a project: time, quality, and cost. In a crunch, the criterion that you rank highest here will take precedence.

  # ___ Time

  # ___ Quality

  # ___ Cost

Phase II: Planning

In this phase, you take some of the information that you gathered in Phase I and begin to see how those details will come together to form a project plan that can be the basis of your project schedule.

1. Write a goal statement. This one-sentence description states the desired result of all the efforts in your project. A sample goal statement may be: "Our goal is to successfully launch a new software product into the marketplace."

   _____

   _____

   _____

2. Write a scope statement. This statement should broadly outline the parameters of your project. A sample scope statement may be: "We will finalize the software according to our internal quality standards and launch it in three major markets by the end of this fiscal year at a cost not exceeding $1.2 million."

   _____

   _____

   _____

   _____

   _____

3. List the major phases of your project:

   _____

   _____

   _____

   _____

4. List any milestones in your project. Milestones are tasks that mark a moment or accomplishment in your project.

   _____

   _____

   _____

   _____

   _____

5. Create a contact list for your project, including each resource's name, title, and department; each resource's manager, contact information, hourly rate or fee; and any other information that you consider useful. You can create this list in a word processing program, such as Word for Windows, or begin to enter this resource information in Microsoft Project. Use the following entry as a model:

Resource Name: John Smith
Title/Department: Engineer/manufacturing department
Manager: Sally Jones, manufacturing manager
Phone: (444) 555-1111
E-mail: jsmith@org.com
Rate: $35 per hour
Comments: Not available in December due to professional association commitments; assistant is Bob James, ext. 5567

_____

_____

_____

_____

_____

_____

_____

_____

_____

_____

_____

_____

_____

_____

_____

_____

_____

_____

_____

6. Outline the standards that you will use for entering information into Microsoft Project, including the following:

- How will you name resources (by name or title)?

  _____

- Who will track progress and how often?

  _____

- What are your organization's standard work hours and fiscal year? This information enables you to create an accurate calendar in Project.

  _____

- What regular reports will you generate and to whom will they go?

  _____

  _____

- How will you track and account for overtime?

  _____

  _____

Phase III: Creating Your Project Schedule

In this phase, you enter information to begin building your project. Use this checklist to be sure you are creating a comprehensive and accurate schedule.

Checklist for creating a Project schedule

____   Enter general project information, such as the project name and start and finish dates.

____   Make any calendar settings for your project based on your organization's workday, week, or year.

____   Enter the names of major phases of your project.

____   Enter the first level of individual tasks in each phase, including task name and timing. If this level task will have subtasks, don't bother to enter timing because the task timing will be derived from subtasks.

____   Enter any subtasks and include timing information.

____   Enter any regularly recurring tasks, such as monthly project meetings.

____   Add resource information to individual tasks, including costs and availability.

____   Establish dependencies between tasks.

____   Study and resolve resource conflicts by using the resource leveling and contouring tools in Project.

_____ Determine whether Project is giving you an acceptable finish date. If it isn't, consider using the following actions:

- Add resources to reduce timing. (However, this action is likely to add costs.)

- Request additional time to complete the project.

- Utilize resource downtime more efficiently.

- Adjust dependencies.

- Start the project earlier.

_____ If possible, add some slack into tasks to allow for delays.

_____ Set up any workgroup resources with whom you will be using Project's TeamAssign, TeamStatus, and TeamUpdate features.

_____ When the project is acceptable, set the baseline and save the file.

Phase IV: Tracking Your Project

Tracking your project involves entering actual time expended on tasks. Use this checklist to help in tracking projects. Don't forget to set a baseline before beginning to track activity on your project.

Tracking procedures checklist

_____ Enter actual start and finish dates for tasks that have been completed.

_____ Enter resource effort expended on tasks.

_____ Enter actual fees or charges incurred on tasks.

_____ Set remaining durations and percent complete for individual tasks.

_____ Use various tracking views in Project, information about earned value and resource usage, and filters, such as critical paths, to analyze the status of your project. Pay careful attention to how much time and money remains by comparing your original estimates and actual activity on the project.

_____ Make any adjustments necessary to keep your project on track, such as adding or reassigning resources, extending your final deadline, or reassessing the remaining budget available for the rest of the project based on cost overruns.

_____ Send out TeamStatus and TeamUpdate messages to keep your team informed of project progress.

Phase V: Preparing for the Next Project

After you've completed a project, don't forget to analyze the project's activities so you can improve your estimation and tracking ability for your next project. Use this worksheet to analyze your completed project.

1. List your baseline start and finish dates and actual start and finish dates for your entire project:

   - Baseline start:_____

   - Baseline finish:_____

   - Actual start:_____

   - Actual finish:_____

2. Write a statement about the major factor that affected your timing and a conclusion about whether you could have anticipated or avoided that factor. Be honest about your own failings. It's the best way to become better at what you do.

   _____

   _____

   _____

3. Enter your baseline total costs and actual total costs for the project:

   - Baseline costs:_____

   - Actual costs:_____

4. Write a statement about the major factor or factors influencing your final costs, including what you can do to avoid cost overruns on a future project (or, if you're lucky, what you can do to have similar cost savings on future projects). What did you do or not do to keep costs in line?

   _____

   _____

   _____

5. Analyze how resources performed on your project. Are there people or vendors you would *not* recommend for use on future projects? Are there people or vendors you feel did exceptionally well? Make a record of them so that you and others in your company can plan resources for future projects appropriately.

- Vendor issues on current project:

  _____

  _____

  _____

- Recommended resources for future projects:

  _____

  _____

  _____

6. List three things you can do more efficiently as a project manager on your next project to improve performance and efficiency:

   _____

   _____

   _____

7. List three things your manager or organization could provide you to make your next project more successful:

   _____

   _____

   _____

8. List three ways you can improve your tracking procedures on future projects:

   _____

   _____

   _____

9. Write statements of what worked and what didn't work in your management of resources in these areas:

- Communication:

  _____

  _____

  _____

- Accuracy of time estimates for resources to complete tasks:

  _____

  _____

  _____

- Resource management:

  _____

  _____

  _____

◆   ◆   ◆

Available Fields and Functions for Custom Field Formulas

This appendix contains three tables that help you identify the fields and functions that you can use when creating formulas to include in custom fields. Table C-1 contains a list of all the Task fields that you can include in a formula. The fields are listed according to the submenu on which they appear when you click the Fields button in the Formula dialog box. Table C-2 contains the same information for Resource fields. In each of these tables, the first column contains a field category. The second column contains either fields within the category or a subcategory. If the second column contains a subcategory, then the fields appear in the third column. Table C-3 lists the functions that you can include in a formula, as well as a description of the function's purpose.

Table C-1
Task Fields Available for Custom Field Formulas

Category	Subcategory or Field	Field
Cost	Actual Cost	
	Actual Overtime Cost	
	ACWP	
	Baseline Cost	
	BCWP	
	BCWS	
	Cost	
	Cost Rate Table	
	Cost Variance	
	Custom Costs	Cost1 – Cost10
	CV	
	Fixed Cost	
	Fixed Cost Accrual	
	Overtime Cost	
	Remaining Cost	
	Remaining Overtime Cost	
	SV	
	VAC	
Date	Actual Finish	
	Actual Start	
	Baseline Finish	
	Baseline Start	
	Constraint Date	
	Created	
	Custom Date	Date1 – Date10
	Custom Finish	Finish1 – Finish10
	Custom Start	Start1 – Start10
	Deadline	

Category	Subcategory or Field	Field
Date	Early Finish	
	Early Start	
	Finish	
	Finish Variance	
	Late Finish	
	Late Start	
	Preleveled Finish	
	Preleveled SW	
	Resume	
	Start	
	Start Variance	
	Stop	
Duration	Actual Duration	
	Baseline Duration	
	Custom Duration	Duration1 – Duration10
	Duration	
	Duration Variance	
	Finish Slack	
	Free Slack	
	Leveling Delay	
	Remaining Duration	
	Start Slack	
	Total Slack	
Flag	Confirmed	
	Critical	
	Custom Flag	Flag1 – Flag20
	Effort Driven	
	Estimated	
	External Task	
	Group By Summary	

Continued

	Table C-1 (continued)	
Category	**Subcategory or Field**	**Field**
Flag	Hide Bar	
	Ignore Resource Calendar	
	Level Assignments	
	Leveling Can Split	
	Linked Fields	
	Marked	
	Milestone	
	Overallocated	
	Recurring	
	Response Pending	
	Rollup	
	Subproject Read Only	
	Summary	
	TeamStatus Pending	
	Update Needed	
ID/Code	Custom Outline Code	Outline Code1 – Outline Code10
	ID	
	Outline Number	
	Predecessors	
	Successors	
	Unique ID	
	Unique ID Predecessors	
	Unique ID Successors	
	WBS	
	WBS of Predecessors	
	WBS of Successors	
Number	% Complete	
	Actual Overtime Work	
	Custom Number	Number1 – Number20
	Objects	

Category	Subcategory or Field	Field
Number	Outline Level	
	Priority	
Project	Dates	Creation Date
		Current Date
		Default Finish Time
		Default Start Time
		Last Update
		Project Finish
		Project Start
		Status Date
	Numbers	Minutes Per Day
		Minutes Per Week
		Resource Count
		Task Count
	Text	Author
		Project Calendar
		Subject
		Title
Text	Constraint Type	
	Contact	
	Custom Text	Text1 – Text30
	Hyperlink	
	Hyperlink Address	
	Hyperlink Href	
	Hyperlink SubAddress	
	Name	
	Notes	
	Project	
	Resource Group	
	Resource Initials	

Continued

Table C-1 *(continued)*

Category	Subcategory or Field	Field
Text	Resource Names	
	Resource Phonetics	
	Resource Type	
	Subproject File	
	Task Calendar	
	Type	
Work	% Work Complete	
	Actual Work	
	Baseline Work	
	Overtime Work	
	Regular Work	
	Remaining Overtime Work	
	Remaining Work	
	Work	
	Work Variance	

Table C-2
Resource Fields Available for Custom Field Formulas

Category	Subcategory or Field	Field
Cost	Accrue At	
	Actual Cost	
	Actual Overtime Cost	
	ACWP	
	Baseline Cost	
	BCWP	
	BCWS	
	Cost	

Category	Subcategory or Field	Field
Cost	Cost Per Use	
	Cost Rate Table	
	Cost Variance	
	Custom Cost	Cost1 – Cost10
	CV	
	Overtime Cost	
	Overtime Rate	
	Remaining Cost	
	Remaining Overtime Cost	
	Standard Rate	
	SV	
	VAC	
Date	Available From	
	Available To	
	Baseline Finish	
	Baseline Start	
	Custom Date	Date1 – Date10
	Custom Duration	Duration1 – Duration10
	Custom Finish	Finish1 – Finish10
	Custom Start	Start1 – Start10
	Start	
	Finish	
Flag	Can Level	
	Confirmed	
	Custom Flag	Flag1 – Flag20
	Linked Fields	
	Overallocated	
	Response Pending	
	TeamStatus Pending	
	Update Needed	

Continued

	Table C-2 *(continued)*	
Category	**Subcategory or Field**	**Field**
ID	Custom Outline Code	Outline Code1 – Outline Code10
	ID	
	Unique ID	
Number	Custom Number	Number1 – Number20
	Max Units	
	Objects	
	Peak	
Project	Dates	Creation Date
		Current Date
		Default Finish Time
		Default Start Time
		Last Update
		Project Finish
		Project Start
		Status Date
	Numbers	Minutes Per Day
		Minutes Per Week
		Resource Count
		Task Count
	Text	Author
		Project
		Calendar
		Subject
		Title
Text	Base Calendar	
	Code	
	Custom Text	Text1 – Text30
	E-mail Address	
	Group	
	GroupBy Summary	

Category	Subcategory or Field	Field
Text	Hyperlink	
	Hyperlink Address	
	Hyperlink Href	
	Hyperlink SubAddress	
	Initials	
	Material Label	
	Name	
	Notes	
	NTAccount	
	Phonetics	
	Project	
	Workgroup	
Work	% Work Complete	
	Actual Overtime Work	
	Actual Work	
	Baseline Work	
	Overtime Work	
	Custom Start	Start1 – Start10
	Finish	
	Start	
	Regular Work	
	Remaining Overtime Work	
	Remaining Work	
	Type	
	Work	
	Work Variance	

Table C-3
Functions Available for Custom Field Formulas

Function Category	Function	Description
Conversion	Asc(string)	Returns an Integer representing the character code corresponding to the first letter in a string.
	CBool(expression)	Coerces an expression to a Boolean.
	CByte(expression)	Coerces an expression to a Byte (0–255).
	CCur(expression)	Coerces an expression to a Currency value.
	CDate(expression)	Coerces an expression to a Date.
	CDbl(expression)	Coerces an expression to a Double.
	CDec(expression)	Coerces an expression to a Decimal.
	Chr(charcode)	Returns a string containing the character associated with the specified character code.
	CInt(expression)	Coerces an expression to an Integer.
	CLng(expression)	Coerces an expression to a Long.
	CSng(expression)	Coerces an expression to a Single.
	CStr(expression)	Coerces an expression to a String.
	CVar(expression)	Coerces an expression to a Variant.
	DateSerial (year,month day)	Returns a Variant (Date) for a specified year, month, and day.
	DateValue(date)	Returns a Variant (Date).
	Day(date)	Returns a Variant (Integer) specifying a whole number between 1 and 31, inclusive, representing the day of the month.
	Hex(number)	Returns a String representing the hexadecimal value of a number.
	Hour(time)	Returns a Variant (Integer) specifying a whole number between 0 and 23, inclusive, representing the hour of the day.

Function Category	Function	Description
Conversion	Minute(time)	Returns a Variant (Integer) specifying a whole number between 0 and 59, inclusive, representing the minute of the hour.
	Month(date)	Returns a Variant (Integer) specifying a whole number between 1 and 12, inclusive, representing the month of the year.
	Oct(number)	Returns a Variant (String) representing the octal value of a number.
	ProjDurConv (expr, durunits)	Converts a numeric value to a duration value in the specified units.
	Second(time)	Returns a Variant (Integer) specifying a whole number between 0 and 59, inclusive, representing the second of the minute.
	Str(number)	Returns a Variant (String) representation of a number.
	StrConv (string, conversion, LCID)	Returns a Variant (String) converted as specified.
	TimeSerial (hour, minute, second)	Returns a Variant (Date) containing the time for a specific hour, minute, and second.
	TimeValue(time)	Returns a Variant (Date) containing the time.
	Val(string)	Returns the numbers contained in a string as a numeric value of appropriate type.
	Weekday (date, firstdayofweek)	Returns a Variant (integer) containing a whole number representing the day of the week.
	Year(date)	Returns a Variant (Integer) containing a whole number representing the year.
Date/Time	Cdate(expression)	Coerces an expression to a Date.
	Date()	Returns a Variant (Date) containing the current system date.

Continued

Table C-3 *(continued)*		
Function Category	*Function*	*Description*
Date/Time	DateAdd (interval, number, date)	Returns a Variant (Date) containing a date to which a specified time interval has been added.
	DateDiff(interval, date1, date2, firstdayofweek, firstweekofyear)	Returns a Variant (Long) specifying the number of time intervals between two specified dates.
	DatePart(interval, date, firstdayofweek, firstweekofyear)	Returns a Variant (Integer) containing the specified part of a given date.
	DateSerial (year, month, day)	Returns a Variant (Date) for a specified year, month, and day.
	DateValue(date)	Returns a Variant (Date).
	Day(date)	Returns a Variant (Integer) specifying a whole number between 1 and 31, inclusive, representing the day of the month.
	Hour(time)	Returns a Variant (Integer) specifying a whole number between 0 and 23, inclusive, representing the hour of the day.
	IsDate(expression)	Returns a Boolean value indicating whether an expression can be converted to a date.
	Minute(time)	Returns a Variant (Integer) specifying a whole number between 0 and 59, inclusive, representing the minute of the hour.
	Month(date)	Returns a Variant (Integer) specifying a whole number between 1 and 12, inclusive, representing the month of the year.
	Now()	Returns a Variant (Date) specifying the current date and time according your computer system's date and time.
	ProjDateAdd(date, duration, calendar)	Adds a duration to a date to return a new date.

Function Category	Function	Description
Date/Time	ProjDateDiff(date1, date2, calendar)	Returns the duration between two dates in minutes.
	ProjDateSub(date, duration, calendar)	Returns the date that precedes another date by a specified duration.
	ProjDurValue(duration)	Returns the number of minutes in a duration.
	Second(time)	Returns a Variant (Integer) specifying a whole number between 0 and 59, inclusive, representing the second of the minute.
	Time()	Returns a Variant (Date) indicating the current system time.
	Timer()	Returns a Single representing the number of seconds elapsed since midnight.
	TimeSerial (hour, minute, second)	Returns a Variant (Date) containing the time for a specific hour, minute, and second.
	TimeValue(time)	Returns a Variant (Date) containing the time.
	Weekday (date, firstdayofweek)	Returns a Variant (Integer) containing a whole number representing the day of the week.
	Year(date)	Returns a Variant (Integer) containing a whole number representing the year.
General	Choose(index, expr1, expr2, expr3)	Selects and returns a value from a list of arguments.
	IIf(expr, truepart, falsepart)	Returns one of two parts, depending on the evaluation of an expression.
	IsNumeric(expression)	Returns a Boolean value indicating whether an expression can be evaluated as a number.
	IsNull(expression)	Returns a Boolean value that indicates whether an expression contains no valid data.

Continued

Table C-3 *(continued)*		
Function Category	*Function*	*Description*
General	Switch(expr1, value1, expr2, value2, expr3, value3)	Evaluates a list of expressions and returns a Variant value or an expression associated with the first expression in the list that is True.
Math	Abs(number)	Returns a value of the same type that is passed to it specifying the absolute value of a number.
	Atn(number)	Returns a Double specifying the arctangent of a number.
	Cos(number)	Returns a Double specifying the cosine of an angle.
	Exp(number)	Returns a Double specifying e (the base of natural logarithms) raised to a power.
	Fix(number)	Returns the integer portion of a number. If the number is negative, Fix returns the first negative integer greater than or equal to number.
	Int(number)	Returns the integer portion of a number. If the number is negative, Int returns the first negative integer less than or equal to the number[CS1].
	Log(number)	Returns a Double specifying the natural logarithm of a number.
	Rnd(number)	Returns a Single containing a random number.
	Sgn(number)	Returns a Variant (Integer) indicating the sign of a number.
	Sin(number)	Returns a Double specifying the sine of an angle.
	Sqr(number)	Returns a Double specifying the square root of a number.
	Tan(number)	Returns a Double specifying the tangent of an angle.
Microsoft Project	ProjDateAdd(date, duration, calendar)	Adds a duration to a date to return a new date.

Function Category	Function	Description
Microsoft Project	ProjDateDiff(date1, date2, calendar)	Returns the duration between two dates in minutes.
	ProjDateSub(date, duration, calendar)	Returns the date that precedes another date by a specified duration.
	ProjDurConv(expr, durunits)	Converts a numeric value to a duration value in the specified units.
	ProjDurValue(duration)	Returns the number of minutes in a duration.
Text	Asc(string)	Returns an Integer representing the character code corresponding to the first letter in a string.
	Chr(charcode)	Returns a String containing the character associated with the specified character code.
	Format(expression, format firstdayofweek, firstweekofyear)	Returns a Variant (String) containing an expression formatted according to instructions contained in a format expression.
	InStr(start, string1, string2, compare)	Returns a Variant (Long) specifying the position of the first occurrence of one string within another.
	LCase(string)	Returns a String that has been converted to lowercase.
	Left(string, length)	Returns a Variant (String) containing a specified number of characters from the left side of a string.
	Len(string | varname)	Returns a Long containing the number of characters in a string or the number of bytes required to store a variable.
	LTrim(string)	Returns a Variant (String) containing a copy of a specified string without leading spaces.
	Mid(string, start, length)	Returns a Variant (String) containing a specified number of characters from a string.
	Right(string, length)	Returns a Variant (String) containing a specified number of characters from the right side of a string.

Continued

Table C-3 *(continued)*		
Function Category	*Function*	*Description*
	RTrim(string)	Returns a Variant (String) containing a copy of a specified string without trailing spaces.
	Space(number)	Returns a Variant (String) consisting of the specified number of spaces.
	StrComp(string1, string2, compare)	Returns a Variant (Integer) indicating the result of a string comparison.
	StrConv (string, conversion, LCID)	Returns a Variant (String) converted as specified.
	String(number, character)	Returns a Variant (String) containing a repeating character string of the length specified.
	Trim(string)	Returns a Variant (String) containing a copy of a specified string without leading and trailing [CS2] spaces.
	UCase(string)	Returns a Variant (String) containing the specified string, converted to uppercase.

✦   ✦   ✦

Project Management Resources

APPENDIX

D

◆ ◆ ◆ ◆

In This Appendix

Associations

Publications

Online

Software products

◆ ◆ ◆ ◆

Project management is a detailed methodology and intricate system of requirements that has evolved over many years for various industries and disciplines. Project management as a topic encompasses concepts of leadership and team building, charting and analysis of data, cost and schedule control, and more.

Many useful resources for project management information, tools, and support can help you work with Microsoft Project. This appendix contains five resource categories: Associations, Publications, Education, Online, and Software Products. It provides phone numbers and, when available, address and fax information. As you can see from this list, project management is an extremely international discipline. Remember to dial country codes before any phone number outside the United States.

Associations

The following associations provide support and information for both general and industry-specific project management issues.

> ✦ **American Association of Cost Engineers:** Counts among its membership those interested in cost engineering and cost estimating.
>
> 209 Prairie Ave., #100
> Morgantown, WV 26505
> Phone: (800) 858-COST

✦ **Association of Proposal Management Professionals:** Can assist you in developing proposals for your projects, whether you bid for government or industry contracts. APMP has local chapters, as well as a newsletter and task force on Electronic Procurement.

P.O. Box 970
Farmington, UT 84025-0970
Toll Free: (888) 772-9467
Phone: (801) 451-2323
Fax: (801) 451-4660

✦ **Association for Project Management:** Based in England, and has chapters in both the United Kingdom and Hong Kong. This association has a certification program for project management professionals.

Thornton House
150 West Wycombe Rd.
High Wycombe
Buckinghamshire, HP12 3AE, United Kingdom
Phone: +44 (0) 1494 440090
Fax: +44 (0) 1494 528937
E-mail: secretariat@apm-org.uk

✦ **American Society of Quality Control:** Focuses on quality issues in project management. This organization offers certification in a variety of specializations related to quality.

P.O. Box 3005
Milwaukee, WI 53201-3005
Phone: (800) 248-1946

✦ **CIPPM:** An international association and center of advanced communication, research, and learning for professional project managers and those interested in project management. CIPPM, founded in 1987, is a nonprofit organization based in Ann Arbor, Michigan (United States) at the University of Michigan. cippm@free.org

✦ **Construction Management Association of America**

7918 Jones Branch Drive, Suite 540
McLean, VA 22102
Phone: (703) 356-2622
Fax: (703) 356-6388

✦ **Educational Society for Resource Management:** (Formerly American Production & Inventory Control Society and still referred to as APICS) Specializes in support and information for those wanting to improve or maximize their resource management skills.

5301 Shawnee Rd.
Alexandria, VA 22312-2317
Phone: (800) 444-2742

✦ **International Project Management Association (IPMA):** A multinational nonprofit confederation of project management associations based primarily in European countries. It offers international conferences on project management.

P.O. Box 30
Monmouth, NP5 4YZ, United Kingdom
Phone: +44 1594 531007
Fax: +44 1594 531008
E-mail: ipma@btinternet.com

✦ **The Japan Project Management Forum (JPMF):** A member-driven, nonprofit organization that promotes project management professionalism in Japan.

CYD Bldg.
4-6 Nishi-shimbashi 1-chome
Minato-ku, Tokyo, 105-0003, Japan
Phone: 81-3-3539-4320
Fax: 81-3-3502-5500
Web: www.enaa.or.jp/JPMF/
E-mail: jpmf-adm@enaa.or.jp
Secretariat: Kosei Watanabe, Takayuki Kyuno

✦ **Project Management Institute:** The premier United States project management association. It has chapters across the country, educational programs, a long list of publications, and online discussion forums. In addition, PMI has a monthly magazine called *PM Network* and a quarterly called *Project Management Journal*. Its publication, *A Guide to the Project Management Body of Knowledge* (PMBOK Guide), is a bible in the project management world.

Project Management Institute Headquarters
Four Campus Boulevard
Newtown Square, PA 19073-3299
Phone: (610) 356-4600
Fax: (610) 356-4647
Web: www.pmi.org
E-mail: pmihq@pmi.org

✦ **Software Program Managers Network:** Established in 1992 by the Assistant Secretary of the Navy to identify and convey to managers of large-scale system acquisition projects proven industry and government software best practices. Operational control of the Software Program Managers Network (SPMN) transferred to the Office of the Deputy under the Secretary of Defense (Science & Technology) on March 2, 2001.

Crystal Mall 3,
1931 Jefferson Davis Highway
Arlington, VA 22202
Phone: (703) 602-0851, Ext. 105
Fax: (703) 602-3560
Email: fergusj@acq.osd.mil.

PMI Special Interest Groups

PMI offers a variety of special interest groups, or SIGs, that focus on different aspects of project management. SIG members are required to pay a small fee to support the group, and all members must also belong to PMI.

These SIGs are either currently available or under consideration:

◆ Aerospace and Defense

◆ Automotive

◆ Design Procurement Construction

◆ Diversity

◆ Education and Training

◆ Environmental Management

◆ Financial Services

◆ Government

◆ Information Management and Movement

◆ Information Systems

◆ Manufacturing

◆ Marketing and Sales

◆ New Product Development

◆ Oil, Gas, and Petrochemical

◆ Pharmaceutical

◆ Quality in Project Management

◆ Risk Management

◆ Service and Outsourcing Projects

◆ Utility

◆ Women in Project Management

Publications

A great many books, newsletters, and journals are devoted to project management and its many facets. Some of the publications in this list are from small presses or associations. You can use the ISBN number — a publishing industry code — to order many of the books from your local bookstore.

Books

The following books provide guidance on general project management principles and industry-specific project management advice.

✦ *The AMA Handbook of Project Management*
Author: Paul C. Dinsmore
Publisher: Amacom Books, A Division of AMA
ISBN: 0-8144-0106-6

✦ *Cost Estimator's Reference Manual*
Authors: Rodney D. Stewart, James D. Johannes, Richard M. Wyskida, eds.
Publisher: John Wiley & Sons, Inc.
ISBN: 0-471-305103

✦ *Effective Project Management Through Applied Cost and Schedule Control*
Authors: James A. Bent and Kenneth K. Humphreys
Publisher: Marcel Dekker, Inc.
ISBN: 0-8247-9715-9

✦ *5-Phase Project Management*
Authors: Joseph W. Weiss and Robert K. Wysocki
Publisher: HarperCollins
ISBN: 0-201-56316-9

✦ *Fundamentals of Project Management*
Author: James P. Lewis
Publisher: Amacom Books, A Division of AMA
ISBN: 0-8144-7835-2

✦ *Managing High-Technology Programs and Projects*
Author: Russell D. Archibald
Publisher: John Wiley & Sons, Inc.
ISBN: 0-471-51327-X

✦ *Project Management: Strategic Design and Implementation*
Author: David I. Cleland
Publisher: McGraw-Hill Professional Book Group
ISBN: 0-07-012020-X

✦ *Project Management for the 21st Century*
Authors: Bennet P. Lientz and Kathryn P. Ross
Publisher: Academic Press
ISBN: 0-12-449966-X

✦ *Project Management Memory Jogger*
Authors: Karen Tate and Paula Martin
Publisher: GOAL/QPC
ISBN: 1-57681-001-1

✦ *Practical Risk Assessment for Project Management*
Author: Stephen Grey
Publisher: John Wiley & Sons, Inc.
ISBN: 0-471-93979-X

Journals and magazines

Many of the associations listed in the first section of this appendix publish magazines or journals. Some of those are listed here, along with a phone number to contact for additional information. Note that many of these publications are available only to members of the organization.

✦ *APICS: The Performance Advantage*
Educational Society for Resource Management
Phone: (800) 444-2742

✦ *Computing Canada* (regular column on project management)
Plesman Publications
Phone: (416) 497-9562

✦ *International Journal of Project Management*
Elsevier Science
Phone: (212) 633-3730

✦ *Journal of Quality Technology*
American Society of Quality Control
Phone: (800) 248-1946

✦ *Project Management Journal*
Project Management Institute
Phone: (704) 586-3715

Education

Educational opportunities exist around the world for certification and degree programs in a variety of project management–related disciplines. The following are just a few of these:

✦ **Center for Management and Organization Effectiveness:** Offers workshops relating to coaching and facilitation.

245 S.E. Madison
Bartlesville, OK 74006
Phone: (918) 333-6609
Fax: (918) 333-5102

✦ **Louisiana State University:** Offers a weeklong seminar through its Department of Executive Education. Go through this seminar to prepare for the PMI certification exam that will earn you the title of Project Management Professional.

One University Place
Shreveport, LA 71115-2399
Phone: (318) 797-5000

✦ **Project Management Research Network:** Runs out of a university in Austria and supports project management educational programs at many technical schools and universities throughout the world.

Extraordinariat Projektmanagement
University of Economics and Business Administration
Franz Klein-Gasse 1 1190
Vienna, Austria
Phone: 0043 1 313 52215

✦ **The University of Calgary:** (in Alberta, Canada) Brought together its manufacturing and engineering courses to create a project management area of specialization.

Project Management Specialization
Department of Civil Engineering
The University of Calgary
2500 University Dr. NW
Calgary, Alberta, Canada T2N 1N4
Phone: (403) 220-4816

✦ **University of New England:** (in New South Wales, Australia) Offers a project management and operations management unit within its MBA degree program. You don't have to fly to Australia to take advantage of these courses (although it's a good excuse to!). The school offers these special programs throughout the world.

Phone: 61 67 733545
Fax: 61 67 733461

✦ **Western Carolina University:** Confers a Masters of Project Management degree from its College of Business.

College of Business
Cullowhee, NC 28723
Phone: (704) 227-7401
Fax: (704) 227-7414

Online

You could spend days online and never run through all the project management and project management–associated Web sites. However, the following list offers a few good places to begin surfing. Please note that Web sites and addresses change frequently; those listed here were current as this book went to press.

You'll find links to all these sites on the *Microsoft Project 2002 Bible* Web page included on this book's companion CD-ROM.

- ✦ **American Production and Inventory Control Society:** www.apics.org
- ✦ **Architecture, Engineering, Construction Business Center:** www.aecinfo.com
- ✦ **Center for Coaching and Mentoring:** http://coachingandmentoring.com/
- ✦ **Center for International Project and Program Management:** www.iol.ie/~mattewar/CIPPM
- ✦ **Earned Value Management:** Sponsored by the Office of the Under Secretary of Defense (Acquisition & Technology) Systems Acquisition/Performance Management. www.acq.osd.mil/pm
- ✦ **FedWorld:** www.fedworld.gov/
- ✦ **The Project Management Forum:** www.pmforum.org/newsindx.htm
- ✦ **Project Management Institute:** www.pmi.org
- ✦ **Project World:** www.projectworld.com/
- ✦ **Software Program Managers Network:** www.spmn.com/

Software Products

In addition to the excellent software products in demo or trial version form on the companion CD-ROM, the following section lists some other project management tools worthy of investigation:

You'll find the links to all these sites on the *Microsoft Project 2002 Bible* Web page included on this book's companion CD-ROM.

- ✦ **Project Integrator (PI):** Great for working with time and process management issues in a workgroup or team. It includes tools for planning, tracking, and reporting on individual resource time expenditures on multiple projects.

System Solvers, Ltd.
30685 Barrington Ave., Ste. 100
Madison Heights, MI 48071-5133
Phone: (810) 588-7400
Fax: (810) 588-7170

- ✦ **Innate Multi-Project:** Innate Multi-Project extends Microsoft Project to a complete program management system, giving a view across projects, offering resource capacity planning, and supporting your business processes whether top-down or bottom-up.

Innate, Inc. Saracens House
25 St. Margarets Green
Ipswich, Suffolk IP4 2BN
England
E-mail: mikew@innate.co.uk
Phone: +44 1473 251550

You'll find demos for two other Innate products on the CD-ROM that accompanies this book. Also on the CD-ROM, on the *Project 2002 Bible* Web page, you'll find a link to Innate's Web site that you can use to locate and order Multi-Project from Innate.

✦ **TurboProject:** From International Microcomputer Software, Inc. (IMSI). A higher-end project management software for design, testing, and production.

IMSI Corporate Headquarters
75 Rowland Way
Novato, CA 94945
Phone: (415) 878-4000
Fax: (415) 897-2544

IMSI (UK) Ltd
IMSI House Printing House Lane
Hayes, Middlesex UB3 1AP
England
Phone: 0181 581 2000
Fax: 00181 581 2200

✦ **Project Administration and Control System (PACS):** The project management portion of a larger financial software suite called Renaissance C/S Financial Applications. If you want to integrate your project costs into your general ledger, check this one out.

Herkemij & Partners
Cypresbaan 6
2908 LT Capelle a/d Ijssel
The Netherlands
Phone: 31 10 4580899
Fax: 31 10 4508233

✦ **Graneda:** A professional graphics add-on package with which you can create exciting project charts. The application includes extensive printer and plotter drivers for printing your charts.

American Netronic, Inc.
5212 Katella Ave., Ste. 104
Los Alamitos, CA 90720
Phone: (562) 795-0147
Fax: (562) 795-0152

✦ **Artemis:** Offers a bi-directional interface between Microsoft Project 2000 and the Artemis Views enterprise project and resource management solution. Using Artemis MSP Gateway, multiple concurrent project managers can seamlessly exchange project data directly with the Artemis Views enterprise project database. In this way, Microsoft Project becomes a complete enterprise multiproject planning, cost control, and resource management solution. With this integration, organizations have the scalability, security, and centralization of the Views client/server architecture, and Microsoft Project users can create projects by using predefined project templates, assign available resources from centralized resource pools, and track project progress by using integrated timesheets. Best of all, the Artemis MSP Gateway operates as a single toolbar inside Microsoft Project, which gets users up and running quickly.

Artemis Management Systems
6260 Lookout Rd.
Boulder, CO 80301
Phone: (800) 477-6648 (United States and Canada) or (303) 531-3145 (International)
Fax: (303) 531-3140

✦ **Cascade:** An Oracle-based project and finance management tool for senior management. This software is especially helpful in decision analysis for mission-critical projects.

Mantix Systems, Inc.
12020 Sunrise Valley Dr.
Reston, VA 22091
Phone: (703) 715-2450
Fax: (703) 715-2450

✦ **Risk +:** Integrates seamlessly with Microsoft Project to quantify the cost and schedule uncertainty associated with project plans. Anyone familiar with Microsoft Project can easily conduct a sophisticated risk analysis to answer questions such as, "What are the chances of completing this effort by 2/28/00?" or "How confident are we that costs will remain below $9 million?" or "How likely is this task to end up on the critical path?" Single point estimates for task duration and cost tend to be optimistic and provide no insight into the uncertainty associated with a task. With Microsoft Project alone, you are forced to make statements such as, "Task X will complete in 10 days." Adding Risk + allows you to make and assess the far more realistic statement, "Task X will take between 8 and 12 days to complete, and will most likely take about 10 days." With Risk +, you are able to identify the high-risk areas of your project, determine the likelihood of risk materializing, assess the impact of possible risk, and more importantly, have the information and opportunity to mitigate risk long before it impacts your project.

ProjectGear, Inc.
2522 North Proctor, #37
Tacoma, WA 98406
Phone: (253) 761-9294
Fax: (253) 761-9289

✦ **SUMMIT Process Management and SUMMIT Ascendant:** Process Management creates Microsoft Project databases using the PricewaterhouseCoopers SUMMIT method. SUMMIT PM has a Web version (SUMMIT Ascendant). SUMMIT is a set of information technology methods, such as "what and how" to deploy a new large package system or "what and how" to set up a client-server system. The software products contain these method descriptions and do process management by building Microsoft Project databases from the method's lists of "what to do" and then letting people track the status of tasks and manage their deliverable documents remotely and simultaneously. Microsoft Project fills in the "when" for the project tasks.

The SUMMIT Center of Excellence
Pricewaterhouse Coopers LLP
600 Lee Rd.
Wayne, PA 19087
Phone: (610) 993-5393

✦ **Enterprise Project:** A comprehensive software solution for multilevel, multi-project planning, optimization, and reporting. It seamlessly integrates with Microsoft Project to enhance it with tightly integrated enterprise architecture, thus adding vital functionality, such as dynamic access to enterprise resource pools, a patented skills-based resource scheduling engine, and robust executive reporting and decision support tools. Using Enterprise Project, project managers continue to work with a familiar desktop tool. Enterprise Project functions — such as access to the enterprise resource pools, skills-based search engine, current task loads, and the task status module — are conveniently accessible within Microsoft Project 2000, giving project managers maximum flexibility to rapidly develop optimal project plans.

✦ **WARP Scheduler:** Also from Enterprise Project, WARP Scheduler automatically performs resource schedule leveling and optimization based on skill qualification, best schedule, lowest cost, and other user-selectable context variables. Its adaptive engine can schedule tens of thousands of tasks in seconds, making it (by far) the fastest project management solution available on the market today. WARP can automatically and optimally assign resources based on multiple individual skills, thus dramatically increasing utilization and reducing overhead costs. WARP makes it possible to re-engineer to suit specific management criteria in seconds, thus providing a big picture of results for every "what if" scenario.

eLabor® Inc.
5153 Camino Ruiz
Camarillo, CA 93012-8601
Phone: (805) 383-8500
Fax: (805) 383.2830

✦ **Hans Tørsleff TimeReg:** A time registration system that updates Microsoft Project with Actual Work entered by the individual resource, sparing the project manager the manual update of the project plan and giving more time to the real management of the project.

✦ **Hans Tørsleff Project Manager:** Allows you to decentralize the planning of the project and resource management but maintain the bird's-eye perspective provided by a centralized project management tool. It includes reporting and a Virtual Project generator.

Hans Tørsleff Management Systems A/S
Gl. Kongevej 161
1850 Frederiksberg C
Denmark
Phone: +45 70 20 08 16
Fax: +45 70 22 08 07
E-mail: mail@htms.dk

✦ **Business Engine:** A resource management tool that helps corporations track and manage people, time, and budgets across hundreds of projects. It integrates project, timesheet, and budget information from a variety of resources.

Business Engine Software Corporation
100 Bush St., 22nd Floor
San Francisco, CA 94104
Phone: (415) 616-4000
Fax: (415) 616-4008

✦ **Project InVision 4:** A Web-based project management repository application that allows Microsoft Project users to access Microsoft Project schedules and project-related data or documents across a corporate intranet or the Internet from any computer equipped with a browser. The application's Time Tracking interface allows users to gather their task assignments from across multiple projects and submit weekly timesheets for posting to Microsoft Project schedules. Project InVision 4 is fully customizable, allowing individual workgroups to configure custom fields, define workflow, and integrate templates based on their unique processes and methodologies.

SME Corporation
1038 Redwood Hwy B7
Mill Valley, CA 94941
Phone: (888) 763-3555

✦ **Project Control:** Uses a centralized database of information about all your projects to help you control multiple projects. You can update a single project or all your projects from this database. Project Control's document manager works with applications such as Word and Excel to help you track all documents associated with a project.

Project Control Software
147 Old Solomons Island Rd., Ste. 513
Annapolis, MD 21401
Phone: (410) 897-0965
Fax: (410) 897-1135

✦ **Project Partner:** Functions as an add-on application with Microsoft Project to present the scheduling data in several very useful graphic formats. The three main options include a timescaled network diagram, an earned-value spending curve, and a resource or cash flow by period summary. Project Partner is designed to increase a project team's ability to easily communicate complex project status information.

Bluewater Project Management Services, LLC
500 S. 336th Ave., Ste. 204
Federal Way, WA 98003
Phone: (253) 874-8884
Fax: (253) 838-1798

✦   ✦   ✦

Glossary

ACWP (actual cost of work performed) Cost of actual work performed to date on the project, plus any fixed costs.

ALAP (as late as possible) A constraint placed on a task's timing to make it occur as late as possible in the project schedule, based on its dependency relationships.

ASAP (as soon as possible) A constraint placed on a task's timing to make it occur as early in the project as possible, based on its dependency relationships.

BAC (budget at completion) The total of planned costs to complete a task (also referred to as *baseline costs*).

BCWP (budgeted cost of work performed) Also called *earned value,* this term refers to the value of work completed. A task with $1,000 of associated costs, when 75 percent complete, has a baseline value of $750.

BCWS (budgeted cost of work scheduled) The planned completion percentage multiplied by the planned cost. This calculated value reflects the amount of the task that is completed and the planned cost of the task.

CV (earned value cost variance) This variance indicates the difference between the planned costs (baseline costs) and the costs after taking into account actual costs to date and estimated costs going forward (scheduled costs). The difference between these two values produces either a positive (over-budget) or negative (underbudget) cost variance.

EAC (estimate at completion) The total scheduled cost for a resource on a task. This calculation provides the costs incurred to date plus costs estimated for remaining work on the task.

WBS (work breakdown structure) Automatically assigned numbers for each task in a project outline that reflect that outline structure. Government project reports often include WBS codes.

actual A cost or percentage of work completed and tracked as having already occurred or been incurred.

actual cost of work performed See *ACWP*.

as late as possible See *ALAP*.

as soon as possible See *ASAP*.

base calendar The default calendar on which all new tasks are based, unless a resource-specific calendar is applied.

baseline The snapshot of a project plan against which actual work is tracked.

baseline cost The total of all planned costs on tasks in a project before any actual costs have been incurred.

budget at completion See *BAC*.

budgeted cost of work performed See *BCWP*.

budgeted cost of work scheduled See *BCWS*.

calendar The various settings for hours in a workday, days in a work week, holidays, and nonworking days on which a project schedule is based.

circular dependency A dependency among tasks creating an endless loop that can't be resolved.

collapse To close a project outline to hide subtasks from view.

combination view A Project view with the task details showing at the bottom of the screen.

constraint A rule that forces a task to fit certain parameters. For example, a task can be constrained to start as late as possible in a project.

cost A cost can be applied to a task in a project. The cost of the task may be fixed, or you can apply a cost to a task by assigning resources, which can be equipment, materials, or people with associated hourly rates or fees.

critical path The series of tasks that must occur on time in order for the overall project to meet its deadline.

critical task A task on the critical path.

crosstab A report format that compares two intersecting sets of data; for example, you can generate a crosstab report showing costs of critical tasks that are running late.

cumulative cost The planned total cost for a resource to date on a particular task. This calculation provides the costs already incurred on the task, plus the costs planned for the remaining, as yet uncompleted, portion of the task.

cumulative work The planned total work of a resource on a particular task. This calculation provides the work already performed on the task plus the work planned for the remaining, as yet uncompleted, portion of the task.

current date line The vertical line in a Gantt Chart indicating today's date and time.

demote To move a task to a lower level in the project outline hierarchy.

dependency A timing relationship between two tasks in a project. A dependency can cause a task to happen after another task, to happen before another task, or to begin at some point during the life of the other task.

detail task See *subtask*.

duration The amount of time it takes to complete a task.

duration variance A field displaying the variation between the planned (baseline) duration of a task and the current estimated task duration, based on activity to date and remaining activity to be performed.

earned value Also called *budgeted cost of work performed*. Earned value refers to the value of work completed. For example, a task with $1,000 of associated costs, when 75 percent complete, will have a baseline value of $750.

earned value cost variance See *CV*.

effort driven An effort-driven task has an assigned amount of effort to complete it. When you add resources to these tasks, the effort is distributed among those resources.

elapsed duration An estimate of how long it will take to complete a task, based on a 24-hour day and 7-day week.

estimate at completion (EAC) The total scheduled cost for a resource on a task. This calculation provides the costs incurred to date, plus costs estimated for remaining work on the task.

expand Opening a project outline to reveal subtasks as well as summary tasks.

expected duration This calculation estimates the actual duration of a task based on performance to date.

external task When tasks are linked between projects, Project displays tasks from the external project in the current project. The external task represents the linked tasks without having to leave the current project.

finish date The date on which a project will be completed.

finish-to-finish relationship A dependency relationship in which the finish of one task depends on the finish of another task.

finish-to-start relationship A dependency relationship in which the start of one task depends on the finish of another task.

fixed cost A cost that does not increase or decrease based on the time a resource spends on a task. A consultant's fee or permit fee are examples of fixed costs.

fixed date A task that must occur on a certain date. Fixed-date tasks do not move earlier or later in the schedule because of dependency relationships.

fixed duration The length of time required for a task remains constant, no matter how many resources are assigned to it. Travel time is a good example of a fixed-duration task.

float See *slack*.

Gantt Chart A standard project management tracking device that displays task information alongside a chart that shows task timing in a bar chart format.

gap See *lag*.

ID number The number assigned to a task based on its sequence in the schedule.

lag The result of dependency relationships among tasks. Lag is a certain amount of downtime between the end of one task and the start of another.

leveling See *resource leveling*.

linking Establishing a connection between two tasks in separate schedules so that changes to tasks in the first schedule are reflected in the second. Linking is also a term applied to establishing dependencies among tasks in a project.

milestone A task of zero duration that marks a moment of time in a schedule.

network diagram A standard project management tracking form that indicates workflow among the tasks in a project.

node Boxes containing information about individual project tasks in the Network Diagram view.

nonworking time Time when a resource on a project is not assigned to the current task.

outline The structure of summary and subordinate tasks in a project.

overallocation When a resource is assigned to spend more time than its work calendar permits on a single task or combination of tasks occurring at the same point in time.

overtime Any work scheduled above and beyond a resource's standard work hours; overtime work can have a different rate assigned to it than a resource's regular rate.

percent complete The amount of work on a task that has already been accomplished, expressed as a percentage.

predecessor In a dependency relationship, the task that is designated to occur before, or precede, another.

priorities Project uses the priorities that you assign to tasks when it performs resource leveling to resolve project conflicts; a higher-priority task is less likely than a lower-priority task to incur delay during the leveling process.

progress lines Gantt Chart bars that overlap the baseline taskbar and indicate tracked actual progress on the task.

project A series of steps to reach a specific goal. A project seeks to meet the triple constraints of time, quality, and cost.

project management The discipline that studies various methods, procedures, and concepts used to control the progress and outcome of projects.

promote To move a task to a higher level in a project's outline hierarchy.

recurring task A task that is repeated during the life of a project. Typical recurring tasks are regular meetings of project teams or regular reviews of project output.

resource A cost associated with a task. A resource can be a person, piece of equipment, materials, or a fee.

resource contouring Changing the time when a resource begins work on a task. You can use contouring to vary the amount of work that a resource does on a task over the life of that task.

resource driven A task whose timing is determined by the number of resources assigned to it.

resource leveling A process used by Project to modify resource assignments to resolve resource conflicts.

resource pool A group of resources that can be assigned as a group to an individual task (for example, a pool of administrative workers assigned to the task of compiling a report).

roll up The calculation by which all subtask values are "rolled up" or summarized in a summary task.

slack Also called *float*. The time you have available to delay a task before that task becomes critical. You have used up slack on a task when any delay on that task will cause a delay in the overall project deadline.

split tasks When progress on a task is interrupted or delayed because the task has been placed on hold, you can split the task into two tasks. When you split tasks, the downtime between the two is not allocated to the total time taken to complete the task.

start date The date on which a project begins.

start-to-finish relationship A dependency relationship in which one task can't start until another task finishes.

start-to-start relationship A dependency relationship in which the start of one task depends on the start of another task.

subproject An inserted copy of a second project that becomes a phase of the project in which it is inserted.

subtask Also called a *subordinate task*. A task providing detail for a specific step in the project. This detail is rolled up into a higher-level summary task.

successor In a dependency relationship, a successor task is scheduled to begin after another task in the project.

summary task A task in a project outline that has subordinate tasks beneath it. A summary task rolls up the details of its subtasks and has no timing of its own.

task An individual step to be performed to reach a project's goal; a project is composed of tasks.

template A format in which a Project file can be saved; the template saves elements such as calendar settings, formatting, and tasks. New project files can be based on a template.

timescale The area of a Gantt Chart view that indicates the units of time being displayed.

tracking The act of recording actual progress in terms of both work completed and costs accrued on tasks in a project.

variable rate A shift in a resource's cost that can be set to occur at specific times during a project. For example, if a resource is expected to receive a raise or if equipment lease rates are expected to increase, you can assign variable rates for those resources.

work breakdown structure See *WBS*.

workload The amount of work that any resource is performing at any given point in time, taking into account all tasks to which the resource is assigned.

workspace A set of files and project settings that can be saved and reopened together so that you can pick up work on a project or projects at the point at which you stopped.

Index

Hungry Minds, Inc.
End-User License Agreement

READ THIS. You should carefully read these terms and conditions before opening the software packet(s) included with this book ("Book"). This is a license agreement ("Agreement") between you and Hungry Minds, Inc. ("HMI"). By opening the accompanying software packet(s), you acknowledge that you have read and accept the following terms and conditions. If you do not agree and do not want to be bound by such terms and conditions, promptly return the Book and the unopened software packet(s) to the place you obtained them for a full refund.

1. **License Grant.** HMI grants to you (either an individual or entity) a nonexclusive license to use one copy of the enclosed software program(s) (collectively, the "Software") solely for your own personal or business purposes on a single computer (whether a standard computer or a workstation component of a multi-user network). The Software is in use on a computer when it is loaded into temporary memory (RAM) or installed into permanent memory (hard disk, CD-ROM, or other storage device). HMI reserves all rights not expressly granted herein.

2. **Ownership.** HMI is the owner of all right, title, and interest, including copyright, in and to the compilation of the Software recorded on the disk(s) or CD-ROM ("Software Media"). Copyright to the individual programs recorded on the Software Media is owned by the author or other authorized copyright owner of each program. Ownership of the Software and all proprietary rights relating thereto remain with HMI and its licensers.

3. **Restrictions On Use and Transfer.**

   (a) You may only (i) make one copy of the Software for backup or archival purposes, or (ii) transfer the Software to a single hard disk, provided that you keep the original for backup or archival purposes. You may not (i) rent or lease the Software, (ii) copy or reproduce the Software through a LAN or other network system or through any computer subscriber system or bulletin-board system, or (iii) modify, adapt, or create derivative works based on the Software.

   (b) You may not reverse engineer, decompile, or disassemble the Software. You may transfer the Software and user documentation on a permanent basis, provided that the transferee agrees to accept the terms and conditions of this Agreement and you retain no copies. If the Software is an update or has been updated, any transfer must include the most recent update and all prior versions.

4. **Restrictions on Use of Individual Programs.** You must follow the individual requirements and restrictions detailed for each individual program in Appendix A of this Book. These limitations are also contained in the individual license agreements recorded on the Software Media. These limitations may include a requirement that after using the program for a specified period of time, the user must pay a registration fee or discontinue use. By opening the Software packet(s), you will be agreeing to abide by the licenses and restrictions for these individual programs that are detailed in Appendix A and on the Software Media. None of the material on this Software Media or listed in this Book may ever be redistributed, in original or modified form, for commercial purposes.

5. Limited Warranty.

(a) HMI warrants that the Software and Software Media are free from defects in materials and workmanship under normal use for a period of sixty (60) days from the date of purchase of this Book. If HMI receives notification within the warranty period of defects in materials or workmanship, HMI will replace the defective Software Media.

(b) **HMI AND THE AUTHOR OF THE BOOK DISCLAIM ALL OTHER WARRANTIES, EXPRESS OR IMPLIED, INCLUDING WITHOUT LIMITATION IMPLIED WARRANTIES OF MERCHANTABILITY AND FITNESS FOR A PARTICULAR PURPOSE, WITH RESPECT TO THE SOFTWARE, THE PROGRAMS, THE SOURCE CODE CONTAINED THEREIN, AND/OR THE TECHNIQUES DESCRIBED IN THIS BOOK. HMI DOES NOT WARRANT THAT THE FUNCTIONS CONTAINED IN THE SOFTWARE WILL MEET YOUR REQUIREMENTS OR THAT THE OPERATION OF THE SOFTWARE WILL BE ERROR FREE.**

(c) This limited warranty gives you specific legal rights, and you may have other rights that vary from jurisdiction to jurisdiction.

6. Remedies.

(a) HMI's entire liability and your exclusive remedy for defects in materials and workmanship shall be limited to replacement of the Software Media, which may be returned to HMI with a copy of your receipt at the following address: Software Media Fulfillment Department, Attn.: *Microsoft Project 2002 Bible*, Hungry Minds, Inc., 10475 Crosspoint Blvd., Indianapolis, IN 46256, or call 1-800-762-2974. Please allow four to six weeks for delivery. This Limited Warranty is void if failure of the Software Media has resulted from accident, abuse, or misapplication. Any replacement Software Media will be warranted for the remainder of the original warranty period or thirty (30) days, whichever is longer.

(b) In no event shall HMI or the author be liable for any damages whatsoever (including without limitation damages for loss of business profits, business interruption, loss of business information, or any other pecuniary loss) arising from the use of or inability to use the Book or the Software, even if HMI has been advised of the possibility of such damages.

(c) Because some jurisdictions do not allow the exclusion or limitation of liability for consequential or incidental damages, the above limitation or exclusion may not apply to you.

7. U.S. Government Restricted Rights.
Use, duplication, or disclosure of the Software for or on behalf of the United States of America, its agencies and/or instrumentalities (the "U.S. Government") is subject to restrictions as stated in paragraph (c)(1)(ii) of the Rights in Technical Data and Computer Software clause of DFARS 252.227-7013, or subparagraphs (c) (1) and (2) of the Commercial Computer Software - Restricted Rights clause at FAR 52.227-19, and in similar clauses in the NASA FAR supplement, as applicable.

8. General.
This Agreement constitutes the entire understanding of the parties and revokes and supersedes all prior agreements, oral or written, between them and may not be modified or amended except in a writing signed by both parties hereto that specifically refers to this Agreement. This Agreement shall take precedence over any other documents that may be in conflict herewith. If any one or more provisions contained in this Agreement are held by any court or tribunal to be invalid, illegal, or otherwise unenforceable, each and every other provision shall remain in full force and effect.